PSYCHOLOGY OF
PERSONAL ADJUSTMENT

John Wiley & Sons, Inc.
New York
London
Sydney

Psychology of

THIRD EDITION

by Fred McKinney

University of Missouri

Personal Adjustment

Students' Introduction to Mental Hygiene

THIRD EDITION
Fourth Printing, January, 1967

Copyright 1941, 1949 by Fred McKinney

Copyright © 1960 by John Wiley & Sons, Inc.

Library of Congress Catalog Card Number: 60–5602

Printed in the United States of America

TO COLLEGE STUDENTS

*Mine, my colleagues',
and the generation contemporary with
Megan, Kent, Molly, and Doyne*

PREFACE

Almost twenty years have elapsed since the first edition of this book was published. Since that time not only have educators accepted the long-felt student need for self-understanding as a means for better adjustment, but also courses called personal adjustment, personality, and mental hygiene have grown until they are high on the list in respect to enrollment. Moreover, psychologists and educators have increasingly accepted the challenge of specialized training and background in order to impart more than knowledge in such courses—encouraging creative activities which stimulate new perspectives, and helping the student to utilize the many outlets open to him for growth toward maturity.

To meet this aim more readily for the contemporary student, this book has been revised for the third time. The specific-problem approach with the use of cases and projects has been retained. The material has been brought up to date and modified so that basic principles of human behavior are more clearly emphasized for students who are learning to face their own problems and to deal with them in groups of their peers under the leadership of a teacher skilled in the use of modern group methods. Certain topics such as values and group dynamics are treated more fully here than in the previous edition.

The material is so arranged that an instructor may omit certain chapters on specific problems, should he desire to concentrate on other chapters, without disturbing the unity of the book. The manual mentioned below has been prepared to assist those instructors who want to use group methods and individual projects in teaching the text.

I am indebted to all of the students and fellow psychologists who have helped me as this material developed. Particular recognition goes to those mentioned in the bibliography that is published in an accompanying volume entitled *Teaching Personal Adjustment—An Instructor's Manual.* I want to thank again my colleagues whose names appear in the prefaces of the other editions. My greatest debt is to my wife, Margery Mulkern McKinney, who has worked on the manuscript at every stage of activity.

FRED McKINNEY

Columbia, Missouri
October 1959

CONTENTS

CHAPTER 1

M ost of us want to improve ourselves in some way or other. We express this desire in different ways. Some secretly wish for more confidence, more success, more popularity. A student may express this need by a remark to his roommate such as "I have to make better grades" or "I wish I knew what I ought to go into vocationally." A young married student may be puzzled over the disagreements he has with his wife and wish *she* would be easier to get along

2

NATURE

AND GOALS

OF ADJUSTMENT

with! Another may be troubled with guilt over his hostility or his sex impulses and consequently strive for greater self-control. One might even strive to discover an answer to "What can I believe?"

To what extent can we human beings direct our behavior and deal with our shortcomings? Most of us believe we can, some overestimate our ability to improve ourselves without help, or expect changes in our behavior to occur by merely wishing for them.

This book is based on the assumption that *as we gain specific knowledge about ourselves, gain insight into our motivation, and build over a proper period of time habits and attitudes to meet our realistic goals that even the most disturbed of us can improve his adjustment.*

Students and Adjustiveness

First let us see some of our contemporaries in their attempts to adjust to their environments, and then analyze the process of adjustment. Here are excerpts from case histories of college students who were judged of good, average, or poor adjustive capacity by trained workers who read their cases. *Read through these histories and formulate an opinion as to the extent to which each student can adjust effectively to his problems.**

Ken F. is one of the fifteen or twenty outstanding seniors in a Midwestern university of approximately five thousand students. He has been elected to several leadership honorary societies and has presided several times during the year at large school functions. His picture may be found in numerous places in the school yearbook.

Ken, at 22, is 6 feet tall, weighs 160 pounds, and belongs to the fraternity which is highest on the student preference list. He comes from a town of about 1000 population. His physical appearance is above average. He is a brunet with a shy, pleasant smile and is neat and gentlemanly. He is liked and trusted as a dependable, capable, and not too aggressive student leader.

He was in the upper 10 per cent of freshmen in college aptitude and had obtained excellent grades in high school in addition to participating in debating, writing, and school government. His grades in college have been superior. He started school with an academic, vocational, and student activity objective, and his reputation in college as a well-rounded student, mature in work habits, might have been predicted from his precollege hobbies, contacts, and summer jobs in business. He has splendid study habits, is conscientious and highly motivated. His free time is spent like that of

---

* It is possible in a course on personal adjustment to do more than just read about the process. Class discussion, small group projects, and out-of-class adventures and try-out experiences, if carried on through one's natural motivation to grow and improve oneself, can assist the student in his personal adjustment at a time when he has an experienced teacher for occasional assistance. For this reason throughout the book suggestions will appear in the above kind of type for students who want to use them. In addition a manual has been prepared for the instructor discussing the use of these methods in teaching personal adjustment. See *Teaching Personal Adjustment: An Instructor's Manual*, Wiley, 1960.

the typical college student in dating, bull sessions, and attending parties and school events.

He is the only child of comparatively young parents. His mother and father are apparently of different temperaments. His mother has been his coach, has given him a great deal of affection and guidance, and has helped him to build social habits and to seek responsibility in spite of his underlying tendency to be like his father in his preference for the background. She has emphasized social and economic success as important to prestige. In high school he had to win this prestige through accomplishments since it could not come through family wealth or position.

In recent years he has been worried because on several occasions he lost consciousness for a brief period. He seems slightly more nervous than the average individual, but this is masked by the way in which he has harnessed his energy.

He has participated in athletics but has won no major honors. He belonged to most of the usual boys' organizations and has had more than his share of the offices. He began dating at the typical age. He dates frequently now but has never "fallen in love." He is quite capable as a hard-working executive type of leader. He shows a strong tendency to adhere to what is conventional, right, and ideal at all times. He is kidded about his "good behavior" and accepts it well. His associates seem to realize that he has labored for all his honors and has merited them.

Few individuals would have predicted after merely meeting this young man as a freshman that he would become such an outstanding leader as a senior. A perusal of his past history and an examination of his ambitions and plans might have given the experienced counselor a clue to his college development. His four years in college have certainly not been free of anxieties, feelings of inferiority, inadequacy, and strong attempts to overcome them through his previously established habits of work in class and on the campus.

Ken judges his adjustment superior, and his associates would probably make the same judgment. However, some of this is a surface phenomenon, and the experienced counselor would judge his adjustment average, even though his accomplishments are superior. Certainly without personal problems, inadequate family income, and a skillful and ambitious mother, he would not have been the individual he has become as a college senior.

What more would you like to know about Ken that is not included in the above description? Is there enough information on how he feels about himself—his inner life?

Katherine E. is a 20-year-old junior with sophomore status; she is 5 feet, 9 inches tall and weighs 150 pounds. She has an unusually good appearance, faultless complexion, regular features, bronze hair, and, except for her size, when well groomed is one of the most attractive girls on the campus. Despite this she has relatively few dates and is not understood by her associates. At present she is in a small sorority, but spent two years on the campus as an independent. She is from a lower-middle-class Irish home in New York City.

She has superior ability. Her grades and study habits have varied from the lowest to superior. She has a number of acquaintances, and there are times when she is rather close to them. She appears somewhat aloof when meeting new people and reports that she knows people do not like her when they first meet her, that she is scared, tense, shaky, and unable to say the right things.

She admits freely to a counselor that she has a number of problems besides that of self-consciousness. One is that she does not know her own mind. She has changed her vocational aims several times since she came to college. She left school in the middle of the year at one time, to the complete bewilderment of her parents. She will work hard for a time and then find it almost impossible to force herself to study.

During the course of a conference she realized that one of her difficulties is that she does not want to grow up. She thinks she was spoiled in childhood. She did not have many playmates. She had an older sister whom she imitated in every detail, yet she felt that she was basically unlike this sister. Her sister was popular, aggressive, and well integrated, whereas she feels that she herself has always been a "willful individual." She describes childish temper tantrums and insubordination in school and at home. Around puberty she attended a convent school, developed many ideals and standards, and two very warm friendships. With time many of her associates disillusioned her by violating her ideals, and in college she has deviated somewhat from the rigorous pattern she wove for herself when younger. She has broken away from her church.

Her parents both work so that she may attend school. They are bright individuals who have taken advantage of their opportunities and have improved their own social status greatly. They seem to be competitive, to be highly conscious of social standards, to wish to conform, and to put great emphasis on the front of the upper middle class. They indubitably had a plan all worked out for Katherine, but she has refused to be contained in the mold.

There is an inner conflict between her own attitudes and those of her parents. She reports that some of her nightmares consist of dreams in which her mother and sister are horribly mutilated and she awakes shocked by the experience. Her parents at times have been very impatient with her, say they do not understand her, and have apparently scolded her severely for her shiftlessness, her moody, dreamy nature, and her inability to make good grades despite her aptitudes. She states that she cannot understand herself, that she realizes she is egocentric, easily hurt, and quick-tempered. She daydreams much of the time and lives in an idealistic world "where life proceeds according to some order." She admits that she is much happier when she is away from home. The greatest conflict with her family at present exists because they are working hard to support her at school and she is not achieving satisfactory grades or striving for any definite goal. Although she freely admits all these problems she does not realize that she is poorly adjusted socially and emotionally.

How would you evaluate Katherine's capacity to adjust to her many conflicts at the time of this description? What are some of the conflicts presented in the above case report?

Henry T. is an 18-year-old sophomore, sandy-haired, 5 feet, 8 inches tall, weighing 135 pounds. He is from the suburbs of a city of 500,000 people, is in the upper 5 per cent of students in college ability, made an inferior record in high school, and is at present taking pre-journalism courses. He is neat, energetic, proud, and of average appearance. His grades in college have improved over those he made in high school. He does not participate in extracurricular activities or in competitive sports. He dates and attends dances regularly. He spends a good deal of time in bull sessions and in "hanging around."

He is an only child. His parents have been divorced, and he lives with his school-teacher mother. As a child he spent a good deal of time practicing music, and his mother made an attempt to rear him as a regular boy by sending him to camp and encouraging interest in Scouts. Otherwise he had few playmates.

It was in high school that insecurity began to assail him. He was physically inferior to many of the boys, unathletic, and emotionally immature. On the other hand, he possessed lots of pride, was individualistic, and realized his abilities. At this time he had a mild case of acne and was undoubtedly more unhappy than he had been at any time in his life. He found fault with his teacher and the school. He said he "did not care what other people thought" of him. He plunged avidly into reading fiction, secured several jobs, developed some warm friendships with "definitely superior people," and started dating. He apparently idealized more masculine boys, although his behavior was not effeminate. He had a little trouble with masturbation and experimented with physical intimacies, probably mainly to prove his manhood.

His college education is being financed by his mother. He is making a strong attempt to obtain superior grades. His manner is somewhat defensive on first contact, as though he were masking a feeling of insecurity and as though his associates did not accept him as he would like to be accepted. Later, as his acquaintances come to know him better they lose their initial impression of conceit.

He fears financial insecurity and a drab existence, yet also dreads conspicuousness. He enjoys people at first, but after a while they grate on him. At that time he prefers to be alone. He has many of the attitudes of the young reporter—liberal, colorful, with strong interest in literature and cultural pursuits, and with an interesting fusion of aggression and introversion.

He judges himself to be of average adjustment, showing good insight into his true status.

How would you evaluate his capacity to adjust? What impressed you about the description of Henry? What do you think his strengths and weaknesses are in respect to meeting frustrations and conflicts?

George N. is a 20-year-old sophomore, 5 feet, 10 inches tall, and quite slender. He is of average physical appearance and neat grooming. He is from a farm near a small German community. He is pursuing a premedical course, has above-average ability and work habits, but is below average in grades. He accounts for this on the basis of the necessity to work for remuneration while attending school.

He describes his family as financially substantial farmers, very frugal, hard-working, and provincial. They attended church, had acquired all the prejudices of fundamentalism, but gave their children no truly religious background. As a child he attended a one-room school and later a consolidated high school. He was the youngest of several children and was teased and belittled by his older brothers. Through their continued ridicule he came to believe that he was horribly ugly. He played little with other children.

He learned early that he could escape his father's punishments by feigning illness, and he recalls that he would stick his finger down his throat to produce vomiting and thereby avoid a spanking. Illness came to be an escape from unhappiness even in high school. His feelings of inferiority were aggravated when he started high school and was unable to date, to get needed haircuts, or to have the clothes that he felt were necessary to mix with people. He was unable to play football because the school had no team. His parents were not the kind to whom he could bring his troubles, so he brooded and worried alone. He states that he daydreamed about all the things he would have liked to have done—the girls he would have liked to date, the games he would have liked to play—and in these dreams he was the Romeo and school hero. Sex was his only pleasurable outlet. He stumbled upon masturbation, was frightened concerning it by older boys who said it led to insanity, and substituted relations with farm animals. At this time, also, he contracted several illnesses and lost weight. He worked hard in summer to convince his parents that he was strong enough to come to college.

College opened new worlds for him. He happened to room with an older boy who became the only real brother he ever had, complimented him upon his assets, taught him good grooming and dancing, and arranged dates for him. Since his father refused to give him money to attend college, he worked at numerous jobs, gaining some knowledge and confidence from each of them. He began to realize that he could get along with people and learned to like them more. He spent considerable time observing people and comparing their lives with the sort of existence that was forced upon him. He became more aggressive and had physical intimacies with girls.

He states that he is still moody. He desires to have the prestige and success of the upper social classes but feels, because of the inferiority attitudes developed in childhood, that he can never achieve them. He fears that he will not become a doctor because of his low grades at present and his inability to finance his education. He is still extremely self-conscious at the boarding table or when he has to perform in any way before a small group of spectators. He wonders whether he will ever forget that he is basically a "country bumpkin" despite the fact that his roommate tells him that this is not the impression he gives to other people. As long as he can be absorbed in his job, dates, and the few contacts he has developed, he is not unhappy, but when he thinks of himself or the goals he wants to reach he is plunged into despair.

Two advanced students who read his anonymous autobiography evaluated him inadequate in adjustive capacity. What would you say the factors are in his life that would tend to strengthen or weaken his emotional balance? He received a score on a personality adjustment inventory which would place him in the same category arrived at by the students.

Larry G. is a 19-year-old sophomore, 5 feet, 5 inches tall, who weighs 130 pounds and is a round-faced, smiling brunet. He is a member of a fraternity and is energetic, sociable, and humorous. He is very bright, obtains superior grades, is well-liked by his fellow students, who regard him as a unique individual. He comes from a town of 35,000 in which there is clear-cut demarcation between economic groups. He is the only child of a family with superior cultural advantages. He is pursuing a pre-law course. He gives the following autobiographical account:

In early life he had numerous playmates, a sensible, affectionate mother and a companionable father. They played with him, guided his development, and encouraged him in all his attempts to express his own talents and preferences. He joined social groups early, went to camp, gravitated to positions of leadership both in grade school and in high school, and, although he was always small and somewhat immature for his age, he was also always one of the outstanding individuals in his class in the eyes of the teachers and students. His standards were high, but he says he was philosophical about any failures to meet them after he had put forth all the effort he could muster. One gets the impression that he experiences life deeply and is interested in all its phenomena. Although born in a town full of snobbery, he is quite democratic.

At college he has drifted into many bull sessions, has treated boys and girls alike, and at the time of this study was beginning to develop a strong affection for one girl. His energy has been channeled into various extracurricular pursuits and interests, particularly debating, student offices, classical music, some athletics, as tennis, swimming, and golf. He feels no strong interest in many of the superficialities like clothes, cars, and playboy activities. He has been quick to see the implications of his courses and relate them to problems of everyday life. He is interested in religion, and church groups are among his many activities. He states that he has normal sex appetites but has always been able to keep them well under control and has not allowed them to overcome his best judgment. He realizes that he has outstanding ability as a student and as a speaker, but this realization merely challenges him to use these talents effectively.

He was evaluated as having above average adjustive capacity by two advanced students who read his anonymous autobiography. This is a student who has achieved leadership status and is liked by most

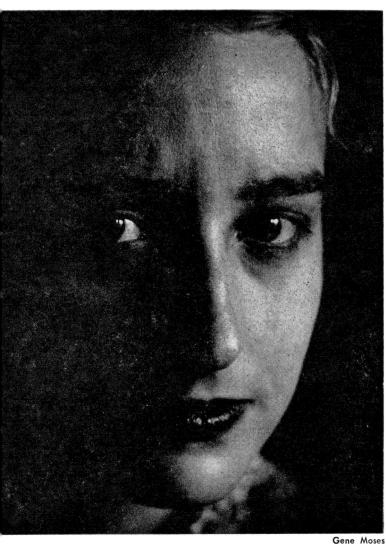

Gene Moses

. . . our experiences and behavior are *caused*.

people who know him. In reading his life story, one is likely to evaluate him as having greater adjustive capacity than he has. However, he received a score on a personal adjustment inventory that indicated "emotional maladjustment." An experienced counselor would notice that he shows nervous mannerisms in a counseling interview and has had more emotional conflicts than the average individual, which he has tended at times to avoid facing frankly. He had, nevertheless, been quite successful in adjusting in college despite conflicts experienced during development.

Several years after graduation, Larry did have some rather serious emotional difficulties. What factors in the description of this man's life as given here may cause you to overlook his emotional weaknesses? What more should we know about him to make a more accurate evaluation?

The Adjustment Process

The Importance of Understanding Causes. The first important idea in understanding others and gaining control of our own behavior is (1) the realization that our experiences and behavior are *caused*. Everything we feel or do is the result of causes or antecedent and relevant events—sometimes quite complex. (2) Controlling or changing behavior or attitudes necessitates an understanding of the nature of the causes of this specific behavior or experience and the removal or manipulation of these causes. This is not the same as deciding that our behavior should be different. All the good intentions we can muster to check certain undesirable behavior may not involve enough of the causes arousing such behavior to make any appreciable difference in how we feel or what we do in a given situation. This realization is fundamental to all our attempts to guide our personal development effectively and in a sustained manner.

Analysis of Adjustment. Of what does the adjustment process as seen in the cases just given consist (695, 779)? It consists of:

1. MOTIVATION. Feelings of inferiority, ambitions toward a specific career, anxiety over failure, and drives toward activities that bring prestige or affection are all examples of motivation. Motives are persistent conditions that dominate and direct the behavior of the individual until he responds in such a way as to remove them. The motive is the *driving force* and direction that keeps the individual at his task. Any basic physical need, any strong desire, any highly anticipated goal is a motive. In considering physical needs, the persistent stimulus is easily described. In hunger, for example, the stomach is constantly contracting until food is eaten. With an anticipated goal, such as reaching a status in a vocation, part of the persistent condition that stimulates the individual is a *tension* set

up in the muscles, which is *relaxed when the goal is reached.* As so defined, the motive is not merely the conscious desire but the *unconscious physical process*—the tension—which drives the individual until it is removed or sufficiently reduced. Motives and their influence on behavior are discussed in connection with study problems in Chapter 2. See Chapter 3 for a discussion of personal motivation.

2. FRUSTRATION AND CONFLICT. An environmental condition or an incompatible motive may block or conflict with activity aroused by the initial motive and prevent the individual from satisfying it. The physical need, hunger, for example, may be frustrated because of the absence of food or the money to buy it. A collegian's desire for popularity, for example, may be frustrated by shyness and previously acquired habits of reclusiveness. The anticipated goal of an excellent grade in a course may be frustrated by slow reading and poor comprehension of difficult material.

What are some of the frustrating conditions in the cases given above? Ken was thwarted in his motivation toward high self-esteem and outstanding social recognition by his family's insignificant social position and his occasional spells of unconsciousness. Henry was frustrated in high school by "inferior physique," immaturity, and acne. Katherine was thwarted in reaching the ideal she felt she must have by life's realities. George's attempt to gain social and athletic success and self-esteem was blocked by his family's attitude, the kind of school he attended, *his concept of himself* as inferior, and his relatively restricted and shut-in life. Notice that in several cases (Katherine and George, for example) the problem was not so much the frustration as such but *what it meant to the individual.*

3. VARIABLE BEHAVIOR. The behavior that results when motives are blocked has been called trial and error. The individual whose motive is frustrated usually performs a number of acts most of which are unsuccessful. The hungry individual or animal searches for food, going first in one direction and then in another, using methods that have been successful in the past. The student who wishes to be popular may behave in a friendly manner, remembering names of new acquaintances, attempting humor in social groups, performing favors, and being otherwise socially aggressive. These means may be effective or, if awkward or overdone, may be offensive or puerile. One of the random acts usually is *successful and satisfying*, at least in part, in reducing the motivation.

What are some of the variable acts performed by the students discussed above when they were frustrated? Katherine was unhappy at home and felt inferior to her sister. She tried to gain recognition through excellence in school grades but did not persist long enough for results to show. Similarly, in social life her conviction that she was inferior made her self-conscious and caused her to flee from the social spotlight. However, under the tuition of the convent nuns and with her own vivid imagination, she built an ideal world in day-dreams. In this world she could be any kind of ideal person. All her dreams were variable attempts to meet the standards of her parents and the accomplishments of her sister.

George sought to gain recognition and develop self-esteem in his childhood but was rebuffed by a busy, stern father and cruel brothers. He felt ashamed of his clothes at school and was afraid to approach girls. He stumbled upon sex outlets and daydreams in which he was not blocked, with the result that he elaborated these behavior patterns.

4. SATISFACTION. The hungry individual finds or buys and eats food, and the stomach contractions cease. The student who seeks popularity discovers after a time that his socially active methods bring him desirable recognition, and he may no longer persistently feel the unpleasant tension of being left out of the group. Satisfaction involves the removal or reduction of the motivating condition, the *relaxation of tension* aroused by the desire. The individual in these cases *is making the adjustment*. It is through this process of satisfying motives that *learning* takes place, the activities that satisfy the motive are learned and tend to be repeated in a similar situation in the future. See Chapter 5 for a more detailed discussion of learning under "Changing Behavior."

For Katherine, satisfaction of motivation toward self-esteem was partially achieved through daydreams. Ken gained satisfaction through extracurricular activities and honors, and George's early outlets toward satisfaction were daydreams and sex activities.

Satisfaction quite frequently is a result of a change in *attitude*, in *pattern of motivation*, and in *a different manner of perceiving the situation*. George came to look at people as friendly rather than as critical of him. Katherine seems to be a different person in what seems to her to be a better world when she is away from home.

5. NONADJUSTIVE BEHAVIOR. We have seen that some of the random activities in these case histories were clearly nonadjustive. They did not remove the motivating conditions. They did not satisfactorily result in reduced tension or they produced later conflict. Usually the individual learns to eliminate these nonsatisfying activities in the

course of his progress. He *learns* not to use them. But, sometimes, they may persist, often because they are *satisfying* in some other way. The hungry hobo may become abusive to the people he approaches for food and thereby delay his satisfaction of hunger longer than if he were meek. He may rant in the street or heave a rock in the show window of a bakery. This may relieve his feeling of aggression, but hunger persists. The student who looks for popularity may develop arrogance or take the "to-heck-with-you" attitude when others do not respond to his overtures. He may become sullen and quietly bitter.

Other activities are only partially satisfying in that they reduce tensions but in addition produce other problems. Such behavior persists possibly because it furnishes *immediate satisfaction* but *later causes difficulties*, or it may satisfy other motives and reduce other tensions without solving the problem at hand, which tends to again increase tension. It is nonadjustive in respect to the motive under consideration, but it may be adjustive so far as other motives are concerned. This is an important point. Much behavior that seems abnormal, incongruous, or socially inappropriate is adjustive from one standpoint. It is merely *nonadjustive in terms of our arbitrary but influential social standards* or frame of reference.

What nonadjustive behavior is found in the cases above? Katherine's and George's daydreams were nonadjustive from a long-time viewpoint. The defensive attitude of Henry was nonadjustive, as was Larry's tendency to avoid facing his problems completely and to write the story of his life and contemporary activities in a manner that glossed over difficulties and indicated adjustment.

6. READJUSTMENT. In order to socialize himself or to satisfy the relevant motive rather than some hidden motive, the individual who uses a persistent nonadjustive reaction must modify his behavior. Simply stated, he must *eliminate the nonadjustive* reactions, those which fail to satisfy the motive under consideration, and substitute those that satisfy the motive under consideration. The hungry hobo, in our social structure, must ask courteously or offer to work for his food. The student who wants to be popular must acquire socially graceful means of getting attention from others and satisfying their needs if he really wants popularity. If, on the other hand, he finds it is not popularity but some other response he wants from the group, the readjustment consists of a conscious examination of his motives and the probable means of satisfying them. Readjustment in the

human being may mean a reorganization of his motivation with emphasis on certain motives rather than on others—sometimes a complex inner adjustment rather than an acquisition of habits.

In George's case, there is evidence of readjustment through his college roommate. This older boy helped him to gain a fresh perspective in a new environment. This roommate appreciated George's assets and by his friendly manner showed respect for the younger boy. He gave George suggestions, helped him to develop social skills, listened to his story, and by telling it George saw himself and all the influences of his parents, his brothers, and his environment in perspective. He came to understand and accept himself more. On his own he ventured where he would never have tried to go before, met girls, went to dances, made friends, and developed in dignity and potentiality.

You may want to discuss with your fellow students the (1) motives, (2) frustrations, (3) nonadjustive behavior, and (4) readjustments of the students described. Your discussion may lead you to a consideration of these processes in your own life.* You may want to list your own frustrations and adjustments to them. Briefly, the adjustive process is an *attempt to satisfy motives*. This becomes complicated by barriers to satisfaction which exist in everyday adjustments.

Summary of Principles—The Adjustive Process. Obviously even the above six-point analysis is an oversimplification of the complex matter of adjustment. It presents only the essence of the process which, as described above, consists of:

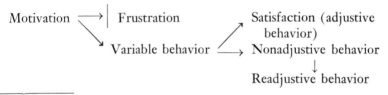

Motivation ⟶ | Frustration ↘ Variable behavior ⟶ Satisfaction (adjustive behavior) / Nonadjustive behavior ↓ Readjustive behavior

---

* A word of caution about analyzing the behavior of your friends and associates. You are already familiar with the abhorrence people feel when someone, even an expert (which most students of psychology are not) analyzes their behavior or their motives. Psychologists discourage this activity in the amateur. Personality analysis is a professional activity and should be undertaken only in that context. For this and other reasons numerous cases are provided which the student may use for discussion. No one will object to the student using the knowledge he gains in a course for the understanding and guidance of his own behavior, particularly if it leads to growth toward emotional maturity and adjustment to his total needs and his environment.

Many problems can be better understood in terms of this kind of simple analysis. It is presented here because it will underlie the discussion in the text for the purpose of understanding our behavior in our attempt to satisfy *motives* for efficiency, vocational success, social activities, sex behavior, and orderly inner experiences as well as the frustration of these motives. Much of the material in the book is presented to prevent persistently *nonadjustive reactions*. In cases in which this inappropriate behavior already exists there are suggestions for activities planned to bring about *readjustment*.

The nature of our nonadjustive reactions is discussed more fully in Chapter 3, and the process of readjustment in Chapter 5. However, before those discussions, Chapter 2 deals with the more immediate problem, study methods.

General Principles of Personality Adjustment. Here, in summary, are some basic principles of human behavior that grow from an analysis of the above cases. They too should provide guidance in the consideration of concrete problems in the text. The basic ideas presented here will reoccur over and over again throughout the book, to provide understandings of the problems considered (777, 695, 563, 422).*

1. All human behavior is *motivated* by needs, and we behave to *adjust* to these needs to remove or satisfy them.

2. Rarely are these needs easily satisfied or thoroughly acceptable to us. Rather they are *frustrated* by conditions in the environment or in our minds which block our satisfaction of them. In other words, *conflict* is inevitable.

3. When conflicts occur the behavior that involves the least possible resistance is often selected whether it is *appropriate for our overall and long-term development or not*. When it is not maximally satisfactory, new appropriate methods of resolving the conflict must be learned.

4. The way we perceive our needs or motives and the situations that satisfy or fail to satisfy them are related to parts of our total experience, past and present. Our problems frequently consist of the necessity for a *new inner* organization or perspective—a more realistic view of ourselves and our world. This is usually attained through actively searching, reading, discussing and writing out feelings.

---

* The numbers found in the text refer to articles or other books listed in a bibliography in an accompanying publication entitled *Teaching Personal Adjustment: An Instructor's Manual.* Usually when reference is made to a title in the bibliography we are calling attention to a study substantiating the statement made in the text.

. . . a more realistic view of ourselves and our world . . . is usually attained through actively searching, reading, discussing . . .

Goals and Definition of Adjustiveness. The average person when asked "what do you want from life?" will answer in words synonymous with happiness. This in psychological language means the *pursuit of satisfactions* of his various needs. In order to continually satisfy needs as they become active each day we must have built up habits, attitudes, and traits that are appropriate. To be a successful public speaker or athlete, for example, we must have learned the necessary skill.

There is more. We must be able to deal with the many irritating frustrations so that strong *conflicts*, which pull us in two directions at once, and the *anxieties* over our possible misdoings will help us *grow* and *develop* the necessary personality traits for dealing with our problems, rather than to withdraw and become immature or offensively aggressive. In short, we need to develop in emotional control, responsibility, and clear understanding of our objectives and hazards. This is called *emotional maturity* and involves such adjustive traits as toleration of frustration and anxiety and the utilization of these states for personal development. We mean by adjustiveness then, the *acquisition of traits and understandings that enable us to meet effectively our personal needs and overcome the frustration or blocks to satisfaction over a period of time*. Chapter 16 is devoted to a more detailed discussion of adjustiveness.

Personal Adjustment and This Book. There will be a constant effort then to stimulate the reader to see what needs or motives are

17

blocked when a problem arises. At times he will be encouraged to see himself and his environment in a different light. The best adjustment consists of more than using experts' suggestions to consciously plan one's life. Much of it consists of seeing the *causes* of behavior, the motivation, and conflicts beneath the surface that make us persist in errors. As new perspectives and insight are seen, the student is better able to use his environment for personal growth. He can relate and interact better with counselors, fellow students, various campus groups and resources. He can use these relationships together with his reading and individual projects to learn new habits, skills, and attitudes that will meet his needs, resolve conflicts, and produce growth toward emotional maturity. The student is therefore encouraged *to seek his own solutions to his specific problems*, using the cases, class discussions, and suggestions merely as a point of departure.

Supplementary Readings

C. Kluckhohn, H. A. Murray, and D. M. Schneider (Eds.), *Personality in Nature, Society and Culture* (2nd ed.), Knopf, 1953.

L. F. Shaffer and E. J. Shoben, *The Psychology of Adjustment*, Houghton Mifflin, 1956.

R. W. White, *Lives in Progress*, Dryden Press, 1952.

In addition see the references cited by number in the chapter and appearing in the bibliography of an accompanying volume entitled *Teaching Personal Adjustment: An Instructor's Manual.*

CHAPTER 2

Are there any relationships between your work in college and later efficiency and self-satisfaction? To what extent are the skills used by the young executive in the commercial world similar to those which bring success while in college? Industrialists who are responsible for production, quality of goods and distribution, and professional men as well, have perforce a wealth of knowledge and personal skills and are constantly acquiring new facts and are thinking in terms of them. Their overall task does not differ widely from your task as a college student.

One of the important demands in our culture is adjustment to responsibilities and duties—one aspect of *maturity*. This involves plan-

ADJUSTMENT TO COLLEGE WORK

ning your time and energy. Adjustment to school work is your most immediate problem, and it is an integral part of adjustment in other areas in the adult vocational world, particularly since learning, thinking, and efficiency are so important to those adult adjustments.

Students' Adjustment to College

Let us review a few cases illustrating students' attempts to improve their adjustment to college. As you read them you may see similarities to yourself or your friends.

Harold T. graduated from ——— High School where he was in the upper third of his class. He had always received good grades but did not remember studying. His father, a physician, is able to pay all Harold's expenses while he is in college. Harold was a member of ——— fraternity although not initiated the first semester because of his grades. He wanted to study medicine, but his motivation was not very strong. His father suggested medicine because Harold would be able to take over an established practice. Three weeks before the end of the first semester he realized that he would not make his grades and began to try to cram. Despite good intentions his habits were bad. He stayed in his room the first night after making resolutions to study, but it was an hour before he really got down to work. After another hour during which there were three or four interruptions, he had accomplished practically nothing; literally hundreds of pages in each of four books were still unread, and his notes, in poor shape, were not reviewed. "How can I ever do it?" was the thought that continually coursed through his mind. The easiest way to banish this unpleasant thought was to do something distracting. The more pleasant this something, the more effective it was as an opiate. So Harold became more active than ever. He went to shows; he spent time in the gym; he lounged in the fraternity house and in pool halls; he tried not to think of his grades; and he cut class more often. At the end of the semester he failed twelve hours. He had another chance the next semester to make satisfactory grades. He changed his room to one on the third floor of the house and roomed with a senior. He scheduled his time carefully to include more study. His roommate helped him to establish a habit of study by suggesting that Harold arrange to study in the same room with him from seven to ten each evening and by refusing to talk with him during this time. Without any special methods, except the urge to make his grades so that he might be initiated into his fraternity, a daily study time, and an interested roommate, Harold's grades rose above passing the next semester. This allowed him to be initiated. When last consulted he was receiving some superior grades.

Martha S.* entered college with an above-average record from high school. Her scores on the entrance ability tests placed her in the upper quartile of entering college students. At midsemester, however, she realized that she was in danger of failing in her college work. In fact, she was so discouraged that she considered dropping out of school. She came to the reading and how-to-study service for help. Through diagnosis of her problem it was discovered that she was spending sufficient time on her work to bring results. However, she had never learned efficient methods of study. As she had always been particularly interested in mathematics and science and had read widely in these fields, she had developed the habit of reading all material as she did a math or science problem. She was unable to distinguish between main ideas and details or to vary her rate and method according to the type of material and the

---

* This case was contributed by Irma Ross formerly of the Reading Clinic, University of Missouri.

purpose for reading. Martha worked in the clinic twice a week for a semester. She was guided in developing methods of attack and was encouraged to report her success in applying these methods to her course work. She was given exercises for increasing her rate of reading and in using efficiently the clues to meaning.

About the middle of the semester Martha reported that she had lost her feeling of imminent failure, and, although she was spending no more time on her work than she had formerly spent, it was now "making sense" to her. By the end of the semester she was making a slightly above-average record and was finding time for social and extracurricular activities.

Sam T. is a slight, erect, well-groomed, mild-mannered, capable 19-year-old sophomore. In grammar school his grades were poor, but they improved greatly in high school and were well above average in college. He was planning to go into medicine and came to a counselor because of his difficulty in premedical courses. Although he was extremely emotional over "failing" a quiz, the counselor learned that his grades were not inferior and that at least one of his teachers realized that some of Sam's quizzes did not reflect what he knew about the subject.

After several conferences, Sam realized that his difficulty was not low ability, poor study habits, or lack of aptitude for medicine, but an emotional problem.

He was the youngest of four boys, all of whom were different in body type from Sam and extremely successful as athletes. He was closer to his mother and more protected than the others. His early vocational choice reflected an ambition his mother had long harbored—art. Although Sam took additional instruction, he soon realized that art as a career was not very promising for him. This decision was crucial for him. His career was filled with compensation for his believed physical inferiority. His ventures in art, in extracurricular activity, and in premedical courses all became a life-and-death matter. There was a feeling that he *must* succeed, that his very existence depended upon success. When he saw, after several conferences, how his early history was influencing his present behavior, his attitude toward his premedical courses improved. In time his grades also improved. He began to prepare for the quizzes by studying with a fellow student. The student quizzed him, and he quizzed the student. They even made written quizzes for each other similar to those given by the instructor. The new perspective, together with these preliminary quizzes, lessened Sam's tension. His improved attitude and accomplishment, which he attributed to the conferences with an understanding counselor, did much to improve his morale.

These cases show some of the typical problems and mistakes that can be made, together with some discoveries that the students made about better study methods. Now let us cover more thoroughly the factors leading to effective study.

There follows a check list of techniques that have been found to be of value as study habits (867). Not *all* good students have *all* these habits, and not *all* poor students lack *all* of them, but these suggestions are valuable in improving the work of a typical student. They also enable the student of superior ability to make the time invested in study more effective. All these techniques do not have equal value; some are many times more effective than others.

An interesting way to use this check list is to *read over each of these suggestions and note on a separate sheet of paper the ones that apply to you.* You might perform a brief experiment. Compare your results with those of students of known efficiency or inefficiency in school work.

Basic Principles and Adjustment to College. Essentially, problems in adjustment to college are the result of other inadequate or conflicting motivations. A student who has difficulties in college may not have strong motivation to learn abstract material, or his motives for social or athletic achievement may be greater and take him from study activities. He may have, on the other hand, associated the school situation with anxiety or escape activities. Furthermore, he may never have gained success through his own efforts in the school situation, he may not have learned to enjoy mastering material in a text.

The problems discussed in this chapter apply the basic principles mentioned in our analysis of adjustment in Chapter 1. An under-

Susan Greenburg

standing of them will stimulate the student to raise fundamental questions as he reads this chapter. What is the nature of my *motivations* for an education? What experiences *conflict* with these motives? Have I learned *satisfying* study skills? If not, how can I best acquire them?

CHECK LIST OF EFFECTIVE STUDY HABITS

Motives and Incentives for Study

* I have several definite, strong *reasons for attending college.*
* I have selected a *vocation* and have planned a tentative course.
* I have found several good *reasons for knowing the material* in each course I am pursuing, and I see its value.
* I have a keen *urge for success in college.*

Class Period Study and Note Taking

* I am *active* all during class—I ask myself questions and try to see why every step occurs when it does.
* I review the classroom work shortly *after the period is over* and before notes are cold.
* I *prepare for class* by anticipating the topic for the day, go into class with certain questions in my mind, and I maintain a critical attitude.
  I get the *essence* of the lecture in a full, organized outline.
* I realize that it pays to *attend class* for I know it will often take hours to compensate for a lost lecture in preparing for an examination.
  My *notes* are neither too brief nor too long and are as personal as possible.

Preparing for and Taking Examinations

My *preparation for examinations* is just a rigorous review in the form of a self-quiz. I try to learn the essentials or the total outline first and get the details later.
* I enter the examination room knowing that I have done my best, and that if I remain *cool* and work hard I'll do well.
I write first the answers of which I am certain—for *encouragement.*
I am sure I *understand* just what a question calls for before answering it.
I have learned not to become *flustered at examinations* by preparing examinations and taking them myself at home, by being prepared, by realizing everyone else is subjected to the same conditions, and by realizing that this examination is just one of many.
I roughly schedule my *time* so that the entire quiz will be covered and *check* all my answers before handing in my paper.

Schedule and Plan of Work

* I have a schedule and have a *specific time* each day for study.
* I have a book all ready to open when the hour for study arrives, and I start with a bang!
* My *study periods* are not too long or too short, but they are regular.
* I take time out for *rest*, but I see to it that I return to study.
* I have a *definite place* to study and do nothing else but study in that place. As soon as I sit down there, it suggests study.
* My place of study is not surrounded by too much noise or too many distracting people. My desk and wall are *devoid of distracting objects*.
* I have a *time for play* and amusement, so I don't feel that I am missing anything while studying.
* I do not try to *do the impossible in one night*. If I did I would fail and continually flog myself mentally for failing.

Habits of Concentration and Daily Preparation

* I always get a *general idea* of the nature of the assignment and what I am to know when I finish studying. Then I go over the material carefully.
* I stop at the end of each section and *review in my own words* what I have just studied. I sometimes outline or mark the book but always get the substance in a form that can be reviewed.
* I utilize statistical tables, graphs, italicized and bold type, topic and summary sentences. With these and other aids I try to discriminate between the important and the irrelevant.
* At the end of the assignment, I *quiz myself* in a fashion similar to the quizzes in class.
* I am careful to get the knowledge *accurately* the first time.
* I always think of the *meaning* of the facts, how they are related to other facts I know and to material of everyday life.
* In memory work, I realize that every word or name has been selected for some *reason*. Knowing that reason helps me to remember it.
* In memory work, I always *overlearn* rather than learn just to the point of perfect recitation.
* I often use dull or odd times to *review* that which I have learned—*between classes* and in the afternoon.
* I am continually checking on my progress, and this tends to eliminate daydreaming.
* I *study with others* only after I know the material and want to be tested, or when there is a particular point I don't understand.

Proficiency in Foundation Subjects

I *read rapidly*, always seeking the main ideas, and without speaking the words to myself or pausing over words.

I am mastering one *new word* each day.

My grades are not being lowered by repetition of a few *errors* in spelling, arithmetic, or grammar.

Other Factors Affecting Study

* I am in good *health;* my eyesight is good or corrected with glasses; I have periodic medical examinations.
* I have good daily hygienic habits—habits of regular hours for sleep, of proper elimination, and of sufficient outdoor exercise. I maintain a balanced diet.

The starred methods in this check list are found to be empirically valuable (867, 100).

Factors Affecting Academic Success. For any individual student the factors causing success or failure in college differ (673). For the group as a whole those with higher *aptitude* and a previous history of school success have the most favorable outlook, but there are exceptions to this (251).

The author took from his roll book the records of three pairs of students who were among the 90 students enrolled in a class in General Psychology. Members of the pairs were alike in intelligence but, as will be noticed in the listing below, widely different in semester grades based largely on objective tests. In two of the cases the difference is almost as great as the range of grades in the course. Obviously it is the *efficient use of ability* because of *motivation,* good *study habits, attitudes,* and *personality traits* that explains these differences in grades.

Initials	Intelligence Test Score	Semester Grade
J. S.	135	F (failure)
A. S.	135	S (superior)
R. T. S.	154	I— (very inferior)
L. P.	159	S+ (very superior)
M. M.	184	I (inferior)
R. P.	187	E+ (highly excellent)

Two groups of probation students of the same intellectual status had received a point-hour ratio of 0.77 when 1.8 was needed for graduation. One of these groups was given instruction in study habits. During the period the ratio for this group rose to 1.79, and for the matched, untrained group to 1.04 (231).

Is the training a permanent acquisition? Approximately three and a half years after the training 58 per cent of the above mentioned study class maintained a passing average, and only 18 per cent of the untrained group had reached this standard (618).

A course in study habits will *not automatically* cause the student to improve in school efficiency because, as stated above, techniques of study represent only one factor in college success. Students who entered college with a poor school history and a below-average college aptitude were grouped together and not allowed to take certain difficult courses, but instead were given instruction in study methods and remedial reading. This course did not change greatly the quality of the school work of these students (350).

Success in college, then, is related to several factors, and it is well for the student to know how he rates in each of these. If he is low in college aptitude and previous school grades, he must rely on improved study methods and strong, sane motivation, and sometimes on a modified program (30) to perform satisfactorily in college (31).

Motivation for Study

Individual Differences in Motivation. Look at the students around you and you will notice how they seem to vary greatly in kind and seriousness of purpose. Some are attending college largely because of the pressures of their social class. Others have a high need for achievement (469). There are those students who want to understand the nature of the world and of man. Others regard courses as a means to professional or business success. There are, in addition, those who see purpose in their school work, but because of insecurity in their background or personal problems, are unable to marshal their efforts to the attainment of good grades. Finally, there are the underachievers who obtain grades only high enough to enable them to enjoy life on the campus (594). It is hypothesized that some students with high ability and low achievement are expressing hostility toward their parents in their poor scholarship (410, 415). A deep understanding of this motivation of students requires a complete study of their personal histories, which is undertaken more thoroughly in Chapter 4.

Aims of a College Education. In order to help you clarify your conscious motivations for obtaining a college education, it may be well to read and discuss a simplified statement of the aims expressed by educators.

1. To understand the basis of *human behavior* for personal and social adjustment.

* 2. To understand other's *ideas* and to express his own.

3. To improve one's *health* and that of one's community.

4. To enjoy *social relationships* widely.

5. To have a basis for a satisfying *family life*.

6. To take some part in *public affairs*, local and international.

7. To enjoy nature, and have a practical understanding of the scientific approach to it.

* 8. To enjoy the *creative arts* including literature and music, as one means of finding one's own creative outlets.

* 9. To develop one's *own standards* and values.

* 10. To *think* critically and constructively.

11. To find the most satisfying *vocation* for both the individual and society.

Sustained Motivation and Temporary Incentives.   As mentioned in Chapter 1, motivation refers primarily to those persistent conditions within the organism that dominate and direct behavior. Motivation strong enough to influence behavior over a period of several months or several years indicates some *stable direct influences within the organism* that usually are the result of development. Such motivation is more than the mental image that the student gets of himself sitting at a desk in his future professional role, or receiving scholastic honors, or enjoying success as a community leader. These daydreams may be supplementary, but the drives which keep the student at work are more deep-seated. Sustained motivation goes beyond a temporary incentive that produces results as the desire to make grades in order to be initiated into a social organization, an occasional thought of one's duty to one's parents, an appreciation of the sacrifice they are making, or the desire to maintain one's reputation. It is more than an interest in or enjoyment of a given course, or the desire to work for a certain teacher. It exceeds even the boost that comes from success and the realization that learning can be fun. It is more urgent than the necessity to obtain good grades in preprofessional courses that are not very interesting in order to get into

---

* Educators differ in the emphasis they place on the above objectives of a college education. Some emphasize total adjustment as a goal, others insist the college curriculum should be largely restricted to items starred above—an emphasis on intellectual development (574, 179, 317, 117).

and succeed in a professional school or to get recommendations for jobs. It is the force that is behind all these signs. Such external *incentives* and experiences can supplement motivation (221). When they are present they improve temporarily and often quite decisively the student's performance.

UNCONSCIOUS MOTIVATION. Although some students are disorganized because of early insecurity and family problems or feelings of inadequacy, many are spurred by problems and difficulties (571). Some students compensate unconsciously for poor health, family background, low economic status, personal inadequacy, or insecurity. The unrest that grows from the social or personal status they experienced in high school may find an outlet in exceptional planning, long hours of work, and participation in college events. Studies have been made on the need for achievement and show that students with a great need for achievement show higher output even on simpler tasks (469). These strong drives then are basically the results of early events in their lives. The motivation may lead to thought and conscious planning and become verbalized into life purposes. We shall discuss this more thoroughly in Chapters 3 and 15.

PURPOSE AS MOTIVATION. A study at Yale University revealed that those students who had a life and vocational purpose and were specifically and constantly planning in terms of them did superior academic work. Cultural and socio-economic factors, as well as intelligence, are also important (176), but they were ruled out as influences in the Yale study by statistical means (160). Students who planned to enter professions, for example, received better grades than those who anticipated business careers. This variation might be explained in part by the students' realization that many professional schools require good preprofessional grades for entrance. The following factors were *not* found to be motivating: the knowledge that a definite position was awaiting the student after graduation; family occupation or family tradition and pressure, and "attainment of unhampered choice of a vocation."

It appears, then, that merely knowing what you want to do is not the important factor. Rather, the inner conditions growing from personal and background factors cause you to recognize that a certain vocation will satisfy your desire for social acclaim and success.

Added to *purpose* as a factor, *decision* was found to be important in another study. The absence of decision is indicated by dependence upon parents, adults, and fellow students for one's choices. A third factor was *social* in nature; it is absent in students who are timid, self-conscious, and who withdraw from social situations. The last factor was named *sensitivity;* it referred to the student's maturity and objectivity, his perspective in dealing with problems that arise, his ability to think about the situations he encounters instead of accepting them blindly. The absence of this factor is obvious in the playboy, the drifter, the provincial, and the individual with the "one-track" mind (301).

Maturity of purpose is evident in students who return to college after military service (298). The factor of *persistence* has been noticed by a number of counselors in accounting for success where ability test results for the given individual may not have predicted success (229, 673). Attitudes toward the school situation, then, are as significant as study skills in academic achievement (131).

MOTIVATION AND STUDY EFFICIENCY. Studies on groups of students do not show that tendencies toward emotional instability interfere with grades. Nevertheless there are cases in which emotional and motivational problems do affect scholarship (153, 868, 554). One study of gifted children indicated that those who were not very successful academically or in life were influenced in part by emotional and motivational factors in their history (787). We shall see in Chapter 14 how these states of depression and listlessness affect behavior.

Some school inefficiency is explained by a conflict in motivation. There are students whose aptitudes and interests push them strongly toward one area of endeavor, whereas their parents, advisers, traditions, or some other force move them toward some incompatible field. There are others who are competing in a field or at a level beyond their present capacity. These individuals might succeed in a different area or in a less taxing situation. We shall discuss them in Chapters 8 and 9.

Finally, there are those students who have a negative attitude toward work, or who lack enthusiasm to carry them through the work-a-day world. They have not clearly envisaged their life goals and purposes, nor have they seen the relationship between these goals and their present academic activities.

If you lack the drive to carry through your daily responsibilities you may try to ascertain the cause of it. Do you need to talk about some of your goals and present habits and discover what is required of you and whether you at present have the habits and attitudes that will enable you to meet these requirements? Or, on the other hand, are you in a field that is foreign to your basic interests and attitudes?

Have you plunged into a curriculum for some superficial reason only to revolt against all that the curriculum means? Are you competing in a curriculum or college where the majority have a background far beyond yours in maturity, preparation, and aptitude, and should you change to a different kind of curriculum or institution where greater success would be assured? Do you have some deep emotional problem requiring solution through counsel that interferes with your efficiency?

Increasing Concentration

Nature of Concentration

My trouble is that I have no power of concentration. If I could concentrate like some of the girls living in our dormitory, I'd get good grades. Why, some of them spend an hour to my five hours of study!

To this student, concentration is a "power" that some have and others do not possess. This is essentially an erroneous view. Concentration is rather a *way of behaving that increases the clearness of the situation* toward which we are reacting and enables us to respond in a dynamic fashion. We always concentrate *on something*—we do not merely concentrate. We concentrate on a situation when we are motivated as shown earlier, and when we have strong *interest, purposiveness, and a more active attitude* toward it. Concentration is the result of strong motivation as well as the capacity to comprehend the material.

Many inefficient students can concentrate well on tennis games, or bridge, are keenly alert in bull sessions, and readily absorb the content of the sports page. Habits of concentration do not transfer automatically from sports to physics. It is necessary to see the value of physics, acquire the groundwork, and achieve interests and attitudes that approach those which are held for sports. Some students, you must remember, prefer mathematics tests to sports pages. Mathematics is fascinating to them. They can do it well; they are prepared and do not evade it.

Importance of Concentration. Several studies have been carried on that involved observing students in the library for ten minutes. The studies showed that students were subject to numerous distractions while attempting to start to study. The distractions can be ranked in order of greatest to least as follows: talking, aimlessly looking around, purposelessly leafing through books, disturbance by a passing student, use of vanity cases, distraction from study by others, daydreaming, reading and writing letters, and attention to personal appearance. A time record showed that over 40 per cent of the total time was given to distraction or to reading material other than the assignment (70). This aimless behavior usually occurs during the "warming up" period before the height of concentration. The shorter this period becomes through heightened motivation the better efficiency.

Producing Concentration. From this discussion what seems to be associated with keen concentration and what is associated with daydreaming and lack of interest in subject matter? Glance over the discussion and that on motivation with this question in mind, and you will doubtless find four or five conditions that improve concentration. Do this and compare your findings with the ones listed.

In order to be able to concentrate well one should:

1. See a purpose in the material before him even if it does not satisfy his purposes.
2. Assume an active attitude.
3. Attempt to eliminate distractions.
4. Cultivate interest in the material.

Each of these conditions is discussed below in greater detail.

SEE PURPOSE IN THE MATERIAL. A problem once started leads one on to its completion. An encyclopedia is just a big uninteresting book to the high school boy until it serves his purpose in supplying him with abundant material for a term theme. The dullest material will become fascinating when it satisfies an impelling purpose. A collegian expresses amazement at the transformation in his attitude toward his economics textbook after his summer experience as a clerk in a broker's office and his decision to select brokerage as a vocation.

ASSUME AN ACTIVE ATTITUDE. The best advice regarding the initiation of the active attitude is to *plunge into your work* the moment you reach your desk. Start going through the motions of study with the genuine aim of enjoying the work as you "warm up" to it. Don't wait for inspiration or for the proper mood to strike you.

A student will find that if he plans, before going to supper, what he intends to do after supper, if he opens his book at the assignment, has his notebook all ready, and begins to work immediately after he reaches his desk, he will soon set up this new habit. The satisfaction growing from his new accomplishment will do much to entrench the habit.

Another specific method of eliciting the active attitude is to read and study with the *intent of reciting the material* to someone else later. One will find that a fact which he wishes to report to his dad is one which is apprehended with heightened concentration.

ELIMINATE DISTRACTIONS. The *third* precept in achieving concentration is to *eliminate distraction* that is subject to your control and to set yourself to resist the remaining minor types of distractions. Distractions are essentially of three major types: those from the *external* environment, such as noise; those from the *intra-organic* processes, such as bodily states resulting from poor hygiene; and those from ideational or *thought* content. We shall discuss the first two under "Efficient body and environment," in Chapter 6.

Ideational distractions consist usually of daydreams. Ideas seem to arise spontaneously and take our attention from our work. These daydreams have causes. It is well to try to learn these causes, to examine the matters that continue to perseverate or "run through the mind." They are usually suppressed worries over money, love, social life, school, or athletic achievement. Try to get at the cause of the trouble, determine your attitude toward the matter, work out a future course, as described in Chapter 5, and then proceed with your study.

After you have removed all distractions within your power, there will still be sounds from the neighbor practicing his saxophone lessons, shouts from the street, a distant radio, and fighting cats, all of which you can and must ignore. This is done more easily when you launch yourself into your work, acquire interest, and try to make yourself superior to petty distractions.

CULTIVATE INTEREST. You usually find no interest in golf clubs until you have driven a few balls down the fairway with them. You have no interest in Korea until you have walked and talked with a Korean and learned to appreciate his customs. After passing through the state of Texas, you find a map of Texas intensely interesting. We do not understand how the meaningless symbols we see on the blackboard of a calculus class can engage the interest of a mathematician until after we have had a well-presented course in the subject and have succeeded in working the problems. Every form of subject matter commands the interest of a great number of people, and *any* form can hold interest and pleasure for us if we have had vivid experiences with it and feel successful in handling it. A subject be-

Susan Greenburg

comes more interesting when we respond fully to it. This likewise enhances its pleasantness (142).

REDUCTION OF DAYDREAMING. We saw that daydreams act as a distraction. Students ask, "How can I keep from daydreaming while trying to study?" The first suggestion, which was given earlier is to find the cause and settle the conflict that produces the daydream. Often, however, after the cause has been removed, the habit continues of its own momentum. The following experiment illustrates how the habit may be broken.

A group of 48 students was trained in concentration by the following method. The students read five pages of difficult philosophical text every day for a period of two weeks. They were instructed to underline on the page the passages where they found themselves daydreaming and to reread those parts of the text. At the end of each page they were required to review mentally the ideas on that page and make sure that they understood them. Figure 1 shows the learning curve that graphically depicts the improvement due to this exercise. This is a group curve, which shows the average trend. Some students improve more than this curve indicates, and some less. *Try this method.* Keep a strict account of your daydreaming. Note your improvement after three or four weeks of continued effort.

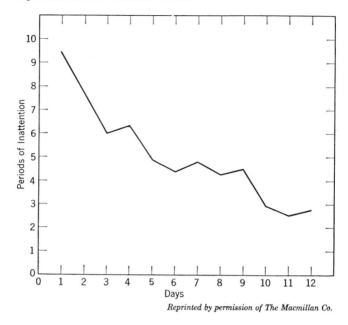

Reprinted by permission of The Macmillan Co.

Figure 1. Learning curve for a group, showing decreases in periods of inattention with time. (After Chant.)

Learning and Memory

The Process of Learning and Memory. We are learning practically every minute of the day. We meet new people and learn their names; we encounter new words in our reading; we hear good jokes we wish to retell later; and there are scientific and other facts we encounter every day for the first time. Most of this is *incidental* learning; we exert little effort in its acquisition. With better understanding of the learning process and the use of most effective methods, our learning and retention activities can become more efficient. Learning that results in profound personal improvement is highly satisfying to us. Learning, like motivation, is a basic process in adjustment and underlies most of the adjustments discussed throughout the book. We will continually return to it.

A student should view learning as (1) the establishment of *stimulus-response relationships* in his behavior or (2) the trial-and-error selection of the proper solution to a problem. Memory is the retention and recall of these responses when the stimuli are presented. To learn that the word "idiosyncrasy" means "peculiarity" is to establish a relationship or association between this stimulus and its response. Memory refers to the *retention* of this relationship and the *recall* of "peculiarity" when "idiosyncrasy" is presented. With this in mind, it becomes apparent that poor memory is due largely to an unsatisfactory association between the stimulus and response; or it may be due to the absence of the stimulus at the time one tries to recall. Most of us have noted that when we try to remember we often search in trial-and-error manner for cues or stimuli that bring to consciousness the desired memory-idea—a response. The more cues associated with an idea, the greater is the possibility of recalling it. It is well to regard memory from this point of view and to seek stimuli to the memories or responses you wish to evoke.

Seeing One's Curve of Learning. A learner is greatly motivated when he can see his progress from week to week. A learning task that extends over a period of time is apt to result in discouragement and loss of interest unless the individual has some measure of his progress. There occurs in the learning curve, sometimes, a period of no apparent improvement. (You will notice such a period in the learning curve on page 36.) Individuals commonly notice in skills, such as target practice, bowling, pool, and even in more complex skills, such as basketball and football, a period in which they seem to be at a standstill or perhaps going backwards. This has been termed a *plateau*, and may be due to (1) a decrease in motivation, (2) interference between and confusion of the material learned, (3) the establishment of errors that tend to reduce the learning score, (4) or the attainment of maximum or near-maximum efficiency with the method used to date and a need for shifting to some new basic mode of attack. The individual should recognize this plateau as a natural phenomenon when it occurs and attempt to learn the cause of the lack of progress with the aim of overcoming it. Some believe that, when their performance is on a plateau, they can improve no further and in thinking so confuse the plateau with the *physiological limit*—the limit of their capacity to improve.

Motives in Learning. Remembering the batting averages of his favorite baseball players is not difficult for the twelve-year-old, nor are the names of movie actors and actresses difficult for his sister. We have no difficulty remembering the people who owe us money and how much they owe us. We seldom forget a dinner engagement when we anticipate a pleasant evening.

We discussed the importance of motivation and an active attitude in learning on page 33. There are numerous studies showing that if animals and humans are motivated and then are rewarded as they move toward the goal or checked when they stray from it, they learn more readily (105, 672).

We defined motivation as a condition that *dominates* and *directs* behavior. Let us illustrate. Read this list of words: painted, hard, useful, new, smooth, manufactured, sliding, and expensive. Suppose you have been given these directions before being given the list. "These words describe a piece of furniture; remember this in listening to them." This statement would have speeded learning and improved retention of the list. A mental set of this type has been referred to as "readiness" to learn specific material. You can motivate yourself to remember a name just before you are about to be introduced to a stranger: "Now I'm going to hear this person's name and repeat it with 'How do you do, Mr. ——.'" Do you think you would forget it easily? Experiments show that motivating oneself to remember rather than just passively learning produced results that tend to last (609).

Meaning and Association. Try to memorize: *mes, paz, hok, kyw, mik, dug, gev, jep.* You will find them much more difficult than a list of simple nouns. But give them meaning, any meaning, and their difficulty largely vanishes. *Mes* is "mess" without the final s; *paz* is a new way of spelling "pass"; *hok* is a short word for "hokum"; *kyw* are the call letters of a radio station; *mik* is another way to spell the humorous, derisive name for an Irishman. Try to supply meanings for the other three. This is an excellent way to absorb the vocabulary of a foreign language. Everything we learn should have or be given *meaning.* It should be associated with something we already know.

Said one student in giving an example of how association aided his memory:

> I associate the mailing of the letter I must post this afternoon with the buying of the paper on the opposite corner. I get an image of the paper man and myself paying him the five cents; then I get an image of the mail box on the opposite corner. This afternoon when I buy my paper I shall be reminded to mail the letter.

The improvement of learning ability for one type of material, like legal cases, by practice with another type of material, like Latin, depends largely upon the *similarity of meaning* between the two materials and methods of attack. The increase resulting from such exercise is not nearly so large as is usually believed. Also, the more direct the associations are, the more effective the learning. For example, if the French *foule* immediately recalls the mental image of a crowd rather than the English word "crowd," the learning is more direct and the meaning readily recalled.

SIMILARITY. This is a convenient type of association. The meaning of the following French words can be remembered because of *similarity* in pronunciation in the two languages: lettre (letter); maire (mayor); monstre (monster); parfum (perfume); caractère (character); finir (to finish). These can be associated with English words similar to their equivalents: lune (moon) can be associated with the English "lunar" referring to the moon; livre (book) can be associated with "leaves" (a book is a group of leaves); commencer (to begin) with commence; éclairer (to light) with clear; inférieur (lower) with inferior; inonder (flood) with inundate; indice (sign) with indicate; menacer (to threaten) with menace.

IMPROVISED ASSOCIATIONS. These also aid in learning. A student found the following helpful to him: foule (crowd)—"A *fool* always follows the crowd"; comparte (tub)—"A tub is a *compartment*"; issue (exit)—"People *issue* from the exit"; mare (pond)—"A *mare* often stands near a pond"; fond (bottom)—"I am *fond* of diving to the bottom of swimming pools." The more vivid and direct these associations are, the better their memory value.

OTHER EFFECTIVE FORMS OF ASSOCIATION. *Imagery* is a good mnemonic aid—use it. One student reports that he has a good memory for lectures because he gets a visual image of the discussed topics placed on a ladder. If the speaker has five points, his mental ladder has five rungs. Other students report other *individual* methods. Some *repeat aloud* the material to be learned; some find *hearing* the material more helpful than seeing it; still others find *writing* the subject matter which they desire to learn most helpful.

It is efficacious for each person to discover the mnemonic systems that assist him most in learning. Remember Mr. French's name by the fact that he does not look at all like any Frenchman you have ever known. This is an example of association by *contrast*, a good way to associate ideas. The five points emphasized in the lecture may be remembered by repeating them to oneself, using one's five fingers as a means of organization. An individual will soon be known for his good memory if he ties the name of each person he meets to a meaningful association; for example, with another who has the same name.

Persons do not forget the telephone numbers 1960, 1776, 1234, or 9876. All of them have meaning; all of these combinations of numbers exist in previous experience. The more he uses the varied exercises, the more he learns. One reason why different types of exercises are used in teaching language is to give the student practice in many associations.

Associate events to be learned with pleasant *thoughts, acts, images, previously established experience, vivid ideas,* your own *interests* or *problems,* and they will be remembered (379). See the *logical relationships* between materials learned, the similar and contrasting items. See the material as a meaningful *whole.* Tie subject matter to be learned with incidents that will be present at the time of recall and that will act as cues or *stimuli* for recall. Remember: the more vivid associations, the more cues, the better for recall.

Survey, question, recite, and review for an active attitude. Experiments show dramatically how effective some form of the active attitude is over mere routine coverage of the material in study. Simply reading and rereading a selection without pause does not aid in comprehension and retention of it nearly so much as a more active method (215, 648). Here are some excellent suggestions for study that arouse an active attitude: (1) Run over the headings in the assignment understandingly and get a general idea of the material before you begin to read (513). (2) Turn the section heading into a question that establishes a purpose for the reading. (3) Write brief summary phrases after you finish reading each section in order to test your comprehension and later relate the ideas from the various sections. Outlining may be substituted for this if it is brief and easy to do and if used for later drill. (4) Look over your brief recitation notes after reading the assignment. Such *self-recitation methods* will definitely retard the forgetting process. Studies in one type of learning show that, when 80 per cent of the time is spent in recitation, twice as much material is learned as when reading only is used (261). A five-minute review after a college lecture was found to double the amount of material recalled (382).

Try to avoid an attitude of unpleasant coercion. Fear, excitement, failure, and such negative forms of behavior are not conducive to efficient learning or good memory, even though vividness usually favors recall (629). Studies show that when students realize that they are failing while attempting to learn, their performance is usually poorer than it might be otherwise.

Other Aids to Learning. Numerous experiments on learning bear testimony to the fact that *distribution of learning activity* is, over a period of time on the whole, superior to continued study without rest or change of activity (360).

JUDICIOUS GUIDANCE. Guidance or coaching seems most profitable in *small amounts in the beginning* of the learning process. Large amounts of coaching and its introduction at an inopportune time have been found least effective (129). If one accepts guidance or coaching one should maintain an active attitude; possibly first try the act voluntarily to set oneself for the guidance. A good tutor is one who spends a large portion of the time raising questions, having the student react to them, and then supplying the solution to the question.

LEARNING CONDITIONS AND RECALL. One of the most annoying vagaries of memory is illustrated by such an experience as turning to your roommate to introduce him to an acquaintance at a social gathering and failing completely to recall his name, to your unlimited chagrin. Other similar experiences: to raise your hand in class to ask a question and then as the lecturer says briskly, "What is it, Mr. ――?" to forget the question; to walk from your study to the living room and find yourself standing in the room ignorant of your mission; or to read over an assignment several times without quizzing yourself and then find that you are unable to answer most of the questions in a subsequent examination. All these are illustrations of attempts to recall items of experience that have been learned under circumstances foreign to those present at the moment of recall.

In studying, try to associate with your method, with your attitude, and even, if possible, with the environment, the *conditions that will prevail at the time of recall of the learned material.*

REWARDS. We learn those acts that satisfy our motives, release tensions, and usually give us pleasure. We tend to eliminate those acts that do not satisfy motives even when they are repeated. A compliment from a teacher reduces the absences from his class and increases the visits to his office. A progressively decreasing golf score entices us to the course more often. The swimming movements that caused us to sink, swallow water, and strangle are gradually eliminated.

Try to engineer the events in your life so that they will bring reward to acts you wish to learn. Reward yourself for accomplishments. Recognize your slight improvements in performance as motivation for further improvement. The recitation, at the end of a study period, of the material learned produces a pleasant effect of accomplishment.

OVERLEARNING AND REVIEW. College lecture material and other meaningful subjects are forgotten *very rapidly at first and thereafter at a slower rate* (336). One method of preventing a rapid drop in the retention of skills and content we have learned is overlearning at the original attack and frequently reviewing the material. Overlearning is repetition even after the material is known so that it can be recited once perfectly. We never forget our own names. We retain well those childhood skills that we have continually reviewed in play, such as bicycling, skating, and swimming. These have been well fixated by their numerous repetitions. If you *must* remember an event, overlearn it. Learn it not only to perfection, but learn it so that it is "second nature."

One psychologist in a startling experiment illustrated the value of repetition even without meaning. He read Greek drama daily to his fifteen-month-old child until the child reached the age of three. Every three months, a different set of material was read. At eight and one-half years of age, the child learned the material previously heard much more rapidly than new material. Apparently, material repeated early exerts a lasting residual effect (113).

NOTE TAKING. It might be well to review the suggestions given in the Check List of Effective Study Habits to see the major ideas that apply to note taking. *Outline your lecture notes.* A portion of material follows in outline and in paragraph form. Both contain the essentials of several pages of a text digested by the same student (168).

NOTES TAKEN IN OUTLINE FORM

I. Arthropoda.
  A. Crayfish is a member of the class Crustacea in Phylum Arthropoda
  B. Structure resembles Annulata but more specialized.
    1. Bilaterally symmetrical body is metameric.
    2. Paired appendages.
  C. For most part, aquatic animals.
    1. From primeval habitat, the sea, migrated into fresh water.
    2. Land-dwelling crustaceans offshoots of aquatic group.
  D. Other great classes of Arthropoda adapted to land.
    1. Insecta, or insects.
    2. Arachnida, which includes spiders and scorpions.

NOTES TAKEN IN PARAGRAPH FORM

The crayfish is a member of the class Crustacea in the Phylum Arthropoda. It is a type of structure resembling that of the Annulata, since the bilaterally symmetrical body is metameric and there are paired appendages; however, the general organization is more organized. Crustacea are for the most part aquatic animals, although a few species are terrestrial in their mode of life. From their primeval habitat, the sea, the ancestors of crustaceans seem to have migrated into fresh water. The few species of land-dwelling crustaceans are clearly offshoots of a group that is primarily aquatic. Two other great classes of Arthropoda, the Insecta or insects, and the Arachnida, which includes the spiders and scorpions, are thoroughly adapted to terrestrial life.

Notice how easily the outline can be perceived, comprehended, and visualized. Contrast this with the difficulty of grasping the same material in paragraph form. An investigation showed that those who used outlines in study were superior as a group to students who did not (46). It has been found that students change their system of taking notes during their college career, and most of them at the end of four years arrive at a similar "best way of keeping notes," which they think should be presented to freshmen. Evidence indicates that the taking of notes aids in examinations, full, clear, definite notes aiding more than brief, vague ones. The immediate value of notes is not so great as the delayed value, although one author suggests taking notes even though they are not to be used later (161).

Efficient Reading. Such a large portion of study in school and self-improvement later consists in reading that it is imperative to be able to read efficiently. A review of the studies on the reading ability of college students reveals some almost incredible facts. Approximately 25 per cent of college students examined in two schools read less rapidly than the median eighth-grade student, and about 7 per cent fell below this standard in comprehension of the material read (27). Consequently, their efficiency in courses demanding reading was impaired, and grades were affected. There is statistical evidence that highly skilled readers earn more credits during the college semester than less expert readers (17).

Improvement in reading speed and comprehension is possible with special training. The rate of improvement is around 25 to 50 per cent for speed and higher for comprehension (444). Consider the importance of any of these increases, with resultant improved grades, to the student who is assigned considerable reading (516). Reading ability has been found to be related to intelligence, and thus this factor would affect the amount of improvement possible in the reading.

REASONS FOR INEFFECTIVE READING. The *speed of reading* and the *degree of comprehension* of the material are two general factors in reading efficiency. In reading, the eyes do not move slowly and uninterruptedly across the page but, instead, move with a series of jerks and pauses. Approximately 94 per cent of the reading time is consumed during these pauses (805).

It is not difficult to understand the reduced efficiency of a reader who pauses often for lengthy intervals and occasionally has to reread lines (805). Furthermore, it is clear that this type of reading does not join meanings rapidly so that they fuse and give rise to larger meanings. Instead the reader joins partial meanings, some of which are forgotten because of the interval between the first and last pause in a sentence.

Another cause of reduced speed is *articulation,* or *lip and throat movements.* The eyes can perceive more rapidly than the speech mechanism can articulate. Silent reading is almost twice as rapid as oral reading. Oral reading further distracts from the meaning in that attention is given to speaking and perceiving the stimulus or word itself. The words are not important in reading—the meaning is.

Good reading, then, is *rapid reading* accelerated by an *extensive intake* at each pause, *few backward motions,* and *absence of vocalization.* Whole meanings are grasped and fused rapidly before forgetting can occur (423).

Improve your reading speed and comprehension. Ascertain your speed of reading. Read a book of average difficulty for five or ten minutes. Estimate the number of words read by counting representative lines, and ascertain the words you read per minute. If your rate is not well above 250, practice will be profitable. The range for college freshmen is from 100 to 400 words per minute. Select a book to read daily, with the aim of increasing reading ability. Ascertain how many pages you can read in a definite length of time. It is well to make calculations in terms of lines. Then it is possible to notice more accurately an increase over a period of a week. It will be interesting to plot a learning curve of your improvement, as shown on page 36.

Daily practice in increasing your perceptual intake, or attempting to grasp groups of words at a single glance, will be helpful. Practice in reading against time and in reading without vocalization to increase speed will reap results. Articulation can be detected and prevented by placing the fingers on the throat while speaking, then placing them there as you read. This will aid in discovering whether the lips move or the throat vibrates while you read. Practice will eliminate these useless distracting vocalizing movements. Daily increase of vocabulary also allows more rapid comprehension and increased reading speed. Your college may be one of the many which have instituted remedial reading clinics.

Vary your attack with the material at hand. Bacon said, "Some books ought to be tasted, others to be swallowed, and some few to be chewed and digested . . ." Sometimes one wants only the meaning, and in such case it is well to skip as many words and read as rapidly as possible as long as the meaning is gained. In other cases, laws, definitions, and principles are to be mastered. There are also books to be read for appreciation, in which case one will want to allow associations to arise as the material is read. For books deserving critical treatment, reflections will intervene between sections read (4).

MISCELLANEOUS AIDS TO READING. Most writers use topics, subtopics, italics, and other devices to place emphasis upon the essence of a paragraph. The wise use of these and the initial sentences in the paragraphs will prove helpful. Tables, graphs, pictures, and diagrams are included in books because they are more vivid methods of presentation and are the most effective techniques for conveying important facts and principles.

Compensating for Poor Preparation. College requires definite skills or tool knowledge, among which are ordinary skills in English composition, mathematics, spelling, and reading. The student should be able to write a discourse without errors in grammar, be able to compute simple arithmetic and algebraic operations, and should have average speed and comprehension in reading.

Many students reach college without these prerequisite tools and are handicapped (42). A review of some of the findings concerning poor preparation for college shows 24 per cent of one group of underclassmen to be below the eighth-grade norm in arithmetic. Similar deficiencies are found in most basic skills. Marked improvement in these deficiencies resulted from remedial training.

Deficiencies will persist in many cases unless the student discovers and corrects them. One college instructor noted that, of 18 courses failed by 30 probation students, 17 of the failures were being repeated. On the other hand, only one of 19 new courses pursued was failed

(619). This indicates empirically that, if a deficiency exists, taking the course a second time does not always remove it. The wiser procedure would consist of drill in those deficient elements that are prerequisite to successful pursual of the course.

Ask your instructor for his opinion of the cause of your failure and some possible exercises for the removal of the deficiency. It has been found that no person makes more than half a dozen errors in the formation of letters in penmanship, but these are repeated again and again. Inability to do a simple algebraic operation may prove fatal on chemistry examinations involving problems (619). Some of the books suggested at the end of the chapter will help you improve these deficiencies. Likewise, a visit to the Reading Clinic or Counseling Service at your college may be helpful in a program of removing academic deficiencies.

A feasible method of building a vocabulary and improving diction is to devote a small notebook to it. Record all new words you hear in lectures, on the radio, at the theater or see in magazines and books. Look them up later, use them in sentences, then in conversation; in this way you will master them, and they will become a part of you. Some word *roots*, such as Latin, Greek, and Old English, are more prolific than others. Some of the Latin stems lead to the meaning of innumerable English words. It is enjoyable to conjecture the meaning of unknown words from their context and then to verify your guess. *Buy a pocket notebook and determine to make an addition of two words a day to your vocabulary in a useful, meaningful manner.* Most of us can well afford to make our speech more definite, vigorous, colorful, and varied. Some words are overused. *Synonyms* should supplant these. *Antonyms* help make ideas more interesting and powerful by contrast. There are available books on making vocabularies more dynamic (492). This is a definite, perceptible method of improving yourself.

Taking Examinations. Instructional words on the examination such as "describe," "criticize," "list," "contrast," should be noted attentively. Answers should be planned mentally before they are written so that they will be well organized, definite, and concise. Technical words, diagrams, and illustrations should be used if relevant. Quantity does not compensate for qualitative deficiencies. When you feel confident that your answers are valid, you will find that writing them with dispatch and vigor is energizing for continued attack. Try to recall by using images from the book, the teacher.

the lecture room, and notes that you may have associated with your teacher.

It is wise to apportion your time allotment, not nervously, but deliberately, and to write first those answers of which you feel confident, and afterwards the ones that need deliberation. Some students report that organizing their answers on separate sheets helps. It is worth remembering that neatness, clearness, and cleverness of organization are factors that influence the grader, whether he recognizes the fact or not. Extra time can be very profitably spent in reviewing answers and noting that all are answered. Partial answers or guesses based on knowledge are better than a blank page, but often a blank sheet is better than a sheer bluff (524).

In objective short-answer examinations it is imperative that instructions be clearly understood, statements be carefully read, and, unless there is heavy penalty for guessing, each question attempted. Watch qualifying words such as "always," "not only," and "usually." Sometimes we arrive at one answer, later read the question again, and feel that another answer is correct. Experiments on recognizing pictures indicate that correct recognitions are quick and produce confidence, whereas false recognitions have the opposite characteristics (693). This suggests a cue for the student who is trying to decide whether his recognition of a true-false statement is correct or not.

PROFIT THROUGH ERRORS. When a quiz is returned, note all corrections and instances in which you failed to get the maximum credit. Determine your weaknesses and plan to correct them before the next examination. Learning progresses through errors. From one point of view, it is far more creditable to progress from a low performance to a high than to maintain a high performance. Use your errors as indications of what not to do next time. Past failure should be used to guide us in the future. Past failure should be used as a means for future success, not as a source of regret and remorse.

Individuals differ in the extent to which they are upset by exams. When they are upset the usual physiological accompaniments are present, and their perception of the material is affected. Students report that if they begin the examination by answering the questions they know they gain some control (99, 617).

Use of the Library. *The value of the library.* The large university and city library systems furnish the means to secure a detailed answer to every question that can be asked, if information concerning the problem is available. Not only are there within the library buildings vast sources of information on every conceivable issue, but catalogs, indexes, and bibliographies give the student ready access to the particular volume in a short time. One of the great acquisitions you can make in college is facility in extensive use of the library. Studies show that grades are not affected by the student's use of the library. Possibly a measurement of *how well* the student uses the library would be more highly correlated with grades.

The library has another aspect—adventure. It has books on travel, hobbies, and your special enthusiasms. It has colorful magazines, the newspapers of many cities, the journals of your chosen vocation, and novels, plays, and short stories through which you can forget yourself and enter the lives of other people.

Acquaint yourself with the functions of the library. Discover how each of the departments can serve you: the reading room contains the current magazines, papers, and journals; the reference room makes available encyclopedias, indexes, and guides; the circulation department houses the stacks from which you may draw books for use at home; in the reserve room are books that are in constant use and kept for consultation on the premises; and the department of special and rare collections offers a treat for the scholarly student. Learn the service that the librarian will render, should at any time your own efforts to secure a certain book prove fruitless. Understand how to use the catalog, comprehend the system of classifying books, and know the call number ranges of the various fields.

Examples of indexes are the *Reader's Guide to Periodical Literature* and Poole's *Index to Periodical Literature*, which serve as indexes for magazine and journal articles from selected periodicals. The *New York Times Index* enables one to determine the date of recent events and is thus a guide to the use of newspapers and news magazines.

An example of a general reference is the *Encyclopaedia Britannica*, which contains in many volumes authentic detailed articles on specific subjects in science, art, literature, etc.

Preparation of Papers. When have you been most successful in preparing papers and when have you experienced difficulties? Read over the suggestions that follow. Do they have meaning for you? Are there other suggestions you would add from your own experience or the experience of your friends?

Collect and organize materials. The more you read on the topic you select, the greater ease there will be in writing.

Write creatively. You have seen other approaches to the topic through your readings; the task now is *yours*. Do not be too hampered by your notes. Freely design your discourse on the topic, your contribution, your interpretation. Do this without too much inhibition. You can correct and criticize for grammar, spelling, punctuation, and sentence structure later, but now create with a free hand.

Success and Education

Success in School and Later Performance. At the onset we must say that *success can take many forms* as shown later. Although some of the early studies pivoting on relationships between single traits and some form of success showed trends, careful review of all of the data leads but to the conclusion there is no clear-cut relationship between *single* personality traits and *overall success* (772).

GRADES AND LATER INCOME. Salaries of several thousand college graduates in the employ of the American Telephone and Telegraph Company were compared for median in four college grade groups: upper tenth of the class, first third, the middle third, and the lowest third. The median of the salaries in each of these divisions showed the *progressively higher income to be associated with higher grades,* particularly after an initial period of service. It will be noted that these results are based on medians or mid-salaries in a group. The study does not show that *all* men graduating in the upper tenth did better than the rest of the men in the upper third. But it does show a definite *tendency* for men receiving good grades in school to be more successful in an institution like the Bell System than those making lower grades (265).

An incidental finding in the Telephone Company study is that there is an initial five-year period of adjustment during which there is slight difference between the salaries of the various scholarship groups. The ambitious should be aware of this period, which probably exists in many vocations.

PERSONALITY AND LATER INCOME. Achievement in extracurricular participation is also predictive of later achievement. The three highest and three lowest ranking students in school grades and extracurricular achievement at Wesleyan University from 1897 to 1916 were studied. There were distinct differences in worldly "success," as rated by classmates, in favor of students who showed achievement on the campus (442). For some vocations, like "business," extracurricular achievement in college is more closely related to "success" than is scholarship. In others such as law, teaching, and the ministry, scholarship is more indicative of success.

One study showed that success in terms of salary is related to father's occupational level, to self-support in college, and to participation in extracurricular activities. Serious reading and membership in college organizations were found more often among those with higher salaries and occupational ranks (798).

GENERALIZATIONS REGARDING COLLEGE RECORDS AND SUCCESS. The upshot of these studies is that *the predictive value of various records and achievements in college varies with the type of work the individual will enter later.* In selling and personal contact work, other factors besides scholarship may be more indicative of future success. On the other hand, if a student is successful in technical classroom and laboratory work, he will probably be successful when he applies this skill and knowledge later; he will have acquired the habits of hard work and perseverance that good grades usually require.

There are some studies of success using broader criteria. It has been found, for example, that members of Phi Beta Kappa and honor scholars appear more often than non-honor students in *Who's Who in America* (a directory of prominent people in this country) (720, 809). Harvard graduates of one class were studied to learn the type of school work that had been done by the individuals judged most successful after graduation. (This success was not due to family wealth or position.) As undergraduate students these successful men had earned 196 of the highest academic grades, whereas a group of individuals selected at random had earned only 56 of the highest academic grades (243).

It should be pointed out that there are studies from other schools which do not find a relationship between later success or job satisfaction and grades (378, 369). One study showed that whether the student graduated or not does not seem to be significant when success is measured by such criteria as job satisfaction, cultural status, morale, and enjoyment of leisure time rather than by economic status (595).

It seems from studies that personality traits related to one's satisfaction in a vocation are not necessarily related to achievement in some other vocation as shown in Chapter VIII (772). Furthermore, there is evidence among both career women and men that mobile individuals (those who "get ahead") are not as well integrated in terms of vocational and social roles and suffer feelings of insecurity. They are said to have *status anxiety* (211, 76, 451).

In addition to success in terms of monetary returns, there are many more *real* forms of success, some of which cannot be measured easily. Success in friendship, marriage, parenthood, and relationships with other persons, attainment of happiness and mental serenity, and *movement toward emotional and intellectual maturity* are all true forms of achievement. Persons rarely realize or take credit for the fact that they are successful, although this kind of success usually is most rewarding in terms of inner satisfaction.

Miscellaneous Educational Problems. *Can a student be too young or too old for college courses?* Below age 21 there is a tendency for the students who enter college at a younger age to receive better grades, probably because they have been accelerated all their lives. Students who enter college after 21 also are good students for apparently different reasons (198). They are frequently students who have had to stay out of school for some reason or other, have had the unusual persistence to come back, and therefore bring with them increased maturity and perspective (756). Carefully selected students who had not finished high school but who showed evidences of maturity did at least as well as and in some respects better than the student body as a whole in college work (67). Studies show that certain students can accelerate their progress through college and finish in three years without apparent detriment to themselves (239).

Do certain home backgrounds jeopardize success in college? Financial handicaps cause students to leave school, and lower economic background produces emotional problems (213). However, if the student has the ability that college work requires and if he obtains the money to attend, through work or scholarships, his home background will not seriously hinder him. This is true whether he be of foreign parentage, of parentage from the lower economic strata, or of parents who lack college training. This generalization is made from investigations that show these students to be either as successful as or superior to those of "better" background. It must be remembered in this connection that the students who come to college from underprivileged backgrounds are often superior mentally to the group as a whole. There is no indication that the offspring of college graduates are superior to other students (760, 690). Granting equality of intelligence, favorable home background will facilitate success in college; on the other hand psychological theory points to compensation on the part of some students who have inferior backgrounds. The socially handicapped student strives for success with all the energy he can muster.

Is a small class a better learning situation than a large class? Small classes in general fall below some point between 20 and 30 students, and large classes would be those above that number. According to survey reports students and faculty both tend to prefer the smaller classes, but, when records are examined, there is a tendency for students in the larger classes to excel in terms of the measures used (364).

Do students fail required subjects more often than optional ones? An investigation of the grades received in both high school and college subjects shows little difference between averages in required and optional subjects (371), despite the fact that students prefer elective courses and say they work harder in them.

Does the location of the seat a student occupies affect his grades? It is doubtful whether this factor affects the naturally alert, intelligent student, but a compilation of grade averages for a number of college classes shows the center of the room to be a more favorable location as opposed to the rear, sides, aisles, and seats behind posts (285).

Does cutting class affect grades? Absence from a well-organized university class lecture and even tardiness has an effect on grades (20, 188). If the student had to prepare a similar discourse from the original sources, many hours would be required. Even the poorest lecture serves to review important material of the course.

Does place of residence affect grades? There is no evidence to indicate that living in a fraternity house improves grades except when the student is striving to be initiated. Dormitory residence in some institutions is associated with higher grades, and in some institutions with lower. In most professional schools place of residence is not significantly related to grade average (608).

How does attitude toward subject matter and teacher affect the student? Many students state that their attitudes toward the teacher influence their learning in a course as much as any factor. It has been demonstrated that one's attitude toward subject matter influences grades and is related to one's attitude toward the teacher (635). If we like and agree with the ideas we read, we tend to remember them better. Certain subjects are dreaded, and these attitudes tend to persist into college. To a certain extent the attitude toward the teacher, like the attitude toward an officer in the Army, is projection of one's own frustration. The teacher becomes the scapegoat. He is viewed as the cause of all the student's own difficulties. There is no doubt that all teachers, like all humans, have inadequacies, and some have many. But usually the teacher cannot and will not be changed during the semester in which the student is taking the course. Therefore, from the student's viewpoint, he must adjust to the teacher.

This does not prevent him from voicing his views privately to his fellow students and perhaps feeling better for having done so.

In many progressive schools students are given an opportunity to evaluate the teaching on anonymous rating scales. Students prefer sympathetic teachers who show evidence of having a sense of humor and knowledge of subject matter and who are interested in them. The attitude of the teacher influences classroom morale (127).

A dislike for a teacher may become an unrecognized asset to the student. It may cause him to be unusually critical of the material and to do much more thinking about it than he would otherwise.

In regard to the teacher's views, the whole gamut of viewpoints will and should be represented by a faculty in a large school. Presumably, in a free educational system, the most valid ideas will survive. It is incumbent upon the teacher to separate facts from conjecture and label them. The mature student will examine evidence for the viewpoints the teacher presents and think for himself. He will achieve an accurate, objective view about his teacher rather than an unanalyzed attitude of like or dislike.

Supplementary Readings

A. Anastasi, *Differential Psychology: Individual and Group Differences in Behavior* (3rd ed.), Macmillan, 1958.

E. Havemann and P. S. West, *They Went to College—The College Graduate in America*, Harcourt, Brace, 1952.

M. E. Bennett, *College and Life*, McGraw-Hill, 1952.

F. P. Robinson, *Effective Study*, Harper, 1946.

C. G. Wrenn, *Studying Effectively*, Stanford University Press, 1950.

In addition see the references cited by number in the chapter and appearing in the bibliography of an accompanying volume entitled *Teaching Personal Adjustment: An Instructor's Manual.*

Complaints and Problems

Youth and mature adults have always "analyzed" themselves and will continue to try to learn why they are unpopular or shy, why their behavior conflicts with their intentions (381). Today, probably as never before, people want to "analyze" themselves. There are available many books of popular variety that have grown from their author's armchair analysis of his own and other personalities. There are also many attempts to interpret for the layman the

CHAPTER 3

UNDERSTANDING ONESELF

scientific techniques in this field. All this attention to personality and adjustment makes the average man desire to *know himself* better. Even when one is making a good adjustment to his desires and environment there is some self-searching (681). Rarely does any young person satisfy himself. Social mistakes and failure to reach cherished goals are keenly felt. At such times we may ask ourselves: What do I really want in life? What are my talents, my assets, my faults? What are my dominant traits? How serious are my handicaps? To what extent can I improve myself?

Problems Prompt Self-Discovery. We seek most to "analyze ourselves," at least superficially, when a problem arises. The problem, complaint, or worry may not be, and usually is not, the real difficulty. It is usually a fragment of the whole personality that is placed in the spotlight of attention. It is a *symptom* or *surface problem.* The real difficulty is often too disturbing to handle alone. This symptom is usually emotional. It may have a physical or mental reference. In some cases it is physical upset: tiredness, lack of appetite, insomnia. In other cases a fear, a worry, a persistent idea, self-consciousness, feelings of inferiority or unworthiness, or depression may be the complaint.

The problem may be related to the family, school, work, finances, discipline, the future, relationship with others (particularly of the opposite sex), health or oneself (254, 55, 749, 34, 79).

The youth or mature adult who becomes conscious of a symptom has been developing attitudes and certain traits for years. He may have been experiencing a conflict for several months, but some recent event has intensified it. It may have been touched off by some experience. This experience usually is a traumatic or unpleasant event, such as a disillusionment, a failure, an embarrassing occurrence, a family disturbance, loss of a friend, unfavorable comparison with another person or being snubbed or rebuffed by someone whose good opinion is desired.

There are some cases in which a less vivid event will arouse a desire for "analysis." One may see a movie, read a book, take a test, hear a lecture and become conscious of a problem and want to understand its nature or "solve the problem." New plans, such as a new vocational decision or change in environment as, for example, going away to college or to a job, may arouse self-evaluation. Even present success that forecasts future accomplishment may be a stimulus for self-searching.

In summary then, the complaint is just a *sign.* Real problems are more *complex*, more *obscure in origin*, with a *developmental past*, and usually represent a *conflict* between basic aspects of the personality that have grown from one's total development. Real understanding consists in knowing these conflicts and seeing their bases in past development under conditions that will allow us to accept them, and deal with them.

Personal Motivation

Basic Causes of Problems

Isabelle is a physically attractive, unselfish, hard-working, serious, 20-year-old coed with a winning smile and gentle manner. She wins people readily and has many girl friends who respect her but who can't understand her devaluation of herself. She has broken a promising engagement because she "wasn't good enough for the boy and would lose him sooner or later."

As a pre-adolescent she had lived in a neighborhood of people of foreign birth. Although her parents are typical, sincere, hard-working, first-generation Americans, she has never accepted them or their group as part of her background. Her models have been chosen from teachers and her associates outside of her parents' group. As she would listen to the boisterous good fun in the neighborhood at night and realize that her parents were a part of it, she would lie in bed and cry. She couldn't escape her background, try as she might. Now and then she had a glimpse of what her life might have been had she been born a mile west in the same city. Boys with taste in clothes and with good manners noticed her, but she knew she "could never belong to one of them." Boys from her own neighborhood disgusted her. Isabelle was experiencing a *culture* conflict. She yearned for life in a suburban American culture. In action and appearance she could pass for one of this group, except that so much of her past was of an orthodox background and its strong teachings. Then there were always her parents who loved her but were puzzled by her. In repudiating her background she belittled much of herself—her ability, her heredity, her religion. She could never forget or cut off her roots, and yet she could never accept them. This conflict was so strong that for a long period she was depressed and remained aloof from most people.

This brief synopsis of Isabelle's plight illustrates the primary source of maladjustment. Strong basic tendencies within the organism *conflict*. These tendencies are organized around *motives* like love, self-esteem, or recognition. Isabelle wanted status or social recognition. Even love and future happiness were associated with status in her thinking, yet she felt that because of her origin she could never merit the recognition she desired. She was hemmed in psychologically. She loved her parents yet hated them inwardly for their lack of social status, but her strong religious training made her repress her hostility toward them so that she was only vaguely aware of it.

When basic motives are thwarted (*frustration*) or oppose one another (*conflict*), symptoms of maladjustment occur. One becomes depressed, hostile, anxious, or withdrawn. Before entering upon a detailed discussion of conflict, it is appropriate to investigate the nature of motives.

Nature of Human Motivation. *Growth of motives.* We are dynamic creatures. We are constantly adjusting to our needs and drives. These motives, as seen in Chapter 1, are any persistent conditions that direct behavior. They begin as physiological urges. When an infant's stomach contracts he feels hunger pangs. He squirms and cries, and his mother comes to feed him. He learns that crying satisfies the motive of hunger. Similarly, the unpleasantness resulting from wet clothing is removed because the mother responds to a cry. Fatigue, thirst, and other inner stimulation, fear, and anger are all among these primary physiological drives or motives that guide our activity in childhood.

Our motives are not all of the primitive type. We are continually developing new needs, wishes, and purposes that must be satisfied. Interest in food and play objects, sounds, attachment to mother and home are seen in the young child. The baby's mother becomes a very strong source of motivation at an early age, because she satisfies and becomes associated with so many basic biological motives. Caressing, fondling, and petting, through their positive responses, add to her value. In turn she guides the baby's behavior toward other goals and also aids in the development of basic attitudes and traits. Mother's "good" and "bad," smile and frown, have motivating value. At about 2 years of age, the arrival of the father in the evening occasions joy. At 10, the father's religion, politics, and mode of dress are defended with fisticuffs. These are learned motives which with time become just as strong as bodily urges. The child's ideals motivate him. The college football player who lives down the street guides his behavior at 12. As reading broadens his world, the nationally known athletes take the stage. The young girl watches and listens intently to the 16-year-old high school student next door. She wants tinted finger nails and rouged lips so that she may be like her older friends. She reads movie magazines and emulates the pictures and poses, and dreams in terms of the men who are the contemporary idols.

Think of all the experiences and situations for which you strived throughout your development. Recall all the people and things that tended to direct your behavior and dominate it at times. When you make an inventory of all these factors you have a *list of some of the motives that were operative in your development.* Then compare your dominant motivation with the persons mentioned on pp. 60 and 61 and on p. 62.

COMPLEXITY OF HUMAN MOTIVATION. The life of a person is primarily an organic unit. It is sometimes difficult to separate certain experiences and tendencies from the rest of behavior and obtain a true picture of a person. Very often we are *ambivalent* to a situation; we both love and hate it. This is a reaction experienced frequently toward a parent or even a "steady date." We may repress the hostility, but it continues to influence behavior. Usually *several motives* stimulate action. The best marriages, for example, satisfy many motives: love, companionship, security, social recognition, and new experiences or adventure.

Motives have *physiological and symbolic aspects*. A young man hates a boss or officer who reminds him of an unsympathetic teacher of his early years or of his father who criticized him severely. His strong hatred has many physiological components as, for example, raised blood pressure, but it also has subjective elements such as images of the disliked person. A college student is enamored of a coed. He gives her his pin or ring. Is this motivation entirely physical attraction? Or do her attractiveness to others, her prestige value, her hard-to-get attitude also operate? Do adventure, curiosity, prestige all influence him? His attraction, whatever its source, is unified. An individual's motivation, as we shall show in our study of development (Chapter 4), is the result of all the factors that have been influential in building habits, attitudes, and traits. An individual's way of life, his wishes and dynamics result from many interacting factors.

PSYCHOANALYTIC EXPLANATION OF MOTIVATION. Lust, hunger, and basic physiological motives are strong, blind, impulsive, selfish, lacking in ethical quality and seek immediate gratification with little regard for consequences or reality. Freud, the first great psychoanalyst, a Viennese physician who treated maladjusted patients, spoke of these as the *id*.

The *ego*, that which we call "me," the conscious wishes of the individual, he said must deal with the id and bring these impulses in line with our standards and "conscience," which he designated as the *superego*.

From this simplified standpoint, life's struggle is mainly to satisfy these biological urges in a manner which we can fully enjoy in terms of our standards and the standards of those with whom we live. Both the libido or race preservation urges, based on sex and love, and the self-preservation urges based on hunger, thirst, and the like, must be satisfied in a manner compatible with the culture in which we live.

Psychoanalysts have pointed to *unconscious* motivation. They show that some tabooed impulses such as hostility toward parents, sex wishes, and other experiences that would lead to shame are repressed but nevertheless influence our behavior unconsciously (777). Throughout this book there will be discussions and suggestions that will bring to light certain insights into your behavior of which you were not previously conscious. *Insights* and new perspectives on our behavior, especially that behavior which arouses anxiety, can best be accepted by us and utilized for growth when we are at the same time relatively secure and satisfying some of our personal needs. (See pages 131–132.)

INDIVIDUALITY OF MOTIVES. Writers have attempted to classify the motives of adults, and there is some value to such a grouping. Before listing the dominant motives of humans, however, let us say that the college student is an *individual* primarily, and as an individual he has motives which, although they are like those of others, have a unique quality. Following we see some of the differences in patterns of motivation among the five college students described in Chapter 1.

Ken puts an emphasis on success. This may be the result of his mother's dissatisfaction with his father's mediocre financial achievement, because his mother has had a great influence on Ken's thinking. He has striven for honors in school work, athletics, and miscellaneous extracurricular activities. Ken wants to do what is accepted and is strongly motivated to win the approval of others. He dates and dances, but girls are not so important for him. He is not, however, a social climber. His mother, through her family, has won a place in social circles for him.

Katherine evades the complexity of modern life. She substitutes the simplicity of daydreams in which she can return to childhood and to idealism. Dates, friends, and social events may lead to disillusionment, so she minimizes them. There is unconscious hostility toward her mother and sister. Although desirous of doing well in school, the fact that her going to college is her parents' idea affects her motivation.

Henry is particularly interested in impressing people. Much of his behavior aims to prove his manliness and to win prestige for himself. He wants to conform to the conventional pattern, but when this conflicts with his individualism the latter wins. Reading is important in his life, and so are other colorful cultural pursuits. Although he is motivated by sex drive his expression or control of it is not on a mature level.

George is highly sensitive to what people think of him. He is easily depressed when he makes mistakes. Clothes and suburban standards influence him greatly. He strongly desires to win status in the upper class.

His desire to be a doctor is largely motivated by this rather than by interest in the subject matter or by his success in scientific endeavors. He satisfies his motives less nowadays in daydreams. He fears being thought of as a country bumpkin, and this fear influences a great deal of his behavior. Girls are stimulating to him from a romantic and lustful viewpoint, but because they are people he fears that he may appear at a disadvantage in their eyes.

Larry wants to be in the center of a crowd. He enjoys humorous repartee with the gang. He usually responds to girls much as he does to boys. Extracurricular activities and their spotlights appeal to him. Ideas are stimulating, whereas clothes, cars, and other things are not so important. Possibly there is an unconscious motivation or conflict which explains some of his nervousness. He gains his popularity by being a comedian and a colorful person in the group.

Each of the above students is differently motivated. Each has certain dominant motives as well as other subordinate motives. The character that our motives assume depends upon our individual experiences and our cultural background, the customs, attitudes, and mannerisms to which we have been subjected (512).

CLASSIFICATION OF MOTIVES. Let us consider some of the motives common to human beings in the American culture. You have learned to desire many of the following conditions:

Social recognition—desire to be known by others, to be prominent in the community, to "amount to something," to have status or to be a power in the group.

Success—desire to master and succeed in school work, social skills that make us popular, athletics, or vocational skills.

New experiences and events—desire for travel, adventure, books, games, new friends, new possessions such as furniture and clothes, social affiliations, membership in groups, cliques, invitations to parties.

Affection—desire for friendship with "the crowd," affection from friends, parents, acquaintances, and the opposite sex, and desire to give affection.

Security—desire for economic status, social status, physical health, and family, and for approval of friends, family, acquaintances, superiors, followers, and of oneself.

ACCENTUATION OF CERTAIN MOTIVES. It has been stated that motives are organized on various levels and that those who gratify basic elemental motives are thereby freed to seek higher gratifications. The physiological drives (1) are most elemental. Then follow needs for (2) safety, or avoiding external dangers, for (3) love, warmth, and affection from others, for (4) self-esteem and recognition from others, and for (5) mastery or self-realization, or being able to accomplish and achieve in accordance with one's talents.

Individuals who grow up without extreme privations, in secure, loving, happy homes with some challenges for growth can turn to self-realization and to the satisfaction of social needs and can better withstand privations in later life. Such a person if so motivated can create, invent, write, appreciate the arts, or make a contribution to industry and society. If one has lacked love, security, or basic physiological satisfactions early in life, he is made susceptible to frustration by these earlier insecurities and privations and will be more easily disturbed by crises in later life. There is considerable evidence that those who have had severe psychic wounds in their early development often succumb later to emotional strain or react in a neurotic manner to them, even after compensating for them (502).

One psychoanalyst has emphasized *inordinate motivation* representing extremes of normal trends that grow from early frustration. A few examples follow (353, 354, 355):

An extreme need for affection and approval, shown in a strong need to please everyone and to be liked and approved by everyone, or shown in a fear of self-assertion.

An intense need for someone, usually a spouse, who will assume all responsibilities, shown in a fear of being on one's own.

A strong tendency to restrict one's behavior and life within narrow borders, shown in an urge to save rather than to spend, or in a necessity to remain entirely inconspicuous, or to belittle one's abilities and to overemphasize modesty.

An inordinate need for power, shown in a lack of respect for the individuality, feelings, and dignity of others and an interest in them only in the role of subordination, or shown in a reverence for strength and an utter contempt for weakness.

A tendency to exploit and to get the better of others, as shown by a great emphasis on money, bargaining, or sexuality.

A need for perfection, as shown in dread of mistakes or personal flaws.

Among other traits found in personal tendencies in their extreme form are needs for prestige, admiration, personal achievement, and independence.

UNDERSTANDING ONE'S OWN MOTIVATION. No aspect of self-understanding is more valuable than a deep knowledge of one's own motivation, particularly in the light of problems or personal unhappiness and confusion. The above-mentioned neurotic trends are no doubt identified in persons known to you (possibly yourself) who are seeking happiness or peace of mind but are trapped in their inability to satisfy their own drives by their present habits. Review the above lists of motives as a means of helping you to *discover your own motivational needs and the extent to which you have developed means to satisfy them.* Can you see why some writers say that the happier, better adjusted, less tense and anxious individual is rather *widely motivated and is satisfying his motives in a manner compatible with the rest of his personality?*

Frustration and Conflict

Frustration of Motives. When any motive is blocked the individual is frustrated unless he discovers a new method of satisfying it. Frustration may take the form of *privation* or *lack.* Insufficient time, knowledge, or intelligence may be extremely frustrating during an exam. Lack of spending money or athletic or social skills, inadequate wardrobe are other situations that frustrate some people. Frustration may be caused by *deprivation* or *loss,* as when one is separated from those he loves, fails in some pursuit, or wrecks a car. Many a war veteran experiences frustration because of a physical handicap due to wounds. Finally, frustration may be caused by an *obstruction* or *barrier.* Examples are seen in the frustrating effect of noise during study, of a low grade when working for a high record, of having to live with an annoying person (664). Young adolescents often feel that their parents' standards are frustrating to their attempts to rate with the gang. They complain that they cannot stay out late, smoke, use cosmetics, and wear their clothes in a certain fashion. The loss of a goal is disturbing, but even more disturbing is *how* that failure occurs (318).

Whenever a lack, loss, or obstacle thwarts a strong motive, such as a desire for love or status or some desire strongly related to the ego, it can be very disturbing to the individual. Not all frustrating situations are external. Some notably personal deficiencies are *within the individual.* When the obstruction becomes a part of the individual, as in the case of fear or guilt, we speak of the process as a *conflict.* For example, a socially conscious sorority girl may want to date a certain boy who has looks, poise, and ability, but who comes from a family "with no background." He does not belong to any fraternity, must work, and has a foreign name. All these factors she regards as barriers to a social relationship with him, and they produce a conflict in her. Frustration has merged into a mental conflict.

Conflict of Motives. Motivation may be blocked because it conflicts with an opposing motivation. This is a more basic cause of maladjustment than frustration, particularly if the motives are strong. The individual is psychologically torn apart. Mental conflicts are the key to most symptoms: unhappiness, irritation, depressions, feelings of inferiority, sex problems, and hostile behavior. Many times the two factions that are at war within the personality are not readily identified. For this reason numerous conflicts will be presented to enable you to identify them in yourself, bring them to your attention, and deal with them.

Experimentally Produced Conflicts in Animals and Humans. Suppose a dog is trained by being rewarded with food to respond to a circle and not to an ellipse. Then the ellipse is changed gradually to look more and more like a circle. The animal discriminates the small changes in stimuli, but, when the circle and ellipse are so similar that discrimination becomes difficult if not impossible for the animal, he tends to "go to pieces." He may squeal, move around in his harness, bite at the apparatus, and bark violently (599). Experiments such as these have also been performed on various other animals with similar results (458). Cats, for example, yowl, crouch in the corner of the cage, climb up the cage, bite, claw, urinate, or fall sprawling on the floor. After the conflict experiment they tend to be different cats, so to speak—less friendly; one habitually hid in dark corners (183). These responses come to be more meaningful when we consider human reactions to extreme conflict.

Students at various educational levels have been given tasks in which they could not or did not succeed. They showed emotion, an increase in errors, nonadjustive responses, and neurotic mannerisms of various kinds (519, 871, 687).

Classification of Human Conflict. How may all our various conflicts be classified psychologically? (456) There are (1) conflicts between opposing desirable motives, sometimes called "approach-approach conflicts"; (2) conflicts between motivation toward a goal and a tendency to avoid it, sometimes called "approach-avoidance conflicts"; and (3) conflicting motivation to avoid a situation—"avoidance-avoidance conflicts." A fourth classification may be added, growing out of the first (1), which becomes much more complicated in real-life situations. Giving up one goal to obtain another makes that other goal partially undesirable (361, 547). This fourth classification has been called "double approach-avoidance," since the individual moves toward one goal and then away from it as he realizes he must lose the second goal if he accepts the first. Let us look at examples of these and the classification will be clearer.

APPROACH-APPROACH CONFLICTS. In these conflicts one is attracted by incompatible goals. Jack wants to room with his boyhood friend, but he also wants to accept the invitation to room with a new acquaintance who is stimulating, different, and seems to be the kind of fellow with whom he would really enjoy living. Mary wants to marry Frank this semester, but she also has her heart set on finishing her course and qualifying as a nurse. It can readily be seen that these are more than approach-approach conflicts, since in their complicated settings there is an aversion to losing one of the alternatives. In reality they become double approach-avoidance conflicts.

APPROACH-AVOIDANCE CONFLICTS. A freshman is attracted to a social group or fraternity he has joined. He likes the brotherhood, idealism, the magnificent house, the prestige and camaraderie of most of the fellows but is repelled by the paddling, pledge duties, and dominance of a few of the older members. A student wants a prominent office, but it will entail electioneering, public speaking, back slapping, all of which he does not particularly like. A girl is strongly attracted to a certain boy who has a car and dresses well, but she has an aversion to his loud manner, his public caresses, and his drinking.

Most inferiority conflicts fall in this category. The individual has strong ambitions to excel in athletics, the social world, or in some enterprise, but he feels inadequate, lacks confidence, and is discouraged by any obstacle or minor failure. Sometimes the thought of an obstruction or possible error serves to discourage him. The motive to compensate for failure is strong, but the fear of failure is also intense.

Sex conflicts are often of this type. The primitive urges (the id) are thwarted by the taboos of society that the individual has acquired—there is an attraction to a girl, a tendency to pet, but there is also the realization that in view of the ideals of both the boy and the girl this behavior will lead to complications, guilt, and eventual loss of mutual respect. Most so-called struggles with conscience represent a conflict between a strong impulse and an acquired aversion to the consequences of acting upon that impulse.

Other examples of these conflicts are shown by the person with overaggressive traits who is impelled by strong drives to get recognition. He alienates people by his aggressiveness, and as he loses

Susan Greenburg

We are concerned lest we make the wrong choice.

friends his aggressiveness becomes greater. There is the 18-year-old who tries to live up to his father's ideals of initiative and social aggression but finds it impossible to become the tough-skinned extrovert who can do door-to-door selling as his father did. The girl who wishes to follow closely the religious teachings of her fundamentalistic or orthodox parents finds that some of her friends belittle these standards in their attitudes.

AVOIDANCE-AVOIDANCE CONFLICTS. Occasionally an individual will be forced or feel forced to respond in an undesirable manner to avoid a situation even more undesirable. An example is the case of the individual who feels that he should try to get an acquaintance whom he does not like into a fraternity because this acquaintance obtained a job for him one summer. He knows that he will lose friends by pushing the case, but he will also seem like a heel if he does not. A boy feels that he must marry a girl whom he does not love merely because breaking the engagement now, he thinks, will hurt her and her parents and make a fool of him and his parents. His mother has emotionally declared that he will disgrace his family if he breaks the engagement. He knows the marriage will not be happy, but he feels that he could not live in his home town if he called it off.

DOUBLE APPROACH-AVOIDANCE CONFLICTS. In these conflicts the individual is torn between two goals which are both desirable and disturbing in some aspects, and he must choose one. The *perfectionist* is easily trapped in this sort of conflict. Harry wants to satisfy all motives, to be highly successful in all pursuits, but time, energy, and aptitude permit success only in some of them. He wants all perfect grades, student offices with prestige, social life—dates, parties and bull sessions—and the sleep that will keep him in physical shape to function happily and congenially. He decides to give up social life, then feels he cannot be without it; relinquishes study time to activities, then is bothered by lower grades; and finally he finds himself unable to make up his mind, so he vacillates from one goal to another. Alice hates to give up her plausible plan for creative writing as a career to go into teaching to please her mother and to provide a definite income. She thinks she will "abhor teaching" and will not do well in it. At present she is undecided and somewhat listless about the conflict.

Anxiety. In many of the above-described conflicts we experience an undercurrent of anxiety. We are concerned lest we make the wrong choice. When the conflict involves our status or reputation, as it usually does when the two forces are strong, and we feel trapped and unable to respond, then we are more likely to feel anxious. We, at these times, feel upset and at fault as a person. There is some evidence to show that when we become anxious we are vaguely concerned about previous failures and shortcomings that we have repressed and that this event threatens to make us face again. The possibility of getting a poor grade in an important college course because one continually substitutes for study talking with friends, going to the motion pictures, or even doing odd jobs, brings back earlier feelings about parents' scoldings, teachers' head-shaking and punishments, and even our own earlier shame about indulgences in forbidden behavior. Anxiety is a generalized state that is the result of many earlier frustrations and threats.

Such anxious feelings are a vague or unclear *anticipation* of further frustrations or punishment. One feels blocked. It is as though "something terrible is going to happen" which can seal one's fate or ruin one's future. The reactions to conflict to be discussed in the next few pages are also reactions to anxiety. They are impulsive attempts to get rid of the disturbing anxious experience.

Adjustment to Conflicts

Reactions to Conflict. Before we discuss the various ways in which the individual reacts to resolve a conflict, let us see how he *behaves during a conflict.* First he vacillates between his desires or urges, or between them and the aversions to them. As he approaches his goal either in actuality or in idea, he is impelled toward it. If he has an aversion to the goal, the nearer he gets to it the stronger his tendency to avoid it becomes. Sometimes the tendencies to reach the goal and to avoid it neutralize each other and produce a block that keeps the individual from responding at all (547). This sort of behavior was seen in the animal in an experimentally produced conflict. As it was hesitating to respond to one stimulus or the other, much vacillation was seen. It would look first toward one, then toward the other, and some blocking of behavior was observed. All of us can recall experiences of great conflict—the "to be or not to be" indecision—and the period in which we are unable to act at all. George wants to phone a girl he has been secretly admiring. He fears she may rebuff him. As he thinks over the idea he moves toward the phone several times, dials the number, and hangs up twice, then dials again but hangs up as she says "Hello."

Vacillation and blocking have been studied in the laboratory. It has been found that the strength of the avoidance tendency increases more rapidly than the approach tendency as one comes closer to the goal (547).

SEQUENCE OF RESPONSE TO FRUSTRATION. How do we usually adjust to frustrated and conflicting motives? What are the various attempts made to remove the frustration and to resolve the conflict? The general answer to these questions is that animals and humans use *trial and error.* These random acts usually include *aggression* or some nonadjustive reaction. Experimentally frustrated animals fought, but they also exhibited fear and trembled (458). Humans become *anxious* when frustrated, possibly because they fear the punishment that so often followed previous aggressions. Both animals and humans *regress* to behavior used earlier in life, or *fixate* some random act that may seem senseless, and repeat it over and over. The frustrated rats ran around in circles or repeated errors they had long since eliminated. The human being finds many methods to *escape* or *defend* himself from the disturbing anxiety produced by the frustration. One easy escape is to *repress* or to turn impulsively away, physically and mentally, from the disturbing situation. Children seek their source of security, the parent, and adopt the behavior, attitudes, and ideas of this model. This introjection of their parents' standards becomes their "conscience" or super-ego that guides them in many situations. However, before long other models with different behavior are introjected, and *conflict* ensues, producing more anxiety, more defenses, and escape. In fact, *adjustment to life* for most people *is not always a logically worked-out plan but a pattern of motivation and frustration and a series of defenses and escape from the anxiety produced by the thwarted motives* (777). These have been called *defense and escape mechanisms.*

DEFENSES AND ESCAPES. We shall review these various escapes and defenses in the language of Sylvia, a college senior, who wrote this summary of her adjustment after a series of conferences with her instructor:

"I see now the basis for many of my problems. I have tried to summarize them in terms of the course material I have learned in Psychology.

"My early frustrations grew out of my parents' incompatibility. Most vivid factors in my life at that time were their fights. When my father left home, my mother spent a great deal of her time belittling him and telling my brother and me that her whole life revolved around us. She may have loved us, but I did not realize it because most of her behavior toward me consisted of restrictions and domination. The fact that I am constantly seeking security and love now indicates to me that these motives were *frustrated*. Since I have been in college I have symbolically fought her by my own type of aggression. I shock her and her friends by saying cruel things.

"As a child I learned (*introjected*) to use my father's method—a temper tantrum—to disturb my mother, and I *regress* to it even today when my security is jeopardized. I suppose, from one standpoint, much of my emotional life is *fixated* at a 10- or 11-year-old level and I am still, as a college student, yearning for the affection and security a child should have at that age.

"Another trait that is a real liability to me today is my jealousy. I presume this grew out of my relationships with my brother. Feeling insecure myself, I attributed some of my unhappiness to my parents' treatment of my brother. Whenever he was held up as a model for me, I became furious. My parents were wealthy, and I came to despise everything that wealth and power stood for (*displacement of emotion*) and began to support the cause of the underdog. I became intensely interested in Negro equality and even gave up my parents' religion. My interest in the underprivileged has almost become my life work. I presume this is an example of *compensation* for my feeling of inadequacy as a child. This trend was facilitated by my relationship with an older woman, a social worker, whose traits I introjected. She was one of the most vivid examples of sincerity, kindness, and affection I had ever known, and she was greatly interested in a better world.

"Until I had conferences with you and took courses in Psychology I *rationalized* much of my behavior. After a temper tantrum I used to say, 'People are so dumb. You need to get tough with them to make them realize issues.' Instead of realizing my real problem, I spent many an hour *daydreaming* about the kind of life I would like to lead, and the kind of person I would like to be. I dreamed of myself as an ideal wife with an ideal family. My goal now is to understand some of my negative personality traits as defenses and to *sublimate* my inordinate desire for affection in a manner which will make me, my future husband, and our children happy."

AGGRESSION. One of the most primitive reactions to thwarted behavior is aggression or hostility. Any strong motive that is severely frustrated predisposes the individual to anger. The very young child shows anger at restrictions to movement and learns to direct his irritability and temper outward. Aggression has been studied to determine its relationship to the motive thwarted and to the degree and number of frustrations (282, 688, 185).

Some of the puzzling violence of the Nazi can be explained in terms of the postwar frustrations of the German people. It has been found that aggression in the form of lynching is definitely associated with economic frustration. As the annual farm value of cotton in southern states diminished, lynching increased. The Negro became the scapegoat (362). This common phenomenon of finding someone, usually helpless, "to take it out on" when frustrated is generally known as *scapegoating*.

A college graduate who worked while he was in school during the depression of 1929 and made very poor grades has since established himself successfully in business. He looked out of his office window one day and remarked, "When I would sit in my boarding house window while in school and see cars pass, I could have socked any of the drivers if one had crossed me. Now I feel differently since I have a business, a car, a wife, and family."

Aggression is sometimes shown in dreams. Katherine, who has been discussed in Chapter 1, relates a dream about her mother and sister, both of whom had frustrated her. She dreamed that they were being mutilated. No doubt she suppressed any aggressive thoughts toward them during waking hours, but these thoughts came to the surface in dreams.

Social upheavals, like depressions, wars, and reconstruction periods, produce aggressiveness. The strength of the hostility may puzzle the person experiencing it. A college veteran who had undergone a rough war experience and an unsatisfactory marriage could not understand why he felt like swatting a fellow who went along the street gaily singing a popular song. This is an example of displaced emotion, which we shall consider now.

DISPLACEMENT. From another viewpoint, acts of aggression illustrate displacement of emotion. Displacement refers to a shift of emotion from persons or situations with which the emotion originally arose to another similar person or situation (346). Often the emotion is suppressed when it first occurs. It has been suggested that some of the resentment against persons in authority is a displacement of repressed emotion toward one's father. One may not feel free to criticize one's boss or teacher, but one may speak disparagingly of his vocation or, if he is fat, of fat men in general, or of his lodge. Loyal friends of Franklin Roosevelt felt that much of the criticism of Mrs. Roosevelt's activities and of his children's behavior was displacement of repressed feeling toward the President.

REPRESSION. An early and easy adjustment to frustrations and taboo situations is repression. When motivation is "stymied," particularly in childhood, the individual is likely to exclude that motive from his consciousness. Consider all the unpleasant aspects of life that you do not dwell upon, the embarrassing moments, the times when you have felt that you acted the fool, or showed unusual ignorance, the times you have taken advantage of another, the terrible sights as accidents or cruelty. Many persons who have been in military service, in prison or concentration camps, or in fascist Europe or Asia, have experienced sights and events they wish never to remember, and which recur only in dreams. Often this material is *too heavily laden with anxiety and guilt to be reviewed voluntarily by the individual.* Experiments on college students show they tend to forget unpleasant memories more than pleasant ones (532). Similarly, an experiment on repression shows that individuals forget more of their selfish choices than of their generous ones (3).

Repression greatly complicates our adjustment to our problems. It prevents us from understanding the forces at war within us. Because of repression conflicts continue to disturb us, but we run from them, substitute pleasure or regression rather than facing them, discussing them and making some sort of temporary or permanent compromise. In addition our repression of aggression may well explain our handling of our many social problems, our insistence upon strong punishment for wrongdoers instead of recognizing the causes for delinquency, crime, and social disorganization and removing them (834).

INTROJECTION. The child's emulation of his parents and ideal persons and *identification* of himself with them is discussed under the development of motivation. Introjection refers to the process of making their behavior and attitudes his own. Some of this is admiration of, or the association of motive-satisfaction or pleasantness with, the parents. These positive attitudes are called his *ego-ideal*. At other times the child follows the direction of the parents to escape punishment or the withdrawal of love. These attitudes were previously seen to be his "conscience," sometimes called the *super-ego*. According to the parents' standards, these admonitions and examples will keep him out of trouble and solve his problems. But, of course, if they are not valid or consistent or if his attitude toward his parents is a negative one, the introjection may lead to conflict instead of relieving anxiety. The case of Sylvia, related above, illustrates this. The college student, in reflecting upon his past experience, particularly his relationship with his parents, and in comparing himself with his associates, can come to realize the strength of his ego-ideal and his super-ego. He may be the kind of individual who has had positive ideals set before him with only the minimum of suppressive punishment, or the kind of individual who is restricted, afraid to venture forth because of stringent discipline in childhood.

FIXATION. Some individuals seem very immature emotionally for their age. Although adults, these individuals show much of the behavior of adolescents or even of little boys and girls. Some youths, like Katherine (Chapter 1), frankly state that they do not want to grow up. Others do not realize they are meeting frustrated motives by *fixating* on an earlier level of emotional development.

There is the boy whose mother praises him for pre-adolescent behavior, his lack of interest in the opposite sex, his child-like devotion to her because she fears the loneliness or dangers of having him grow up. All the pitfalls of love, sex, and adventures in the world are depicted to him. His initiative and aggression are suppressed subtly, and he remains immature, often without realizing what the difficulty is. The young war widow who had just a few romantic months with her husband before he left may fixate on this period, live completely in terms of their plans for the future. Similarly, the alumna who takes more interest in sorority affairs than do the girls who are active in the chapter may be fixating emotionally at the college period. Fixation protects the individual from the effort of assuming greater responsibilities and of solving new problems. The term "fixation" is sometimes used more broadly to mean resistance to change in learning new habits. Under frustration and emotion, animals and humans are known to repeat ineffective habits rather than to try new ones (482, 458). Laboratory studies have indicated how this resistance to change is related to such factors as strength of motive, reward, and punishment (686).

REGRESSION. Some individuals, in times of frustration, substitute behavior that formerly was appropriate; they *regress*, sometimes wisely, to an earlier stage of development. In regression the individual usually returns to fewer, simpler, and more primitive goals, and possibly less realistic goals (40). The individual may return to any group of habits or any stage previously discussed as a point of fixation. Regression in memory is illustrated by the oldsters who refer to "the good old days," "we don't have the good old . . . we used to have," "the old home place." Many a military man, in a culturally strange Oriental or European city, under frustrating conditions regressed in memory to Mom's pies, the drugstore gang, the girl in her light spring dress, ice cream sodas, and Bill's convertible. All these represented an earlier day of less stress. Temper tantrums, self-pity, boasting, and egocentric stubbornness in adults all represent regressions.

Regression may involve only certain aspects of the personality. It may be only a temporary escape from present vicissitudes for a later fresh start rather than a permanent retreat from reality and the problems of the present that must be solved for progress. The antics of grown men on a convention trip or at the college homecoming, the play-acting of an entire city as at the New Orleans Mardi Gras, the club initiation pranks, and the behavior during a vacation to the seashore or mountain cabin—all are suggestive of regression.

Regression has been demonstrated experimentally with children by removing toys that they have enjoyed and allowing them to select less interesting toys and games. The more the child seemed frustrated by the removal of the more desirable toys, the lower the constructive level of his play (40).

FANTASY. If motives cannot be satisfied in everyday existence, they may become a reality in a dream world, either after one has gone to sleep or during a dull moment in the daytime. Everyone daydreams somewhat, and some people lead an active life of imaginary existence. Among college students 69 per cent admitted daydreaming frequently.

In a study Negro boys were found to daydream more than white boys, probably because of greater frustration (57). The silent child daydreams more than the talkative one, probably reflecting less overt satisfaction of motives. Many who have not been successful enough from their standpoint with the opposite sex daydream of a very pleasant date or of accomplishing some extraordinary feat in the presence of an important person. Romance is a frequent subject for the daydreams of the adolescent boy, as are themes of violent aggression and of wealth (777). The martyr type of daydream is also prevalent; it accompanies the "they'll be sorry" theme. One collegian who has few acquaintances tells of an imaginary acquaintance to whom he boasts and who is impressed by him. He even imagines opening doors and allowing the imaginary chum to enter the building before him. The child's play is largely fantasy. He can readily imagine riding in a play car and locking his playmate in an imaginary jail. The appeal that movies, novels, art, television plays, and games like Monopoly hold is to some extent due to their satisfaction of motives for adventure, affection, and security not otherwise experienced (35, 643).

PROJECTION. There are always certain aspects of our personality that we come to despise through discipline or taboos. In dealing with these, we learn to deny the traits as part of ourselves. We discover that we can attribute them to someone else and feel relief by so doing. This "misery loves company" process takes many forms. Seeing dishonesty, immorality, and ruthless, self-seeking behavior in others, discovering evidences of forbidden impulses clandestinely satisfied by them, are a few examples. Pointing to guilt in others is so satisfying when one is troubled with impulses that lead to feelings of guilt in oneself. The many excuses for being late, making errors, etc., fall in this category. "The majority of the class is flunking the course, too," the socially busy sophomore tells his dad. "She had a bad reputation before I ever saw her, so she better not talk about me," argues the fellow who feels guilt for the shabby behavior toward a girl whose future he blackened; he tries in this manner to attribute the initiation of the undesirable behavior to her. "There are more immoral fellows on this campus than I have ever seen before." All illustrate the projection mechanism.

RATIONALIZATION. Finding reasons for our failures and evading the real causes and consequences of our difficulties can take many forms. Hardly an hour passes without most of us substituting rationalization or false reasons to explain some event that would cause anxiety and loss of self-esteem if faced frankly.

Sometimes whole areas of thinking are in "logic-tight compartments" which the individual cannot expose to free thinking. Religion, for some people, remains in a logic-tight compartment. The mother whose son or daughter can do no wrong will hear no criticism of the child, no matter how valid it may be. Most prejudices are supported by rationalization rather than by examination through reasoning.

Selfishness is bulwarked by statements like "The Lord helps those who help themselves," "You have to protect your family"; or it is bolstered with statements like "Our country was built on individual initiative," which are expected to defend all kinds of exploitation. The individual who finds that his affiliations with Christianity conflict with his week-day hostilities and shrewd practices belittles the "wild-eyed idealist" and says, "You must be practical."

When all the effort that we can muster fails to achieve a goal, we decide it wasn't worth having anyhow. In addition to the "sour grapes" rationalization there is the "sweet lemon" approach. The *status quo*, no matter how undesirable, assumes new value when changing it involves more talent or courage than we possess or means that we lose cherished perquisites by the change. It is shocking sometimes to see how good, moral adages are quoted out of context to justify some basically immoral practice. Elaborate expenditures on church buildings, when the man for whom the religion was named emphasized good works instead of property, is often justified by saying that "nothing is too good for the House of God." The nature of valid reasoning versus rationalization is discussed more fully under "Effective Thinking" in Chapter 7.

COMPENSATION. A real or imagined obstacle or defect results in substitute behavior or attempts to overcome it. This type of process is a widespread biological phenomenon. A defective thyroid gland by compensation grows larger; with exercise, breathing and heartbeat becomes faster to accommodate the greater need. Stories of individuals with physical or social handicaps who have attained greatness are legion and are mentioned in Chapter 15. Sometimes, from a motivational standpoint, the greatest asset a high school or university student can have is a feeling of inadequacy, if it is antecedent to appropriate compensation. The process of turning a handicap into an asset is called *overcompensation*. The actor with the large nose or big mouth or prominent eyes who uses these as a mark of distinction is well known to the American public. Similarly, the self-made man who grew up on the other side of the tracks is an example of compensation.

A deficiency may lead to direct or indirect compensation. The individual may achieve success in some realm other than the one in which he is handicapped, such as the borderline student who becomes an outstanding extracurricular leader, athlete, or successful manipulator of campus business deals. Arrogance, loud talk or clothes, cut-

Susan Greenburg

outs and weird gadgets on cars, as well as superior accomplishments in music, art, or scholarship may represent compensation for an earlier feeling of inferiority.

SUBLIMATION. It has been previously stated that the greatest conflict occurs not between basic motives but rather between *methods of satisfying* these motives. Therefore it is quite possible to substitute socially accepted means of satisfying impulses that push toward asocial satisfaction. If aggression and hate are the results of accumulated, frustrated motives, then all means by which motives are satisfied prevent the more violent types of aggression and hate.

There are many socially approved methods of satisfying basic motivation. All the various forms of play and sports, social gatherings and parties, service to others, hobbies, art and creative work, outings and travel are socially approved methods of satisfying motives. Sports, for example, are an outlet for aggression and frustrations; social gatherings and religion are outlets for affection.

The whole process of readjusting when we are emotionally disturbed consists in *finding avenues through which our basic motives may be satisfied in a manner that will merit our approval as well as the approval of society.* Motives differ with the individual; they represent the personal history of an individual. The creative means of satisfaction will vary from person to person. As an individual expresses himself in a hobby or social activity, he releases basic tendencies within himself in a desirable form. He feels more secure and is better able to accept and redirect those of his traits that produce anxiety.

A most important function of society is to help individuals to find a source for satisfying their strong motives, and to help them organize their experience in a manner to handle their anxieties effectively. If one is able to do this, he will have less need to project his shortcomings onto others, to become hostile toward them, to rationalize his prejudices, to compensate in a manner that will injure his fellow man, and in other ways to bolster his own ego and appease his own guilt by belittling those around him. Even a sublimated activity, if it leads to a holier-than-thou attitude, may become a disguised hate. It has been pointed out that a given form of sublimation might become fanatical. In such cases it usually is the result of repression and failure to face one's real problems. It is an escape from life as it really is.

MISCELLANEOUS ESCAPES AND DEFENSES. It has been seen that *any* random attempt at adjustment may assume extreme and abnormal proportions. We saw that some motives may be accentuated until they become compulsive and dominative of the individual as, for example, an extreme desire for perfection or an intense need for affection and approval, or an overpowering tendency to exploit others. As indicated above, even sublimations may become fanatical. Such defenses are well illustrated by tendencies toward *self-punishment* and *reaction formation.*

One psychiatrist has written a book devoted entirely to *Man Against Himself*, illustrated by examples of martyrdom, neurotic invalidism, addiction to alcohol, depressions, self-mutilation, and accident-proneness, and even impotence and frigidity. All of these are presented as methods by which the individual punishes himself as an escape from or defense against anxiety (536). *Self-punishment* is aggression or hostility turned upon oneself rather than against another.

Reaction formation is the term given to behavior that is the opposite of that which the individual desires to express. The exceptionally pleasant individual may be using pleasantness as a façade for inner tendencies to be aggressive. Reaction formation consists of compensating for negative impulses by substituting behavior that will best mask these impulses. The individual who just cannot face his tendencies to be aggressive or lustful feels that he must go to the opposite extreme to prevent this behavior. Many idiosyncrasies that separate an individual from others fall in this group. The person who must be overly neat, overly careful, or overly honest may be fighting impulses that he does not dare express even in their mildest form.

Many apparently nonadjustive or queer reactions, then, do have an adjustive basis if we thoroughly understand the subject's motivation. Self-punishment or martyrdom may not seem so silly if it has given the child parental sympathy that was otherwise withheld. Likewise puritanical traits are understood if they offer solace to the individual made anxious by strong lustful impulses within himself. Even depression and suicidal tendencies, regarded as punishment for suppressed guilt, assume meaning.

Evaluations of Escapes and Defenses. At this point in our discussion the individual who has been taught to believe that certain types of behavior are *always* right and others *always* wrong will be somewhat confused. As he sees certain behavior that he may have cherished being criticized as a defense or an escape, he may be disturbed. Let us reiterate that life is filled with frustrations and conflicts and we are constantly in a process of adjusting to them. Defenses and escapes are inevitable and universal, and they represent a kind of adjustment to unbearable anxiety at that point in growth. We are all in the process of adjusting to conflicts and escapes, and defenses are among the means of adjusting. It has been pointed out that defenses and escapes merely indicate that one's personality has strength and is *in the process of adjusting* to a disturbing situation.

We must now raise the question: When do defenses and escapes become dangerous or serious? These adjustive reactions must be evaluated in terms of the *total personality* and eventual *growth* toward maturity. There are times when a brief regression or compensation in one segment of experience may enable an individual to make a better total and long-term adjustment. Their *social value* is also important. If an individual's aggressions, compensations, or even displaced emotion results in a better adjustment for other people, its value is enhanced.

The adjustive reaction should not *absorb so much of the individual's energy* that he cannot carry on the functions of everyday life. Chapter 16 deals with this question. It may be briefly stated here, however, that, if the escape or defense seriously *interferes with the overall development* of the individual toward a mature, happy, sociable, integrated, plastic, zestful person living in the present real world, its value tends to be negative rather than positive. Stated more bluntly: Adjustive mechanisms are undesirable when they *jeopardize the physical or mental welfare and growth* of the individual or of society. Certainly an understanding of these adjustive mechanisms that enables the individual to deal better with his own inner life and guide it toward future adjustment has great value.

Conflicts and Mental Health. It has been said previously that conflicts and anxiety are the primary base for maladjustment and abnormal behavior and illness (691), and many of the above reactions to conflicts have been shown to be *symptoms of maladjustments* as well as intelligent or blind and stupid *attempts to adjust.* These questions arise: Do conflicts *alone* produce serious maladjustment and neuroses? Does the *constitution* of the individual play a role? Is the basic constitution of the individual weakened or strengthened by his *earliest experiences?* The experimentation on animals has shown that not all animals are deeply disturbed by the experimentally produced conflict. Furthermore, a certain emotional response of a convulsive nature caused in rats by subjecting them to high-pitched noises has been shown to be inherited and related to temperament (287, 482, 486, 501). There is also some evidence that temperament is related to types of physique (704).

It is highly conceivable that the *kind of temperament* the individual has, as well as the *frustrations that occurred very early in life,* could act to influence the later susceptibility of that individual to abnormal and neurotic behavior during conflict. It is thought that the extent to which the individual breaks under conflict depends upon the *kind* of conflicts, how *deeply seated* they are in terms of the individual's drives, their *frequency,* and *intensity. It is the nature of the conflict rather than the amount of strain* that is most important.

Certainly the conflict becomes much more important when it involves the *ego-status* of the individual. If the person feels that his whole reputation as a personality depends upon the outcome of the conflict, then it is very serious and involves anxiety. Those who emphasize the importance of constitution would insist that the extent to which the conflict affects the individual depends primarily upon the constitutional susceptibility of the individual to these influences; that there are some persons of apparently high resistance who may be subjected to almost any of life's experiences without suffering an emotional or mental break (436). Many others regard structural physiological and biochemical pathology as minimal, and personal and social factors—conflicts—as most important (121).

The Inevitability of Conflict. Conflicts are an intimate part of life itself. In fact, life would be colorless without them. They add to the zest of living. Conflicts in and of themselves are not undesirable. It is because conflicts exist among our loyalties and strong inclinations that we stop to think and formulate a way of life. A better integration of our personalities can result from an intelligent approach to conflict. If we learn early in life to face and deal openly with the inevitable choices and incompatibilities in thinking and behavior that do occur, we will learn how we stand on basic issues. We will formulate our governing values. Presumably such a frank approach to problems produces a strength to deal with problems in the future if the problems are not emotionally overwhelming.

A distinction must be made at the outset between *objective* and *subjective* conflicts. Objective conflicts represent the clash between our attitudes and events in the external environment toward which we can react with unanimity. A college student may despise cheating and may have resolved with his whole being not to cheat and to make his attitude toward cheating clear. He may find himself gravitating toward others who feel as he does, and as a result they may together create a moral atmosphere. He has *no great conflict within himself.*

Objective conflicts are not too taxing to the individual because he can put the whole force of his personality behind his reaction to them. He may sense the ill will of those who oppose his idea but this he faces at the *outset.* The individual who is torn within himself about the viewpoint he is to assume is the one who is disturbed. The person with the to-be-or-not-to-be attitude, the individual who vacillates between loyalties and who does not know where he stands on an issue, is troubled. The presence of objective conflict may not be too disturbing if it leads the individual to gain insight into his basic personality.

Some subjective conflicts can take on the characteristics of objectivity as we become aware of them and their consequences. The boy who feels he needs his mother even though her constant companionship makes it impossible for him to become one with his contemporaries—a goal he deeply cherishes—is more usually disturbed when the nature of his conflict is not clear. As he clearly sees the forces pulling within him, he is better able through discussion and experience to strengthen one, weaken the other, and make a compromise. He knows the nature of his inner battle.

We may conjecture that certain conflicts early in life that involve the ego and self-esteem of the individual, if they are prolonged, may be very disturbing. Other conflicts which, when solved, help one to build adaptability and a pattern of reactions to the world, may be fortifying for later living.

Review of Adjustment Process

How Frustration Leads to Aggression and Punishment. Let us attempt to summarize the most important ideas presented in this chapter and diagram them as we did in Chapter 1. These concepts are basic to the explanation of most of our daily behavior. First, many of our feelings, attitudes, and strivings are reflections of *our physical and psychological motivations, our needs which drive us to action.*

We cannot satisfy all these needs. Our motivation is constantly being blocked or *frustrated.* We may diagram frustration of motivation in this manner:

1. Motivation → | Frustration.

Frustration of ongoing motivation leads to restlessness or variable activity, one form of which (especially in the case of high motivation) is *aggression.* When we express our aggression to the injury of others we usually receive in return counteraggression or *punishment* from another person. In early life a parent may punish with a slap, later, a look or a word; still later a boss, a rival, or even a friend may punish us in some kind of counteraggression. We even punish ourselves when we review our wrongdoings. Counteraggression or punishment consists of *further frustration*. Let us diagram this process as we have traced it so far.

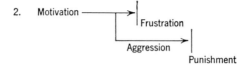

Frustration May Result in Learning. As pointed out in the diagram in Chapter 1, there is another course this activity may take. Our restlessness or variable behavior may lead to activities that get around the original frustration. We may find other satisfactions for the blocked motivations. Then learning takes place. The variable behavior in this case becomes a learned activity to satisfy a frustrated need. Let us diagram this:

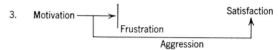

To illustrate this: A school boy of limited intelligence is blocked in his efforts to succeed in the classroom and through his variable activity may become the class comedian. The clowning may produce satisfaction to him if the students and teacher are amused by it, or it may lead to further frustration through the teacher's punishment or the class's laughter "at" him rather than "with" him.

Anxiety as Anticipation of Punishment. The concern over possible punishment obviously leads to further problems as discussed previously in this chapter. The first of these problems is *anxiety*. For example, the boy referred to above, who is unable to comprehend the school lesson or answer the teacher's questions, may experience fear or anxiety over what will happen if his restlessness or aggression leads to a remark or other disapproval from the class, punishment from the teacher and shame within himself. His emotional concern, his lost feeling, may go far beyond the realities of the punishment or ridicule he actually receives. He is then experiencing *anxiety*. Let us diagram this:

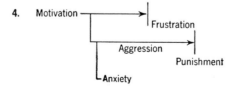

This boy is also in *conflict*. Should he speak out, be a comedian and take a chance on being amusing? But what about the disgusted look on his classmates' faces or the scolding from the teacher? This conflict also arouses anxiety in him. This is an approach-avoidance conflict as discussed previously.

Nonadjustive Activities are Partially Satisfying. The boy mentioned above may engage in any kind of adjustive activity while feeling anxious even if this activity is not entirely satisfactory. Any of the reactions to anxiety or conflict mentioned in this chapter may be used by him. He may project (blaming others for the conditions in the class), rationalize (find excuses for his behavior), or displace his feelings (show irritability toward an innocent pupil). These nonadjustive reactions and the others mentioned below partially reduce the anxiety if for no other reason than these activities reduce tension. When this happens the activities aroused tend to be learned. Anxiety under such conditions acts as motivation for nonadjustive or, in more fortunate conditions, as need-satisfying behavior. Let us diagram this:

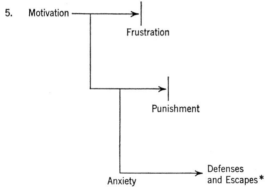

Conflicts Lead to Anxiety. Sometimes the above-mentioned aggression and anxiety is due to a trapping conflict rather than to the frustration of motivation or the blocking of ongoing activity. For example, it may be that the individual is not deprived of affection or success but fears the source of this satisfaction. A girl may want to show her love for her father but cannot approach him because of her fear of him. Similarly, a young salesman may want to sell his

---

* Aggression	Introjection	Projection
Displacement	Fixation	Rationalization
Repression	Regression	Compensation
Reaction formation	Fantasy	Sublimation

company's commodity, it may even be a commodity that can be sold easily, yet he dislikes or dreads making the necessary calls. These are approach-avoidance conflicts and may be diagramed as follows: $M_1 \rightleftarrows M_2$. In the first case, Motivation$_1$ is the love for the father, and Motivation$_2$ is fear of him. Thus $M_1 \rightleftarrows M_2$ becomes the first line in the previous diagrams. The remainder of the diagram is identical to that drawn for frustrated motivation on page 83. These diagrams when understood should help you comprehend and organize the basic processes underlying all of the personal problems discussed in the remainder of the book.

Personal Problems as Conflicts and Anxiety. The personal problems, then, which we do not solve readily are basically conflicts with some underlying anxiety. This anxiety, we have seen is unpleasant and motivating, drives us to discover ways of relieving it (225). These relieving activities, or habits, that may be difficult to explain otherwise, are called "defense" and "escape mechanisms." They are the nonadjustive reactions mentioned in Chapter 1—"nonadjustive" because they relieve anxiety and therefore tend to persist and disguise our motives. They do not satisfy, however, the frustrated or conflicting needs (motivations) that caused our difficulty in the first place. Our real conflict is not solved by them. We are usually merely diverted.

Individual Differences and Anxiety. We differ from one another in the degree to which we are susceptible to anxiety and threat and the manner in which we perceive and react to it (343, 730). Jack may not be easily threatened by his fellows, his superiors, his mistakes, or events. Jack, because of his temperament and total development (to be discussed in Chapter 4) may experience such security that he can accurately perceive the dangers in any situation confronting him and react to them accordingly. Bill, on the other hand, may be quickly aroused to a highly anxious and disorganized state. He may respond to the anxiety by running away from the situation, by refusing to face it, or by becoming rigid and defensive about any matters that arise.

Take a situation like a highly frustrating or threatening oral quiz that has been designed to produce a feeling of failure and anxiety and think of the various ways the people you know including yourself might perceive the situation and react to it. As you speculate on the reactions you will doubtless include such responses as terror and pain, tensions and mental blankness, bluffing, anger and aggression toward the teacher.   Another possible response is an effective rational attack on the problem consisting of trying those parts of the examination that can be answered and frankly rejecting after trial those parts that are beyond your powers.   Obviously, the last of these reactions is the most effective and is found as reactions to stressful and threatening situations only in the case of persons of the greatest of stability and maturity.   The reactions may likewise be found in those situations in which the individual has, because of training or circumstance, taken a *goal-centered* or *problem-solving* rather than a *self-centered and defensive attitude* (483, 605).   The self-centered behavior is often self-defeating and inappropriate in so far as solving the problem is concerned (391, 511).

The *major theme of this book* is an attempt to enable the reader to deal with his conflicts, frustrations, and emotional states in a manner that reduces the anxiety, tension, self-centeredness, and aimless defensive activity and redirects his activity toward a perception of the cause of his condition and a discovery of the activities that may possibly remove it and satisfy his needs (505).   We originally as children

Anxiety is lowered by others' understanding . . .

Susan Greenburg

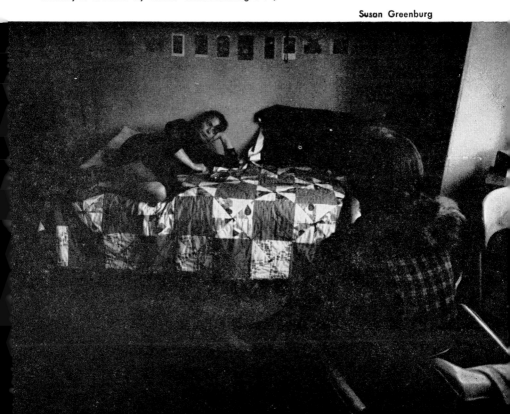

acquire our sense of confidence and self-trust by dealing effectively with problems and conflicts (220). If this is not acquired in early development it must be attempted in the same manner later.

There have been some interesting experiments performed to gain data on this problem and to discover the personality traits elicited in anxiety situations (518, 446, 248, 676). Some of these traits are high and low anxiety proneness, rigidity under anxiety, and perceptual defense (not perceiving those elements of a situation that are productive of more anxiety). One's concept of one's self, or one's self-image, has also been studied and related to the amount of anxiety experienced and the manner in which it is handled throughout one's previous life history.

Readjustment to Conflict and Anxiety. An individual can learn nonadjustive defenses and escapes that take the edge off his anxiety but still leave him unhappy and immature. What is the solution to his predicament?

The solution consists of conditions that lower his anxiety so that he does not need to escape or defend himself but instead can use the motivation produced by his problems to learn new ways of satisfying his needs. Anxiety is lowered by others' understanding, and environments that allow some success and satisfaction of needs. Many of the remaining chapters of the book (particularly the chapter on Creative Adjustment) deal with *conditions that reduce the individual's anxiety and guide his activities in the acquisition of skills and attitudes that lead him toward maturity and satisfy his basic personal needs.*

The initial difficulty, then, as shown in the diagram on page 87 is that the satisfaction of the individual's motives is frustrated. This leads to various other problems: aggression and anxiety. We can move toward the solution of any of these problems if the intensity of the problem can be reduced, be it aggression or anxiety. Then if trial and error and problem solving can be stimulated, there will be greater likelihood of finding ways of meeting needs originally blocked.

Let us reproduce the diagram, placing an emphasis on reduction of the tension and strong emotion (*reduced anxiety*) and simultaneous trial and error toward the satisfaction of needs (*learning*). At any stage in the adjustment process the emotion (aggression or anxiety) may under proper conditions become motivation for learned activity that will enable greater satisfaction. Even the defense mechanisms may lead to effective adjustment if they satisfy needs and result in the acquisition of mature personality traits.

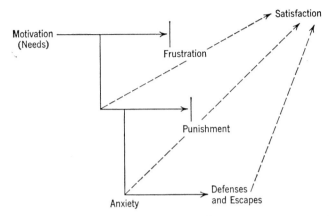

The broken lines in the diagram represent a condition whereby (1) strong emotion and tension are reduced, and (2) activities are directed toward learning habits and attitudes that satisfy motives and needs.

Supplementary Readings

J. Dollard and N. E. Miller, *Personality and Psychotherapy*, McGraw-Hill, 1950.
C. S. Hall and G. Lindzey, *Theories of Personality*, Wiley, 1957.
G. A. Kelly, *Psychology of Personal Constructs*, Norton, 1955.
N. R. F. Maier, "Frustration Theory: Restatement and Extension," *Psychological Review*, **63**:370–388, 1956.

In addition see the references cited by number in the chapter and appearing in the bibliography of an accompanying volume entitled *Teaching Personal Adjustment: An Instructor's Manual*.

Developmental Factors and Patterns

Most of our difficulties in youth and maturity have their roots in our childhood. As you read in the next chapter cases of individuals with difficulties, you will see that frequently the circumstances of early life seem related to present shyness, anxiety, feelings of inferiority, restlessness, or some other difficulty in youth and early maturity. Regardless of your present stability, confidence, efficiency, or purposefulness, you will find it interesting and valuable during your reading of this chapter to think of your own development. We shall discuss the many factors that occur during the years of growth and that make people what they are as adults—factors such as the family, neighborhood, school, play experiences, and various ventures and projects. Better still, you may refer to the pre-interview blank in the accompanying volume *Teaching Personal Adjustment: An Instructor's Manual* or obtain a similar blank and *write your own*

CHAPTER 4

DEVELOPMENT

OF PERSONALITY

autobiography or think over the factors in your development before proceeding with this chapter.

Cases: Developmental Patterns

Tom G., a 19-year-old college sophomore, is a handsome, well-dressed, mature-appearing, poised young man. He is 6 feet, 1 inch tall, weighs 175 pounds, is a brunet, and has a clean-cut, manly appearance. He seems to have the respect of his fellow students and to possess easy social relationships. He is neither extremely introverted nor extroverted and is temperamentally stable. People tend to seek him out as a companion.

At present, he is slightly above average in grades. He tells the following story of his life: His family is urban, well-established in an upper economic bracket. His birth was normal. His mother is an even-tempered woman who reared him in a regularized, modern manner. She was careful to supervise the servants to see that Tom did not acquire any fears, and his early life was a healthy one. He was rarely spanked. Discipline consisted in withholding privileges. He showed no nervous habits, was very fond of both parents, who played with him, and the three frequently went on trips and camping expeditions together. He idealized a young uncle who often took him flying and on similar adventures.

He enjoyed the luxury of an excellent neighborhood, extensive play equipment, friends, and many playmates. He states that he had no sex curiosity, was not much interested in girls until after puberty. His father was his pal, gave him adequate sex education when he was about 13 years old, and at that time corrected a few misunderstandings. His rigid, extra-family religious training, he feels, produced some anxiety, but, by and large, his childhood was very happy, without any worries or maladjustment.

Toward the end of the grade school period, he began to lose interest in school work and had a hard time maintaining the attention required by his subjects. He was not particularly interested in athletics, although he was a good swimmer. He went to camp each year.

In high school he was allowed excessive freedom, cut classes, joined a fraternity, associated with older, more mature boys, and began dancing and dating. He felt that his childhood was cut off prematurely. At first he felt ill at ease with girls, but this was soon overcome. At about this time his father suffered financial reverses. This, he states, brought the family even closer together. He found himself trying to make events in life intelligible. He experimentally sought a new religion and, much to his satisfaction, persuaded his parents to join the Unitarian Church with him. As a high school senior, his father allowed him to work as a laborer in his business. This was a profitable experience, and he came to respect the men who worked with their hands. He believes this experience also gave more meaning to his religion. He worked very hard and lost weight, which he regained as soon as he came to college.

At college he joined a fraternity, went to quite a few parties, in general had a good time, was very popular, spent more money than he thought he should, and nearly flunked out of school. Although *his parents were patient with him,* he viewed this period as a crisis. He began to *take stock of himself* and saw that his old tendency to drift and to shirk his responsibilities was coming back. He realized that he was not building intellectual interests or substantial hobbies. Neither did he put his schemes to make money into effect. These *arresting realizations and resolutions to change brought about an improvement.* He now regards his year of shiftlessness as a valuable experience because of what he *learned* from the various types of boys with whom he was thrown in contact. He was given an "average" rating by two mature contemporaries in terms of his total adjustment to life. His score on a personality inventory blank indicated good emotional and social adjustment.

Ned J. is a 21-year-old senior of above-average physical attractiveness, but slightly below par in grooming. He is a conscientious, hard-working student who obtains superior and excellent grades, seems shy and nervous, but is friendly and sincere. The story of his life runs as follows: He is the eldest of three children of a high school teacher who had only a very modest income when Ned was small. His mother is a rather high-strung, exacting, nervous individual, who disciplined him rather vehemently but fairly as a young child and taught him to be quite helpful around the house. His father is a shy, sincere, kind-hearted, hard-working, tense individual who spends all his spare time working on the small farm on which they live.

The home atmosphere was frugal and regulated, but his parents encouraged the children in many creative ventures on the farm, involving the raising and marketing of produce. He evaluates his parents' activities very highly and does not at present resent their stringency or the superior social adjustment of a brother who is a few years younger. Although the parents were well knit as a family, they had frequent minor quarrels. Despite the pervading tensions in the home, Ned regards his home life as ideal.

His health was good until he was about 10 years of age, when he was seriously ill for several weeks. As a child he learned to play the piano, had many friends, and enjoyed activities with them. In school he tended to be shy and serious. In pre-adolescence he belonged to clubs, teams, Boy Scouts (but did not pass many of the tests), participated actively in athletics in the neighborhood, and developed two warm friendships which were terminated upon graduation from high school.

He fell in love with a younger girl in high school, became far too serious, daydreamed about their life together, and has not yet been able to forget the affair which her parents ended.

The family traveled widely. They were very active in church work. With adolescence his parents allowed the children much greater freedom and opportunities to make their own decisions.

The hardest adjustment Ned had to make was in college. He felt immature, was not interested in the social activities of the fraternity, and regarded the change as sudden and strange, felt ill at ease in large social gatherings like parties, yet wanted to attend them. He did not enjoy fraternity house activities like smoking, drinking, and loafing. Intramural sports were the only fraternity activity in which he participated. He turned to a young people's church group and more compatible companionship. He preferred girls to boys and spent more time with them. At this time, too, there was a conflict between his early religious training and college science, which he came to enjoy greatly and in which he attained excellence.

During his college years Ned regarded himself as physically unattractive, owing particularly to a very slight case of acne and a cheek mole, and he felt self-conscious about his curly hair (which in reality is attractive), and generally inadequate. As a matter of fact he had a well-developed body. His self-consciousness, although not at all socially obnoxious, was noticeable. Had he made any effort at all to become one of the group, he would have succeeded because he was extremely modest, conscientious, sympathetic with students who were having difficulties, and helpful to them. His fraternity brothers recognized him as a loyal member and a "nice fellow." Two mature contemporary students judged his total adjustment to life as very poor. His score on a personality adjustment inventory indicated maladjustment.

Ned later took graduate work, and although he was constantly fearful that he would not succeed and would never be able to teach a class, he has achieved superior success in terms of his responsibilities, even though he does not have the ease of some of his colleagues.

Nita N. is a 17-year-old freshman of average height and weight, moderately well groomed, and above average in appearance. She grew up in a town of 2000, went to a small high school, and ranked third in a graduating class of 20. She was liked by all her teachers, and she won a scholarship awarded by a national firm interested in youth on the farm. She received a great deal of recognition in the town for her 4-H activities and the various trips and awards she earned.

She had many acquaintances but rather few close friends. She was highly competitive in her relationship with her contemporaries and felt that she had to make very good grades to uphold her reputation. She says she is studying hard, but, after she spends three hours a day working for remuneration and attends a full class schedule, she is not very efficient in the evening hours. She has several dates during week ends and studies very little then.

She is one of three girls in her family. Both parents are young—her father a hard-working, introverted farmer who has had very little contact with people. Her mother, on the other hand, is a vivacious person who is always in the limelight and in recent years has been very active in young people's groups. Both parents have always expected a great deal of Nita, have overprotected their children, and have given them full instructions about what they should do, with few liberties. Although Nita had shown a great deal of initiative in 4-H work and extracurricular activities in high school, she had to account for her time rather closely. Her home is conventionally religious. Apparently she has received rather little real affection from her busy parents, and the response that she has obtained from her contemporaries has been the result of her successes rather than of any warmth or personal charm. As a college student, she seems somewhat tense, aloof, and is likely to give her fellow students the idea that she is conceited.

Although in conferences she discusses quite freely her concern over her future vocation and grades, she avoids mentioning anything about her social or inner life. The counselor hypothesizes that Nita is excited by the new freedoms at college and the varying standards she sees among her associates. No doubt, she finds it difficult to accept the fact that many of her associates can handle this freedom intelligently. Boys seem to interest her more than she will admit to herself. The closest that she will come to discussion of her problem is to indicate on her pre-interview blank that she is idealistic, weak-willed, moody, and does not show "oneness of purpose and consistency and stability of attitudes and desires." The counselor has the feeling in talking with her that she has never been able to confide in anyone, and because of her background fears to face and verbalize some of the matters that are disturbing her deeply. She was doing poorly in a course in Zoology, and this threw her into an emotional state somewhat like panic. The counselor had the feeling that she was concerned about more matters than the Zoology and had displaced some of the anxiety associated with the problem of handling her new freedoms to the problem of school work. Her ability, her previous record and interest in school work indicated that there is very little reason why she should have academic troubles if emotional problems were not a disturbing element.

We now turn to conditions contributing to the development of *maturity and unity of personality* traits and motivations, and those conditions that give rise to conflict, anxiety and *nonadjustive responses*. Before reading ahead *you may find it valuable to list conditions so influencing your own development and compare it with the list on page 94 and the discussion which follows.* These brief sketches of the development of three college students should give you an idea how students and counselors label certain factors very important in total personality development. We must admit at the start that personality is so complex that it is doubtful whether all aspects of any individual have been thoroughly understood. Nothing specific is stated in the above cases about the *heredity* of these individuals; their body chemistry related to their *endocrine glands*, which in part affect their temperament and moods; their *earliest* development, which goes beyond their own memories and may have been a routine matter to their parents. Surely some of the *social and emotional atmosphere* around the home, neighborhood, and town was missed. It was also difficult to ascertain how important each of these factors was because the factors interacted. Tom, Ned, and Nita were individuals or persons all during their lives, and they were treated as, and they behaved as, integrated individuals—not as a group of influences. All the many influences that affect our ongoing growth fuse. Not one of these personalities discussed above is the result of a *mechanical accretion of factors*. *They are living, striving, growing individuals* with certain hereditary influences in the cells of their bodies *interacting* with the environmental nurture that began nine months before their births. They are persons with self-esteem, and the potentialities for rational thought, and the extension of their personalities through their activities and plans. Growth continues always, determined partially by inner forces and partially by outer pressures. Any one trait, aptitude, or tendency of Ned, Tom, or Nita is not the result of heredity or environment, or of this failure or that encouragement, but *is a product of all these factors* and perhaps many which remain undiscovered *as they interact and fuse* (52).

Despite the limitations of your knowledge it is possible for you to gain insight into your development. We shall, in this chapter, try to help you by calling your attention to factors that are known to influence the course of development of the individual. On the basis of objective studies we shall indicate the external and internal forces that affect adjustment.

FACTORS CONTRIBUTING TO DEVELOPMENT

A. Constitutional factors—reflected in part in body build, temperament, and basic reactive trends.

B. Prenatal life and birth.

C. Early maturation.

D. The mother—who may be loving, understanding, overprotective, inconsistent or unreasonable in discipline, tense and dominative or anxious, reject the child or play favorites.

E. The father—similar to mother.

F. The family unit—whether parents were compatible, home broken, affected by relatives, reputation, offered warmth and security.

G. Aspects of the home and neighborhood—such as cultural level, rural or urban, kind of neighborhood.

H. Play, social contacts, and recreation—group activities as outlets and sources of growth.

I. School experiences.

J. Extraschool experiences—movies, television, work.

K. Religious and moral influences.

L. Health and physical factors.

M. Self-impressions and evaluations.

N. Affection and sex.

O. Pubertal changes and adolescence—attitudes produced by changes, newer social and parental relations.

P. Plans and future goals.

Q. Maturity—vocational establishment, independence of family, philosophy of life, heterosexuality.

R. The individual's integration of traits leading to a learning attitude rather than conflict, anxiety, defense and escape.

Early Development

Constitutional Factors. You have noticed extreme physical traits running in families. Two or three people in the same family will have a strikingly similar build or some noticeable facial feature. Cases are known in which twins develop a mental disorder even though they have been separated for years by distance (402). However, heredity and constitutional factors must always operate in any environment that affects them one way or another. Not all twins for example will develop a mental disorder when their identical brother or sister enters the hospital. When this is the case, a difference in the environment and way of life seems to explain the disparity (341). Whereas certain aspects of temperament and social behavior seem to remain remarkably alike in twins reared apart, other forms of behavior of a social nature differ in these separated twins (110).

Observation of young children, even of the same family, indicates that temperaments differ quite early in life. Children differ in speed and extent of movement, ease with which they become excited or irritated, responsiveness to environment, smiling tendency, tenseness, and such traits. Undoubtedly some of these differences are due to basic temperament; others can be explained in terms of early environment (708, 575).

At present it is difficult to generalize about the extent to which these constitutional factors affect emotional life and individual ways of behavior, but evidence is available to show that these background influences work together with environmental factors in making us what we are (568).

A number of attempts have been made to connect physical types with temperament without conclusive success. Some studies show a tendency for certain temperaments to be associated with certain body types such as the fat, soft, and easygoing, the long, slender, and sensitive and the muscular, energetic, assertive person. More critical studies show body build and temperament are only slightly associated (16).

Prenatal Life and Birth. Very little of our psychological development is directly due to prenatal influences. The development in these nine months is mostly a matter of physical growth, which includes the structure that is basic to later capacities and temperament (128). There is a great change in the child's life at birth, when he leaves the mother's body—but is this emotionally disturbing? Apparently not, from studies comparing children delivered by Caesarean section with others (250, 845). There are rare cases in which physical injury or instrument delivery at birth has affected later behavior (845).

Temperament is doubtless more important than we can demonstrate with empirical studies today. It is almost impossible to separate what is learned from birth on from our individual innate temperamental tendencies. Much of our behavior is due to the particular way in which our basic tendencies are fostered or negated by the environmental factors to be mentioned in this chapter. It has been demonstrated experimentally in rats that tendencies toward brightness and dullness, wildness and tameness are inherited (303). How much our constitution governs how quickly, deeply, and strongly we can be emotionally aroused, whether we are high or low in energy level, the ease of control, and our energy and other characteristic moods and expression is left to future research.

The Mother. The question we wish to raise is: How is the child affected by the mother who does not *love* the child and *rejects* him emotionally; by the one who *overprotects* him, is *dominant,* exemplifies *unreasonable* or *inconsistent discipline;* by the one who has a favorite among her children or makes *unfavorable comparisons* between them; or by the mother who is *emotionally unbalanced* herself and reflects her own conflicts in her children?

The child needs the affection of the mother in order to develop *stability* and to feel *secure* (874). An investigation of numerous young babies indicates that adequate handling and fondling prevents tension and persistent crying, and fosters better physiological activity (638). Separation from the mother can give rise to *anxiety* in the child (111). It has been argued that affectionate mothering bridges the gap between the dependent existence before birth and the many frustrations of the outer world (561). Well-adjusted college students speak of their mothers as being gentle, agreeable, and even-tempered more often than do students with emotional problems (520). It might be asked whether the importance of these factors is limited to middle class Western civilization (284). Furthermore, how important is affection in comparison with constitutional factors and all the other influences in play, school, and adolescence?

OVERPROTECTION. Obviously a parent can continue babying the child too long. There are many indications of the negative effects of overprotection. In nursery school such children are described as lacking initiative, crying easily, demanding adult attention, and avoiding other children. The minimum effect of overprotection is encouragement of traits such as *dependence, lack of cooperation* in situations requiring give-and-take, and poor work habits (320). The overprotected child may show the effects of parental domination or indulgence. He may do well in school because of parental emphasis on marks and his own tendencies to withdraw from child play. The constant use of fear by the parent to control him can produce an anxiety state (455). The other children may ridicule his shyness or punish his insistence on taking the center of the stage. This makes him unhappy and withdrawn from others. If this treatment continues, he may always have an inadequate personality. If his social contacts are not compensated by some other achievements, he may in extreme cases develop a seclusive personality.

MOTHER'S REJECTION. The opposite extreme in the parent's attitude exerts even greater disturbing forces. When the child is unwanted, neglected, or rejected by the parent, insecurity and resultant over-aggressiveness, pugnacity, flight from home, and delinquency may result (471).

There are other conditions that jeopardize the mother's affection for the child, in the eyes of the child. If a baby is born into the family when the child is 18 to 42 months of age, his position in respect to attention from the parents and unshared affection will be disturbed, and aggressive symptoms may result. A child who has established many habits of self-control may regress to infantile habits and become a problem when *jealousy* occurs. Case studies show that the disturbance growing from this sibling rivalry may continue through a great portion of his life (403).

MOTHER'S DOMINANCE. The dominant mother tends to produce traits such as obedience, courtesy, modesty, carefulness, and attentiveness, but her child lacks initiative, depends upon authority, and is better adjusted to older people than to his age-mates. Children of submissive parents, on the other hand, tend to be disobedient, disorderly, selfish, and aggressive, but they are also more self-confident, talkative, and independent (561).

PREFERENCE FOR AND INFLUENCE OF MOTHER. Both boys and girls are as a rule closer to the mother, at least during the first decade of life, than to the father. She exerts a prodigious influence on them. The young child identifies himself with his mother and reflects her fears and her ideas of right and wrong (299). She influences these ideas more than do father, friends, club leaders, or teachers (315). Stable male students say their mother was nondemonstrative, mild and even-tempered (740, 521). Nervous, tense, insecure, self-centered mothers with conflicts tend to produce an unhealthy atmosphere and anxiety and tension in the child (289).

SUMMARY. It appears that the mother's role in the life of the healthy child is to give the child affection and security and to guide it early in life. She is a better mother if she is calm and secure herself and allows her child to grow up and exercise his own initiative. She becomes the model of the girl if she is worthy of this ideal, and thus influences development. Anything that alienates the girl too much breaks this identification with the mother as a model.

The Father. The father apparently exerts his direct influence upon the child later in childhood. His role as well as the mother's is determined in part by their relationship to each other, their compatibility (289, 476). There is no doubt that the mother who idealizes the father to the child while he is at work or away in military service is adding to the real or imaginary influence he may have.

If the mother rejects the daughter whereas the father is protective or varies between love and sternness, the daughter becomes submissive (581). On the whole the girl of the family is more stable if the father is not too stern with her (740), but encourages a relationship that furnishes her with an ideal for her choice of a husband rather than an emotional fixation that prevents interest in other men (790).

The father's relationship toward his son produces a wholesome development if he shows interest in the boy's development, plays with him, punishes him wisely, and becomes an ideal which can be emulated.

The Family Unit. When the histories of individuals who have developed emotional and mental disturbances are examined, inadequate family backgrounds and attitudes are frequently found (38, 84). This includes such factors as loyalty toward the two parents in broken homes. Within the normal range homes will differ. There are acceptant, democratic, indulgent, rejective, and autocratic homes. Combinations of certain of these conditions may arouse rivalry among the children. Relatives may affect in some way the emotional adjustment of the children—possibly creating a source of friction or of inspiration. On the other hand, personality stability and later mental happiness is associated with a happy home (740, 790, 521).

POSITION IN FAMILY. Whether a child is the only one in the family, has an older or younger brother or sister, or is a member of a family of six or eight undoubtedly influences his personality. It is obvious that not all "only children" or "youngest" or "oldest" are alike. Ordinal position in a family does not necessarily correspond to psychological position. A resourceful parent with one child may arrange events so that the child will never experience what strongly affects another only child. The most important factors in development are answered by questions like this: Is the child accepted and loved? Is the child overprotected or rejected?

Aspects of the Home and Neighborhood. Childhood emotional explosions have been found to be related to the number of adults and children in the home, rivalry between them, the presence of visitors, the attitudes of the adults—critical, anxious, nagging, emphasizing badness in the child, domination, inconsistency—as well as organic states of fatigue, hunger, and poor health (278). A parent may harp on some behavior, giving it undue significance. Parents and teachers studied some years ago were found to differ from clinicians in what they regarded as a problem (750). It has been said facetiously that there are no problem children—only problem parents!

Crowded living conditions are thought to cramp the child's personality growth. They prevent idealization of people, emphasize physical sex life rather than love, and act as a strain on emotional life (613). Children of lower economic status fight more in nursery school than those of a higher status (385). The extent and kind of crime and mental disorder are related to neighborhoods even though

Rollie McKenna

there is a constant flux of population (226). Cultural conflicts between the standards of the parent, usually foreign born, and the child who reflects the pressures of the neighborhood cause disturbances. These conflicts are accentuated if the child represents a minority of his group in the school he attends (782). Whether a child lives on a farm, in a small town, or in a city is also influential (754).

Shame and feelings of inferiority may result as the child compares his home with those of others. Shame about one's home has led to rebellion and delinquency. A girl may escape from the home and compensate for her feelings about her home by trips with other girls downtown to visit movies, lunch rooms, and walking the streets. Such a practice may develop into nocturnal street cruising, drinking, and being picked up to be taken to hotels.

Inferiority feelings are slightly less in children whose parents have vocations with financial and social prestige (725). The contrast that the child feels between his status and the status of those around him is no doubt a big factor. Security and personal dignity have come to be associated largely in our society with the possession of money and goods (420).

Other factors are important in the *atmosphere of the home*. There are free, creative, colorful, cultural, or gregarious attitudes, and constricted, provincial, rigid, traditional, or materialistic attitudes. Mention must be made of the parent who has the future role of the child planned despite the physique, temperament, or talents of the child which may caricature the role. Conversely, there is the understanding parent who helps the less athletic or the aesthetic boy or the mechanically inclined, unfeminine girl to find himself or herself and to develop talents to achieve a creative adjustment.

DESIRABLE CONDITIONS IN EARLY DEVELOPMENT. Let us stop at this point and see what a good home is, psychologically, from the standpoint of personal development. It should *lead to individual initiative, a learning attitude and away from anxiety, conflict, defense, and escape* (123). What is indicated above seems to be a good developmental climate including (1) affection that gives security but does not lead to fixation at any stage in development or regression to a safer easier stage (842, 80, 591); (2) discipline that is not overpowering but consistent and results in learning; (3) good models in parents or older individuals for identification and sources of standards and understanding when difficulties arise (424, 150, 682, 135, 29, 735). In summary, effective conditions for growth for the individual allow

him to develop *inner strength to combat anxieties* when they arise. This is reflected in a *strong ego and good self-regard*. (See Chapter 7, p. 202.)

Later Development

Play, Social Contacts, and Recreation. *Early play.* To what extent is a child who learns to play and to deal with his contemporaries early in life different from one who meets another child only occasionally until he enters school? Many events that occur very early during play speed the social development of the child. It has been found, for example, that contact with other children in nursery school has these effects upon the child: as a rule he becomes less an onlooker and shows more active participation in social contacts with others. There is an increase in *social poise and spontaneity* in social situations. He loses some of his tendency to fear others, to shrink from notice, or to hover near adults. Sometimes nursery school reduces tensions that may have arisen between the child and someone in the home. In addition there is an increase in the child's tendency to show *independence*, to stand up for his interests and rights (382). Contrast the child who has learned sociality with the child who sits alone, daydreams, and has so few outlets that any emotional experience becomes the subject of persistent brooding.

Play has another effect, which all of us have observed in our own experience but has recently been subjected to elaborate investigation. It *releases tensions*, is an outlet for frustrations and anxieties. It is a means of assimilating disturbing experiences by repeating them in a mild and controlled manner. Children in bombing areas did not talk about air raids at first, but later rehearsed the experiences in spontaneous play (82). Even adult reading of detective stories and viewing of exciting movies may be a playing out of fear situations in order to release anxiety.

FRIENDSHIP, POPULARITY, AND LEADERSHIP. Play activities allow the child to establish the bases for friendships, popularity, and leadership in their later development, discussed fully in Chapters 10 and 11. They allow him to acquire the social habits and attitudes that may give him poise, confidence, initiative, and a knowledge of the social give-and-take. In addition, if his experiences are wide, his whole horizon will be broadened, and new interests and talents will be discovered.

Children develop friendships during play for different reasons, depending upon the pairs. Physical, mental, and social factors are among those found to be alike in friends. Friends tend to behave similarly, too, in situations such as those requiring honesty and generosity (314). Popularity or acceptability by others is related to energy, if this energy does not annoy the other child. Listless and uninterested children are less acceptable to their peers. On the whole, the popular children are those who are superior in intelligence, grades, classroom behavior, playground skills, and pleasantness in attitude toward work and play (310). They are not necessarily the most cooperative (314).

Children who are *leaders* are above the average in scholarship, are rated as extroverts, are more intelligent, and as a rule are somewhat larger, better dressed, more fluent in speech, better looking, more self-controlled, and more daring. It appears that leaders tend to be conspicuous even though they are not conspicuously good (382). Children can learn to maneuver their way to leadership just as adults can, and children through their choice of associates pave the way to later election to leadership.

The value of release of tensions with play and free contact with others in development is shown by lowered delinquency rates where there are increased recreational facilities (847). In later life these values are demonstrated in the better adjustment in college and in military service of individuals who have a history of sports, team memberships, and social activities (521).

School Experiences. What effects besides socialization through contact with other children may school have upon the child? A child may withdraw emotionally because of a serious handicap in some subject or because of some situation which makes him feel inferior to others. He may be absent for long periods or transfer from one school to another with some effects (569). The personality of the teacher and her attitudes will affect children differently. Teachers who are able to secure cooperation and the good will of the children have students who cheat less, it has been found, than those who are more rigid and conventional in their methods (314). Similarly, when teachers create an atmosphere that allows students increased freedom and opportunities for responsibility, these privileges are used to advantage. Parents have found the personalities of their children to change when they go to school. A child might conceivably get warmth or objective treatment there that he does not receive at home (569).

If you go back in your experience and list events, periods, successes, and failures, and explore abilities and interests in your school career that seemed to influence your present traits, you will doubtless make some discoveries.

Extraschool Experiences. These include jobs, camp experiences, hobbies, membership in clubs, loafing, travels, visits to relatives, city adventures like museum trips, and reading (37, 570). What effect do these have throughout the years of growth? Every college student, upon reflection, will realize the effect of them on his life. *Jobs* hypothetically can inculcate responsibility and good work habits, arouse interests, test aptitudes, broaden one's horizon of life's scope, or they can disillusion the child early, corrupt his standards, or produce poor work habits. *Camps* theoretically can teach skills, hobbies, appreciation of nature and can socialize and influence character traits (330). *Hobbies* can become the source of a life interest or vocation. If broad in scope they may have educational value. If they include other people, they are socializing. *Travel,* either within the vicinity or over wide geographical areas, is educational and broadening in per-

spective at least. Veterans of World War II show this effect in their college work. The effect of *loafing* will depend upon the influences, human or otherwise, that operate during the period.

SOCIAL ATMOSPHERE. If a group has an authoritarian leader who is dictatorial, makes all the decisions, and is personal in his criticism or praise, aggression or apathy is the result. Aggression crops out when restraint is removed later. The democratic leader is better liked by children (457). Younger children around 6 and 8 years old tend to choose their ideal persons from their immediate environment (339). At about 10 years of age and above, historical and public characters become their ideals. Although parents have great influence as models in early years, at about the tenth year this influence yields to that of other persons whom the child knows directly or indirectly.

MOVIES AND TELEVISION. Some children miss very few movies which are shown in their area; others go only on rare occasions. Movies have been found to influence children's attitudes and ideas concerning customs, dress, manners, and morals. They also produce or accentuate fears. Movies affect the sleep of some children and produce nightmares (200, 636). Restlessness during sleep after seeing a movie increases 26 per cent in boys and 14 per cent in girls. Under proper management, movies can stimulate the child's imagination and give concrete form to educational materials that are difficult to present otherwise. Movies may serve as a safe means of facing anxieties and as wish fulfillment for some children. Much that has been said above
104

also holds for television. Movies and television do not seem to be the origin of emotional problems but a focal point for problems of the disturbed children. Most children spend considerable time watching television, but there is little evidence that it affects the typical child's scholarship or interests in other recreational and social activity. Parental control and shorter viewing time tend to be found among children with higher IQ's (147). We must raise the question: Do children with certain traits and backgrounds see television and movies more often than others, thereby reflecting these traits in the results of the experiments?

Religious and Moral Influences. Children usually are born into a religious group. It may be of the orthodox or fundamentalistic kind, or it may be one which puts its emphasis mainly upon morals and ethics. In various parts of the country any given religion may be the dominant one, or it may represent a minority and thus influence only the adherents. Religious leaders and educators differ in the intensity with which they use fear and coercion to mold behavior. Religious teachings differ in the extent to which they conflict with typical Western culture, which is largely materialistic, and with science, which emphasizes natural causes rather than supernatural that intervene between events and the individual. Clergymen vary in the degree to which they will encourage their flocks to make contact with those of different faiths and to prepare children for a complex, heterogeneous world. They differ in the extent to which they teach or discourage prejudices and bigotry. One of the worst accusations that can be brought against some avowed religionists is that they shroud with a cloak of righteousness their hostility toward those who think differently, and they propagate this unbrotherly attitude in the children of their congregation. On the other hand, some religious leaders hold up models of strength, courage, and conviction blended with love and understanding of the erring but searching human beings.

The home, school, clubs, movies, community centers, books, playmates, and major social upheavals have influence on moral development as well as on total personality adjustment (130, 323). The breakdown of morals, ethics, and character is seen in the delinquent. Next to the home, intimate companions are mentioned as most important in bringing about delinquency. On tests of honesty and generosity, children tend to resemble their friends in behavior. Club members are more cooperative than non-club members, but not necessarily less prone to cheat (314). Attendance at various church schools improves slightly, but consistently, scores on tests of honesty and helpfulness, either because of the school influence or of the kind of family that sends children to these schools (491).

It is interesting that an economic depression does not show negative effects on children so far as delinquency rates can be used as an index (670). War, on the other hand, probably because it breaks up the home, does seem to produce more delinquency (622).

Real moral growth is more than a memorization of rules, more than associating unpleasantness with a certain act. It also involves reasoning on the part of the child as he tries to integrate his own experiences with the rules and actions of parents and playmates. It will require more research to learn what factors bring about genuine affection for one's fellow man (despite marked physical and social differences among individuals), self-sacrifice for others, and a faith amid difficulties—granting, of course, that this is the real aim of religion.

Health and Physical Factors. Some children have more than their share of the childhood diseases and their aftereffects. One of these aftereffects may be parental overprotection or emphasis on health, which keeps the child out of the normal childhood rough and tumble. Other children meet with frequent or serious accidents. Poor or good health and bodily conditions may show themselves in variations of vigor, social manner, or appearance and thus influence the early life. The importance of pain in building fear of doctors and of other situations cannot be minimized. Health may affect the child's dreams, his disposition, his popularity, and his total personality adjustment (310, 311). One psychiatrist states that in 75 per cent of problem children health is a factor. College students who have emotional problems speak more frequently of illness than do others (521).

Affection and Sex. How do we explain that some people seem almost oblivious to sex; others ask numerous questions, get information, and seem satisfied; and still others, through curiosity, indulge in childhood experimentation in the form of masturbation, homosexual or heterosexual contacts? Individuals vary in the extent to which they think, worry, or daydream about sex. We cannot separate sex from affection or love. In fact, in considering the sexual development in Chapter 12 we must consider the child's total personality because, as will be shown, this aspect of his life depends upon many other developments.

Self-impressions, Evaluations and Goals. Not only are we influenced by the events that occur around us as we develop, but we contribute to this influence. During our development we gain certain impressions about ourselves as we react to other people. We feel unworthy or inferior, or lack confidence. We fail to meet our own level of aspiration or that set for us by those we admire (685). All the factors mentioned before, physique, health, abilities, and interests which influence personal adequacy and feelings of security, contribute to our evaluation of ourselves—*our self concept* (569, 683, 41, 259, 398, 403).

An individual may have interests usually attributed to the opposite sex, feel too submissive, be inadequate as a student, or be influenced by his minority status in race, religion, socio-economic level, vocation of his father, or reputation of his family (614). Individual play roles and one's actual role may conflict with one's ideal. The person's attitude toward himself is a factor in the development of *delinquent behavior* as well as ambitions toward and the achievement of goals of *self-responsibility* and personal growth (403).

Adolescent Development

Pubertal Changes and Adolescence. In the course of normal human development there occurs first a period of very rapid growth and then a period of body change in which the boy becomes more manly and the girl more womanly. Secondary sex characteristics, as they are called, become prominent—the deeper voice, the broader shoulders, the beard and the pubic hair in the boy, and enlarged mammary glands, pubic hair, and broadened hips in the girl. In primitive societies at about this time there is a distinct transition from child to adult, but not so in civilization. The youth often has many years ahead of him before he can take his place as a fully recognized adult, economically and emotionally independent of his family, trained for a career, and mature in attitude toward himself and the opposite sex and toward society as a whole.

Puberty and the period in the teens known as adolescence in Western civilization is a departure from childhood even if it is not full adulthood. The personality retains most of the traits that have been developing since infancy. There is rarely a sudden change in basic traits in the teens. Of the adolescents who are delinquent, for example, a large percentage showed these traits before puberty (275). Some marked changes in outward behavior appear, however. They are mainly social in nature and result because (1) the youth usually seeks *independence from parental guidance;* (2) there is an attempt to establish satisfactory *relationships with the opposite sex;* and (3) the teen-ager attempts to *integrate* the various new and old elements of his personality. Such a social development signifies a growth toward emotional maturity.

The process of becoming psychologically weaned from the family consists of independence in decisions and plans, preparation for a vocation, and, sometimes, in earning part of one's education for this goal. Adjustment to the opposite sex involves in some a change in attitude, and often new social skills which are important in the process of rating and dating, as discussed in Chapter 12. The integration of one's own personality includes the formulation of a philosophy of life, or adopting those customs and modes of thinking among the welter of varying viewpoints and behavior in America that he can accept while remaining a part of the group with which he has chosen to align himself. This integration is discussed in Chapter 7.

Adolescent Physical Changes and Their Influence. Many of the problems that the adolescent has to meet are intimately related to the marked physical growth that occurs just before puberty. Girls as a rule reach pubertal changes before boys, and this difference among children in the same grade makes for conspicuousness and teasing. The average age at which the girl menstruates is about the middle of the thirteenth year. There is no comparable measure for boys, but the average age of the appearance of pigmented straight hair on the body is around the middle of the thirteenth year. There is an uneven development of various organs and physiological functions (356), and some writers have attributed a part of the instability at puberty to this cause. It must also be remembered that in addition to the uneven growth within the body and the changes that the adolescent shows to the people around him, there are also the changes involved in his social world as he moves from childhood to adolescence.

Interests, attitudes, and behavior of adolescents are related to the physical changes and development at puberty. Girls, after the beginning of menstruation, are much more interested in physical appearance (752). At puberty boys tend to play less vigorous games, do more daydreaming, and have more conflicts with the family. In one study physically mature boys had greater interest in personal adornment, the opposite sex, and strenuous sports than did immature boys (734). Pubescents are also taller, heavier, and stronger than pre-pubescents.

Contrary to popular belief, they are not more awkward or less dexterous (542). The awkwardness that we seem to observe in the adolescent is due to hesitation and self-consciousness rather than to lack of real skill after he gets started in an activity.

Individual Differences in Pubic Changes. Go into any large group of 15-year-old boys and you will find them differing greatly in physique. Bill will measure 5 feet, 3 inches, weigh 122 pounds; Tom will be 5 feet, 10 inches tall, and weigh 125 pounds; and Bob, 5 feet, 3 inches, and weigh 140 pounds. Girls will vary similarly (711). For boys, body size is a source of self-esteem (399). Differences will also appear in most other physical features. The face, which is a major object for attention from the individual himself and from others, changes at this time. For some this change is greater than for others and, in certain individuals, upsetting (150). Acne, an eruption on the face, is frequently more disturbing than its seriousness warrants. Even the amount of perspiration increases and has been known to be a subject for worry. Adolescents may center their attention on any one phase of their growth if they are at all anxious in nature and emphasize it beyond all normal proportions. The most important difference will be the difference in *attitudes* produced by these physical variations. An individual is likely to feel that *he is different* from others.

There are individuals of either sex who have shown precocious pubic changes. The large mammary glands or enlarged sex organs might cause self-consciousness. On the other hand, there is the boy or girl who wonders whether he or she will ever mature sexually. This is particularly important to the boy because of the cultural premium upon size and strength among men. Boys and girls at puberty are quite ready to joke about changes in voice, fuzz on the face, prominent breasts, or other noticeable physical conditions.

No doubt the attitude that arises will be largely conditioned by what the parents and fellow playmates have engendered. There are parents who look with fear toward the child's maturity. They feel that their boy or girl has grown out of their influence, and they are upset by change. Some fathers and mothers do not prepare the child for pubic changes and assume a hush-hush attitude about normal development such as menstruation and nocturnal seminal emissions.

Sex Development. Since most of the physical changes at puberty are associated with changes in physique that distinguish the sexes as well as with the development of the sex organs themselves, the adolescent becomes more conscious of sex functions than before. The adolescent's sex life is a continuation of his earlier attitudes and behavior, and the pubic changes merely reinforce these drives and attitudes. We have seen that there are wide differences in background. Some parents give full sex education as it is requested and allow the children to observe them freely and naturally as they dress and bathe. In addition they instill sensible taboos and provide vigilance so that the child is not exposed to sex stimulation. Other parents, because of overcrowded living conditions, a morally impoverished neighborhood, or their own lack of information on the subject, are unable to give their children the proper kind of background. Parents differ in the degree to which they make the child feel that he may come to them freely to discuss sex problems. Therefore, before and during puberty, sex experience differs as well as do the extent and force of the inhibitions governing sex. Some adolescents have nonrealistic ideals and feelings of guilt in relation to sex. Others have no ideals. Still others are able to control sex impulses and sublimate their sex energies in widely diffused, satisfying play activities. These differences tend to produce in our society the sex delinquent, the individual with severe conflicts, and the individual who experiences a wholesome love life (366).

Some youths who have not been given satisfactory sex instruction have been disturbed by puberty changes associated with sex. Menstruation can upset the girl who has not expected it or who does not understand the naturalness of the process. Bleeding is so strongly associated with fear and pain that it can produce fear and embarrassment if the girl does not develop the proper attitude. Nocturnal seminal emissions and the dreams accompanying them have been puzzling and sometimes productive of feelings of guilt in boys. The boy may believe that he is losing his manhood or that this emission is a punishment for sex thoughts or actions. If menstruation varies in any manner from the average, it may also be disturbing from that standpoint. Obviously, rape, attempted rape, or seduction of either sex by an older individual has traumatic effects. Experimentation with sex organs in play may lead to strong guilt reactions which may persist for some time.

Adolescents and Home Influence. College students report in their autobiographies many differing parental influences, and various attitudes toward their parents that they think have affected their development. About a third of the adolescents studied mention *con-*

flict with parents (753, 625). The student may be ambivalent toward his parents—love them at one time and dislike them at another. His parents may have inculcated in him certain traits of submissiveness, seclusion, fear, and hostility. He may feel that his parents are too old to understand him and his age group. He may be unable to meet the ideals they have set for him. Their accomplishments may seem so great that his only reaction is to enjoy some of the reflected glory. He may be very proud of his parents, their accomplishments, appearance, and social habits, or he may be deeply ashamed of them. His parents may quarrel and later separate. Both may try to gain his confidence and malign the other parent. He is confused by the conflicting loyalties.

The influences mentioned earlier on pages 96 to 97 have their effects in adolescence: *overprotection,* which may keep him close to home now; earlier sternness and parental *perfectionism* may account in part for his overly active conscience or personality disturbance (753). He may have *introjected* traits of either parent that he dislikes, or he may have gained from his parents traits that are incompatible with his present way of life. He and his parents may be in conflict because they live in different cultures. The parent may regard play and social life as a waste of time, and stylish clothes and possessions a waste of money. Dating and coming and going may be rigidly supervised (78).

Studies of the behavior of adolescents also agree with those of younger children in that they disclose that broken homes (167), homes of low income, and families with constant friction between parents, overprotection, dominance, or rejection all produce undesirable effects on personality (858).

Adolescence is pre-eminently a period in which the offspring needs a wise model. Often, when given an opportunity to express himself, he says that he has longed for a parent who could be a friend and a companion, *who would understand him* and be a credit and a source of prestige to him (753). There is evidence that a good, confidential relationship between youth and the parent, particularly the mother, is important for personality adjustment. The opposite—antagonisms with the parents over clothes, money, freedom in going and coming, and social activities—is disturbing to the personality (625, 78, 18). In extreme cases the adolescent may "run wild," violate moral codes, and break the standards of common decency.

The adolescent regards freedom as a symbol of maturity. It is the most obvious sign of maturity to him, and he strongly wants to grow up, particularly as he sees that he *is* mature physiologically and resents the restrictions of childhood. Many of the most conscientious parents fail in the early years to allow the child to assume responsibilities, fail to *wean him psychologically*. The child has meant so much to the parents emotionally, the time since babyhood seems so short, that it is difficult for them to see their physically grown John or Mary as anything but a child. A parent, fearful of losing her role as mother, and thinking of "the other kids" as those without restraints, tightens the reins. Friction between parent and child is the result.

When college students describe the characteristics of a successful family, they emphasize much that a professional worker might mention (150), namely, (1) absence of great tension and presence of affection between parents and between parents and children; (2) entertainment of friends in a home attractive to young people; (3) moderate parental counseling and supervision and moderate consistent discipline (150). It is interesting, however, that about two-thirds of youths who have taken part in studies say that they have no criticism of their parents at all! (753)

Adolescent Social Life. Crowds. Just as the pre-adolescent has his *gang* for adventure and excitement, the adolescent has his *crowd* of both boys and girls, which congregates at a congenial home or some commercial establishment or church building (691, 356, 432, 245, 164, 260, 493). Amid what appears to adults as silly chatter, teasing, bantering, social skills are developed. The members feel that they belong to a cherished group, find satisfaction in the banter with the opposite sex, learn small talk, the current dance, and the self-confidence and social ease which some adults, who have developed outside one of these groups and feel *social isolation or rejection*, greatly miss. Social rejection can have serious consequences in later life (177). It is claimed that youths learn loyalty to a group, practice in judging people, and experience in love making under protected circumstances. The one negative aspect is their antagonism toward those outside their group. Sometimes this snobbishness seriously interferes with activities of the larger community or the school as a whole.

In adolescence there are numerous kinds of *social relationships.* Individuals differ in the number of friends they have and the closeness of these friends to them. There is the almost inseparable friendship, the close friendship, the familiar friendship—the friend toward whom there is little warmth—the various degrees of acquaintanceship, and finally the role of spectator, knowing one by name but not to speak to. There are all degrees of relationships between members of a crowd or clique. Usually the inclusion or exclusion in the clique is not a matter of family position but depends upon the relationships between different personalities. In individual cases these relation-ships influence future attitudes and social behavior between an indi-vidual and his fellows. Attitudes of social rejection, persecution, loneliness, snobbishness, popularity, inferiority, leadership, social con-fidence, compensatory drive, and work are to some extent influenced by these teen-age experiences. Some adolescents, because they do not have a wholesome source of adventure and contact with the opposite sex, turn to delinquent activity (387). In Chapters 10 and 11 there will be a fuller discussion of popularity, friendship, and leadership, especially as they are found in college.

In addition to the group relationship, dating frequently begins dur-ing adolescence. Numerous attitudes yet to be investigated arise as the result of dating or the lack of dates. Individuals report the follow-ing as influential in their development: desire for more numerous or more desirable dates, conflict between dates' behavior and their own standards, tendency of dating to lead to deep affection too quickly, inability to get repeated dates with the same person, lack of confi-dence on dates, feeling that he or she is not coming up to the date's expectations. Some individuals' later relationships toward the other sex are to some extent influenced by successes or failures at this time.

Besides the informal social activities of adolescents, there are the activities promoted by adult-supervised groups—the *extracurricular activities* of the school, and clubs and other extraschool groups of a religious or secular nature. In Chapter 10 the value of these activities in building social traits and habits that will function in later life is discussed. Many an adolescent learns from these activities citizenship and skills which he can use in later group work.

Athletic activities, particularly for the boy, are of special import-ance at this period. The participant in athletics shows greater physi-cal prowess, and prestige develops from his success as an athlete in high school and college in the eyes of the community. Often athletic success enhances traits like self-esteem and confidence. In addition to those who excel in competitive team sports, there are those adoles-cents who develop extraordinary skills in minor sports and gain recognition through them. There are also youths who feel a strong aversion to sports and a sense of inferiority because they are not skillful. Others develop a "don't-care" attitude and along with this show superior motivation toward some nonathletic youth activity. Because of their failure in sports, they achieve success in the other activity.

Developmental Goals

Integration of Personality—a Goal. As a teenager develops physically, moves into a new type of social activity which is closer to the adult form, and is given greater freedom and responsibility, he begins to realize that he is no longer a child and that the days of adulthood are not far off. He looks to the future, a job, independence (see Chapters 8 and 9) and preparation for marriage and for creating a home (see Chapters 12 and 13). He also must think through many of his standards as he comes in conflict with standards different from those his parents have given him and as he attempts to cope with new urges and temptations. Finally, he should be preparing to meet the new responsibilities of citizenship and social maturity. He will move more surely through adolescence and thence into adulthood if he understands himself, what is expected of him, and how to meet these expectations. In short, as he comes *to perceive himself as a responsible mature adult he is reaching one of the goals of development.*

Maturity. Adolescents in America have been criticized for their lack of maturity and their lack of knowledge concerning important issues that they should learn to deal with decisively in a democracy. Schools, even universities, differ in the degree to which controversial issues are presented and facts pro and con are discussed. Schools and communities vary in the extent to which they thrust upon young children responsibilities and opportunities for self-government to prepare them for citizenship and suffrage. The nature of maturity is discussed in Chapter 16.

The background of parents and associates are factors that prepare or retard us in the teens for the later necessity of confronting various different customs and attitudes, and of deciding for ourselves what moral, ethical, and religious standards we shall accept as guides in our thinking and acting. Apparently work experience matures the youth more than does school. According to one study, unemployed students show least maturity (836). Some youths live in culturally sterile environments without purposiveness or inspiration; such environments discourage responsibility or self-discipline. These youths may turn to vivid sensations—thrills—for stimulation.

Even in America there are individuals who believe that the basic problems of life cannot be solved by the common man himself, that he needs to be told what to think and how to act. No matter how authoritarian an individual's background may be, if he develops in a complex culture he will be compelled to make some decisions for himself. The extent to which he is prepared to do this will influence his future development. Studies of the activities of young people some years ago showed a need for greater personal growth (866, 56). Religion, books, radio and television programs, movies, periodical literature, club activities, conversation, travel, military service—all are possible sources of stimulation and new perspective. Lacking stimulation from these, he may turn to thrill activities or even vice for diversion.

Goals, Pitfalls, Atmospheres—A Summary. As we look back over the many facts and principles presented above what can we say the individual is developing toward? It is *maturity and the capacity to adjust effectively* to himself and his environment (see Chapter 16). This means, more specifically, the ability to satisfy his needs effectively over a long period of time (see Chapters 1 and 3). It also includes the reduction of persistent frustration and trapping conflict, both of which arouse anxiety. It further involves the use of any residual anxiety for the development of traits that will enable the individual to satisfy his needs later and deal with future frustrating conditions more effectively.

The second question we might ask is, What are some of the *pitfalls* in development? One is prolonged fixation on, or regression to, an immature level of development. This is represented by marked dependency, self-defeating hostility and aggression, withdrawal and unrealistic fantasy, guilt feelings that result in self-punishment rather than growth, egocentricity, and low self-esteem. These conditions are among the symptoms of inadequate development and usually represent strong unresolved conflicts and attending anxiety. They are the converse of ego strength, sociality, and confidence, which are based on personality traits and roles that meet the individual's needs so that he can continually grow to reach his highest potentiality.

The *mature individual*, in summary, reflects an early environment that builds in him basic trust of his world, and a later atmosphere that encourages self-acceptance, initiative, and security. He will need these attitudes as he works through the conflict occurring when he gives up childhood habits to attain the youth and adult habits, attitudes and roles which he sees displayed by effectively adjusted models in his surroundings.

Supplementary Readings

A. L. Baldwin, *Behavior and Development in Childhood*, Dryden, 1955.

G. S. Blum, *Psychoanalytic Theories of Personality*, McGraw-Hill, 1953.

C. S. Hall, "The Genetics of Behavior," in S. S. Stevens (Ed.), *Handbook of Experimental Psychology*, Wiley, 1951.

J. W. N. Whiting and I. L. Child, *Child Training and Personality*, Yale University Press, 1953.

J. E. Horrocks, "The Adolescent," in L. Carmichael (Ed.), *Manual of Child Psychology*, Wiley, 1954.

In addition see the references cited by number in the chapter and appearing in the bibliography of an accompanying volume entitled *Teaching Personal Adjustment: An Instructor's Manual.*

CHAPTER 5

Stephens College, Misso

CREATIVE

ADJUSTMENT

Self Actualization

Meaning of Creative Adjustment. People develop. They occasionally turn liabilities into assets, take themselves in hand, adjust to difficulties, discover the response that will most effectively meet their needs, and as one clever author has stated it, even learn "how to be happily maladjusted" (555). Stated more technically, individuals can learn to deal with their conflicts and anxieties and grow some as the result of them.

When one is disturbed about some aspect of his personality, is troubled over some personal problem, or battles with impulses that clash with the ideals he holds for himself, he has little *perspective.* It is hard for him to see the problem as it really is, to realize that many others have faced it and that it is but one aspect of a total personality and a total life. He more often escapes the problem by plunging into some activity which may or may not enhance his development. It may bring him recognition, for example, but not a feeling of personal consistency and esteem. Before one can proceed to experiment with his difficulties, to use trial and error to solve his problem and build new traits, he often needs *security* to understand better the basis for the problem. Sometimes a person he respects enters the scene or he gains success and recognition in some project that utilizes his interests and given talents in a purposive, original, self-satisfying, useful manner (9, 502, 777, 535). It is less often a highly planned routine program and more often a meaningful adventure with people or a project we find interesting.

This *self actualization* differs from a passive adjustment to forces that play upon us. It is personal growth that has individual meaningfulness. It involves purpose, thought, and striving for consistency and integrity in our own characteristic manner (447, 400, 505, 304). This we might call *creative adjustment.*

Creative adjustment then is *individualized and meaningful growth toward emotional maturity, becoming the most effective individual one can be in terms of one's abilities and interests.* It is discovering and developing one's self. It is not a sudden, mysterious change, although on rare occasions surprising new insights and new ways of life do arise. It is not a matter of exerting more "will power" some one day, of merely "wishing it were so." A single book or lecture may start the process, but adjustment to difficulties requires more than a sudden inspiration. Platitudes and soothing verbiage may sometimes be an escape from oneself rather than an understanding and acceptance. Effective creative adjustment is an extended quest to discover oneself, knowing that what is found is a human development arising from basic temperament and early experiences. Although creative adjustment is a dynamic and individual process, with a large creative and inspirational element, it follows hypothetically a describable course with changes in the sensory-neuro-muscular system. New habits are built, others eliminated, new interests and attitudes are developed, traits are extended, substitutions are made in responses and effective stimulations. This may all occur in the framework of an adventurous project such as athletics, debating, or the preparation for a career (781, 522, 604, 829, 660, 786, 709, 247, 769).

Pattern of Adjustment. The pattern described in Chapter 1 holds both for the acquisition of behavior that is nonadjustive and for satisfactory or readjustive behavior. 1. The individual is *motivated* to satisfy his developed needs. 2. *These needs are frustrated.* 3. *Learning* with trial and error or variable behavior ensues. 4. Some *reaction results that satisfies this need,* whether or not it satisfies him as a whole. If it is satisfying to him as a personality, he has adjusted to the situation. If not, a later *readjustment* must take place. Shyness, for example, satisfies a need. It is learned through trial and error. It protects its possessor from many social situations with which he is not prepared to deal, but in excess it also hampers his development. Eventually he must cope with it if he is to be happy.

Most problems and emotional disturbances are *nonadjustive* in terms of our total personality. They exist because they satisfy some motives. They have been acquired in a previous trial-and-error manner, possibly in a crisis. To eliminate them the motivation that originally caused them to arise should be satisfied in a different manner. If the original motivation is satisfied, this problem behavior may be eliminated if it is followed by unpleasant or unsatisfactory consequences. A case will illustrate this point.

Edward C. is 5 feet, 11 inches tall, well on the good-looking side, with average grooming. He comes from a small town and a family of below-average means. In childhood he contracted infantile paralysis. He recovered and walks without any orthopedic devices and with only a slight limp. The muscles of one of his legs are atrophied, and Edward is extremely sensitive about this.

He is most sensitive about his mild handicap before girls. All during high school he would date only girls who were not asked by anyone else. He firmly believed that he would never marry. He probably realized that girls were attracted to him but, fearing rejection, he apparently repressed much of his attraction to them. When he came away to college he became quite active in one of the larger young people's church groups, assumed leadership, and had social contacts with many more girls than ever before.

He came to the counselor to discuss his change in vocation from Law to the Ministry. Inadvertently, the talk veered toward dating and social activities. During the conferences that followed, Edward began to see himself more as a total personality with many assets. Both the counselor and Edward's roommate strongly encouraged him to date more than he did, and during the period of his college years his attitude toward himself seemed to change. His handicap gradually assumed somewhat less importance. This was probably due to the fact that more people regarded him as a person rather than as a boy who had been crippled earlier in life.

His retirement, particularly from members of the opposite sex, was an escape from the unpleasantness associated with his feeling of being unmarriageable. He felt rejected, "different," at that time, and if a girl, particularly one of whom he thought a great deal, refused him a date, this rejection on the background of the earlier rejection was very disturbing. The retiring behavior, then, satisfied the need for self-protection, but it failed to satisfy the larger motivation to be like all the other fellows in his own eyes and in the minds of his associates. His coming away to college, an understanding and admiring roommate, a counselor who saw him as a total person, and his successes with the religious group, all tended to satisfy that strong childhood desire *to be accepted and to be like others.* His attempts to get dates with the girls he really liked were successful. The few times his timidity got the better of him were very unpleasant and went a long way toward killing his diffidence. As a senior he became engaged to a very attractive girl with charm and many ideals similar to his, whom he later married.

Conditions of Creative Adjustment. Turning to the practical side of this matter: What, specifically, can one do to make an adjustment to relieve, for example, feelings of inferiority, anxiety, or emotional instability in a way that means self enhancement? When all the suggestions for personality readjustment and self-actualization are considered they involve basically the following:

1. A concern about oneself that leads to an exploration of resources for personal growth rather than to ways of defending oneself or escaping from the problem.

2. Persons or environments that encourage us to *express ourselves freely,* either verbally or through some activity. These we may call *conducive human relationships or environments.*

3. Free discussion at our own rate of our problem, our background, and inner tendencies, or the *spontaneous activities of a social or creative nature* that release inner tendencies previously unsatisfied or repressed.

4. With ventilation of our problems, or with accomplishment and success in social and creative activities, there usually arises amid negative feelings some success and some feeling of *self-worth.*

5. Discussion or projection of ourselves into activities, often brings about a different *perspective,* possibly better *understanding* and a better adjustment to our problems.

6. As self-confidence and self-understanding grow, and as we are freed from fighting inner tendencies, we begin to *experiment with events* around us and within us; through trial and error or a planned program we strengthen certain traits, reduce some anxieties, and resolve conflicts all of which allow us to satisfy our needs.

You will recognize these suggestions as a practical application of the learning process previously mentioned. The statements represent motivation, trial and error and satisfaction, and learned attitudes and responses.

Cases of Attempted Readjustment

Each of these aspects of readjustment may be seen in the cases that follow. The student will find it interesting to see which of these aspects of the process of effective adjustment are prominent in each of the following cases. He may find it profitable *to discuss this with his fellow students*. Then he can compare his impressions and conclusions with the discussion dealing with each of these aspects of adjustment.

Irwin M., an 18-year-old, slightly built, well-dressed freshman, who looked more like 15 years of age, referred himself for "psychoanalysis,"

Susan Greenbyrg

as he called it. When he came into the office, he seemed shy and awkward, but talked quite readily. He said that at first he makes a very good impression on people, but later they seem to prefer others to him. This pattern has duplicated itself on a number of occasions. It happened when he went to camp. In the fraternity he was elected to an office the first few weeks; now he thinks none of the fellows respects him. He told this with considerable concern and emotion.

No doubt many of his fraternity brothers treat him more as a kid brother than a contemporary. He is a likeable, conscientious fellow with good facial features and complexion. Having been the only child of a large, wealthy, successful family, he admittedly received great attention from both parents and relatives early in life and was sheltered, so that going to camp and coming to college are really the first experiences that he has had in making decisions for himself. It is difficult for him to profit from the typical trial-and-error experience that grows from the necessity to direct one's own affairs. He broods over his errors rather than using them for future guidance. Furthermore, he was in the lowest quarter in ability in terms of an entrance test (ACE scores: total 25, Q 19, L 15).

His parents apparently have reared him in a sheltered manner. He has a high regard for them and for their reputation and feels that he should, in view of this, be preferred by some of the most popular boys in the fraternity, rather than taken casually by them. He feels particularly inferior to some of the older fellows who are very poised and socially capable. He observes these older men in their effective banter with each other and in their easy relationship with girls and feels that he can never achieve that. He is self-conscious, regards them as critical of him, has difficulty maintaining conversation with them. He worries about his reluctance "to look the fellows straight in the eye," his desire to get away from them and go up to his room alone, and his inability to carry out many of the plans he envisages. He thinks about dating a girl, then feels that she will not enjoy his companionship.

Many of the boys in the fraternity have a very materialistic and cold attitude toward life, and this philosophy conflicts with his early training and sentimental views. He said that he became jealous of his friends, wanted to possess them, was analytical of the motives of others, realized that he was pretty much of a "baby" at heart and self-centered. He complained about vacillating between friendliness and withdrawal and irritability. He said that he thought that hard knocks would be good for him.

He said that at first he thought the attitude of others toward him was anti-Semitic, but his experience at camp and in his fraternity has convinced him that the difficulty lies within himself. He always remembers being less well received by his contemporaries than by elders. Much of this dates back to his first attendance at school. The other children seemed to pick on him.

After the conference he had a talk with his father, who apparently choked off his discussion of emotional and subjective symptoms by telling him that there was nothing the matter with him; that he was better than most of the boys in the fraternity; and that self-analysis is a bad idea. This was helpful for a brief period, as were the conferences with the counselor.

For a while he constantly imitated the older fellows, took advice from them, and tried to follow it but stated that inwardly he felt inadequate. From his standpoint he was failing in everything—school work, relations with fellows, dating—and he felt that, because he did not have to work, was in one of the "best" fraternities, and had so many opportunities, he should be distinguishing himself.

He told the counselor that he needed advice and needed it badly. He admitted that he looked forward to the conference periods and felt better for a while, but needed to be told just what to do because his own efforts were so fruitless. He was told that he had received plenty of advice from a number of people and what he needed more than advice was an opportunity to talk out his feelings and act out the behavior of which he was most capable. This impressed him, but the disturbing feeling of inadequacy that he experienced many times a day was overpowering. He was extremely sensitive to any slight, and one of the more critical boys accentuated this *feeling of rejection by the group.*

As time went on and the conferences continued, the negative statements about himself decreased, and he showed a greater tendency to be realistic about his traits and possibilities. When he saw the movie, "The Razor's Edge," he felt that the central player had many of his traits but showed much more character and assurance. He, on the other hand, felt that he was a coward, afraid to face the world. He decided to see this movie again and came out with a number of insights. This is what he wrote to the counselor:

"I saw the picture again, and I have come to some definite ideas. I think if you will straighten out these ideas for me I will hit upon something. The *first* thing that I have surmised is that I am divided into three parts: *first*, the part that makes me so anxious to make friends that I leave myself open (to criticism). I don't act natural. I think that everything I do offends someone. I am afraid that I will do the wrong thing. The *second* part is the bad part—the deep cowardice—the part in which I think that a person is my friend only because of what he can get from me. This is the suspicious part of me—judging things for their money value—the cheap part. This is the part that will not allow me to love anybody, to be true to anybody, because I think that this will lower my status; that people won't like the persons I go with, either boy or girl—the part that looks at people's faults instead of their good qualities and affects my conversation and feelings. Then there is the *third* part—the part that feels that I can't get enough knowledge, the initiative part of me—the part that I hope some day will be natural—the part that wants me to do things but is conquered by the other parts, the good intention side of me, the part that judges a man by what he is, the part that is not like the second part that judges a man by what other people think. The problem then is to determine what I should do to eliminate the first two parts and strengthen the third. The way to do this is to find a cause of the two parts and try to eliminate it. That is where I need your help."

At one of the interviews he became hostile to the counselor and said that the counselor was being too nice to him and because of this he went out of the conference feeling that his problems were not so great as they really are. This ability to express aggression without penalty seemed to improve later relationships. On the whole, as the result of five months of counseling he felt that his attitudes had improved a great deal, that whereas he had not changed very much he was not so upset by his own behavior. He stated that he realized now that he could change some things about himself and other things he could not, and he would just have to learn to put up with them.

He saw the role his early life played in his development and the pressure that the fraternity was exerting upon him. He was initiated and, the pledgeship ended, he won an office. This occurrence helped his confidence somewhat. Apparently he was rather well liked by the boys in his fraternity, but most of his difficulties grew out of his *high level of aspiration*, his *lack of well-established social habits*, which brought about a very disturbing feeling of inadequacy. In addition there were earlier childhood experiences of being *rejected* by the group after the contrasting warm relationship that he had within his family. He was an individual who had been given inordinate attention by relatives and by teachers at a small private school. This was *overprotecting*, and it prevented him from developing on his own initiative the habits he needed in order to get along with his contemporaries. When he did not receive the affection he got at home, he felt rejected *when in fact* many of his fellows liked him.

After this academic year he did not return for counseling and he seemed from casual contacts to be making a better adjustment on the campus. He graduated after four years despite his low aptitude scores, went into military service as an officer, and was later married. When he had marital difficulties he again sought counseling.

This case shows very well the processes that occur in reaching a more effective adjustment assisted by counseling: release of tension, facing oneself as one really is, making discoveries and accepting aspects of oneself that previously caused one to run away, and, finally, planning a course for future action.

Steve D. was known to the counselor through his parents and sisters. His father was a faculty member; his sisters were all very successful. Steve was always a very poor student, even in grade school, and had caused great concern to his mother. He also was smaller than most of the boys and preferred to play alone. His experience in the Army took him out of the home and relieved him of the ignominy of poor grades in school and of his previous overprotection. While in the Army he received an injury that incapacitated him. When he returned home he was told to rest. He said he was beginning to like this rest, but he realized that it would result in invalidism. The rest probably satisfied his previously built non-aggressive habits. Yet he wanted to mature and become self-sufficient. This conflict resulted in guilt, depression, and suicidal tendencies. He said that he has always been good at mechanics, but he didn't think he could hold a job because of his physical condition.

The counselor asked him if one of his difficulties wasn't that he felt inferior to his sisters and his parents; that, although he could be successful in mechanical pursuits, he felt that they were not in keeping with his parents' status. Furthermore, he constantly thought of how successful his sisters have been in school and all throughout life in their relationship to other people and in their professional fields. Their success was a great contrast to his career. He replied: "You've hit the nail right on the head."

The counselor went on and attempted to verbalize the effect of the recent "crisis" on him. "Now this recent trouble, namely that of having your girl's mother tell you that you shouldn't see the girl so much, may have caused you to feel even more inferior. Possibly you felt that she realized that you would not be able to support the girl; that you were a failure." He said, "That's exactly what I thought." His whole attitude changed with these prompted realizations. The counselor went further, since the student seemed to take such a passive, defeated attitude. "Why don't you find out from a physician just what you can do and what you can't do, what kind of job you can take, and what kind you can't? Then talk with the Veterans Administration about some on-the-job training. Go some place else to get this training and spend a reasonable amount of time in activities that you enjoy. You have to live your life, and it should be a good one. Don't compare yourself with anybody else. Instead of seeing how many negative traits you have, as compared with some imaginary ideal, remember what a good mechanic you are, the success you have had in the Army, and build on it."

He was definitely encouraged by this advice. He took out a notebook, jotted down suggestions that the counselor gave him, and left the office saying, "You've given me new hope."

The follow-up showed that he had made use of these suggestions, and that he was moving to a larger city and would have contact with an outpatient V.A. psychiatric unit.

This student came in somewhat helpless in attitude and not disposed to face his problem himself, nor did he have the ingenuity to plunge into some pursuit. He needed to be *directed*. The counselor fortunately knew a great deal about him and his background and could direct the interview without stirring up excessive anxiety or taking away his initiative.

Betty N. is an extremely bright, well-groomed, dynamic, and rather attractive girl. She grew up in a small town. She was the eldest of three children. Her father became very ill about ten years before her entrance into college, and he developed deafness as a result. He was unable to do anything but putter around the house. This was extremely frustrating to him since he was an honor graduate himself and had been an outstanding leader when in college. He became extremely critical of the children. Betty's mother, who was a teacher, undertook the support of the family and spent a good deal of time out of the home.

Betty noticed her feeling of insecurity when she went to high school, when the family was most insecure financially. There seemed to be a close relationship between her and her younger brother and sister. She felt that her father was too critical of her and that her mother was too busy to give her much attention. She complained a great deal because she had to wear braces on her teeth. She said many people treated her as a "child of the braces age." She had a poor complexion at this time. Trying to keep up with the other children in high school in clothes and other social necessities was a disturbing experience. She dated very little. Much of her relationships with boys were platonic.

A very close chum of hers died after a brief illness when she was in high school, and this death upset her greatly. She feels that she has never had as close a friend since then.

She came to the counselor first after one of the girls living in the same house had berated her, saying that she was selfish, egotistical, overaggressive, and needed to be taken down a notch or two. This threw her into a panic, and she had a talk with some of the other girls. Then she came in to see the counselor. The counselor listened as she related some of her earlier experiences, and when she had finished he reassured her frankly and sincerely, as he could well do in view of her aptitude and previous accomplishments, her grooming, and ingenuity. The counselor realized that her problem was not due to any objective deficiencies because she had many assets, but were due to the many family conflicts during her growing period and probably to some rejection both at home and at school.

Her next visit concerned vocational advice. She felt that she had to have a career and she had to be important in something. She complained of being very unhappy, not having much purpose, and not getting along too well with her fellow students of either sex. She still worried about her complexion, although it was not noticeably poor to the counselor, and was sensitive about her mistakes and her unpopularity.

She said she had tried everything—being a mouse, a loud-mouth, a social climber, a hostess, and a pal, but none had overcome her feeling of inferiority about her social status. She said, "I don't really seem to have any special person to be near to or to care what happens in my life. I want someone or something definite to work for . . . I don't mind doing the dirty work but I like a little recognition. Perhaps that is what my heart is crying out for—recognition. Just for someone to be aware of me." Much of this attitude persisted throughout several semesters, despite the fact that she was busy with a job, was taking a full load, and was studying long hours.

Toward the end of her college career she met a boy who was probably more emotionally upset than she. He was an only child who had seen the counselor at the suggestion of his fraternity brothers because he was such a "stinker." He did not react well to the hazing, went to pieces once, and began sobbing. He wanted to be around the fellows but was constantly bragging, and when they called his bluff he was hurt. He and Betty seemed to have a great deal in common. They were both interested in music and creative writing. He was not so good a student as she, but they studied together a great deal and apparently confided in each other.

She consulted the counselor one more time, not about herself, as she thought she had straightened out pretty well in the course of her college years, but about this boy who now became her charge. He had been "in the dumps" for several days, had gotten some poor grades, and wasn't getting along too well with other people. She wanted to know what she could do to help him. As she talked, she answered her own questions.

Although she was quite aggressive for a girl, she was wise enough to realize that any help she would give him would have to be indirect; that she would have to be merely on the scene as he helped himself. But it was clear that she had now found someone who cared, who was interested in her as a person, in whom she could confide, and who really needed her. They married. They seemed to complement each other. A follow-up after several years indicated that they had been through his Army hitch together. She had been working while he served his enlistment. Now she was again working to help him get an advanced degree. She seemed much happier than before. Their marriage seemed to be successful.

Betty shows us something that is frequently observed: that individuals seem to grow in maturity and self-control when their needs for affection and understanding are satisfied, when they can build a warm but realistic relationship with someone who cares.

Utilizing Relationships and Activities

Reluctance to Face Problems. It has been said that those who most need to come to grips with their problems are sometimes least willing to face them. All of us know a shy, self-centered, serious individual with few social outlets whom we feel could develop more effectively through counseling or group participation. We can also probably recall a brash, overactive person who bluffs or offends people and seems to be the only one unaware of his ineffectiveness. It is easy to find others who do not face their personal problems and attack them effectively—but do we need to look beyond ourselves? Have we developed to our full capacity in *emotional maturity* and *social effectiveness?*

Why is it difficult to see ourselves as others see us, or, once we see our escapes or defenses against unpleasant reality, why is it difficult to persist in trying to remove them? The answer to this question is readily seen when we refer to the last line of the diagram on page 83, which reads "Anxiety, Defenses, and Escapes." Take away our *defenses and escapes* and we experience *anxiety*, a very disturbing emotion. We often prefer our quirks, symptoms, and undesirable traits to raw anxiety over what we are and what we might become. For this reason a conducive environment is important. It allows us to take the *first step toward self-improvement:* recognition of a personal problem and a willingness to work toward it.

Conducive Human Relationships and Environments. A warm, understanding friend, sponsor, or counselor can do more to help the individual to find and to express himself than almost any other human relationship. This does not imply that the individual should find someone to do things for him, but rather someone to encourage him to do things for himself. A friend may open new possibilities to him or provide opportunities for his initiative to operate, but solving his problems for him may be masked domination. Similarly, an environment that is conducive to the expression of the individual's talents and motivation may be a deep source of development and self-realization. An extracurricular pursuit, a hobby, dramatics, debating, sports, creative writing, drawing, or a developed talent—all can serve as conditions for self-expression and self-realization. This has been called a "permissive" relationship or environment (660).

Free Expression through Abilities and Interests. Through the sponsorship of a friend, coach, or counselor, and by the use of a stimulating environment, the student should be able to explore freely a field of interest or a talent. He may try his hand at student government, writing, art, athletics, community work, or group activity. He may discover those avenues through which he can best develop, those that release tensions for him and bring him recognition and success. In counseling he can freely talk about or around his problem and inadequacies. He can "blow off steam," "get it off his chest." In an activity like athletics he releases energy through muscular activity. This is an avenue for the expression of repressed aggressions and adventure. In dramatic activities he can become emotional, play a repressed or thwarted role. Through creative writing he can face his anxieties through the characters he creates or through the poetry he writes. Artistic production may express the inner life of the individual satisfyingly.

Achievement of Self-Acceptance. Permissive human relationships, if they provide an avenue for the expression of real interest and talent, and particularly if this is appreciated by others, produce an increase in the evaluation that the individual places on himself. This occurs along with the usual mistakes, disappointments, and unpleasantness. He comes to feel that he is not entirely a failure or is not inadequate in all realms of endeavor; that he has some intelligence, writing ability, or athletic skill. Others give him recognition for this and sometimes warmth and friendships grow out of it. Inwardly he develops an acceptance of himself—not only of his positive traits, but also of his negative features. If he is not a "complete flop," he can more readily accept the failures he experiences. This is a definite kind of inner and outer growth, however slow it may be.

Discoveries About Oneself—Insight. If the project one plunges into is pleasant and successful, his negative traits that come to mind are not so disturbing. As the individual faces these inadequacies instead of suppressing them, their origins are understood. They can be handled without so much anxiety, and the student begins to make generalizations about how he came to be the person he is and what he may do about it in the future. He sees "what has been the trouble," why he has behaved in certain ways. Many different aspects of his behavior now make sense. He is gaining perspective about himself and his world.

Morris, for example, understands now after several conferences why he has been the clown. He could make others laugh when inwardly he was sad. He sees why he always had to be in the center of attention. Sitting still, listening to a lecture, or studying made him restless. It was all a pattern of escape, from himself, from his inadequacies, by constantly getting the approving laugh or smile of others. Emotionally he was still a little 10-year-old boy seeking the attention of those around him. He felt inadequate but he could never face the fact. It was too depressing. Being with others made him forget. His family life "had been a mess." His parents fought, his mother was too wrapped up in him. He was ashamed of his home and wanted to get away but was emotionally tied to it in order to keep his parents together. He started out late socially and was very backward as a small child and felt inferior. He had some insight into the fact that his present behavior is compensatory. He is the bluffer, the big front. He shows little responsibility, cuts classes, gambles away the money that was to put him through school. He is a high-pressure salesman. If he weren't so unstable he might make an excellent comedian.

Many of the processes and factors related in Chapter 3 on "Understanding Oneself" and Chapter 4 on "Development" are here seen as they occur in the individual's own life. Insights occur during successful participation in projects, activities, and discussions with others, or even while writing a short story in which one loses himself— while painting, doing handicraft, or listening to music or attending a good movie. Here are some examples of such student insights from four different persons:

A coed said, "I don't understand why, but when I take a trip after a hard season's work, ideas just come to me. As the telephone poles whiz by, I see myself more clearly. I understand what I am and what I am not."

"I made a discovery one day while in the midst of writing an English theme that was coming right along after several weeks of procrastination.

I said to myself, 'Dub, you old fool, don't you realize that running away from things you've got to do is much worse than doing them? It is the idea you're fighting, not the work. Sit down and start to work next time, and if you can't work, do what Dr. X. suggested: start writing what's on your mind. This will probably bring to light your defenses, the unpleasantnesses connected with the task. Once they're out of the way you can carry the mail.' "

"I'm beginning to see the light. I can see now that it pays to expect to make errors, and when I make them say, 'Well, this is one on today's account.' That's better than freezing up in such situations, fearing that I'm doing something wrong. Furthermore, I'm going to expect kidding. They can't dislike me and yet spend so much time riding me."

"I find it helps to settle matters instead of stewing over them. Now take the matter of losing my cigarettes. I've spent several precious minutes brooding over that until finally I said, 'What the hell—thirty five cents! I'll just charge that up to profit and loss.' Then the idea struck me. I'm going to take out mental insurance. I'm going to expect trouble; that's the premium I'll pay when the trouble comes. Then it won't bother me. I've been saving up for it—really toughening myself—facing my problems instead of running."

It has been observed frequently that insights are not of great value unless the individual discovers them himself (341).

Putting Ideas into Use—Experimenting with Events in One's Life. As this process of emotional release, frankness, self-discovery continues, the individual is more likely to try new ventures in daily living. New zest and motivation are more likely to arise. He seeks new methods of growth and change in his environment. He makes new plans, branches out into novel areas, and tries different schemes. Suggestions and ideas for self-development like those given in various later chapters of this book are accepted and tried with verve now instead of being sources of dread. He begins to extinguish some of his anxieties and aversions. The swimmer, for example, who was discouraged by the coach's outline of efficient methods when he was so inefficient begins to show new interest in them when he is able to stay afloat for a while and knows he is not a complete failure as a swimmer. Now he can experiment with greater confidence and gain new habits.

With the new zest he is not so withdrawn. He is more aware of his environment and of the correct or erroneous nature of his activities. He has more of a learning attitude. As his anxieties and aversions lessen, the conflicts between what he ought to do and what he is afraid to do or dislikes to do are more easily resolved. When these uneasy balances (conflicts) are broken, many of the escapes and defenses are no longer necessary. The individual does not spend as much time in vacillation, confusion, and impulsive plunging into activities that do not adequately satisfy his needs and motives. Many needs mentioned on page 61 are satisfied by his activities in this new state.

We shall now examine counseling and group activities as means of effective adjustment, and then review some of the specific techniques and processes through which old traits, habits, and attitudes are eliminated or new ones acquired, usually as a part of some such project as those discussed earlier.

Counseling

Nature of Counseling. It is extremely difficult for one to gain perspective when thinking alone about one's problems or plans. Problems often become magnified when one considers them alone and the "thinking" or "self-analysis" becomes brooding and worry. The "success-in-three-lessons" articles speak of developing by self-determination and by mottoes and platitudes. Real personal growth usually involves some means of *losing oneself* through a social venture —a counseling situation or a group or a creative activity.

Counseling is a professional source of contact with another person (94). It involves seeking one who is understanding, who can be trusted, and who is usually regarded with respect and warm feelings. With time, under this relationship the process outlined on page 122 occurs, *problems can be ventilated, tensions can be released, anxieties can be gradually discussed, morale can be developed,* and, sometimes, *interpretations of behavior can be offered, insights can be experienced, discoveries can be made, perspective and objectivity can be gained. Impulses for action usually result,* which provides a basis for personal growth (235, 746, 626, 661, 300, 689, 151, 778).

The fact that there are so many psychological charlatans such as fortune tellers, astrologists, and self-styled psychologists without professional training who seem to prosper indicates the demand of the public for an analysis of their personal assets, liabilities, needs, and conflicts (745). It is not necessary, however, for the interested person to go to the charlatan for his information.

Counselors Aid Understanding, Self-Acceptance, and Control. Today students expect counseling on personality development, the nature of their aptitudes, and interests (674, 872). Those who have applied for such services represent the typical college student, and in some respects the superior student. The groups who have been counseled report that it has been valuable and that they achieve higher grades afterward and improve in their adjustment to college (851, 579, 45, 413, 262).

Counselors differ in the methods they use. Some will have you take the major responsibility for solving your problem. These counselors will encourage you to discuss your problem as you see it and to express freely your feelings and inner states (728, 729). Others will be somewhat more directive. Whereas the more directive counselor will encourage you to discuss your difficulties or tendencies at length, he may also give you various *tests*, *interpret* now and then the meaning of what you have stated, *reassure* you by indicating that many other students have the same problem that worries you occasionally, and relate cases of others to lend *perspective* to your problem (758). Finally he may *suggest* methods that have been helpful to others (87, 606, 531, 610, 701, 407). Instead of individual counseling the counselor may arrange for individuals with similar problems to meet in small groups for a discussion of their common difficulties (157). Whether directive or nondirective, the goal of counseling is understanding of yourself to the extent that you will *accept your basic traits and tendencies and become less emotionally disorganized and more effective* in your attempt to deal with them.

The background of training of counselors differs somewhat. The clinical or counseling psychologist has a scientific background with an emphasis on the facts that have grown from child study, learning and habit formation, emotion, attitude and trait development, mental measurement, and counseling. The major emphasis in his training has been on normal development and functioning. The qualified psychiatrist has a medical degree with additional training in a mental hospital or adjustment clinic. He is well acquainted with the development, treatment, and prevention of mental diseases and emotional disturbances. Most clinical or counseling psychologists are connected with public institutions like schools and clinics. Psychiatrists work in private practice and public institutions.

Discussion Provides an Emotional Outlet. Discussion of one's emotional problems has been referred to as the "talking cure." It has long been known that, if we talk over with an understanding listener those matters which disturb us, we are greatly relieved. This procedure is known as *emotional catharsis*. The discussion of the problem, whether or not it is accompanied by weeping, tremor, or some other overt expression of emotion, results in released tension (562). Many a man in military service learned the importance of talking over anxieties rather than brooding over them (149). The individual as well as the counselor is aware of the relief that follows after the story is told. This initial success should bring him back for further counseling and some of the more lasting effects mentioned below.

Discussion Desensitizes the Individual to His Problem. When the individual discusses his problem with an able, experienced counselor of any kind, the counselor assumes *a calm attitude*. He is acquainted with similar cases; he has heard this story in another form before. To the counselee the matter is very serious and unique; the thing that has happened is overwhelming. He sometimes does not see how life or the world can go on. To the counselor this is only one case in many, and the disturbing episode is only one event in the lifetime of this particular individual.

The student who is relating his problem cannot help being impressed by the counselor's calm. He is often *associating his difficulties* for the first time *with a cool, composed attitude*. At all times during the interview the counselor is sympathetic and understanding, but his sympathy is more intellectual than emotional. He sees the student's problem. He knows how the student feels, but he goes further; he sees it *in relation to the student's environment* as a whole and to his lifelong experience. To him there are ways out. The disturbing event is not an insurmountable block. It is a problem that may be met in one of many ways.

Discussion Changes Attitudes. Discussion also causes other changes in attitude. When one broods over a problem, he usually recalls it and all its unpleasantness time after time. He sheds very little new light on it. When he worries he relives the predicament without any solution in mind. In order for his story to carry over to the counselor he must be *objective*. Immediately he realizes that there are other people in the world; that what seemed to him to be all-important might appear trivial or perhaps foolish to someone else. He may even say to the counselor, "This might seem foolish to you, but it is important to me." This admission is worth much to him. He has already made a *fresh, different association* with the problem.

Furthermore, the discussion of the problem *encourages new ideas* and feelings to emerge, new possible causes for the difficulty to present themselves, and *new solutions* to appear. The student may say to the counselor, "This doesn't seem as bad now as it did before." He has changed his attitude.

In telling his problems to someone else the student tends to be more *logical;* he need not be logical when he runs over his difficulties in his own mind. He makes realistic rather than anxious associations. He understands more fully the situations open to him for exploration (568, 407).

Discussion Allows the Discovery of Repressed Material. There is evidence that, from early childhood on, human beings repress experiences that are shameful, punished, and not acceptable to them. We do this, as we saw in Chapter 3, in order to prevent anxiety. But this repressed material does not remain repressed. Events in life rearouse it. If it is associated with emotion, the stirred-up bodily state associated with emotions can continue even though we banish the ideas from consciousness. The psychoanalysts have pointed out that repressed experiences may be a source of motivation and may explain much of our behavior, peculiar and otherwise.

. . . the discussion of the problem encourages new ideas and feelings to emerge . . .

Susan Greenburg

The understanding, warm counselor makes it possible for the individual to face some of these repressed experiences. He may come to see in the interview that a person may be on the whole a fine person and yet have had some shameful experiences. As the individual *integrates* the repressed material with the rest of his personality, he can better deal with this repressed material. It does not represent a segment of himself, so to speak, walled off from the rest of his personality and operating independently.

Discussion Helps to Organize the Personality.* It is not difficult to see that if dominant motives are repressed under some conditions, when inhibitions are removed they may seek expression, and the individual may behave noticeably out of character. These repressed reactions are functioning without the benefit of the morals, standards, and guiding force of that person's total self. His conscious, organized self represents one side of his personality; the repressed, unacceptable motives and experiences represent another. He is not an integrated, well-organized person. In fact, there is civil war within him. In the conference, over a period of time, these forces that cause inconsistency may be reorganized. Then the force of his whole personality can act to inhibit and guide those aspects which he previously repressed and would not acknowledge as part of himself.

As the counselor responds sympathetically and understandingly to the story, the person who has brought the problem to him seems to gain *new strength*, increased *morale*, and more active *motivation to find a solution*. The counselor provides an atmosphere somewhat rare in our culture, one in which the individual consulting him may accept himself, may see his negative and positive traits as a part of this total personality. He can dare to see himself as having certain "bad," undesirable, previously unmentionable traits, but also good traits. As he discusses himself more he comes to see how these "bad" traits were developed quite understandably. He assumes less the attitude "this can't have happened to me" and more the attitude "this is indigenous to some human development. If it is a part of predictable development, it can't be so bad. If it developed originally maybe it can be eliminated."

Discussion Provides Information and Interpretation. The counselor also inadvertently and casually supplies *information* with

---

* Personality may be defined as the dynamic organization within the individual of those psychophysical systems that determine his unique adjustment to his environment (12).

an interpolated "I think you're right," "That may not be true," or "Do you *think* so?" Problems frequently arise because of erroneous ideas, false information, and lack of perspective (800). The counselor's off-hand *assurance* that the matter that worries the student has occurred in the lives of 70 per cent of the persons of his sex and age certainly gives perspective. Without interrupting needlessly the on-going process of self-discovery, the counselor might, during a lull, hand the counselee a book, state some interesting facts, mention a service available to all students, or indicate the extent to which a given problem is prevalent. Now and then, when it is appropriate, the counselor will interpret a certain form of behavior for the student or remind him that an experience illustrates something that he has learned in one of his courses.

Case Illustrating Discussion

Frank is a student who ranks in the upper quarter of college students in respect to college aptitude, yet he found that he was unable to study. He exerted all the will power he could, but this usually resulted in disgust with himself and constant daydreams about his girl. He had just about decided to leave school despite the fact that he was strongly ambitious to go into law and liked the subjects that are preparatory to it.

He came to see the counselor. After talking around the subject for twenty minutes, he came to the real point. He said that he found out that his fiancée had had previous intimacies. One of the boys concerned was a very good friend and a fraternity brother. This relationship occurred before he went with the girl. She was assaulted sexually at puberty. He admitted that she seemed to love him very much, was very frank with him and loyal to him. All of this he understood, yet his doubt of her persisted. His own standards emphasized continence until marriage. His preoccupation with this problem kept him from studying or from doing anything well.

He continued to talk and again came to a subject which he had evidently been trying to avoid. He said, "There is another matter which may be related to this, but I am reluctant to talk about it. I have discussed it with only one person, my father. I don't want to bring it up again with him." He continued, telling the counselor that he is an adopted son; his birth was illegitimate. His parents were of good stock, however. Apparently at the back of his mind there was an association of his girl's behavior with that of his mother. He did not realize this before he began to discuss the matter, but, after he had talked about it, he saw that his own origin was the source of his disturbance over his girl rather than her actual behavior.

The counselor listened as Frank related the story and then asked him if he sometimes felt insecure because of his illegitimacy, even though he knew no one was aware of it except his foster parents, who had a very sensible attitude toward it. He had, it seems, suppressed the matter in his thinking. The counselor helped him to face the fact that his origin is unconventional, but that the conditions of his birth should not in any way affect his future, particularly since he has talked it over with his girl and she is not at all disturbed by it. The counselor reminded him of outstanding individuals with unconventional origins and suggested that Frank face this fact of his biography and realize that, although some people regard his origin with prejudice, there are others who are much more intelligent about it. The matter should never come up except in his own mind. If he makes an adjustment to it, that is the only adjustment necessary.

Discussing this whole matter with someone else seemed to help Frank greatly. He left, and returned for another appointment a week later. He said that seeing the cause of his confusion and inability to study was what he needed. His whole manner at the second interview was much freer. He was much more cheerful and was much better able to study. He was told to come in again if he had any more difficulties, but he has not returned. Other aspects of his adjustment seemed good. He enjoyed the men with whom he was living. His foster parents had made a good adjustment and loved him deeply. He had had a history of success as an officer in the Army.

The Student Is to Assume the Initiative. The good counselor will not interrupt too much the student's own initiative in finding himself through the counseling experience. He will not go off on a tangent and give a lecture. He will not indulge too much in technical terms or in some other fashion leave the impression that solving the problem presented is his responsibility rather than the student's. His main purpose is to *provide an atmosphere* for the counselee to make discoveries, gain perspective and objectivity toward his problem, release tensions, and experience growth.

Does Counseling Make One Too Analytical? Some emotionally tough individuals, in reading case histories, may have the attitude expressed by the father of Irwin M., as related in the case illustrating effective adjustment. They may say,

"It is bad for an individual to think about himself. Seeing a psychiatrist or a clinical psychologist makes one create problems that were not there originally. It aggravates emotional disturbance. All that junk that they talk about can have no good result. One should be discouraged from being so analytical."

So we raise the question: "Can one be too analytical?" Most individuals who are preoccupied with mental symptoms are not analytical in the psychological meaning of that word. It is true that they may be *too introspective* and are undoubtedly *egocentric*. Discussion of these matters with someone else should not have the effect of increasing their egocentricity and subjectivity. As they relieve tensions, become less sensitive to matters by exposing them, and relate their problems to a social world by discussing them with someone else, they should gain *objectivity*, if, of course, they have consulted a trained, competent counselor. Many an individual has become emotionally free and more capable of dealing with problems in the external world after such a conference. On the whole, courses in Psychology have the same effect. There may be individuals who are stirred up by taking courses in Abnormal Psychology or by reading psychological books prematurely, but it must be remembered that they had problems before they took the courses or read the books. The fact that they are upset by them indicates that they may need counseling and professional assistance rather than additional repression.

Activities in Adjustment

Some Effects of Social and Special Interest Activities. Sometimes entering into group relations, becoming a member of a club or an organization or activity such as a team or drama group provides a means of *releasing tensions, projecting one's inner life outward, seeing oneself in a new light,* and *obtaining the human support one needs.* With the success that such a venture brings, the individual is more able to accept his negative traits. He may see that after all he is not too different from others. The social situation, in the form of a congenial group, club, extracurricular activity, or even informal bull sessions, is usually required for development. The program, formal or informal, afforded by these groups together with the social stimulation and commitments made by the individual entering them usually furnishes the needed persistent stimulation (motivation) to development. The development becomes a dynamic, spontaneous acquisition of new habits, attitudes, and traits built in a social *milieu,* usually accompanied by a sense of satisfaction.

Every college counselor has seen the effect on some students, over a period of several years, of being on their own, living and working with others, taking responsibilities, participating in group ventures, having contact with lectures and the humanities, and growing generally in knowledge and perspective. Sometimes a student will gravitate over a period of time toward situations that will be conducive to building habits.   One student may take a job in the college cafeteria if he feels that he needs to have experience in dealing with other people.   Another may arrange an athletic program for himself or a summer manual labor job that will build him physically.   A third may go out for debating or dramatics with the purpose of developing traits.   Others may select writing, art, and crafts.   Extracurricular activities, jobs, hobbies, lecture programs, or art exhibits and informal social groups like bull sessions, all have sometimes the value of helping the individual *project his inner life* outward and of *developing new attitudes and habits.*

Avenues of adventure are discussed in Chapter 6, page 161, in connection with budgeting time, and also in Chapter 8, page 225, in connection with avocations, and in Chapter 10, page 291, on social adjustment.   These stimulating events, which differ in specific character with the individual, tap numerous individual motives, keep the participant close to real living events, give him satisfactions, and yield success to many motives.   The individual is sublimating usually when absorbed in these activities and in so doing is usually adjusting to his conflict in one of the more effective ways (777).

There are times when a solitary project or responsibility will have many of the above effects.   Even then, however, the social element is frequently present.   One decides to write a book, develop a career, invent a gadget, pursue a hobby.   Invariably the individual is dependent upon the writings or products of others, and there is the anticipation of the response from others as he works on it and when his project is completed.   In short, he is behaving in terms of a real rather than an imaginary world.

Project as a Training Program.   In the most effective kinds of social activities the individual becomes deeply absorbed in the venture. It is not a rigid, mechanical training program but rather a dynamic, interesting adventure in some activity.   The rigid training program is often too mechanical and for that reason frequently loses its interest for the individual.   The activity has more of the play spirit.

It is a fact that many of the traits the individual wishes to acquire consist of specific habit patterns, but these habits are best acquired indirectly through a stimulating informal *project.*   For example, grooming involves an attractive arrangement of hair, frequent effective cleansing of the face, shined shoes, pressed suit, clean apparel.   Harmonizing colors and patterns must be chosen.   Good grooming can be achieved more successfully by associating with others who are well groomed and by trial-and-error observation of people and pictures than by making a serious training program out of it.

There are times when the more *formal training program* yields good results, as for example in athletics and dancing. In those cases there is usually a structured course with a trained, personable leader or teacher. On the other hand, many individuals acquire most of their skills in a trial-and-error manner. For example, no one can tell us exactly how to roller-skate. We put on skates, go to a large, smooth surface like a sidewalk or rink, and *try*. We might move into it gradually by trying the skates on a lawn so that we do not fall too frequently and get hurt too badly. We learn to balance by balancing. This is true of such activities as swimming, cycling, and similar skills. It may be that a fusion of the planned program and the informal project can be achieved.

The same processes are involved in learning social and personal skills. The ease and conversational art that a charming hostess shows at a reception has been learned over the years through trial and error. It consists of patterns of habits and attitudes such as smiling graciously, remembering names, finding the guest's interests and freely talking about them or stimulating them to talk. It also includes unlearning tensions, fears, suspicions, and sensitiveness over awkwardness and *faux pas*.

Extracurricular Activities and the Humanities as Free Expression. *Dramatics* is one example of a social outlet. It enables the participant or the observer to live different roles and at times to give vent to aspects of his personality that were previously repressed. It brings him in contact with others of similar interests. It allows him to satisfy such motives as social recognition and adventure. It has been said that this fantastic type of play, like talking about one's problems, enables the individual to face his anxieties in a safe manner (777). He can play a new role.

A psychiatrist dealing with children discovers that he can learn quite a bit about the child's problem and, too, the child can relieve some of his repressions and experience overtly some of his anxieties, if he is allowed to play freely with various toys. The boy or girl is encouraged to play as constructively and destructively as he wishes. If he desires he is allowed to squash the dolls, take them apart, and even discuss his aggression. With consecutive periods of *play therapy*, the child makes a better adjustment to the disturbing situation. Play

therapy is becoming more extensively used among children and somewhat among adults (219, 47, 30, 840).

Psychodrama is the use of play by youth and adults in a dramatic setting in which tensions are released and the individual is prepared for real situations (553). Sometimes individuals are aided by watching others perform. The possibility of constructing films for individuals with problems, so that they might see actions on the screen similar to their own about which they are anxious, has been discussed and used to some extent.

Group therapy, as it has been called, has been used extensively in the service and among civilians. Carefully arranged sessions are planned for individuals with similar difficulties so that they may listen to each other discuss aspects of their personality and growth (794, 717). Experiences are shared, and the person in charge acts as leader in integrating the contributions made during the meeting (393, 447).

Athletics has advantages similar to dramatics. It is a socially approved outlet for aggression and adventure. Some individuals who do not receive recognition or achieve success in school work or social activities may do so through this avenue (611). The other activities, such as debating, special interest clubs, hobby groups, professional fraternities, have the same values.

Success in these activities gives the individual confidence and allows him to face more readily the negative aspects of his personality and to tolerate them at least temporarily as part of himself. This is a natural growth under the circumstances, particularly as he sees similar traits in some of the other members of the group for whom he has high regard. Assuredly, the opposite tendency to fight a vital part of oneself, to disown it, despise it, and think of it as shameful or worse is inimical to personal unity and self-respect. It defeats integration, a major goal in personality development. Activity groups are realistic and provide real adventure rather than fantasy in which erroneous impressions of oneself and others remain uncorrected. In fantasy an individual himself or others may appear all good or all bad; in real contacts the fusion of good and bad traits can become more apparent.

The fine arts are a good source of self-discovery. The individual, through writing fiction, may *project his own feelings and attitudes* into the persons he creates on paper or the persons others have created in literature or art. He can experience vicariously through them adventures and emotions which he does not allow himself in reality. He can meet his anxieties in a similar way, in a safe manner. He experiences accomplishment and release, and possibly some emotional freedom which may allow him to get away from his own problems into the real world outside himself. Music also acts as a background upon which an individual may engage in reverie, project himself outward, identify himself with others, as in group music, and often get relief and possibly some insight. As a result music is customarily associated with pleasantness and repose (541).

A full program of the above-mentioned activities including jobs, reading, music, and recreation has been of help to individuals with emotional difficulties (288).

EXPRESSIVE OUTLETS AND FREE WRITING. The process basic to play therapy underlies some poetry, art, crafts, athletics, and *free writing* and might well be used among youths and adults as a means of projecting outward their feelings and tensions.

Kurt L. is a tall, well-built, fair-skinned fellow with light red hair. His striking appearance wins for him much secret admiration from members of the opposite sex. He appears to have dignity and reserve, but when one talks with him one is struck with the fact that he is extremely shy and ill at ease except when with a group similar to his former drinking buddies. Practically no one except a few teachers realizes that he has unusual creative ability. He has developed it to an appreciable extent by his strong need to unburden his frustrations and repressions.

His parents separated when he was young. His mother is apparently a poorly adjusted woman who has turned to fanatical religion for solace, has taught him repression of all his feelings. All his life he has yearned for an older brother or the companionship of his father, whom he has idealized in perspective. He went out for sports but was awkward and, despite his splendid physical build, was not too successful, yet he persisted. It was in high school that he received the encouragement to write, and he has been doing so ever since. Now as a college junior he has turned out numerous short stories which compare quite well with published material. He is very reluctant to submit his writings to a publisher because so much of it reflects his inner life.

His greatest anxiety and disturbance is his social maladroitness. He feels that he makes a fool of himself every time he meets persons whom he wishes to impress. He cannot say what he thinks is expected of him and what he feels. Therefore he thinks he is not up to par as a man. Some of this is due to the complex emotional thinking associated with his father. His grandparents pointed out to him all his father's shortcomings, yet as a child he idealized him in his daydreams. On real contact with this parent, however, Kurt always seemed to fail in what was expected of him.

Another frustration was in his relationship with girls. The only time he could impress them was when he had been drinking, and then he became sexually aggressive to the point of frightening even himself.

The counselor encouraged him to continue writing and asked to see some of his products. Kurt was willing to bring most of them. One or two he thought he could not show anyone. He wrote these stories under compulsion in a single sitting. Sometimes he did not want to read them after he had finished them. When he completed them he felt greatly relieved. It was through his conferences that he began to use them as a means of understanding himself better, as well as a release.

One of his stories dealt with a man who secretly admired a girl who worked in a Chicago office near his and who went to lunch at the same time he did. The story described quite realistically the introspections and the mental ruminations this man experienced as he admired the girl from afar and planned to meet her. The story is climaxed when he has collected enough courage to talk to her and has bought some tickets for the opera which he plans as a surprise for their next meeting. Since they had not planned to meet, she did not appear either that day or subsequently. The story beautifully depicts Kurt's own problems in this area and ends as his experiences usually end, in frustration and disappointment. Yet projecting this experience outward into a creation of his imagination had realistic value for him.

In counseling, the client is often encouraged to *write* in whatever manner seems appropriate to him. Some students, like Sam who is described below, *find relief in writing down all thoughts as they come to them, very much as in an interview* (522). Others who are interested in creative writing write short stories, projecting themselves into them. Painting and drawings may be used in a similar manner.

Sam N. is the son of a high school principal in a small city. He has on several occasions started to college and then has left in the middle of the semester, remaining out of communication with his parents. He has always been an enigma to those who know him. Though attractive physically, he seems to be poorly groomed purposely. Whenever there is a chance that he will succeed in any venture, he spoils it, seemingly deliberately. When he reluctantly came to the counselor, he admitted emotional upset and inability to discover the nature of his difficulty. He admitted being cynical, disliking everything on which society puts a premium, having been judged a juvenile delinquent despite his father's attempts to shield him.

He talked freely during the entire interview. He was encouraged by the counselor to try to write out his thoughts and feelings for relief and possibly to gain some understanding of himself. The following are free explorations of his feelings. They indicate how a college student may use this technique for emotional release and self-discovery.

"I resent the fact that my father would not let me play football in high school and thereby let me be a part of the group. I resented his asking me bluntly if I loved him. I thought he was a good father to me, so what could I do but say 'Yes'? . . . I resent his saying as he whipped me violently that it was hurting him more than it was me. I hate that falsity in his character—something which I can never really tell him and make him understand. I hate his insensitivity to his wife. I despise his childishness, his fits of violent aggression and anger. . . . This process of analyzing my past is leaving me *bare;* it is freeing me by leaving me utterly devoid of everything except a feeling of new potential, new possibilities, new horizons. . . . I am afraid that the very persons and processes that are attempting to help me will fail—will let me have a vision, then dumbly, unconsciously let me again suffer from frustration. . . . I remember one time, when I decided impetuously to leave home, Dad said to me, 'Please, Sam, don't leave tonight. Wait until morning, anyway.' He said this in a pleading, almost crying tone. Why—why did I cry then? Was it because I felt myself caught, imprisoned in the sentimentality, the possessive love of my parents? The fact that I would never be able to express myself freely as long as they lived? I know I have wished that they were dead so that I might smoke and drink and be an atheist and act without their false, puritanical values imprisoning me. But would I escape then, even if they were dead? I am caught in a trap. I have run away from religion, from them, from all convention because I thought distance would separate me from these horrible, inconsistent values. I wanted to be bad. I wanted to suffer. I forced myself to suffer. I wanted to know the pains of life.

I want still to know life. My dad could not understand why I threw away all the good things of life, friends, college, warm clothing, etc., to place myself consciously in a position where I must suffer and fight and feel the pains of hunger. He did not realize that I wished to come to a life of maturity myself, not being assisted all the way. . . . In many ways my father kept me from being a part of the group. He used to visit me when I was in grade school. This was a source of tremendous embarrassment to me. I like the badness in me. It was my adventure, my expression, but my expression was thwarted, repressed, because of lack of understanding. I want to be accepted and loved by the group or maybe by a select group of people interested in ideas and basic real feelings—but I don't want social position, that prison, that slavery for the sake of power. I want to be loved, yes, but I want more to love and love with all my heart and soul some real object. I will never be able to release this terrible pent-up emotion on a compromise or falsity. . . . Since I could not have free expression of my impulses in my own environment, I had to run away to seek this expression, but even when I was away from my parents I could not escape their puritanical indoctrination."

Through these writings Sam not only got relief but came to understand himself better. He realized he hated social standards because social standards were represented by his father. He further realized that in hating his father he also hated himself because underneath he loved as well as hated his father. Many of his own traits were those of his father. In one conference he said with considerable insight: "I know now why I am so hard on myself, why I love pain and hunger and failing. It is because I am trying to punish both my father and myself, particularly that part of myself which is my father."

Autobiographies are a source of emotional release and of knowledge about oneself. Even fragmentary material like "An Evaluation of My Semester in College," or "The People Who Have Interested Me Most," or "My Philosophy of Life" has value in self-discovery and self-acceptance.

Counseling and Group Activities Are Interrelated. You have undoubtedly noted in this discussion that there are many similarities in the effects of counseling and of activities such as hobbies and interest projects. Both are sources of knowing oneself better and of building a better attitude toward oneself. Both furnish means of projecting one's inner life and relieving tensions. They can well be integrated. Group activities may implement counseling by furnishing a field of activity in which the individual may test his hunches about himself and try out sources of skill and interest that he has discovered to be basic to his personality. Counseling is a more direct means of discovering one's inner tendencies. Group activities, on the other hand, have the characteristic of being more lifelike. There is no reason why the individual who wants to know himself better and is desirous of developing an effective adjustment cannot use both. In counseling, the individual discovers his basic motives and personality trends. Group activities can furnish him an outlet for these strivings as well as successes. Furthermore, group activities are a means by which he may convert the discoveries about himself into the daily social habits of which life is essentially built.

In both of these processes—counseling and free expression through creative activities—there is an opportunity for *imprisoned emotions connected with repressed and sometimes forgotten disturbing experiences to be released properly and placed in perspective.* The individual faces rather than denies certain impulses and feelings and comes to accept them as part of himself.

In the relationships and activities discussed above, changes of a growth or maturing nature usually occur in the individual. Under what conditions are these changes pronounced, and what is basic to their occurrence? To these questions we now turn.

Changing Behavior

The Question of Changing Behavior. A fact that we must realize at the outset is that our behavior is changing somewhat all the time, regardless of what we do. There is a continuity to personality, which forms the central core (12). Nevertheless, modifications in the form of learned behavior constantly occur (647). In the early years parents reward or punish behavior in order to eliminate or perpetuate it. An individual will imitate and introject the behavior and attitudes of some person he idealizes. He will join a group, adopt its standards, be criticized or praised for desirable or undesirable behavior. All of this may occur inadvertently as part of everyday events.

As adulthood approaches we desire to assume more initiative in this process of maturing and of developing the traits that we believe to be ideal. Essentially, this will occur by the same process found in childhood development, except that the groups to which we belong will be more adult and there will be more verbalization of our traits informally or in counseling. As youths or adults we seek principles and methods; we want to take ourselves in hand and change ourselves (71).

An individual may center his attention on a symptom without gaining much insight into his entire personality. He may feel that the symptoms of shyness, feeling of inferiority, impulsiveness, or inability to make people like him are his difficulties rather than a more complicated underlying process. After several counseling conferences one may find that understanding oneself may reduce the verve to change, or, on the other hand, that seeing oneself as a whole and feeling that one is less objectionable as an individual may make the whole process of acquiring new traits and habits easier and more dynamic.

John N. came to a consulting psychologist stating that he wanted a book or instructions that would make him a public speaker. He knew that there were courses which made speakers out of men, but he did not know how to avail himself of them. Without using the exact words, John made it clear that he thought that once he became a public speaker most of his problems would be solved. To him a man who was not a public speaker was a weakling, had the kind of personality that people do not respect, and he felt that if he could "just learn those principles which transformed one into the kind of person who made a good public speaker," he would be a much more effective individual. John really was not so naive as his words might indicate. He was emotionally upset over his inability to speak in a group, and in his emotionalized thinking he viewed it as causal to his ineffectual personality.

In the course of a series of conferences, John began to discover why public speaking was so important for him. He began to feel that his learning to speak in public was not a life-or-death matter, that the great urge to acquire this skill grew out of his inner relationship to his father. His father was an extremely dominant person, unkind and at times brutal to John's mother, a charming, cultured, intelligent person who succeeded in finding a social outlet outside of her home. John learned early in life to knuckle under, keep his mouth closed, read, and daydream, and although he grew to be over 6 feet in height, with massive shoulders, he was extremely introverted, and all his initiative revolved around obtaining good grades. Speech had literally been choked off in him as a child. Without his realizing it, the ability to be an outstanding public speaker had become a symbol of regaining extroverted initiative and individuality which he felt had been taken from him by his father. As he began to discover the source of this inferiority he realized that he was not such a flop, that he had achieved scholastically, had won an assistantship which he was thoroughly capable of fulfilling, that he had gained in a quiet way many skills and a number of staunch friends and admirers. Fantasy of himself as a great public speaker did not have to become a reality within a week. He could experiment with speaking and improve through the course of time. The desire to change himself so that he could become a public speaker led to something far more valuable than skill in public speaking—a better understanding of himself plus a steady, progressive, nonmiraculous growth in his ability to perform in public.

The Essentials in Changing Behavior. We have seen in the preceding pages that behavior can be changed in a substantial way under strong motivation through counseling or activities in school or extracurricular avenues. This involves *needing* and *wanting to change, reducing resistances to this change, patiently exploring what it takes to bring about the behavior we desire, and producing the surroundings that will enhance it.* Let us look more thoroughly into motivation, conflicts in motivation, and the trial and error arising from the motivation which reduces it and also helps us to grow as a person. First let us look at one successful and well-known program of self-improvement, the Alcoholics Anonymous movement.

The Alcoholics Anonymous Program of Changing Behavior. When the alcoholic becomes a good member of A.A. he changes his whole attack. Instead of egotistically saying, "I can take it or leave it" (and usually taking it), or instead of suppressing the whole matter of addiction or emphasizing the drinking habit alone, he now does this:

He comes to understand and admit that he is "allergic to the stuff," that he is powerless to deal with it. He may show insight to the point of realizing that he has an immature personality, that for him alcohol is an escape. However, as he attends A.A. meetings, sees and hears former alcoholics who tell of having been wet for years during which they lost everything they had, he believes that "a Power greater than ourselves could restore us to sanity," and he turns to religion—*the kind that will be meaningful to him.* He has faith in the Deity. He feels that he can associate himself with something bigger than himself. This process is highly motivating to him, particularly as he meets others who understand him, who have faced the same problems. We can see that this process so far is a form of group therapy. Similar to other group therapy, the alcoholics "made a searching and fearless moral inventory of ourselves," "admitted to God, to ourselves, and to another human being the exact nature of our wrongs." However, the program goes further than *understanding* and *accepting oneself* as one who differs from others in being unable to drink moderately, and that is why it interests us in this section. They "made a list of all persons we had harmed, and became willing to make amends to them all." This whole program is kept alive by the members constantly finding new alcoholics to whom they may tell their own story and to whom they make the program of A.A. available (6).

The Alcoholics Anonymous program illustrates rather well the ideas mentioned earlier. It arouses in the individual an understanding and acceptance of himself, the building of new traits and experimenting with events in the environment for positive development. This program is a combination of a guided plan and informal activities. The *group* is important in this personal improvement program (826). Let us turn now to the basic condition in all personal improvement.

Understanding Motivation. The primary factor, then, in learning and developing new behavior or changing old behavior is motivation. We have seen previously, in Chapter 2, in connection with motives for study and, in Chapter 3, in a discussion of the nature and development of motives, that motives are *individual,* that they are frequently *unconscious,* that they are the greatest factor in explaining the individual's zest and the direction his behavior takes. It has been shown that all of us are motivated in some direction and that even the frustration of a motive may be stimulating. Therefore, it may not be as important to acquire new motives as to recognize what our present motivation really is.

Whereas all of us, as has been previously indicated, are striving to satisfy needs, it is necessary to know, of any given individual, what specific form this motivation takes. Some of this motivation is expressed in our strong interests, our personal ambition and life purpose, our hobbies, and in the people and situations toward which we gravitate as well as those toward which we have strong aversions.

The reason that certain of our traits are distasteful to us is usually that they satisfy certain motivations and not others. This statement is illustrated in many of the cases above. Steve D. on page 126 was getting satisfaction from his invalidism; but he also wanted to be self-sufficient. Irwin M. on page 123 wanted to be accepted by others, to have close friends; but previous experience caused him to suspect those who became close to him. This may be diagramed: Wants acceptance → ← Fears others. This basic pattern of two opposing motives that block each other and cause anxiety is found when we analyze many of our problems. *Understanding oneself, then, means knowing one's motivations and discovering the events in life that will satisfy them,* the behavior that helps to achieve goals, and the behavior that is thwarting or conflicting. Let us turn to the usual situation—conflict in motivation.

Breaking Conflict in Motivation. One reason that we do not break habits we dislike is that even though we dislike the habit, it is also satisfying to us in some way. We are thus in conflict. Usually some aversion keeps us from carrying out the activity that will result in a new habit to take the place of the undesirable one. Edward C. on page 121, for example, had to reduce his resistances to going out with girls or else suffer the feeling of being unmarriageable. Irwin had to extinguish some of his sensitiveness to what he believed was rejection by his fellows. In these and other cases either motivation to acquire habits must be increased, or *resistance and avoidance to the activity—fear of embarrassment or rejection—must be lessened* by changes in the individual making the adjustment. Often this reduction is accompanied by introducing the individual into the activity he dreads in its milder and less threatening form. In counseling he does this by discussing the feared situation. Sometimes after talking over the matter and fearing it less one gets into situations he previously dreaded, as Edward C. did. In all such cases of reduced conflict learning takes place. There is trial and error, which results in acquiring the desired attitudes and traits or in reducing the hampering attitudes or traits. This, as indicated in the list to follow involves reward of the desired activity and checking or punishment of the nondesired behavior.

Consolidating Motivation. What often seems like increased motivation is a consolidation of all the motivations toward a given goal. After discussing a goal we have been quietly wanting to achieve, we often find many "reasons" for attaining it and avoiding the opposite choice. Here is a list of conditions that are motivating or rewarding in a program of personal improvement:

Clearly state your goals.
List the disadvantages of present behavior.
List reasons why you want to change.
Get someone else to learn the new behavior with you.
Pick some "model person" and observe him.
Keep a record or diary—see weekly success.
Be alert to any progress, however small.
Talk with others who started where you are and have progressed.
Recall your previous successes and use your present advantages.
Expect the learning process to take time.
See the frustrations and conflict in your motivations.

Habit Breaking and Forced Disuse. This method of forced disuse, or "will power" as some designate it, is not so effective psychologically when used alone as is often claimed. Forced disuse of some strong habits may create more problems than it solves. The individual may become nervous, emotional, and irritable, and thereby begin a new series of bad habits. Try for example *not* to think of food for five minutes, and you will notice that you think of it more than you would otherwise. On the other hand, become absorbed in some interest for five minutes and you are unaware that time has passed, and the thought of food has probably not entered your mind. Voluntary control of behavior is important, but it does not consist in inhibiting a strongly motivated act, putting attention on the act, and ignoring the underlying motivation. Understanding the motivation and trying to find a new avenue for it makes much more sense, psychologically. This new source of satisfaction affords opportunity for the previous undesirable habit to fall into disuse.

The members of Alcoholics Anonymous *renounce* drinking. They don't repress their alcoholic tendencies; they continually talk about them and their means of controlling themselves. They accept wholeheartedly their conclusion that they cannot drink, and they seek new ways to spend their time and energy. They continue to enter bars, but now they look for alcoholics instead of alcohol, and for comradeship based on common problems rather than on common escapes. The renunciation is part of a new orientation.

It is a commonplace that individuals who are seriously handicapped, as through blindness or loss of a limb, seem to adjust better than those who have minor defects. One factor in this better adjustment is renunciation and clarification of motivation. The seriously handicapped know what they can do and what they cannot. They have frankly faced their problems and the adjustments to them.

Trial, Error, and Success. Everyone has had the experience of changing behavior through trial, error, and success. Most of us no longer fear the dark, suck our fingers, wet the bed, or lose our tempers as in childhood. Some have learned to concentrate, speak up in class, or eat food they once abhorred. These habits have been acquired because rewarding conditions have followed these activities. The undesirable activities were checked and new, satisfying ones substituted.

In all examples given, motives were aroused in acquiring the habits, whether or not the individual realized it. Disturbing behavior can be eliminated and more desirable habits and attitudes acquired *if* strong motives are aroused, *if* responses occur which satisfy these motives (reward), and *if* the undesired behavior is no longer satisfying (515, 338, 337).

People embark on new diets, for example, and lose weight for health's sake when the new diet is rewarding to them. It can become rewarding *if* they can see loss of weight in a few days, and *if* they can eat all they want of low-calorie food when they crave food. Then they tend to become enthusiastic about the project. They feel they are reaching their goals without too much dissatisfaction.

Many students have found that if they keep an accurate record of the time they have wasted each day and show it to the counselor each week they tend to eliminate the time-wasting habit. The chagrin that results from admitting even to themselves that they waste time deters them.

The *reported-record* method may be used in facilitating the elimination of habits, such as nail biting, tension, fear, disturbing mannerisms, and some attitudes such as worry or brooding, provided of course that the motivation for them has also been altered. The tally or reported-record method has been helpful to some because it makes them conscious of their *success*. Some laboratory studies have shown that undesirable habits as speech defects, fingernail-biting, and spelling errors can be reduced by practicing them consciously (600). In such cases, the *undesirable consequences of the activity* are made highly conscious. Serving an emetic with alcohol produced abstinence in 74 per cent of a large group of chronic alcoholics. The emetic severely nauseated the individual and built up a strong aversion to the sight, odor, taste, and thought of alcohol (448). Unpleasant events such as pain, embarrassment or censure frequently operate to weaken a given tendency (566, 68).

Whereas punishment can check errors if appropriately used, if too intense it can arouse anxieties, withdrawal and "behavior without a goal." These are detrimental to functioning as an effective person, as shown in Chapter 3.

Summary. Most of us cling to undesirable habits for some or all of the following reasons.

We are not strongly or widely enough *motivated* to break them.
The consequences of the habit are not *punishing* enough.
The motive that instigated the habit in the first place is *not satisfied* by a more desirable habit.
The habit satisfies immediately or strongly some *hidden motives*.
We don't *practice* the new habit long enough.
We are not in the kind of environment that will *arouse* the desired and *inhibit* the undesired activity.

With strong, consolidated, ego-involved (pride) motivation, persistent reward of the new habit, checking of the old, and desirable satisfaction of the need that aroused the undesirable habit, many habits can be broken.   Think of the habit you want to break in these terms, see why you have not broken it in the past, and what a program of breaking it and substituting new habits will involve.

Supplementary Readings

G. W. Allport, *Becoming: Basic Considerations for a Psychology of Personality*, Yale University Press, 1955.

R. May, *Man's Search for Himself*, Norton, 1953.

E. R. Hilgard, *Theories of Learning* (2nd ed.), Appleton-Century-Crofts, 1956.

J. A. McGeoch and A. L. Irion, *The Psychology of Human Learning* (2nd ed.), Longmans, Green, 1952.

In addition see the references cited by number in the chapter and appearing in the bibliography of an accompanying volume entitled *Teaching Personal Adjustment: An Instructor's Manual.*

Susan Greenburg

CHAPTER 6

PERSONAL

EFFICIENCY

Tom, Dick, and Harry may have roughly the same intelligence, income, and physical make-up, yet they may differ markedly from each other in the success they achieve in the use of these assets. We all have the problem of learning to use effectively and creatively our bodies, our time, and our income. We must learn how to spend these resources wisely for our maximum development and happiness.

Basic to our personal efficiency are the attitudes, motivation or blocks in motivation for the task before us. Interacting with motivation are the presence or absence of learned skills—two major factors we have seen as important in previous personal problems. Let us see how attitudes and motivations influence the efficiency we show.

Budgeting Time

Importance of Time. The following statement comes from the pen of a young teacher who when in college attempted to win, by the end of his sophomore year, a competitive scholarship and at the same time earn his room, board, and fees through remunerative work.

"Those two years of hard work and planning did more to teach me the value of time and life itself than all my other experiences. As a student, free hours were a truly appreciated joy. A dance or a movie in which I indulged about once a month was not just another party or show, as it had been in high school, but was an event upon which I feasted in imagination for weeks ahead. Even today I budget my time and fill it with work in order to experience 'that indescribable pleasure which issues from a change from work to the freedom of play.' I not only learned to enjoy work in those two years but for the first time I appreciated the refreshing nature of play—the freedom and relaxation following work."

Time cannot be saved as is so often claimed; an hour of this day cannot be tucked away for consumption tomorrow. It has been suggested that the more money we save, the more we have, whereas time is more subtle stuff; if we start saving it we no longer have a moment to spare.

Time can, however, be invested. A few hours of time can produce an inspiring experience to be carried in our memories for the rest of our lives. During an interval of time we can create something in the scope of our talents and motivation. The experiences that grow from the investment of time may be those that emerge from reading a good book, visiting a quaint town or a picturesque scene, conversing with a great character or congenial person, or developing a strong friendship. The creations may be the result of a hobby. They may be represented by a homemade bookcase, an automobile paint job, a poem, an essay, a collection of guns, or proficiency in playing tennis. The difference between a truly great personage and "just another individual" is largely the use of time. We all have some type of capability as raw material. The advantageous employment of time converts these capabilities into a fund of knowledge, understanding, and proficient skills.

Biographies reveal that youth is a time for creative work. The Persian Empire was conquered by Alexander when he was 25; Bryant wrote "Thanatopsis" at 17; Madame Curie began her search for radium while still in her twenties; da Vinci in his eighteenth year painted the famous angel in Verrocchio's canvas; Gladstone made his first speech in Parliament when he was 24; at this age Goethe published the tragedy, "Gotz von Berlickingen," and at 18 Hamilton attracted wide attention as a pamphleteer and was shortly after made a member of Washington's staff. Schubert, the great composer, had just passed 30 when death visited him. The lives of Keats and Shelley were shorter than thirty years (325).

How do you use your 1440-minute allotment daily? You will be surprised at the number of minutes for which you can give no account. Wasted time is not often relished time. Time fully enjoyed is not wasted. Checking how you spend your time is an illuminating survey every college student might undertake. It can be as interesting as a golf or bowling score. Take a blank sheet of paper for each day and record the time intervals at the extreme left and in the blank across the sheet note the activities carried on during these periods. For example:

Time	*Activity*
7:00	Bathe, dress, breakfast, see morning paper, walk to school
8:00	Class (English)
9:00	Study History in library

Then note the time you spend in the various activities such as shown below:

Activity	*Hours*	*Activity*	*Hours*	*Activity*	*Hours*
Classes	4½	Meals	2¼	Extracurricular	
Study (English)	¾	Athletics	0	(school paper)	½
Study (History)	1½	Remunerative		Time	
Study (French)	2	work	1	unaccounted	
Sleep	7	Extracurricular		for	3½
		(chorus)	0	Personal care	1

In this survey, time consumed in getting to and from an activity was included in the activity. The item that deserves the greatest analysis is "time unaccounted for." In the case of the above individual, on the day represented here, this time was lost after meals and in the afternoon. (A time of day most students might watch.) Most of it was spent around the house. Although this individual could have reached and attended all his classes in 3¼ hours, he consumed 4½. This schedule was selected because it is exceptional in the amount accomplished. This student studied 4¼ hours, worked 1 hour, and wrote a news item for the school paper in ½ hour. You can make such an analysis for yourself. It has been found that many students do most of their studying on four days of the week. The week-end then, may be watched for available hours and half hours (375). After some such survey one might critically ask oneself whether his time could have been spent more profitably or enjoyably.

Susan Greenburg

We all
have some
kind of
capability
as raw
material.

Avenues of Adventure with Time. How can one get the maximum return in happiness through the investment of time? The answer in general is: *by a variety of activities and some appreciable accomplishments in each one.* College offers as great a variety of activities as one can desire. Here are a few of them: athletics, using the facilities of the gymnasium and playing fields; the library, which includes the periodical room and phonographic records; lectures, plays, concerts, art exhibits; Student Union facilities; and religious activities.

In addition there are casual reading as furnished by newspapers and magazines; shows, games, conversation, relaxation, dates, picnics, and dances. Discussed more fully in Chapter 10 are such extracurricular activities as debating, dramatics, school paper, school politics, band, and pep clubs. Consult handbooks or pamphlets on "information for new students" for assistance in choosing the organization you wish to join.

It has been suggested that man can gain balanced satisfaction if he "splits his day three ways": eight hours for sleep and rest; eight for serious work; and eight for recuperative and recreational activities.

Traditionally 2 hours of *outside preparation* has been considered as the requirement for each credit hour in college. The question arises, How much time do students *actually* spend in study? The *average* college student (who spends about 16 hours a week in class) devotes about twice as much time to study than does the high school student. Study time varies greatly with individuals: some spend less than 10 hours and others with the same credit load consume 50 hours (835). It appears, then, that the student must readjust his study schedule upon entering college. The exact time devoted to study will depend upon *his individual* ability and habits. If the student finds that he must devote much more than 48 hours a week to school work, it may be wise to select a lighter schedule. One extra year in college sometimes makes the difference between four years of frustration, fear, and remorse, and five years of more serenity, success, and satisfaction.

An inquiry has shown that students with lower college ability scores spend considerably more time in study and yet receive much less credit. Intelligence is a far more significant factor in school achievement than time spent in study (835). Reports show that there is a relationship between grades and well-planned time budgets (865). It behooves you to learn your college aptitude score or relative intelligence and take this into consideration when you compare yourself with students who spend less time studying or do not have systematic study habits.

AVOCATIONAL ACTIVITIES. A *faculty-student committee* of the University of Chicago suggests these standards: a four-hour-a-week minimum for serious reading; for formal social affairs, dances, and teas, a five-hour maximum; for movies, shows, attendance at games, a six-hour maximum; and for religious and social service work, a two-hour minimum (637). How do these standards tally with your expenditure of time? Are some activities top-heavy in your schedule?

The value of extracurricular activities will be discussed in Chapter 10 under Social Adjustment. Moderate participation in the activities of the campus is found to be associated with good scholarship (160). Among athletes, however, there is evidence to show that grades decline during the season of competition (631).

REMUNERATIVE ACTIVITIES. Often a student is in continual conflict about the wisdom of working while at school. He sees others with a broader social program and more time to devote to the accumulation of grades and credits, and this bothers him considerably. A review of the surveys of the *working student* shows that these activities curtail fraternity and sorority activities and attendance at parties rather than participation in other extracurricular activities. There is some evidence from a Yale study to indicate that the working student earns higher grades, probably because of greater motivation— greater desire to gain a preparation for a future career (160). To work more than 12 hours a week has been found harmful by a University of Michigan study. The generalization from a Minnesota survey indicates that earning more than 75 per cent of school expenses tends to affect grades unfavorably. The university hospital seems to be used more extensively by students with greater earnings (813). Students who receive federal aid prove to be worthy of assistance on practically all counts. Such aid is regarded as an effective means of conserving human abilities (115). Students themselves, alumni, and many college administrators have a favorable attitude toward part-time employment. In general, the differences between groups of working and nonworking students are slight. The benefits of working depend upon conditions specific to given cases (583).

Among the possible advantages listed are (1) the attainment of more education than could be achieved otherwise; (2) the acquisition of habits of industry and thrift and the greater utilization of mental abilities; (3) a test of character and ambition; (4) acquisition of occupational experience; (5) acquisition of a sense of independence and economic values (757).

MAKING TIME SCHEDULES. Students sometimes object when a somewhat fixed daily schedule is suggested to them. They claim this takes the joy from life and tends to make machines of men. A program should do the opposite. It may help eliminate procrastination, assist one to see his progress, provide varied activity, and prevent last-minute frantic activities. Some programs fail because they are too rigid and do not allow for rest periods, changes of activity, and human frailties. It is imperative in planning a program to make it *flexible,* to allow for *unexpected events,* to plan long periods for that work which requires a warming-up period and short periods for fatiguing work, to *alternate* entirely different types of activity so that one type will have recuperative value for the other, and to plan for no more work than can be successfully accomplished in an allotted period. Play can be scheduled at the hours when there is a natural tendency to "let down." A clever plan is to reward yourself for unusual accomplishment. Treat yourself to a show or a favorite magazine after a period of hard work.

A model schedule may be worked out by a student using a form similar to that on page 159 indicating the planned activity for each hour. One secret of a full life is to salvage odd moments and fill them with pleasurable experience.

Budgeting Money

Importance of Budgeting Money. In this symbolic age money represents time, talent, and efficiency. Some persons consider budgeting money even more necessary than budgeting time. Those who consistently fail to live within their incomes suffer in reputation and self-respect. Businessmen are sometimes intolerant of persons who are unable to regulate their personal finances. A well-planned budget fosters a smoothly running daily existence and releases time for the consideration of more serious problems.

Wise spending, which means *satisfying one's deeper wants by the use of one's money,* results in an enriched life. The basic value of money, in the last analysis, is how best it can satisfy our broader needs. The amount is not important; its effective use so that it will increase our comfort, enjoyment, and security, is significant (395).

Students with Financial Problems

Here is a happy-go-lucky young student who must have *everything he sees*. If a student down the hall buys a new sport coat at a bargain price, Jimmy thinks he ought to "save money" by taking advantage of this bargain too. He forgets that he took advantage of three or four other bargains this month and he is now spending next month's living allowance on this month's luxuries. If he carries these habits and attitudes into business he will violate some of the basic principles of budgeting.

Lewis and Maurice both enjoy "games of chance." To Lewis it is a possible means to recoup his unwise expenditures. Maurice, on the other hand, gets a great emotional thrill out of winning and has an interesting way of forgetting his losses. *Gambling* to him is almost like a drug. Neither he nor Lewis has learned to look upon a game of chance as a form of play which may place his finances in jeopardy. Neither has learned to set aside a certain amount when he enters a "friendly game," and to quit when this amount is gone. Neither has learned to stay out of games beyond his limit, and Maurice has not even learned to stay away from sharks.

Marie is *dissatisfied with her allowance*. It is already in excess of what her parents should give her, in view of their income. All her friends, however, have large allowances. Her parents have unwisely sent her to schools in which most of the students are from families with larger incomes than theirs. Marie therefore continually objects to her small allowance and is unhappy because she cannot have that which other girls enjoy. She often spends all her allowance around the first of the month and does without necessities the rest of the time. Should Marie frankly face the facts, select companions with allowances like her own, and budget carefully, she would have ample funds to dress herself well and enjoy life thoroughly. Furthermore, she could lighten the financial burden her parents now carry.

Karl's financial problem is that he voluntarily *keeps his expenditures too well within his allowance*. He imposes upon his friends without any intention to reciprocate. He will drop in frequently on a group of boys who are "baching" and lunch with them. Not once will he invite them to lunch with him. He does not buy textbooks, but borrows from others. He frequently goes on double dates with a friend who has a car but never offers to buy gasoline. He smokes cigarettes but rarely buys them. At the end of the year Karl is $200 or $300 ahead financially but far below par socially.

Mark is the *chronic borrower*. His allowance barely covers last month's debt. Every acquaintance has an equity in his wardrobe. He never contracts commercial loans or gives his friends collateral. Although he is a pleasant and potentially popular person, most of those who know him soon lose respect for him on account of his shoddy financial habits.

Suggestions for Good Financial Habits. A few well-tried principles for building good financial habits follow.

Assume financial responsibilities and experience the consequences of poor budgeting. Responsibility can be achieved by earning some of one's spending money. A college student will not spend $25 for a dress that is suitable for only one occasion if she has to earn the $25 at the rate of 75 cents an hour. The same results can be gained by living within a fixed income. If one overspends his allowance, he must do without necessities for the rest of a designated period or supplement his income by employment.

Devise a detailed budget for income, and check daily successes in meeting it. It is surprising what a simple device like a budget does for the individual's peace of mind. It tentatively solves in advance many of the problems the individual will meet. It makes the individual face the reality of his actual income as well as his needs. It forces him to decide before it is too late which of the many desires he may satisfy.

Suggestions for a Planned Budget. Budgets vary in extent and complexity. A simple budget consists merely of a statement of the income on the top line followed by a list of needs and desires and their cost. The total of the costs of needs and desires must not be more than the income unless the individual has a means for augmenting his income.

The budget should first list *fixed charges.* These consist of rent, food, and the like. It is well to pay them in advance or at least deduct them from the bank balance. A student can obtain a more valid basis for next month's budget if he keeps a notebook of the present month's expenditures. Some students have large enough capital at the beginning of the year to open a checking account, which gives them experience in banking.

The good budget provides a *sinking fund.* The budgeter should always allow for emergencies. A clever budgeter saves for future buying. He can always buy to greater advantage if he has a *reserve* when bargains are available. He can buy in quantities and take advantage of cash discounts. Saving for future security is not an important item in the student budget, but it is well to begin thinking about it early.

Economy within the Budget. Another suggestion that many have found valuable is: *be your own producer* when it is economical.

Many college students apply this principle extensively. They form groups to organize cooperative houses. They plan their budget cooperatively, and each devotes a certain amount of time to the preparation or planning of meals. Some handle their laundry cooperatively. A few raise part of their food supply.

One may economize by *serving oneself* rather than paying someone else for the service. If one is skillful in the use of dye, shoe polish, electric iron, needle, and carpentry tools, many a dollar may be saved wisely. Early repairs are thrifty. Many savings may be made by buying the material and producing the end commodity.

Wise buying is the best way to economize. Make buying a hobby. Read consumer periodicals * and the many fascinating books written to inform the consumer of the ingredients of many of his purchases. The thread count of the material in a garment is a much better index of quality than a brand name. It is not true that "you get only what you pay for." Some of the more expensive suits are inferior to cheaper brands. Carry on a little experimentation of your own.

It is a good suggestion to find a means of *enjoying yourself without too great expenditure of money*. The greatest pleasure comes from events and products that are the result of our own creative efforts.

Another suggestion for buying is to *imagine that you have possessed the object for a week*. If you still want it after you have spent hours in imaginary use of it, perhaps you should buy it. Think of the many things you have bought that have meant very little to you a month later. Recall these incidents when shopping. Remember that the more variety of experience an object will afford, the greater its value, regardless of cost. Remember, too, that some of your neighbors get as much variety out of an $800 second-hand car as you will out of a $2400 car. There may be more relaxation and pleasure in using the cheaper car because of freedom from anxiety to keep it scratchless and to meet the instalment notes.

Individual Differences in Economy. You have no doubt known some individuals who have the same income as their neighbors, yet they appear to have more to spend because they buy wisely. Such a person has a better home, better furniture, better clothes, and more books and objects of art. He and his family shop extensively before

---

* Consumers' Research, Inc., Washington, N. J.; Consumers' Union, 17 Union Square, New York City.

they buy anything. They learn all they can about an article. They never buy luxuries at their original cost because they realize that the resale price is much less than the original. They save so they may have capital to take advantage of bargains. They always secure detailed prices before contracting debts. They buy clothes at odd seasons, preferably at the end of the season. Buying is one of their hobbies. They frequently visit the second-hand shops. They go on tours of old barns and attics. Some of their choicest furniture was covered with layers of dirt and ill-chosen paint when they first saw it. These articles cost practically nothing except the time and energy to restore them to their original beauty. Several books that were worth many times their price were discovered in a junk heap. To find them was an adventure.

There is another variety of individual who buys stintingly, who makes every purchase an unpleasant relationship for all concerned. He differs from the other person in that the former buys with a plan, takes lots of time, and creates his bargains. He serves the seller by purchasing goods which are valueless to him. The stinting kind of buyer makes purchases under pressure, coercion, and shrewd tactics. Such an individual is unpopular and loses in good will far more than he gains in dollars and cents.

Many of those who believe themselves to be thrifty are "penny wise and pound foolish." They will save a 50-cent taxi fare and as a result pay a $1.00 cleaning and pressing bill. They will buy note paper that costs 10 or 20 cents less per 500 sheets but tears and discolors in less than a year. They will economize by eating starches rather than milk, fruit, and vegetables and be poorly nourished as a result.

There is the person who feels that he must "put on a front" in excess of his income, the person who values only a rich crowd. False pretenses such as these cause an emotional strain and usually defeat their very purpose—pleasure and relaxation. It has been found that expenses of members of Greek letter social organizations during normal times are several hundred dollars higher than those of other students.

Data from actual budgets of college students show very clearly that a *college education may be obtained on varying incomes* (64, 644). Use the items below and compute a range of costs of education for your own campus and sex group. Your budget will be more interesting and valuable if three or four students work out this information together. The administrative offices in your school will be pleased to furnish you with information. Some of it no doubt is published in the college bulletin. Here is a list of items that should be included in a student's budget.

Tuition	Fees (courses and activity)
Room	Books and supplies
Board	Laundry and cleaning
Recreation	Personal necessities

Source of Student Income. A democratic ideal is to make education available to all those capable of receiving it. Because higher education is expensive and frequently involves self-maintenance outside of the home, it is important that financial opportunities be made available for all those who are in the higher ability brackets. Society suffers when capable students are denied higher education because of their financial status (349). At one time in one Midwestern city, 42 per cent of the high school graduates of the upper 15 per cent in ability were not in school at all. Seventy per cent could not go to college because of lack of funds (276).

EXTENT OF STUDENT SELF-SUPPORT. Even during a prosperous period about two-thirds of the men and a half of the women students in the universities of this country were working part-time, and one-fifth of the men and one-tenth of the women were earning all their expenses (349). There are marked variations among different groups of students and different schools.

Students work about 20 hours a week on an average. There is, however, wide variation (757). The amount earned by students also varies with the institution and the training of the student. At Yale, for example, during one year about one-fourth of the working students earned less than $50. The upper fourth in earning, on the other hand, received six to twenty times this figure. Rate of student pay was higher in privately controlled colleges than in state institutions (468).

NATURE OF SELF-SUPPORT. It has been previously indicated that the remuneration which a student receives from work is closely related to the type of skill required by the position. College students have found numerous ways to finance an education. A list of miscellaneous ways to earn sufficient funds for some degree of self-support follows.

Waiting on tables	Yard work	Musician
Kitchen work	Coaching	Entertainer
Janitor	Boys' work	Church work
Care of children	Laboratory assistant	Typing
Selling	Canvassing	Attendant or
Caretaker	Chauffeur	Companion
Carpentry	Barber	Usher

Many students have originated novel and interesting means of financing college education. Some form small businesses to serve varying student needs as for laundry, evening snacks in student housing, and photographs taken at student parties.

Some colleges have cooperative dormitories at which students can earn a reduction in college expenses. Other colleges have made use of part-time employment as a vocational guidance program. Several colleges are well known for their provision for vocational work. The Antioch plan allows students to go to school part of the year and to work the other part. Berea College provides means by which students may earn college expenses in a bakery, broom factory, press, creamery, and the woodwork and sewing industries (549). At the date of writing, universities have assumed more responsibility concerning the housing and personal welfare of single and married students than ever before in the history of education. Although many of these provisions are temporary, others will continue for many years after the military veterans have received their education.

TYPES OF FINANCIAL ASSISTANCE. In addition to savings and part-time jobs, students should investigate the following sources of organized financial assistance available through their college or through national sources (697, 427, 230, 257).

1. Scholarships
2. Fellowships (usually for graduate study)
3. Student loan funds
4. Federal aid
5. Work plans

It is not unusual for a college to have available $50,000 or more in scholarships and $150,000 in loan funds. Usually information about financial aid is found in the catalog of the college.

Financial Behavior and Adjustment. The way one uses money may reflect inexperience and lack of training regarding its use or may be one of several indexes of inner difficulty. Students have been known to use money for objects that increase their prestige and decrease their feeling of insecurity. Others have a narrow span of interests and hobbies, and the spending of money and the acquisition of objects is one of their few sources of pleasure. Squandering the money of parents has been discovered in counseling to be a means of expressing hostility toward the parent. Impulsive and erratic financial habits have frequently been part of a total personality pattern. A desire for affection and security has sometimes been satisfied by showering oneself or others with expensive gifts. The connection between money and power must not be overlooked. Stinginess might also reflect restrictiveness in personality. It is well for the student whose behavior with money and possessions differs markedly from that of others to try to discover the inner motivation of this behavior.

Efficient Body and Environment

Summary of Studies on Efficiency. There are studies that indicate that almost every aspect of the environment can influence our personal efficiency and morale to some extent, particularly when they exert their influence on us for long periods. Let us summarize the implications of these studies for the student who is attempting to obtain the greatest effect with least fatigue from the hours he spends studying.

1. Lighting should be bright, even, and without glare or shadows (472). Headaches or difficulties in vision with good light suggest the need for physical examination.

2. Noisy and distracting circumstances should be avoided when creative work is to be done. If they cannot be avoided the student can be assured he will adapt to them, possibly at the expense of more energy (803).

3. Air of the optimum temperature (around 70 degrees), humidity, and circulation is most desirable but in this case too, with strong enough motivation one can carry on mental activity even at higher temperatures (114).

4. The early morning hours are first in terms of efficiency, the hours after noon rank next; there is a drop before noon and a greater drop in late afternoon, as shown in the curve in Figure 2 (114).

5. Having all school materials conveniently near and using bookmarkers in books that will be referred to later eliminates distracting movements which are bound to cut down efficiency in industry (74).

6. A rest pause or change of activity is effective when efficiency begins to wane (74).

7. Sleep is the best form of relaxation, and adequate sleep reflects itself in individual efficiency. When motivation is high, temporary loss of sleep does not seem to affect efficiency except in prolonged, complex tasks (89).

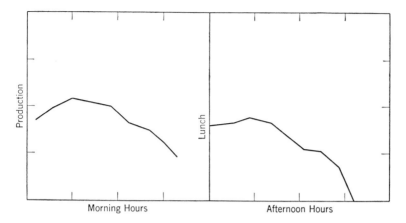

Figure 2. Typical daily production curve. (After Burtt.)

A student who is constantly falling asleep despite 8 hours' sleep at night should consult a physician.

8. Healthy dietary practice consists of eating a wide variety of food in moderate quantities in pleasant circumstances. Studies indicate mental processes are not affected by a diet that reduces weight 10 per cent below normal (59). Fasting for periods of from 10 to 33 days produced losses in mental and muscular functions (273). A twenty-four week period of semi-starvation (famine area diet) produced a 30 per cent loss in body strength, and social and emotional changes such as decrease in sociability, tactfulness, humor, romantic tendencies, and increasing feelings of depression and inferiority, but no marked change in intelligence (409). Efficiency increases with light midmorning and midafternoon snacks. There is less accomplished after a heavy meal than a light one (359).

Some argue against regulations of one's environment implicitly suggested in the above data, especially in creative work. It must be remembered, however, that most creative work involves detail. As efficiency is increased in executing details, more time is available for thought and inspirational activities, which are fuel for the creative flame. The biographies of many of our great creative workers testify to long hours of arduous work, which undoubtedly involves some type of planning.

Drugs and Efficiency. Although there are numerous experiments on the psychological effects of drugs, scientists working in this field have encountered difficulties that are partially responsible for the equivocal nature of some of the results. This is largely due to the differences between individuals in physique and *attitude*, the complexity of the processes studied, and the variation in the amounts of the drug administered.

Alcohol is classed as a *depressant* and not a stimulant, even though it seems to stimulate the individual. It is generally stated that this pseudostimulation is the result of the *removal of certain inhibitions*, as alcohol affects the higher and more recently acquired mental functions. The individual seems to care less what he says or does. He is less critical of himself, less self-conscious, his troubles diminish, and he feels freer. The alleged increase in efficiency is probably due to this removal of inhibitions. An individual may report that he makes a better speech after drinking an alcoholic beverage. This he attributes to increased ability, when in fact it is due to a decrease in the tendency to analyze critically and curb his actions. At this time, too, judgment is less keen. He apparently makes a better address because of the spontaneity and bouyancy resulting from the abeyance of certain self critical attitudes (255).

Alcohol is known clinically to be a form of escape—particularly for some individuals, an escape that may become more attractive with time. These people must recognize that they cannot "take it or leave it" and must find other ways of relaxation. Alcohol blunts judgment, including the discretion as to when to stop drinking.

It is often asked whether an individual can be excused for certain atypical behavior under alcohol, whether one becomes different or more truly like his inner self when inebriated. There is not an abundance of data bearing on this question, but when patients of various mental disorders were given alcohol intravenously (injection in blood stream), they tended to show the same symptoms but to a greater degree (582).

TOBACCO SMOKING. A general evaluation of smoking is difficult, particularly since it is a different problem with different individuals. There are individual differences in the extensiveness of use of tobacco, its meaning to them in terms of personal morale and the ease with which they can give it up. Heavy smoking can hardly be defended on any grounds and it is probably a symptom of a tense way of life. It is believed to contribute to stomach and duodenal ulcers and patches of retinal blindness. The experimental results on the negative effects of tobacco are not all conclusive (89). The correlation of lung cancer and smoking is a matter at present of serious discussion (588).

Smokers have been found by several investigators to have lower grades in school than nonsmokers. Only 5 per cent of 130 high honor students in a large eastern university were smokers (335). What does this mean? How can this be reconciled with the above findings? Smoking certainly does not cause low grades, and abstinence from smoking high scholarship. The explanation probably is this: one youth studies hard, spends little time on drugstore corners and in social gatherings, gains his social recognition by obtaining good grades, and does not acquire from his fellows the habit of smoking. Another is a more social type. He acquires the smoking habit from the other fellows in his many hours of association with them. He spends less time in study, and his grades are lower.

The smoker will tell you that he enjoys his cigarette or pipe. He is "not himself" without them. Smoking *sets* him. It seems to make him more efficient. He is probably right; smoking has been *associated with his activities* many times a day for some time. It has become a well-fixated habit. His actions are conditioned by it as they are by other constantly recurring conditions. Without his pipe he feels like the dignified businessman who has lost his hat and must appear in public without it. Smoking seems to add to social poise because it is a well-established, smooth habit that can be introduced into a situation when one may feel awkward and at a loss to know what to do otherwise. If one wishes to curtail smoking he should substitute an approved, established habit using similar activities.

CAFFEINE IN POPULAR BEVERAGES. Much that has been said above about tobacco as a social habit holds for coffee, tea, and the cola drink in which caffeine is found in small amounts. Two questions usually arise concerning these beverages. Do they increase or decrease efficiency? Do they keep one awake? Mild doses, such as found in single servings, usually have a stimulating effect. Speed of movement is increased, and mental tasks show slight improvement after a quantity equivalent to that found in a cup of coffee is taken. In typing, speed was increased and errors decreased after a small dose of caffeine; ability to do addition was increased, and reaction speed was decreased. Larger doses, however, disturbed motor coordination (255).

Caffeine or benzedrine sulphate, which gives the feeling of pep (241), taken in tablet form before examinations, or at other times when sleep is to be forgone, certainly cannot be generally recommended without a physician's advice.

Small doses of caffeine such as found in a single cup of coffee can hardly be named as the causal agency in sleeplessness in all cases. If it is taken late and on an empty stomach or by a person of low body weight, it might serve to prevent sleep. Suggestion is a powerful agency. One who is convinced that the coffee he drank or the benzedrine tablet he took will stimulate him will probably not be disappointed! (240)

Attitudes and Efficiency

The Individual Who Lacks Habits of Work. There are some people who fear work, who have a strong conflict between the need to get down to school work and the desire of getting by, and this pattern becomes so strong that it eventuates in a personality trait (428). This person usually is not fighting work—he is fighting his attitude toward a certain kind of work. Often a student will spend time reading material just as difficult as his assignment but feel a strong disinclination to study. Usually this individual has not experienced enough success resulting from systematic work on the assignment. Sometimes this is a student who has not had to work earlier to obtain passing grades. Now when he approaches a study assignment, he does so with dislike, tension, and other unpleasant negative attitudes.

Sometimes this attitude of escape has developed because the individual has been conditioned against reality, has been punished for his errors, and therefore fears to submit the products of his work to the judgment of others. He fears their ridicule. Very often this individual is perfectionistic in attitude. For him, no work at all is better than criticized work. The case of Bill H. illustrates this.

Bill H., after several conferences in which he talked quite freely about his inefficiency, was able to verbalize the specific nature of his poor work habits. He said, "I am never satisfied with what I am doing. I always want to be doing something else. When I am studying, I think about dating; when I am dating, I think about playing basketball; when I am playing basketball, I think I should be studying." The counselor asked him if his real problem might be the use of daydreams as an escape from the activity of the moment. Bill agreed that was exactly the process. When he was studying he thought about the ideal date, not the specific activities that occur on his own dates. When he thought of basketball, it wasn't the caliber of game he usually played, but championship basketball with himself as a star. "But why do I dislike reality?" asked Bill. Then he proceeded to answer his own question. "As a child, reality was grim. I lived on the other side of the tracks and had to work. My mother worked outside our home, too, and came home at night worn out. I was constantly being punished. It seemed that nothing I did around the house was right, yet I was working all the time. I suppose I came to the place where I couldn't attack a task calmly, carry it through to completion, and then label it either a success or a failure, or point to certain aspects of it that were wrong. To my mother's perfectionistic standards, any failure was abhorrent, any departure from the ideal was intolerable. So I would doodle, beat around the bush, fear to attack the task, and daydream during the task. That is the approach I now have toward work. The fear of failure is too strong for me to work whole-heartedly. Even though the atmosphere here is different, my mother with her standards and punishments is still a part of me. That's it!" said Bill with obvious elation. "I punish myself with delays, depression, doodling, doing things the hard way, and not coming to grips with the problem because I have the fear that punishment is inevitable as it was when I was a child, and I may as well give it to myself and get it over with." Bill put in his own language discoveries that were quite helpful to him. He learned why he was inefficient and could not attack a task with verve. Although he had strong motives toward law and the material he studied, his whole approach had been one of emotionality and distaste.

Let us consider people who are less involved emotionally than Bill. An individual may be immature in motivation and may not have developed a need for a source of success, such as a vocation or a life purpose. He may not see the importance of his present activities in terms of a vivid future goal. Sometimes he is one who has not learned satisfying habits of work that will run along automatically and pleasantly. This problem of purpose was discussed in Chapter 2 under "Motivation for Study." Below are the contrasting cases of Pearl R. and Julie K., who differ in efficiency.

Announcement is made at three o'clock that a short paper must be handed in the next day. The student has no other required activity that day. Below we find the application of two systems of habits and attitudes to meet this problem.

Pearl R. realizes that she can best enjoy the remainder of the day and assure herself of a good grade by going to her room immediately, making an outline of the entire theme, ascertaining what references must be consulted, estimating the time that will be required, and immediately beginning to plan and write the theme. She finds that after the first hour she cannot leave her work, she has become so ab- sorbed in it. At supper it is prac- tically complete, and one hour after supper it has been retouched, put in final form, and checked.

She has the satisfaction of having completed a task well and now has the time to relax in any manner she desires. She may turn either to a new job, utilizing the zest that re- sults from a completed one, or she may go to a show, engage in some game, or read for pleasure.

Julie K. says, "I have all night to do this. I am tired after the day's work. I ought to go get a coke." There she meets some friends and spends the time until supper in light conversation. She eats a heavy meal, remains in the living room a half-hour after supper looking through the papers and magazines, goes up to her room, decides to take a nap. She sleeps an hour, wakes up almost too befuddled to work, and decides to set the alarm clock and wake for an early morning session. She wakes at four, goes to her desk, spends half an hour trying to recall some of the specific requirements of the paper, becomes panicky as daylight broadens, writes as well as she can under the strain she is experiencing, and finally tosses a poorly written theme over to the corner of the desk with the statement, "I'll do better next time."

Attitudes That Produce Work. The individual who finds that he cannot get down to work, who sits at his desk and experiences an aversion to the task at hand, will not solve the problem by immediately rushing into some escape activity and feeling remorseful later because he has not accomplished anything during that period. This might be an excellent time for him to discover why he is temporarily blocked. What are his inner resistances to work?

The following is recommended: Let him sit at his desk with a pad of paper before him and write out everything that comes to his mind, possibly beginning by describing just how he feels. It might begin with something like this: "Here I sit, knowing I have this assignment to complete, but finding it very unpleasant to open the book and deal with the material at hand. . . ." As he writes on he will make some discoveries about his aversions. He might even go back to earlier experiences, might find, buried below consciousness, some unpleasant associations with the subject matter or with the teacher. He might discover that he has been driving himself too hard and not allowing periods of relaxation when he might indulge in activities that he thoroughly enjoys. He might find a conflict between his basic motivation and the activities in which he is at present engaged. Eventually positive attitudes will emerge.

How does one get the success from study activities which build positive habits? Simply stated, a student's motivation to study must increase and his aversion to it decrease. We have suggested a method for understanding and reducing the intensity of aversion to study. How can one increase his motivation for study? Some suggestions are given for consolidating motivation in connection with Changing Behavior in Chapter 5.

Students suggest different methods for increasing motivation for study. Here are a few:

1. Recognition that the work itself is not necessarily unpleasant. The unpleasantness springs from the necessity to study and the aversion to it. The use of escapes with later guilt is also unpleasant.

2. The use of methods that cause the student to plunge into the required activity has been helpful; for example, making a game of study has helped some. "How much can I cover in a half hour?" has been challenging to some people. Studying with other students or in an environment in which others are seriously working is sometimes valuable. Breaking the material into smaller units is an encouraging device.

3. Clearly facing the *consequences of not studying* at the time of decision or of escape may heighten motivation or lower the aversion to study. In addition, seeing the value of the material studied or the value of learning habits of concentration may likewise be motivating.

In summary, good study habits result from strong motivation: success and reward associated with study on the one hand, and the reduction of unpleasant attitudes resulting from previous failure, boredom, and deprivation of pleasures associated with the *idea* of study (not necessarily the active searching for salient facts) on the other hand.

Here we have a pattern of *conflict*—a pattern we have discussed previously. The opposing forces are blocked, and this block can be removed only by strengthening the drive, or as is often more necessary, by *reducing the aversion to the desired behavior*. The case of Russ N. indicates the effect of a change of attitude.

Russ N., a student whose major interest is in dramatics, English literature, and the arts in general, had prescribed for himself a second-semester freshman program of a science and a foreign language, both of which he viewed with strong distaste. The electives that he was allowed proved later to be disappointing. At the end of the semester he had inferior grades in both of the 5-hour required courses. He was discouraged and thought of the large percentage of college students who did not get a degree and wondered whether he ought to pursue higher education any longer. At a counseling conference he discussed many matters which troubled him. He talked of the work to which he was best adapted in terms of aptitudes and interests, his academic capacities, and the reasons for his poor study habits. With a new perspective gained through this discussion, he continued to take the foreign language for another semester but elected one course in English, which he knew he would like, under an instructor he admired. After two weeks of the new program he found that his attitudes had changed markedly. The teacher of the foreign language remarked, "Mr. N., you are not the same student. You never come late to class any more, and you always have your lessons prepared. What has caused the change?" Russ described his change in attitude as due not only to change in perspective and a renewed hope of graduating, but also to the inspiration value the English course held for him. It allowed him to experience directly the material with which he will deal in his vocational life as a high school English teacher. His perspective was improved somewhat by acquaintance with a high school English teacher, a graduate student on the campus, who encouraged him in his interests.

Relation of Feelings to Output. Very often we feel fatigued, and a job becomes monotonous long before our output drops. An interesting experiment shows the relative disparity between feelings and efficiency.

Twelve individuals worked continuously for about 5½ hours at inserting words into sentences in order to complete the meaning. The work was divided into 15 equal units with a rest pause before the last unit. At the beginning of the experiment each individual reported on a scale how he felt. He reported his feelings again as he completed each unit of the job. The scale upon which this report was made ranged from "extremely good" to "extremely tired." Fig-

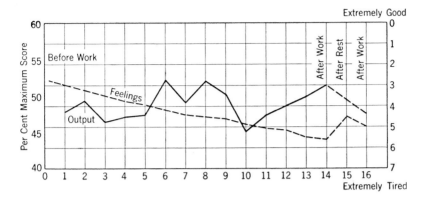

Figure 3. Relations between feelings and output. (After Poffenberger.)

ure 3 shows the relationship of feelings to efficiency. At first the individual feels fine, then, as output begins to rise, feelings fall and continue to fall throughout the task. Output is practically always above feeling, except at the beginning of the job (615). We should realize that when we are tired *our feelings of fatigue are not an indication of our level of efficiency.* Furthermore, with a change of attitude and increased net motivation these negative feelings are reduced.

It is well for the individual to study himself in respect to monotony, a disinclination to work distinct from actual fatigue. Specifically, he should study his likes and dislikes toward various tasks. Those tasks which he finds monotonous but which must be done may be made more interesting by some rearrangement of conditions. For example, substitution of piece-rate for time-rate payment was an adjustment that proved satisfactory in one industrial situation. This no doubt challenged the individual and made him exert more initiative on the job. Interest in the details of the work, as well as dividing the task into smaller consistent units, has possibilities. Numerous suggestions have been made in the preceding sections that may help the student to *make a game of his study responsibilities* and thereby heighten interest and reduce monotony.

Supplementary Readings

D. A. Fryer and E. R. Henry (Eds.), *Handbook of Applied Psychology*, Rinehart, 1950.

E. V. Hollis and Associates, *Costs of Attending College*, U.S. Department of Health, Education and Welfare, Bulletin No. 9, Washington, D. C., 1951.

C. E. Lovejoy, *Lovejoy's College Guide*, Simon and Schuster, 1954.

In addition see the references cited by number in the chapter and appearing in the bibliography of an accompanying volume entitled *Teaching Personal Adjustment: An Instructor's Manual.*

CHAPTER 7

VALUES AND THOUGHT

Personal Philosophy of Life

How do we acquire our beliefs? We acquire the attitudes that mold our values from many sources, often unconsciously. Our mothers, fathers, persons whom we have idealized, our school, church—all mold the deep attitudes we hold. The wide influences in our present culture, including motion pictures, magazines, songs and television are also effective, especially if they arouse us deeply. These various influences are necessarily conflictory in a free democratic society. We are aware of inconsistencies in our beliefs at times, and make choices between them. Choices must be made throughout life. Youth outgrows childhood superstitions and simple answers to complex questions. Childhood religion becomes a mature faith compatible with modern science, allowing personal and societal growth. Moreover, with more education early attitudes may appear parochial and limited in scope.

Many distinguished persons have worked out a *credo* or living philosophy, as a test of the consistency and realism of their attitudes and values. College students have also found this a challenging and valuable exercise. Let us look at what we might call the "personal philosophies" of two students who are quite different in many respects. Their papers are selected not as ideal or typical but because they are forceful, interesting, and more complete than the average. They might well arouse group discussion. Students may find some of the attitudes expressed in these papers diametrically opposed to attitudes they hold. *The class may be profitably divided into groups of six or eight students to discuss critically these papers as a preparation for a paper on personal philosophy which individuals of the group may want to write.*

Student Personal Philosophies

Martin N. is a tall, well-built, mild-mannered, mature student. He had been in military service and is married. He has a small group of mature friends. His well-written philosophy carries added punch because of its humor.

"I believe in leading a full life. That is my entire philosophy of life in the proverbial nutshell. Put in such brief manner, it is not very enlightening or edifying, so the question arises—What in God's little green acres is my definition of a full life and why is it a philosophy of life?

"There are three phases of life—the physical, the mental, and the spiritual. As to which phase should predominate or whether all three should be developed equally in one's design for living is up to the particular individual. But no one phase should be left entirely dormant in the leading of a full life. Of course Fate plays a large role in our lives, and we can't always mold Fate to suit ourselves. In so far as we can mold ourselves I believe:

"A strong and healthy body is essential for a proper zest and exuberance for living. The body with which we have been endowed was meant to be taken care of. Of course, a strong back and a weak mind is frowned upon by the intelligentsia and rightly so, but the powerful intellect and the neglected tissue should be equally frowned upon.

"Proper education and development of brain power is a must. It is a means of intelligent guidance through life, appreciation of beauty even in the commonplace, and the ability to distinguish between the lasting, wholesome pleasures and the superficial. Ignorance is not bliss but slap-happiness, the kind of happiness which can rear up and kick one when his back is turned.

"The spiritual side of life cannot be neglected either. By the spiritual life I do not mean going to church on Sundays and dropping two-bits in the collection box while the fingers itch to filch sixty cents in change. I do mean that, in one's daily boundings about the horizon, an adherence to the Christian principles and faith in some higher power is conducive to the full life. It takes faith in something besides one's self to safely weather the crises of adverse circumstance.

"I do not believe that any one certain religion is the true road to God. I do not believe that everything in the Bible is the truth simply because it is in the Bible. I do not believe it is necessary to live up to the dogmas of any chosen sect to live a Christian life. I do not believe that it is necessary to be a church-goer to have a spiritual life.

"I consider the complete spiritual anarchist whose philosophy is, 'The King can do no wrong, and I'm King,' as a drifting soul; but I also consider it a fallacy to develop one's spiritual life to the point of neglecting the physical and the mental, to substitute blind faith for any constructive thinking, to forgo all physical pleasure in the belief that one's reward will come in the after-life. An after-life may or may not be true. If it is, it is still no excuse for not living the present life which God has given us for the purpose of living."

Isabel T. is a brilliant, hard-working, purposive student who seems to care little for the external values that many college students emphasize, such as clothes, dates, pins, and keys. She makes arresting contributions to every class and raises stimulating questions. Whereas her philosophy of life is unorthodox in some areas, it reflects the serious, sincere, idealistic thoughts of a more mature student.

"My philosophy of life cannot be definitely stated. A 'philosophy of life' is synonymous with 'perspective,' and my perspective is constantly expanding. The only definite belief I hold is that this dynamic state is good.

"I do not think that a personal God exists. I do not accept any causal hypothesis as a palliative of my future, definite death.

"I think man is the order presently supreme on earth and that, as other orders were once supreme, it is possible that others may in the future be so.

"I think that, as individuals, we die completely, and our only means of immortality (while the species retains its present position) are through the germ plasm and through the transmission of and addition to our cultural heritage.

"Since life is short and is had but once by a particular combination, I think that personal happiness is the most desirable state and the only reason for continuance of existence.

"I think that happiness is the state of self-willed absorption and expression of a capacity expanded to the fullest extent possible.

"To achieve this, I think absolute freedom of thought is necessary; thought is 'free' only when there is access to every source of knowledge which can be acquired. Also necessary is freedom of action; this cannot be absolute for anyone, however, as it would then limit action of another. Freedom of action of the individual should be curtailed to the extent that the freedom of the group demands.

"I think that each individual, in order to enhance and safeguard his personality as an individual, must enhance and safeguard the personality of the group, for only the group aware of its responsibilities and potentialities can enhance and safeguard the individual.

"I acknowledge no standard of 'right and wrong' as intrinsically true, but as commanding observance only to the extent that group welfare demands. Individual action is conditioned by cultural commandments colored by emotion and experience; I see no reason why the standard of any individual should be applied to the action of another as a basis for judgment. By this I do not mean mere 'tolerance,' but an acceptance of people as they are with the realization that as I am, and wish to be, myself within the confines of group welfare, so others are.

"I think that in order to bring all the above to the level of practicality, it is necessary to have a strong labor movement, a strong cooperative movement, and a strong educational program; and as I consider my personal happiness inextricably bound up with these, I enhance my happiness by helping in any way in which I am capable to bring them about." *

Personal Philosophies of Contemporaries. There have appeared in periodical and book forms personal credos by mature well-known individuals. As one sample, let us look at excerpts dealing with the problem of good and evil in addition to some of the accepted contemporary materialistic ideals.

Lewis Mumford (203), American critic, known as a social historian and student of architecture, has said,†

. . . the evils of life have a large capacity for good; and the mature person knows they must be faced, embraced, assimilated; that to shun them or innocently hope to eliminate them all together is to cling to an existence that is both false to reality and essentially lacking in perspective and depth. Like arsenic, evil is a tonic in grains and a poison in ounces. The real problem of evil, the problem that justifies every assault upon war and poverty and disease, is to reduce it to amounts that can be spiritually assimilated.

This doctrine is just the opposite of certain "optimistic" life-denying attitudes and habits of mind that have become popular during the last three centuries; particularly, the notion that comfort, safety, the absence of physical disease are the greatest blessings of civilization, and that as they increase evil will be automatically abolished. The fallacy of this view lies in the fact that comfort and safety are not absolute qualities, but are capable of defeating life quite as thoroughly as hardship and disease

---

* A Princeton University professor collected the anonymous credos and biographies of eleven seniors, which may be read profitably for a wider range of student attitudes and beliefs (116).

† In the volume from which these excerpts were taken and its companion volume can be found the personal philosophies of many well-known and outstanding contemporary thinkers. Included are such diverse thinkers as Albert Einstein, Theodore Dreiser, Bertrand Russell, Jacques Maritain, H. L. Mencken, and William R. Inge (203, 224).

and uncertainty; and the notion that every other human interest, religion, art, friendship, love, must be subordinated to the production of increasing amounts of comforts and luxuries is merely one of the dark superstitions of our money-bent utilitarian society. By accepting this superstition as an essential modern creed, the utilitarian has turned an elementary condition of existence, the necessity for providing for the physical basis of life, into an end. Avaricious of power and riches and goods, he has summoned to his aid the resources of modern science and technology. As a result, we are oriented to "things," and have every sort of possession except self-possession. By putting business before every other manifestation of life, our mechanical and financial civilization has forgotten the chief business of life, namely, growth, reproduction, development. It pays infinite attention to the incubator—and it forgets the egg.

Student Goals in Life. After reading over the list that follows *you might want to write on your most cherished values.* This activity may appeal to some students more than writing an essay on their personal philosophy.

A method has been devised by which one might place in a rank order the values he regards as most significant in his life. Below are such values listed in order of importance by one girl (192). It will be noted that she emphasized pleasures for herself and others, self-development, and placed relatively minimal value on security, changing society, duty, and self-discipline.

INVENTORY OF GENERAL GOALS OF LIFE

"Score"

18	Getting as many deep and lasting pleasures out of life as I can.
17	Promoting the most deep and lasting pleasures for the greatest number of people.
17	Self-development—becoming a real, genuine person.
16	Fine relations with other persons.
15	Making a place for myself in the world; getting ahead.
14	Handling the specific problems of life as they arise.
13	Peace of mind, contentment, stillness of spirit.
11	Power; control over people and things.

Values Considered in Personal Philosophy. What were some of the values considered in the writings of the quoted students and the excerpt from Lewis Mumford? What would you include in such a paper if you were writing one? A list follows of possible life goals taken from papers written by students and teachers:

Pleasure	Self-sacrifice
Self-development	Serving God
Relationship with others	Immortality
Getting ahead	Self-discipline
Handling problems	Duty
Contentment	Finding one's place
Power	Security
Service	Acceptance of hardships

One might notice certain possible omissions from this list such as the appreciation of beauty, the seeking of truth, or openmindedness. A search for the factors underlying the standard we may hold as guides in our lives may reveal these or other values such as: utility and authority.

Maxims Expressing Guiding Beliefs.   Some people in stating their guiding beliefs quote one or two well-known maxims.   An investigation was made among persons of above-average educational and socio-economic status to learn their guiding maxims.   Over six hundred people were questioned, and about a hundred maxims were considered.   Below are the six maxims that received the highest preference (741).

1. Do unto others as you would that they would do unto you.
2. Know thyself.
3. Anything that is worth doing at all is worth doing well.
4. If at first you don't succeed, try, try again.
5. The great essentials of happiness are something to do, something to love, and something to hope for.
6. The only way to have a friend is to be one.

Values and a Way of Life.   A value may be defined as (1) a preference for objects or behavior, (2) as *what is desirable*, or (3) as *foresight* of the outcome of behavior.   Below are thirteen ways of life expressing values; five of them are described briefly.   These are ways to live which various persons at various times have advocated and followed (557).   You may find it interesting to rate each of the five described below using a scale ranging from 1 to 7 (7 meaning "like very much," 4 "indifferent to," and 1 "dislike very much").   Should one or more of the ways listed but not described seem to appeal to you more than the ones described, rate them too.

* ***Way 1:*** Preserve the best that man has attained.
    (In this "design for living" the individual actively participates in the social life of his community, not to change it primarily, but to un-

derstand, appreciate, and preserve the best that man has attained. . . . Restraint and intelligence should give order to an active life.)

* *Way 2:* Cultivate independence of persons and things.

Way 3: Show sympathetic concern for others.

Way 4: Experience festivity and solitude in alternation.

Way 5: Act and enjoy life through group participation.

Way 6: Constantly master changing conditions.

Way 7: Integrate action, enjoyment, and contemplation.

Way 8: Live with wholesome, carefree enjoyment.

(Enjoyment should be the keynote of life—not the hectic search for intense and exciting pleasures, but the enjoyment of the simple and easily obtainable pleasures, the pleasures of just existing, of savory food, of comfortable surroundings, of talking with friends, of rest and relaxation. . . . Driving ambition and the fanaticism of ascetic ideals are the signs of discontented people who have lost the capacity to float in the stream of simple, carefree, wholesome enjoyment.)

Way 9: Wait in quiet receptivity.

Way 10: Control the self stoically.

* *Way 11:* Meditate on the inner life.

(The contemplative life is the good life. The external world is not fit habitat for man. It is too big, too cold, too pressing. Rather it is the life turned inward that is rewarding. . . . In giving up the world one finds the larger and finer sea of the inner self.)

* *Way 12:* Chance adventuresome deeds.

(The use of the body's energy is the secret of a rewarding life. The hands need material to make into something: lumber and stone for building, food to harvest, clay to mold. . . . Outward energetic action, the excitement of power in the tangible present—this is the way to live.)

* *Way 13:* Obey the cosmic purposes.

(A person should let himself be used. Used by other persons in their growth, used by the great objective purposes in the universe, which silently and irresistibly achieve their goal. . . . One should be a serene, confident, quiet vessel and instrument of the great dependable powers which move to their fulfillment.)

The five ways of life briefly described and starred were found by factor analysis † to be basic to all thirteen possible ways of life on the list. These five express values common to all of the others and for that reason were expanded beyond a single statement.

---

† This refers to a statistical method of determining the number of factors or dimensions that will account for the intercorrelations among a number of variables—in this case five factors were found.

Students from the United States are found to differ from students living in other countries in the values they stress. The values of American students center around a rich, full, well-rounded life with an emphasis on vocational and social adjustment (372). French, German, and Italian students put greater emphasis on the intensity of their *inner experience*. Despite environmental difficulties these students develop a definite personal character (268).

Attitudes toward Politics and Contemporary Society. One method of testing the consistency of the values we hold in life is to come to grips with real, everyday issues in connection with the institutions that influence our lives. Politics is one such area. Children begin with the attitudes and viewpoints of their parents, neighbors, and teachers. In high school and college young people are usually exposed to free discussion and debate of issues, and they may begin to formulate their own positions. They read articles or books espousing given points of view which appeal to them or which they reject. They find there are systematic and somewhat integrated thoughts or "isms" on current issues.

An article appearing in *The Saturday Review* is an example. The editors of this journal asked several well-known writers to discuss briefly the current "isms." Contemporary political points of view were treated in this article: *fascism, capitalism, nationalism, liberalism, conservatism, colonialism, communism* and *socialism* (784). (The reader often finds he identifies his views with fragments of several of these viewpoints.)

If one is searching for how a creed can be expounded in book form, Frankel's *The Case for Modern Man* is worth examining (245). Here the position of the *liberal* is stated—the belief that reason is sufficient to solve our problems, that ordinary men can govern themselves through discussion and gradual reform. In religion, the liberal believes that dogma should be adjusted to the insights of science, which change with time. In economics, he supports the *laissez-faire* doctrine up to the point of exploitation and government control from there—all in the interest of the larger group. The author presents briefly in addition to the liberal view the views of some outstanding thinkers like Niebuhr, Maritain, Toynbee, and Mannheim who would qualify this creed to varying degrees.

Books such as Whyte's *The Organization Man* (843) and Lerner's *America as a Civilization* (450) or Riesman's *The Lonely Crowd* (641) will help the student think about and see more objectively

the contemporary society in which he is living. Reading and discussing such materials with his fellow students will better enable him
to verbalize the values that he absorbs as he lives actively in our American society. In *The Organization Man* the author points out that
the *Protestant ethic* represents the American ideal of yesteryear.
This emphasizes the sacredness of property, the enervating effect of
security, the virtues of thrift, hard work, and independence. Pursuing
these values, man forcefully tried to mold his environment to his individual purposes. The contemporary emphasis, particularly in our
organization-oriented society, is to make morally legitimate the pressures of society against the individual. With this emphasis the group
is viewed as a source of creativity, there is strong belief in belonging

191

as an ultimate need of the individual and an emphasis on the application of science to achieve this belonging. This belonging emphasis, the author believes, we must learn to resist when it conflicts with our *rationally* developed individual plans. *The student might well read books such as these to see the extent to which he has absorbed the values of one or another emphasis.*

Student Attitudes about Society. Studies in the 1930's dealt with the extent to which the college student is reactionary, conservative, liberal, or radical—conservatism meaning "attachment to things as they are, perpetuation of the *status quo*," and liberalism meaning "preference for some degree of modification." Seniors, on the whole, were found to be more liberal in their views than freshmen (11–13), and there was a persistence in this trend for several years after they left college (104, 578). Certain courses were interpreted to be "liberalizing" agents during a given semester (722, 487). There is evidence that liberalism and conservatism are related to certain religious preference, to parents' attitudes and vocations, and slightly to intelligence (394, 228, 126). As far as political attitudes are concerned, prejudice and conservatism seem to be associated with lack of information (10).

Opinion pollsters interrogate people of all classes more now than ever before (473, 102). One author, in evaluating the attitudes of the American people, defends the thesis that they are generally right in their thinking about public issues and show more common sense than their leaders in Washington. He indicates that in recent issues the people have been the leaders and argues that with more objective information their judgments would improve (473). This, it seems, would hold too for the college student. He, like the general population, reflects change in attitudes over the years toward greater liberalism (102, 96).

Student Values and College. Students as a result of college attendance do (1) become less dogmatic, (2) show greater capacity to think critically, (3) show less prejudice, (4) become more permissive and show greater flexibility in human relations. These tendencies were reflected in the studies quoted above conducted mainly in the '30s, and one might well generalize that colleges in the main liberalize student values. A recent critical review of the literature related to this subject indicates emphatically that college experience itself barely touches the student's *standards of behavior, his quality of judgment, sense of social responsibility, and perspicacity of understanding* and *guiding beliefs* (372).

When college graduates are compared with others their outlook differs negligibly from them on many questions (322). They are, for example, along with their social class more conservative on economic issues (755). The changes mentioned in the preceding section are viewed in terms of changes occurring at the time and represent merely a sample of issues in vogue during the generation. The studies did not show that the student becomes a more liberal person in college, but that he acquired some social and political attitudes which are representative of an outlook of his time rather than those of his parents (372).

The author of this survey further states these attitude changes observed in most of the studies are surface changes. The student has modified his opinion on certain questions, has learned how to tolerate and get along with people differing from himself, has become more self-reliant—but he remains basically the same person with substantially the same value judgments. College has *socialized* rather than liberalized him. It allows the student to live more smoothly in his time, but it does little to help him evaluate the appropriateness of this way of life in a broader and more fundamental perspective. These results are surprising at first to many teachers as well as to students, but few upon reflection deny their validity. It might be well *to discuss their implications and possibly have a group of students report on the original study*.

Liberalizing Influences. There is a positive note to this study. The conclusions stated are estimated to hold for 75 to 80 per cent of the students. There are a minority of students and a small group of institutions that have a more liberalizing impact. These students have participated in experiences that vividly bring them face to face with value issues and often demand decisions the consequences of which they can experience directly. These may include actual and responsible practice of citizenship with the successes and failures that arise from it. They may consist of one of the following vivid personal meaningful experiences: living in international setting, a provocative work-study curriculum, or a well-planned field study. The colleges that have more liberalizing influence at first seem to have nothing in common; however, further analysis indicates that they have this in common: they have a *high level of expectancy of their students* even though what is expected differs among them. They may stress intellectual initiative, profound respect for the worth of work, world-mindedness, or a dedication to humanitarian service.

These colleges seem to have a campus climate that arouses the student and moves him from his previous frames of reference.

The Authoritarian Personality and Values. One group of psychologists and psychiatrists have isolated a personality pattern or syndrome to which they have given the name "authoritarian personality" (5, 75). This syndrome has been studied by various methods such as interviews, questionnaires, and laboratory tests. A scale is available for determining degrees of authoritarianism in an individual. Persons representing the pattern in the *extreme* form are highly rigid, stereotyped, and dogmatic in their thinking. They show extreme deference to superior authority and act authoritatively with those in subordinate positions; they are intolerant of minority groups. They tend to manipulate and exploit people as objects rather than human beings and expect to be exploited in return. Extreme authoritarians are emotionally unstable and seek security by adhering to established order and what to them seems right and basic. Deviation from conventional behavior is uncomfortable. Those who receive scores on tests that place them in the higher authoritarian groups emphasize neatness, importance of dress, dependability, rules, and strict adherence to them. They tend to belong to orthodox fundamentalist and evangelistic churches—tend to be economically conservative.

CHARACTERISTICS AND DEVELOPMENT OF AUTHORITATIVE ATTITUDES. In attempting to find a generalization to describe this pattern of behavior it has been hypothesized that these individuals cannot tolerate ambiguity—they must have certainty and absolutes. They feel better if they can place people and events into clear-cut categories (75). They have difficulty shifting from one frame of reference to another. For example, they find it difficult to classify items that describe their "best self" and "worst self." In stress experiments designed to make them emotional, they often deny expression of emotion and exert great control over their behavior. They stress their own moral rightness and lack self-insight. They ascribe their difficulties to events outside themselves (256). A study of their personality syndrome suggests that this pattern of behavior arises from severe discipline as a child, with great stress on rightness of parents' rules and values and with insistence on absolute obedience without regard for the individual personality of the child. It is a form of emotional rejection of the child. The developed submissiveness later extends to authority figures. The engendered hostility is repressed and aggression is displaced toward more helpless persons in minority or inferior positions.

Traits that are in contrast to the authoritarian pattern are flexible thinking, ease in changing frame of reference, an emphasis on frank self-understanding, tolerance of groups with different standards, liberality in religious and social views, a willingness to take responsibility for choices involving value conflicts.

The scales that measure degrees of authoritarianism were factorially analyzed and were shown to have at least these three components: (1) "Religious Conventionalism"; (2) "Authoritarian-Submission"; and (3) "Masculine Strength Façade" (an outward display of toughness) (590). It has been pointed out that *extreme* highs and lows on the F scale (authoritarianism), those who are prejudice prone and those who are prejudice resistant, are similar in many respects. We are cautioned that we may be able to explain the relationship between the above-mentioned traits on simpler grounds than assuming an "authoritarian personality." Is what is called "authoritarianism" often merely acquiescence? (48).

AUTHORITARIANISM AND PERSONAL GROWTH. Students high on the authoritarian scale when placed in a homogeneous class under a patient and ingenious teacher changed from a class that resisted discussion and preferred "being told" to a less inhibited group with greater discussion and spontaneity. Such a change does not take place when students high on the authoritarian score are placed indiscriminately with other students (747).

Objective students of behavior should be cautioned at this point to see authoritarianism as an aspect of personal development in a segment of our culture, a personality pattern with potentialities for growth and service rather than a stigma or fixed personality trait (511).

Attitudes toward Religion. After World War II investigations were made of the religious attitudes of the college student. The results of these studies highlight some of the religious issues and trends in collegiate thinking: about 70 per cent of the students feel that they require "some form of religious orientation or belief in order to achieve a fully mature philosophy of life." About 25 per cent are essentially orthodox in their adherence to Christian dogma. The majority are dissatisfied with institutional religion as it exists. When students shift their religious preference, it is practically always in a liberal direction or out of organized religion entirely. Present-day college students are less concerned about apparent conflicts between religion and science than were their predecessors, and more disturbed about "the failure of institutional religion to prevent war or lessen human misery." Only 12 per cent subscribe to the Marxian doctrine that religion is the opiate of the people and should be actively contested. The majority believe that the denominational distinctions between Protestant churches are outworn and should be abolished. Ethics, humanitarianism, and social reform are endorsed more frequently than traditional theology. Young adults tend to return to the church after marriage and upon encountering the responsibilities of parenthood. Older students with military experience do not differ dramatically from younger students. Modern college instruction offers little in the philosophical aspects of religious doctrine. If the present-day student achieves a mature system of rational theology, it is not through college instruction (13).

Mature Religious Sentiments. It has been said that man has a natural hunger for religion; he cannot know but he must believe. In many aspects of his private life man is alone. There are sorrows, disappointments, pains, dreads, and guilts that he has difficulty sharing. Death is an experience that is indeed solitary. Man often finds an omniscient, omnipotent, and merciful God is the answer to his need for belonging, acceptance, assurance and guidance (477).

Religion has quieted the anxieties of many human beings, but in doing so has it narrowed their lives and serving as an opiate, lulled them into unreality? Has it restricted their thinking or their search for truth? The religion of an individual can be childlike, self-centered, and immature. As such it does not encourage free thinking or judgment of one's own behavior. It contains false or incomplete intellectual views and promotes rigidity and intolerance. It excludes regions of one's experience by encouraging repression rather than gradual understanding and guidance of certain forces in one's personality (368, 11). The repressed material in many cases tends to arouse later and produces anxiety and personality disturbance.

Much of the criticism by youth and by lay thinkers of *institutional religion* has been directed at the immature forms of religion that seem to impede personal growth, unity, and consistent morality rather than to promote values and behavior exemplifying love, mercy, sacrifice and humility. Mature religion is *heuristic*, which means the believer holds tentatively but wholeheartedly to his beliefs until they are confirmed or until they lead to the discovery of more valid ideas. A mature religious sentiment has been *defined* as a disposition built through experience to respond favorably in certain habitual ways to conceptual objects and principles and whatever an individual regards as ultimately important in his own life and central in the nature of things. A mature religious sentiment, it is argued, assists the individual in his quest for purpose outside of himself, can enable him to unify his thinking and values and help give consistency to his morality. Man in part is determined by his make-up and his society, but a mature religion emphasizes the free aspects of man's life—the choices and aspirations open to him.

It is argued that the more aware an individual is of his total being and his possibilities, the more dynamic he is, and the greater his perspective. Men of purpose, hope, and faith are more likely to stand outside the rigid chain of stimulus and response, it is argued, and by this stance to throw the weight of their feelings and attitudes toward their choices. Such religious attitudes strengthen the sense of one's own dignity and worth and aid in building confidence with which to affirm values in life. This awareness enhances personal freedom and responsibility (505, 742). (See on page 105 the discussion of religion and personality development.)

Formulating a "Philosophy"

Personal Philosophy—Difference between Philosophy and Way of Life. Your philosophy of life is your deliberate effort to make sensible your beliefs, morals, and behavior and to unify them so that you may have a basis for action when you are confronted with problems.

A personal philosophy probably should be differentiated at the start from the *less conscious* forces in an individual's behavior. For example, most persons reach maturity without having raised or answered very many questions concerning behavior, and yet they consistently act in definite directions. Habits and attitudes, although not clearly formulated and rarely stated by them or their acquaintances, guide their actions. Their behavior toward their fellow man, their sincerity, and their dependability suggest certain attitudes. These attitudes, traits, and daily habits are responsible for their consistency and stability as persons. These attitudes and traits may or may not be socially oriented. A criminal may justify and rationalize his behavior as he orients himself to others in his antisocial environment.

Let us call these directive motives, traits, habits, and attitudes your *way of life* because of the undefined element that is present, and reserve the term *personal philosophy* for your conscious statement of your credo and the attitudes that are formed and re-formed in an attempt to unify your thinking in a total pattern.

Organized personal views may be so complex and so fascinating to their author that they become top-heavy and abstract and assume an existence that is *independent of everyday life*. Some of us may become more interested in principles than in their application to life. We have all seen the person who is so absorbed with pencil-and-paper morals that he has never entered real life situations. He has never put his morals to a test.

There is a tendency, too, for one to keep his morals in a logic-tight compartment, where standards remain intact and unexamined from childhood to adulthood. When crises arise, moral standards do not operate in them. His standards are idealistic and relatively unmodifiable. Any behavior that violates them is to be disowned. Such individuals may vacillate between "saint" and "devil." The case of Horace is illustrative.

Horace N. is a member of a family of good, solid reputation, known for their sincerity and their adherence to conventions. He is the youngest child, the only boy in the family, and was quite close to his mother. He found early in life that it was not difficult to win her favor and at times to receive special attention and privileges. She was prone to excuse his failures and very solicitous of his health. Horace accepted all his mother's standards without question. Following his mother's wishes he accepted warmly the religious instruction and practice of the family's church, and his religious experiences in childhood and adolescence when in a religious environment or in the home were genuine.

Despite his position as favorite in the home, he became a hanger-on of the neighborhood gang. He developed the habits and attitudes of the group, which were incompatible with some of his religious training. The two patterns of behavior were never compared. When he was with the gang, he lost himself in the group's pranks but, when with his mother, he was a "perfectly good boy." It was not until he reached college that he became clearly conscious of how strong were his tendencies to violate the standards for sex behavior indicated at home, how weak he seemed to be in his efforts to live up to what he thought was right. It was puzzling to him that moral standards could be so vivid when he considered them at home or in the church and yet so ineffectual when he was with people whom he considered immoral.

At no time did Horace think through the whole problem. He thought that if you pay allegiance to morals and ethics they should function at all times. Religion to him was like a rabbit's foot or talisman that works automatically. He did not realize that, in order for a code to function, it must be dominant in attitudes and behavior. He suffered many depressions, particularly when he was unable to repress the memory of his derelictions.

Horace had not worked out a personal philosophy. He had accepted a code of standards and, because he had always been sheltered and allowed to follow his own pleasure in the family, he had carried this pattern of behavior outside. His moral standards were principally verbal, or at least confined to a pious setting, and were never associated in thought or action with his daily life. He grew up without sex education. Sex to him apparently was a compulsive outlet, involving little consideration for the other person as an individual. He strongly despised his misbehavior and everyone who behaved similarly. After a breach, he plunged fervently into his moralistic rituals, obviously as an escape from his guilt. There was no attempt on his part to discover and understand the source of his behavior or accept it as a vital part of his personality with which he must deal. Rather, he thought that if he rigorously denied it and repressed it, it would cease to exist. He certainly did not question the standards his mother had passed on to him or his ability to live up to them. Horace was an island of insecurity surrounded by his mother's perfectionistic, inviolable standards and his own violent passions. He had not discovered how poorly organized he was as a person, that there was not much he could call his own self.

One should have the experience of freely choosing between right and wrong. The individual can then experience some of the consequences of each kind of choice so that the right behavior is learned as the kind of behavior that is most deeply satisfying and the wrong behavior as productive of far-reaching, undesirable consequences. This does not obviate, however, the importance of building positive and negative attitudes, sentiments and emotional reactions in the child.

In short, a personal philosophy should be realistic in order to function in one's life. A group of principles is not a substitute for well-developed traits and inner security. The principles must represent the individual's inner demands and the pressures of his environment as well as a code of values. A set of verbal standards assumed without reference to the rest of the personality is dangerously fragile.

Development of Personal Philosophy—the Process. Values and their organization into a personal philosophy grow like other human products, in a random manner through *trial and error* as we try to *solve problems* that confront us. If the solution is of a motor nature, so that we do not think in terms of ideas and do not verbalize our solution, it probably does not become a part of our philosophy of life. Much of this philosophy may be taken from a writer, from the Bible, or from proverbs of an unknown source. If these ideas are to function as ideas in life, we must experience real satisfaction as we see their roles in our behavior. They must have the vividness of insights or discoveries, discussed in Chapter 5. As hackneyed proverbs repeated without meaning, they are of questionable value. The admonition, "Do unto others as you would that they would do unto you," means little until the individual has found through experience the meaning and value of it. Rarely does a personal philosophy come from single experiences. Single books, courses, or essays may sum up one's attitude and the reaction tendencies that have grown from numerous previous personal experiences. One then would be encouraged to read widely in current magazines * and enjoy lectures and educational radio and television programs which are available to him. One does not build a philosophy of life during one week-end in which he writes a term paper, but he can bring to consciousness attitudes that have had a long previous existence.

PERSONALITY FACTORS. An individual's personal philosophy, like all such complex patterns of experience, is influenced in growth by the many *other aspects of his personality*. His intelligence, his temperament, his physique, his physiological urges, his emotional experiences, his contacts with other people, with books, with plays, with sermons, and with lectures, his friends, enemies, and teachers—all play a part. No doubt the compatibility of his philosophy and behavior is dependent upon the extent to which *his philosophy has taken into account his basic constitution and important past experiences*. The degree of *inner security* one experiences also influences one's philosophy. Comparison of the systematized attitudes of a college student with those of a previously admired teacher or friend will reveal many similarities.

PERSONAL SECURITY. The bases for one's values go back into his early life where he learns trust or distrust of others, self acceptance or personal insecurity. Later in school he begins to verbalize these attitudes. In high school his horizon broadens. He sees a wider range of standards, interpretation of right and wrong, his courses raise questions about social standards and practices. To many the problems of drinking, smoking, late hours, luxuries and extravagances, popularity, undesirable associates, petting, and class distinctions become very real. With conflicting views apparent among their associates, they search for their own beliefs. The student who comes to college from

---

* Some of the well-known and established better magazines are: *The New Yorker, The Atlantic Monthly, Fortune Magazine, Harper's, The National Geographic Magazine, The Nation, Newsweek, Time, The New Republic, The Saturday Review.*

a restricted environment may note more liberal trends in organized religion, meet cynicism and skepticism about established practices, see incompatibilities between ideals and institutions. He may find concepts he has regarded as established being examined critically, as, for example, authoritarian religion, capitalism, the profit motive, and ideas that he previously regarded as radical given open consideration, as race equality, socialistic legislation, divorce, and subsidized housing. These and many other problems and unsolved questions press him toward verbal solutions and make the formulation of a personal philosophy important.

Although he does not realize it, frequently his own anxieties and suppressions exaggerate his observations. One of the discoveries he may make is that he is really dealing with his own problems when he thinks he is concerned with the standards of others.

VALUE OF PERSONAL PHILOSOPHY. A philosophy of life should *guide* behavior. It should allow one to act on the basis of rational principles, rather than through fear, selfishness, and external force, such as parental or social pressure. As indicated above, however, it cannot ignore inner tendencies as anxiety or outer forces such as social standards. These should be realized in developing one's philosophy. If the philosophy helps self-understanding and involves a certain amount of acceptance of oneself as one is, it can be a real source of direction for the future. A personal philosophy brings relative *serenity* to most people. It provides *perspective* and allows one to see oneself in retrospect and to *project ambitions* realistically into the future. It can *organize* or *integrate* our derived values so that they will form a "united front" and *strength of conviction* when a conflict arises and a decision must be made. History shows that those men who have received the gratitude of society espoused a worthy movement, spent their lives developing it, and so merged their own personalities in the movement that they and the movement became indistinguishable.

Certain students have no choice but to formulate their views into a system. Their past training and their systematic mode of thinking make them unhappy unless they see order in their beliefs.

In short, a realistic personal philosophy can assist those who are in difficulties, should *give perspective* of one's self and of the world, *foster personal integration and growth*, *aid adjustment*, and *increase creativeness* (328, 190).

Ego Identity and Strength. A discussion of persons who have formed a philosophy of life is not complete unless it calls attention to men known to be of "strong character." It is significant that individuals have had the force of thousands in the history of man's adventure with life. Examine these forceful personalities and what do you find? They have usually identified themselves with a somewhat consistent way of life, which has given them unity and direction. This has been called the process of ego identity and is discussed again on page 450. They usually know too their potentialities and weaknesses and attempt to act in terms of them. Often they stand alone against many other individuals who are unguided. When they are supported by others who believe as they do, their strength is prodigious. Let us look further into this matter, into self-control.

SELF-CONTROL. Self-control consists of a *realistic plan* of action and the *forcefulness (motivation)* to carry it through. It has grown from many experiences of free choice in which certain selections have led to failure and unpleasantness and have thereby been discarded, and in which other selections have been rewarded. This is what has popularly been called "will power." Those who show less control of their own behavior have not based their plans upon knowledge of themselves or have not developed motivation, attitudes, and strong desires toward the goal. On the contrary, they have some strong feelings and tendencies (often unconscious) in opposition to what they *say* they want. Personal control is not a mystical matter. It consists in having or acquiring through vivid experience motivation in a given area of behavior. One may or may not possess this motivation at a given time, but his status at that moment does not seal his destiny for life. It might be well to review at this point the discussion under "Changing Behavior," Chapter 5. There it was shown that the elimination of undesirable behavior involves, first, a clear understanding of what that behavior consists in practical applications; second, a marshaling of all of one's attitudes toward that behavior; and, finally, planning a course of events that will strengthen the desired behavior and weaken the contrary activity. Such a process is not developed rapidly. It is a substantial heightening and consolidation of motivation and a selection of practical situations and associates that enhance certain types of behavior and weaken others (550, 512).

It has been found that attitudes, for example, may be changed through vivid experiences—experiences that are novel, emotionally charged, and realistic, and that occur in the absence of counter influences. These attitudes will blossom through contact with other individuals, groups, or institutions that have prestige value and that are satisfying to our other motives. Speeches, pamphlets, knowledge of the majority and expert opinion, debates, radio programs, moving pictures, courses, social gatherings—all have been found to change attitudes. When these attitudes are organized, they have influence in helping us to carry through our decisions. A strong organization of attitudes, feelings, and beliefs around realistic plans that are associated with ourselves and that are aroused when we make choices and strive toward goals is what we think of as self-control.

Beliefs in Transition. It is clear that *growth toward maturity and establishment of ego strength and self identity* require that childhood beliefs undergo a change. Conflicts between old and new standards are troublesome to the average developing person and when conflict occurs he may throw overboard all old beliefs. He then finds himself at a loss about what to believe. Friends and older advisers serve as a sounding board while we discover for ourselves which of our strong beliefs are most basic and most valuable. Determine them, and hold fast to them while you gradually discard those which fail to meet the test of living.

A new belief may be only a different interpretation or statement of an old one. This situation is seen in the alleged conflict between religion and science. If religion is the search for that which is central to the nature of things and science is the statement of natural laws, then there can be no basic widespread incompatibility. It is true that an immature religion may have certain elements in its ritual that are incompatible with science as interpreted by a dogmatic graduate student. Further search into both religion and science will reveal many similarities. The bewildered student will find indisputable common grounds which he may accept while his beliefs undergo a gradual adjustment.

Effective Thinking

Not all of the beliefs and attitudes that make up our initial philosophy of life represent valid thinking or meet the test of reality. Ideas, like actions, are used to adjust to our needs, to make us feel secure whether they are valid or not. We shall examine in this section some examples of this "wishful thinking" that usurps the function of valid, effective thinking. Mental activities which satisfy us but are not dependable as real guides to future action are: daydreams, suggestions, prejudices and emotional biases, superstitions, erroneous beliefs, analogous reasoning and unwarranted generalization, and hunches and intuitions, all similar and having certain elements in common. Let us see the operation of some of these mental activities which are *satisfying but invalid* in so far as solving the problem at hand.

Substitutes for Effective Thinking. *Daydreams.* Daydreams about get-rich schemes, "being discovered" as an outstanding talent or personality, or suffering martyrdom for a cause and thereby changing the attitudes of many, all represent the use of ideas to adjust to a feeling of inadequacy and to meet a need for self-esteem and success. They cannot, however, be classed as a form of effective thinking. Daydreams are subjective and are molded by the needs of the individual who experiences them. They are not subject to the controls of logic and correct reasoning. They frequently hamper rather than advance the individual's future development. Daydreams become effective thinking when they lead to plans that can be checked by events in the real world. They become creative when they assume some concrete and acceptable form as a story, play, invention, painting, job, musical composition, gadget, or realistic plan of action.

SUGGESTION. In buying clothes, cars, and even in selecting roommates or voting for individuals for public office the process of suggestion rather than thought may operate. Factors like *beauty, prestige, habit, the size of the group which behaves in a certain manner, reputation or prestige of the individual making the appeal, emotional associations, previous positive response tendencies* all tend to make us respond to a situation impulsively rather than critically. These factors are especially effective in cases in which the individual has scanty knowledge about a situation. They are all potent factors in advertising but poor stimuli to rational consideration of a proposition. Most of the other errors of thinking mentioned below involve an element of suggestion.

HUNCHES AND "INTUITIONS." Hunches and "intuitions" may fall in this general class of fallacious thinking particularly if they do not have a rational basis. They may prevent the thoughtful, successful attack of problems. They are illustrations of suggestion. Usually they are *conclusions growing from some superficial or emotional element of the situation* and not from a thoroughly rational, critical treatment. They are sometimes correct but are often wrong. We remember the times when our hunches were effective and forget the failures. We usually favor hunches, among other reasons, because of our memory of their previous success or because they are opinions we are eager to hold. One has a hunch to make a certain bet in a card game, to take a certain job or to believe a certain proposition. One is confident not for any logical reason but possibly because the situation resembles one in which he was formerly successful (although he is not clearly conscious of this). Or, he may be confident because of an unconscious association; he is in a mood similar to that which prevailed when on another occasion he made an effective selection. The mood has been associated with success and prompts him to act now. Or, there may be some other element in the situation that suggests through previous experience an expansive, self-confident attitude. If reason could work, hunches might be discarded early, but rationality is excluded because of the positive emotional element.

PREJUDICES AND EMOTIONAL BIASES. Much of that which passes for thinking is rationalization or defensive thinking to justify an emotional bias.

A sample of the operation of prejudice and of the complete absence of rationality is in the process of voting. Notice below the lack of cogent evidence upon which this student's choice is based.

Representative Doe is a member of the solid old Blank party which Jack has linked with his father's good will, the best people in the community, and other favorable associations. The representative is six feet tall, pleasant, has a good smile, never makes one feel uncomfortable by raising troublesome issues, is always willing to run little errands in Washington, and convinces his constituents that he does his best for the home folks. He never misses an opportunity to praise them and to tell them that he is a foe of all evil that may touch them.

Jack knows very little of Doe's voting record in Congress or his philosophy on vital domestic, foreign, and economic policies. When Jack steps up to the voting booth for the first time, he carries with him a warm feeling toward Representative Doe. He does not hesitate to vote against Doe's opponent, who has angered people and who talks continually about social problems and complicated domestic and foreign issues.

All of us have biases that we must recognize as operative in our thinking. Most of us are *ethnocentric*. As human beings we are biased to favor human beings against nonorganic features of the universe and the infrahuman animals. Man is the greatest animal, in our minds, because we set our own traits as standards. If we are white men, to us the white race is greatest in achievement; if we are of Germanic descent, we believe the Nordic is superior; if American, America and all its institutions and ideals are the greatest. *Real* history began in 1776, from this point of view. If we are members of the Alpha Alpha Alpha fraternity, then "Alfs" are superior to all other groups. As our affiliations extend, so do our allegiances and prejudices.

In addition, we assume the individual prejudices of those we admire within these groups—the individual Germans, Americans, Holy Rollers, and Alfs.

Our many individual fortunate and unfortunate experiences bias us for or against events, places, and people and certain ideas. Periodicals, pictures, plays, and conversations all give us points of view *which we usually accept uncritically if we approve of the medium* from which they spring. We do this often without a rigorous analysis of the bases for the belief.

The whole question of what makes a person hold a given prejudice or a bias in favor of the *status quo* (things as they are), or a bias against tradition and for innovation was discussed earlier in the chapter.

SUPERSTITIONS AND ERRONEOUS BELIEFS. Which of the following statements do you believe true, and which false? Check those you believe true.

> The number of man's senses is five.
> Man is superior to the animals because his conduct is guided by reason.
> Chess and checker playing develops one's power of concentration.
> Intelligence can be increased by proper training.
> The study of mathematics is valuable because it gives one a logical mind.
> Conscience is an infallible guide to conduct.
> No defect of body or mind can hold us back if we have will power enough.

Erroneous beliefs, such as *all of the above*, modify the accuracy of the thinking of students. In most studies of students' superstitious beliefs, girls were slightly more credulous than boys. The more intelligent students hold fewer false beliefs. Such beliefs are influenced by parents and socio-economic status and are therefore acquired in development. There is also only a slight tendency for the students with higher grades to hold fewer erroneous beliefs. Fortunately, courses in science reduce the extent of these false beliefs about man's mental life. Even courses in which specific training was not given to contradict the false belief caused a drop in the percentage endorsing it (214).

ANALOGOUS REASONING AND UNWARRANTED GENERALIZATION. A common fallacy that explains some unclear thinking is to *isolate one element of a situation and attribute to it the cause of the entire situation*. Because a friend who has red hair proved disloyal, one need not worry that a newly acquired red-haired acquaintance will also be untrue. In the realm of ideas, the loud support of an issue by a few unstable people does not mean it is invalid. Social schemes and events are complex, and they consist of complex causes and effects. Single elements in the situation may be merely incidental events and not causal antecedents. *Reasoning by analogy,* of which the preceding fallacious type of thinking is an example, is grossly unreliable if some superficial element is the influential factor. Because two situations are alike in some details, they need not be alike fundamentally, and it is illogical to reason from one to another.

Another pitfall of thinking is that of *generalizing too widely* from the facts at hand. Because three members of a given fraternity have borrowed money and have not repaid it, one man asserts that all the other 47 members are not honest, yet it does not follow from the data. Similar generalizations resulting from college students' use of insufficient data are:

"Whenever I use a pen to write an exam, I do poorly."
"If a girl agrees to accept a blind date, she is neither pretty nor popular."
"Young teachers are always hard on the student."
"More students flunk in required courses than in elective courses."

Many of these reactions are emotionally conditioned. The individual has associated an event in experience with an emotional consequence. He does not consider the matter rationally but merely verbalizes his feelings in such an "all-out" statement, not delayed for thought or consideration. Many other processes operating to adjust the individual to his personal motives, but that do not produce valid thought, are rationalization, introjection and projection, discussed in Chapter 3.

Attitudes That Aid Clear Thinking. The individual who prides himself on clear thinking should be sure he can answer these questions in a manner to indicate that he has a solid ground for his thinking.

Is your thinking conditioned by what you *want* to believe, or by what is rational?

Are you more concerned with *winning your point* than with thinking clearly, even at the cost of your first opinion?

Are you willing to go anywhere and accept any conclusion to which clear thinking leads you? If not, what limits do you place on your thinking?

Are you critical of your own thinking, and continually asking if it will stand attack?

When you reach a conclusion are you willing to look for errors, and on finding them begin solving the problem all over again?

Do your answers to these questions indicate that you have the *truth-seeking* attitude rather than the attitude of accepting the beliefs of the group or those which give you emotional satisfaction?

Thinking and Adjustment. When the methods by which teachers solve their personal problems were examined, intellect and reason were *not* found to be primary factors. Their adjustments, as well as the adjustments of most of us, are primarily the results of reactions to frustration and attempts to avoid anxiety (781).

Thinking or verbal and covert problem-solving is used to satisfy needs. The insecure person thinks in a manner that will make him feel secure, not in a manner that is necessarily valid. If this thinking releases his tensions, satisfies his motives, and enhances his ego, it seems valid to him. Most of the forms of thought exemplified above illustrate the use of ideas to satisfy personal needs, not to reach correct conclusions. It might be said with some assurance that it is rare to find valid critical thinking in an area if the results of this thinking will cause the individual to feel insecure or to lose face. To a large extent "thinking" is the servant of one's self-esteem, one's motives, and the less rational aspects of one's life.

It is relatively easy for us to see the invalid thinking of the Nazi, or of the Communist leader, or of the highly zealous religious leader of a faith with which we are not sympathetic. It is very difficult, however, to see some of the inconsistencies in our institutions in respect to race relations or economic exploitation of others, especially if these practices benefit us. Valid thinking in such areas jeopardizes our "way of life" and makes us feel insecure.

Perceptual Defense. A number of empirical studies have been made on defensiveness and its effect on perceiving and thinking, which give validity to the foregoing statements (103, 388). *Rigidity* is the tendency to hold to a viewpoint and not accept new facts, or to refuse to take a different perspective. It arises when one's position is threatened enough to make him feel anxious. Anxiety interferes with the flexibility so important for free thinking. Many attempts at thinking that fail illustrate *functional fixedness.* This retention of inadequate solutions occurs because the prevailing emotions, attitudes or perspectives at the time influence what we perceive and block what we dare not perceive. This greatly hampers effective problem solving (2, 217, 857).

This phenomenon was mentioned in discussing the authoritative personality (159). As a means of dealing with human rigidity it has been suggested that the old adage be reworded to read: "If at first you don't succeed, don't try again; try another problem" (481).

Thinking and Personal Problems. The personal problems discussed in this book exist largely because the individual involved with them was unable to think effectively about his problems. Either he is substituting quick means of relief for the discomfort he feels or, when he attempts to use more effective methods, he arouses so much anxiety that he discontinues logical thinking. He becomes disturbed when he perceives where his thinking may be leading him.

The solutions suggested in this book are basically an application of valid thinking at a rate at which the individual can accept and use the conclusions of his reasoning. As suggested in Chapter 5, it is usually necessary for the individual to begin his thinking about his basic values and attitudes in a secure context—a hospitable environment. He needs to see his sources of personal strength and security along with his unrealistic ideas. As in counseling, the substitution of realistic and valid points of view for self-defeating and inaccurate ideas will often take time and some kind of emotional support by other individuals or groups.

Maybe it is too much to expect of an individual that he reach a logical position rapidly if this conclusion will gravely undermine his stability. To be sure, our best ultimate guide for our own welfare and the welfare of society is critical reasoning. But the ability to accept it depends upon the total adjustment of the individual or security of his society.

The thinking of abnormal individuals demonstrates the potency of insecurity in the warping of thinking in order to achieve security. The person who believes that he is great and that other people are persecuting him uses these beliefs to guard his self-esteem and to explain the lack of warmth in his reception by others.

Valid thinking or knowledge is that which has survived the tests of criticism, that which has been substantiated by laboratory experiments or by logic, that which has withstood over a period of time the open attack of critical adversaries. It is objective thinking—thinking that is not governed by individual desires and feelings. Our real hope for clear thinking on complex domestic and foreign issues which cannot always be subjected to experimentation or to the tests of time is in the existence of a situation that *will allow all ideas to be expressed freely* so that they may come in conflict and the best may survive. True democracy is framed to produce valid thinking by setting up a situation in which all viewpoints can be given equal expression. Any power that tends to limit free expression of ideas through the press, radio, schoolroom, pulpit, or platform jeopardizes democracy, valid thinking, and man's adjustment to his future.

The Process of Thinking.   Valid thinking, of either the problem-solving or the creative type, involves the following stages:

Clear statement of the problem.
Search for solutions.
Critical test of these solutions.
Tentative acceptance of tested solutions.

Susan Greenburg

. . . a situation
that will allow
all ideas to be
expressed
freely so that
they may
come in
conflict and
the best may survive . . .

Allowance of Time for Ideas and Insight to Arise. On numerous occasions people who have created music, poetry or a mechanical invention have stated that after hours of hard work with no success there arises in or after a period of relaxation, a solution to their problem or a burst of creative beauty. The period of relaxation served as an incubation period. A clear *insight* into the problem occurred, and a solution was reached that would bear criticism. This insight into the problem sometimes arrives at an unpredictable moment when they are engaged in some activity entirely unrelated to the task at hand. Cases have been reported in which a rest has aided the solution of a problem. However, the role of hard, systematic work in creative or practical thinking cannot be too strongly emphasized. It is the factor that prepares the way for insight.

Analysis of Daily Thinking and Application of Principles. You will enjoy reviewing decisions, judgments, generalizations, or plans that you have made today or yesterday. Label them in terms of processes discussed in this chapter, as "hunch," "syllogistic reasoning," "suggestion," "prejudice," "analogous reasoning," and the like. Subject a number of daily acts and decisions to this analysis, and you will be convinced of how little you think. It may even make you more critical of your actions and lead to wiser decisions on your part. The college student's life is replete with situations in which he can practice identifying valid and invalid thinking. There is the bull session, the visiting lecturer, the newspaper, and even the classroom at times.

Supplementary Readings

G. W. Allport, *The Individual and His Religion,* Macmillan, 1950.

R. R. Blake and G. V. Ramsey, *Perception: An Approach to Personality,* Ronald, 1951.

J. S. Bruner, J. J. Goodnow, and G. A. Austin, *A Study of Thinking,* Wiley, 1956.

J. M. Gillespie and G. W. Allport, *Youth's Outlook on the Future,* Doubleday, 1955.

P. E. Jacobs, *Changing Values in College,* Harper, 1957.

In addition see the references cited by number in the chapter and appearing in the bibliography of an accompanying volume entitled *Teaching Personal Adjustment: An Instructor's Manual.*

Planning for a Career

Careers. Lawn cutting is a job, landscape architecture is a career; wall papering is a job, interior decoration is a career; bookkeeping generally speaking is a job, accounting is a career; and so on through the 42,000 different occupations known to investigators (181, 700). Work for many people is just a job; it is drudgery. For others, work is the mainspring of their very existence. It is romance; from it they derive their greatest pleasures. Work offers to them adventure, thrills, and new experiences. Stories of the indefatigability of such men as Pasteur, Napoleon, Steinmetz, and Edison are legion. These differences in point of view are due to fundamental divergences in the organization of experiences. Often the whole vocational horizon of the individual can take a different form through orientation.

212

CHAPTER 8

CAREERS AND PERSONALITY

AN EMPLOYED YOUTH WHO PLANNED FOR A CAREER. The following is a case of orientation accomplished by the work of a vocational counselor (416).

Donald S. was a clerk in a shoe store in a small Kentucky town. He had taken the job two years previously at the end of his formal education. He showed his dissatisfaction with it by interviewing a traveling vocational counselor. He confided that he was in a line of work which did not interest him. He had liked the job when he first took it, but was tired of fitting people's feet for $20 a week (a good salary at that time). When asked if there were other occupations which interested him, he said "No." He went on to say that he knew one should be working in a stimulating calling, so he knew the shoe business was not for him.

The counselor explained that in order to become interested in a field one must obtain information about it. It was recommended that he read the history of shoes: learn from books in the library or from an encyclopedia that shoes probably started as a crude sort of sandal and evolved through many variations to shoes of mail worn by knights of the Middle Ages, to pointed shoes affected by the dandies of the eighteenth century, to wooden sabots worn by the French peasants, to shoes made like stilts, worn by Chinese ladies.

He was told to examine one of the shoes he showed customers daily and see cropping out the features that have been carried over or evolved from the styles of other centuries and other peoples. This information should be fascinating to a salesman of shoes as well as practical and useful. It should make him style-conscious and alert to niceties in design. He was also told to learn that the cow, the calf, the elk, the deer, and the antelope, to mention just a few, all contribute to the manufacture of shoes. Tracing the manufacture of shoes from the artisan shoemaker to the present-day factory process would offer enjoyment, and a visit to a modern gigantic bootery on his next vacation would allow him to point out the intricacies of manufacture to his customers. By this time the zest of discovery would lead him on to new aspects of the study of shoes.

These suggestions were readily accepted by the energetic youth. He became a constant reader in the library, quizzed the traveling men from the wholesale shoe houses on styles and construction. One of these sales representatives who visited the store happened to be the sales manager of a large manufacturing company. He was struck by the fund of solid information that the boy possessed, as well as his urge to learn more. He offered Donald a position with a salary double that which he was receiving. Donald has since been promoted to the position of assistant sales manager of this company.

Such a case, which is a paradigm of growth in any field, illustrates how a job may become a career, as the terms are used here. Furthermore, it shows how knowledge makes an individual indispensable in any sphere. The man who commands one of the greatest funds of knowledge in a given line can hardly fail in it. Suppose, for example, there were a position open in the advertising department of a large shoe house. Who would be better qualified, so far as being informed regarding shoes, than Donald S. whose vocational history is sketched above? In addition, consider the personal satisfaction derived from being such a source of knowledge, virtually an authority in a field.

Alfred L. was a sophomore, superior in academic standing, about average in athletic ability, and of good physique. He was a well-mannered, neat, alert 19-year-old college student. He had worked as a salesman for a summer, and in addition had held several odd jobs as waiter, yard boy, furnace boy, and errand boy. Although he came originally from a town of 12,000, he had also lived for several months in a large city. His acquaintance with industry and commerce in American cities was very superficial, however.

As a sophomore he began to realize, with some trepidation, that he must find a vocation. He had thought casually of several vocations: selling, the ministry, teaching, law, and medicine. His consideration and elimination of these vocations as possibilities for his life work had been very superficial, although he did not realize this until he had talked with a vocational counselor. The counselor suggested that he make an inventory of the aptitudes that had shown themselves either in the schoolroom, on the playground, in hobbies, in Scout work, or in odd jobs. He was told to consider every possible aptitude, whether it be manual, intellectual, or social. After he had made this inventory he was to bring it to his counselor for a critical evaluation and check, lest his evaluation be inaccurate and superficial. Should he find, through his frank survey of his past experiences, that certain aptitudes seemed to be promising, he was to test them by securing summer employment. He was to do the same in connection with his interests. While considering some of his abilities and tendencies, he was to survey all possible vocations and not restrict his attention to six or seven.

His efforts produced encouraging results. He considered his ability in athletics, which, although never leading him to stardom, had supplied him with a general interest and knowledge of athletic games. He had been greatly interested in biology in high school. He was interested in hygiene and public health and had read several articles concerning the need for general improvement of public health. He kept in his room several catalogs of athletic equipment. He had concluded from his reflection that he was at least average in his ability to deal with people, and probably above average. His teachers had told him that he wrote well.

These were the vocations he considered in view of his interests and accomplishments: director of physical education in high school, Y.M.C.A., men's clubs, or church; teacher and author in the recreational field of public health; recreational director in the municipal park system; research work in recreation; dealer in, and promoter of, athletic equipment; private instructor in sports in a wealthy community. He was convinced that his future lay in recreation, athletics, and public health. He built up a bibliography in this field; acquired college catalogs, catalogs of equipment, books on hygiene, athletics, etc. He is at present writing an article to be published in a boys' magazine on the construction of a homemade tennis court.

Characteristics of a Career. The individual who arrives at a decision regarding his life work and sees how college courses help to prepare and mature him for the job after realizing the great untouched possibilities in the field can come to view work in his father's stationery business, or box manufacturing company, or coal enterprise, with new enthusiasm. He may learn to derive some of the satisfaction and interest from such pursuits as the artist or scholar does from his work. A course in geology, which previously had little to offer, if related to his life purpose can take on more meaning.

A career suggests (1) working with *purpose;* (2) *growth* in a vocational field, planning, and using imagination; (3) making a game out of work; being *creative*. It is not merely work, but work directed toward fulfillment, and it involves interesting experimentation and exploration.

A man or woman may teach English in a high school or do book-keeping for a firm and be forced to go through the same prescribed duties year after year. Such a person may get in a rut and need to turn elsewhere for the satisfaction of dominant human motives, even if it be toward excessive drinking or other dubious means of "pepping up life." Another may teach English in a high school and see promise of larger satisfactions within the limits of the position. He may write; he may see the young personalities before him as characters in a novel; he may experiment in methods of teaching and publish the experiments in pedagogical journals; he may be interested in devising a textbook that suits the needs of his students, or he may furnish professional leadership on the staff or in organizations of teachers. In short, he can grow and create in his vocation. Similarly, the accountant may escape the bounds of his immediate job. He may see the figures on his ledgers as having meaning, as an index to trends in the behavior of the customers of the firm, and as signs of future events. They might be used as a basis for changing policies in the firm. He, too, may make his work creative and grow personally.

Job Satisfaction. Studies have been made of the satisfaction people find on their jobs. Twenty-five per cent of college graduates apparently do not find job satisfaction. They wish they had studied something else in college (322).

Workers prefer certain jobs to others. The men studied indicated that such factors as the opportunity to assume responsibility, show initiative, and gain prestige are among the most important reasons for their preference. They also mention as important congenial working conditions with pleasant social contacts and opportunity to reach vocational aspirations (829).

It is very clear that one's work is one of the important ways in which an individual can gain self actualization and fulfillment (679). We feel satisfaction if the job in some way allows us to express our interests, use our abilities, satisfy our needs and be the kind of person we aspire to be. Some objective factors influencing job satisfaction are job status, salary, continued employment, retirement plans and a relationship between duty and education (369).

Present Dearth of Planning.   Many students select as their vocation the one remaining out of the six or seven that they have considered and eliminated.   The train of thought is something like this:

"Now, I don't think I would like medicine.   I never did care to be near hospitals, or to visit the offices of physicians.   Law doesn't interest me. I am not a good speaker, and a lawyer should be able to sway a jury.   I am not mechanically inclined, so that eliminates engineering.   I know I would never make a good minister, and I would not want to be a teacher all my life.   I cannot write, although journalism ought to be interesting. Well, what is left to choose from?   Business.   Yes, business—I'll enter the business school at the university."

This man thinks he has *selected* a vocation!   Of 50 students in an Industrial Psychology class, 70 per cent admitted that the process through which they made their choice resembled the one above. Only 8 of these 50 students said that they had planned for a specific vocation.

When the aspirations of groups of students are compared with their later achievement many fall short of their goal (545).   About 60 per cent of a group of high school students studied reached occupations of a rank similar to their high school aspirations (623).   On the other hand a goodly percentage of our very bright students who on the basis of intelligence could do well in the difficult areas as science and language if motivated to seek professional careers do not go on to college when scholarships and loans are available to assist them.

Another illustration of these facts is shown in the responses to a brief questionnaire given to a General Psychology class of 85 students. These students, it is believed, were above the average of the student body in seriousness of purpose.   Thirty-nine per cent of the group had not definitely chosen a vocation, and half of the group who had made a selection merely recorded the name of a curriculum which had been elected rather than a specific goal in the field.   It was the rare individual who stated a *definite* vocation, such as cultural anthropologist, probation worker, dietitian, psychology instructor, psychiatric social worker, or packing-house executive.   Of this class 32 per cent had *not* read any books or pamphlets on vocations, 63 per cent had *not* initiated any interviews in preparation for a vocational selection.

Reports from five other colleges and universities in various parts of the country show consistently that 28 to 55 per cent of the students are *uncertain about future vocations* (736, 832).   There were, however, several significant reports that deviated from these trends. At one school in which there is a good personnel division, 87.8 per cent of the students had made a vocational choice. At a girls' college as many as 57.8 per cent had not chosen a vocation, and at one co-educational university the percentage was 47.2 (50).

The Individual May Not Be Able to Reach a Certain Goal. Inadequate intelligence and special aptitudes, interests and certain inappropriate personality traits limit vocational attainments (713). A student who desires to be a doctor may not have the abstract intelligence necessary to complete the premedical courses with satisfactory grades. An individual who aims for a goal beyond his capacity will surely suffer bitter disappointment in the future (795). Such unhappiness may be prevented by a judiciously planned diversion of the interests, plans, and daydreams of the student into channels through which he may be certain of attaining success, happiness, and the respect of his community. The store manager is not unhappy because he is not a lawyer, if he has never had a serious desire to be a lawyer; and he is happy if he sees a future in his business, and a distinct goal which he approaches daily by his hard work.

Socio-Economic Factors Play a Part. Parents reflect in their behavior their economic and social class and this influences the offspring's vocational attitude early in life whether he realizes it or not. Family conditions as pointed out in Chapter 4 can affect our security, our social or withdrawal tendencies, our inclinations to find some outside activity that is distracting or absorbing. There is evidence, for example, that students from the middle socio-economic class outdistance upper class students in academic achievement (173, 510). It has also been said that the middle class individuals stress "doing something" whereas the upper class stress "being somebody" (508). The belief as to what contributes to success—ability, pull, luck, opportunity also varies with economic status. Corporation executives, for example, in greater frequency mention ability as high in importance; unskilled laborers do not have the same faith in ability. Such differences in opinions could well be related to the aspirations the individual expresses.

We must face the reality that despite our open educational system and the strong emphasis in our culture upon upward social mobility (every person should try to better his position in life), not everyone who is capable of utilizing his ability does so, and not every person of limited ability in a given area falls to his level. Studies show our

American society as stratified and that social and economic conditions operate to keep many of the lowly placed vocationally down, and many of the highly placed up. There is, therefore, considerable frustration and vocational maladjustment on the one hand and manpower waste on the other (772).

Perspectives in Planning

Generalizations Concerning Vocational Planning. *Capable professional assistance can improve vocational selection.* No one should select a vocation for you, but you can secure professional assistance. Vocational planning consists in furnishing the student with a source of *information* and a method of *procedure*. He may investigate vocations that are open or inadvisable for him in view of the facts discovered by valid tests about his capacities and propensities (521, 87, 363).

Basically in planning for a vocation one is seeking a *source of personal growth through a vocation—a growth that will be integrating and realistic in terms of one's aptitudes and interests. This growth ideally will allow satisfaction of deep personal needs and a means of contributing to society.* This usually involves a prolonged trial-and-error process of testing one's aspirations with the realities within oneself and the world in which he lives (772).

Many schools and colleges employ a counselor trained in psychology and related subjects to aid students in obtaining facts about their abilities, interests, and personality traits. Other institutions have set up testing and counseling bureaus. These counselors are in a position to help the student obtain perspective by reviewing the facts about their interests, aptitudes, and personality traits in the light of certain occupational information.

Parents are known to have projected their unrealized vocational desires upon their children quite often. The youth should seek to understand the parent's point of view but remember withal that it is he, himself, who must later meet the demands of the field. A frank, unreserved talk with the parent, pointing out cogent reasons for the vocational selection, and possibly suggesting that an arbitrator be consulted who will consider both the offspring's and the parent's viewpoints, will be effective. This arbitrator may be a professional man, a teacher, a clergyman, or a friend of the family.

Vocational Choice and Planning Requires Realistic Exploration. The student has but to look at his instructors to find variations of attitudes toward a vocation. Some mount the rostrum with enthusiasm and interest in their subject matter. Others, it is obvious, approach their teaching merely as a means of earning a subsistence after obtaining all the college degrees they can. The satisfactions that a field affords to the worker are not intrinsic to that field but are to a great extent resident in the suitability of the individual for the field. There are disagreeable aspects to all positions. One vocational counselor advises students not to expect to find a "perfect niche," or to be naively deluded by the "attractiveness of the remote" or by the "glorification of the unusual." Nor should the student believe that *any* position can be reached by *any* person who merely works hard and lives properly; this is the "fallacy of perfectibility." One must learn to regard the practical, occupational world realistically (850).

PREPARATION DOES NOT BEGIN OR END AT SOME DEFINITE TIME. The prelaw course is just as much a preparation for law practice as the course in contracts or evidence. An advertising writer once confessed that the course most practical in fertilizing ideas in his daily work was one in classical mythology. There are hundreds of lawyers in every large city, but how many of these have had three or four years of chemistry as prelaw students to prepare them to handle effectively cases involving such chemical processes as those used in the manufacture of dyes, foods, or explosives? Just as all preprofessional school work is preparatory for a profession, so are early practical experiences preparatory for later success.

Nowadays, in many universities, *previous records* are used as a basis for admission to certain professional schools. One examination of records of students who intended to enter a school of medicine showed that 50 per cent did not have grades high enough to admit them to any medical school in the United States. Of those who planned to become teachers 75 per cent had grades below 80 in subjects that they intended to teach. Of students who had chosen dentistry, 50 per cent would not have been able, with their undergraduate grades, to gain entrance to dental schools in New York City (736).

MAN CAN ELEVATE CAREERS AS WELL AS CAREERS CAN ELEVATE MAN. Suggest to a college student that the position of a detective is open to him, and he will reply that one does not need a college education for such a position. No, neither does one need a degree to preach or to practice law, but how many great ministers are there without college training, or how many successful lawyers without college backgrounds?   There was a time when the profession that we know today as medicine could be entered without a college degree.   As the number of men who had been formally trained in reputable institutions increased, those who lacked such training found themselves of inferior standing in their profession.   There are pursuits traditionally devoid of college men that may be elevated to the status of a profession by superior preparation.   A few definite examples are companions, governesses, private secretaries of executives, camp directors, fine gift merchants, and managers of employment bureaus.

ONE OF THE OBJECTIONS TO EARLY CHOICE OF A VOCATION IS IMMATURITY AT THE TIME OF SELECTION.   Maturity in respect to an occupational selection, however, is a matter of experience and personality and not of age.   A boy of 15 years who is well *acquainted with his own attributes*, has made an extensive *study of vocations* in general, and has conducted an exhaustive study of a few specific vocations (including *interviews* with successful men and *trial work and readings*) may be more mature from this point of view than a 30-year-old man who has held few positions and has neglected other sources of vocational information.   A follow-up of college men shows that early vocational decisions made in line with family tradition and boyhood hobbies tend to be stable (196).

Other interesting facts are that students who have used vocational planning are also somewhat above those who have not chosen a vocation in: *age*, number in *fraternities*, amount of work *experience*, extent of participation in *athletics*, *intelligence*, extent of *parental education*, and number of *mothers* who pursue the vocation of *homemaking* (736).

Another objection to early choice is the resultant early specialization (714).   Vocationalism has been rightly criticized because it precludes a broad liberal background as a basis for higher education.   However, it is not so easy to specialize in the average college as some claim.   All the first courses are general courses and, furthermore, present college and university regulation tends to prevent such specialization.

The *mature and successful student*, however, who has a strong interest in his courses and current events, and who may be particularly interested in some general area of knowledge, probably *need not be too concerned over the fact that he cannot reach a choice early in his college career*.   He is obtaining for himself a good general education which can be the basis for leadership status in a number of occupations. Studies of college students indicate that there is a goodly percentage of individuals who do not enter fields closely related to their college work, yet they consider their college training valuable (324).

Belated choices may preclude, to be sure, possibilities that could have been realized had the individual made the choice a few years previously. A senior cannot start anew as a freshman and elect the courses that would prepare him for a vocation upon which he has recently decided.

As many authors have insisted, there is too marked a tendency today to prolong the dependence and infantile attitudes of the child. The early search for a vocation under competent guidance is an opportunity for the youth to assume responsibility. Too many young men 18 to 23 years of age are as naive as children concerning the need and means of supporting themselves and planning their lives.

No one will criticize the youth of college age for inability to make conclusive choice. In some respects a tentative choice or a choice of a general vocational area is preferred to an established decision, particularly if the decision was not preceded by a valid selection process. Excellent vocational decisions have been reached after several tentative decisions have been discarded as results of reading, interviews, and try-out work in the field. Some may doubt the wisdom, however, of allowing events to make a decision for one, or to arbitrarily choose a vocational field without deliberation.

Studies on the Effectiveness of Vocational Testing and Guidance. Evidence of the inadequacy of tests used alone as a basis for vocational guidance is shown by a follow-up of over 1000 New York school children who had been given, at the age of 14, intelligence, clerical aptitude, and mechanical adroitness tests (467). These test scores were correlated with such criteria of occupational success as average yearly *earnings*, average *satisfaction* on the job, and the average occupational *level* of the job. These measures of success are not absolute, and they depend upon many variable factors in the complex nexus of worker and position. They represent one approach, however, to a study of success on the job. The correlations obtained between tests and success are quite low for mechanical work (0.00 to 0.25).* They are slightly higher for clerical work but still too

---

* One common method of computing relationships is the *correlation* technique. A "correlation coefficient" may vary from $+1.00$ to -1.00; the *positive* correla-

low to allow much prediction on the basis of them (0.05 to 0.26) (799).

In contrast to the low correlations between tests and success there is a substantial relationship (0.60) between scores on the clerical test and the future possession of abilities required for clerical work. Also, the various tests, together with certain items of school record, including the age until which the family plans to keep the child in school, correlate highly (0.90) with the grade the individual will reach at a later age. This correlation gives us a clue to the reason for low relationships between ability tests and vocational success, namely, that in the work-a-day world success is not measured in terms of ability alone (799).

Tests, then, have predictive value for certain human behavior (528). For the higher brackets of vocation considerable education is necessary. Therefore tests are valuable in a basic form of vocational guidance, namely, the guidance of education.

It is difficult to test the effectiveness of a well-conducted vocational guidance *program*, but several attempts have been made in this direction (417). Most of the studies show the student appreciates counseling services and seems to be helped by them toward greater realism (811, 666, 414). As one writer in the field has maintained, it is necessary to compare students who have availed themselves of vocational information and guidance and ones of similar attributes who have not, and note differences. Then, a number of extraneous factors must be considered, such as economic conditions, social influence, illness, and accidents, which might alter individual cases (772).

It is equally difficult to evaluate the relative success of *individuals* who have been given guidance, as compared to those who have not. Take, for example, the problem of evaluating success. Success may be divided into two phases: efficiency on the job, and self-satisfaction. What measure should be used for efficiency on the job—earnings, quality of work, quantity of output, length of time in the occupation, length of time on the job, promotions? Again, all these are influenced by factors not involved in the individual's performance, such as economic cycles and the complexities of the specific job situation.

---

tions indicate direct relationship; the *negative* inverse relationship; a 0.00 correlation indicates no relationship between the two measures. If two traits have a substantial negative relationship, a high score in one indicates a tendency for individuals to obtain a low score in the other. Correlations between 0.80 and 0.99 show substantial relationship.

Writers have pointed out weaknesses in all these criteria (851). Despite the complexity of the problem and the errors that exist in the present methods of evaluating success, studies have been performed and in the main have produced evidence that guidance, counseling, and judgments based on tests are superior to no assistance (405, 833, 652, 365).

Investigators in England divided students into two groups. One group was studied rather thoroughly by tests, interviews, and analysis of records. Vocational advice based on these data was given. The students in the other group were not subject to the complete guidance program. After two years, elaborate follow-ups were arranged. From these, information was gathered about whether the individual remained in the occupation recommended, the extent to which the employer was satisfied with him, and the degree to which he felt that the job was suitable. These studies seem to show that detailed vocational guidance is quite worth while in terms of the criteria mentioned (405, 365).

Avocations

In the present complexity of civilized life, many individuals must make a compromise in their choice of a vocation and thereby leave some strong motives unsatisfied and some aptitudes unutilized. Furthermore, in spite of careful planning one may be *forced into a vocation* that does not satisfy him. It is in such cases that a man may make advantageous use of avocations or hobbies. Hobbies can well satisfy the personal needs which are not met adequately in a particular vocational situation. Avocations are important because available leisure time is being increased with the specialization and mechanization of industry. Stereotypy is encroaching upon even the more complex fields, reducing the opportunities for creative expression. Avocations, then, become the avenue for satisfaction of urges to create (771).

List of Avocations. The members of a class in applied psychology, in listing their avocations and those of acquaintances, named hundreds. A few are listed in groups below. In each group are included some mentioned quite frequently and others that are rather rare. Beside the groups mentioned below the avocation of social and charitable work was mentioned. Sports are not included below because they have been discussed already.

Collecting—stamps, books, insects, objects for home.
Pets—dogs, fish, monkey.
Indoor games—cards, billiards, chess.
Appreciative activities—music, art, nature study.
Social groups—discussion, dancing, study.
Creative skills—dramatics, photography, cookery.
Miscellaneous—aviation, metal work, travel, lecturing.

Selection of Avocations. Several questions at once arise: Should one deliberately choose avocations? Should they spontaneously grow out of one's life interests? Should they be the activities one enjoys when not working?

In the main, avocations grow out of the *spontaneous activities* of the individual, but there are many bored individuals who have no personal resources to call upon to supply amusement. Americans are criticized because of their stereotyped, passive methods of finding diversion. It is uncommon to find a man with a well-developed creative hobby for which he is noted locally and from which he receives his fullest happiness. Occasionally one will be found who claims that he has the best amateur set of marionettes in the state; another, a banker, the owner of the oldest and most complete library on banking in the city; another, the best amateur pastry baker in the community. There are persons who have several clever hobbies that consume their energies and broaden their personalities. Hobbies are being used by at least one adult-education group as a method of stimulating persons to acquire knowledge systematically. Vocational interest blanks described on page 239 may be used to explore one's avocational interests (771).

If an individual has not found the joy which it is claimed may be gained through the pursuit of a certain hobby, the selection for trial of one or more absorbing activity like those mentioned above may not be out of order. The basis of selection of an avocation is practically identical with that of a vocation. Both call for an analysis of ourselves and the activities in which we are interested, and, finally, a selection growing from the comparison of these two analyses. Other lists of students and adult hobbies might be consulted (576).

Personality Evaluation

The initial step in vocational choice and planning is to acquire knowledge of oneself. In order to choose wisely one must be aware of one's interests, attitudes, motives, and preferences, as well as abilities and aptitudes. Put in simple language, a man must answer the questions: "What can I do well?" and "What do I like to do?" Once the individual has some knowledge of himself in this respect he is better able to review a list of vocations and study some of them intensively.

Exploration in Self-Understanding. We have mentioned previously the pre-interview blank presented in the accompanying volume: *Teaching Personal Adjustment: An Instructor's Manual.* This is a device that you may use to assist you in collecting information about your personality. This blank can aid you in understanding yourself for the selection of your vocation.

Before this blank is evaluated, certain *cautions* are in order. The self-understanding method has been criticized with justification by some vocational counselors on the grounds that *the average student is incapable of evaluating objectively his own abilities* and, sometimes, his own interests. When students' ratings were compared with tests, wide discrepancies were noted. The students' ratings, however, improved after they had completed the test (28). There is always the danger that the student may overemphasize certain aspects of his personality in order to justify a strong false belief. We urge that this method be regarded as *merely supplementary* to the clinical methods used by a qualified counselor as outlined. When a vocational counselor and objective tests are not available, this method may be substituted, but allowances must be made for its limitations. Some of the limitations of this method may be overcome by having a critical, qualified person check the student's evaluations of his abilities and interests, as was done in the case study on page 257. The self-understanding method, when critically used, is far superior to drifting into a vocation.

The Clinical Method. Two cases studied by a counselor with the use of the clinical method follow. The profile charts present *profiles* that show the students' ranks on *ability* or *achievement* tests and *interest* tests. The profile chart should be consulted again after

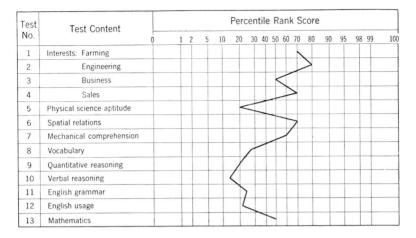

Figure 4. Profile of interests and aptitudes for Warren F.

the material on aptitudes and interests has been read. Thus the student will be enabled to see how test results are interpreted for a specific individual.

Warren F., age 22, is the son of a farmer with an eighth-grade education.* When Warren was young he spent considerable time "tinkering"— repairing machinery, farm equipment, and electrical appliances. He did not read a great deal except for an occasional *Popular Mechanics* or other mechanical magazine. He engaged in some sports but was not otherwise active in high school affairs—work on the farm consumed too much time.

In high school he liked plane geometry and made a 94 in this course. His grades in agriculture were high; English, physics, and social studies were low average. His graduating class was small in high school, and his overall average placed him close to the middle of his class.

After he finished high school he entered the College of Agriculture to study Agricultural Engineering. His grades were below average, and it seems probable that he would have failed one or two courses if he had not been excused to enter military service. He joined the Marines and was selected for training as an aviation electrician. He completed several courses along this line and served about three years in this type of work, achieving the rating of sergeant before his discharge.

On his return to college he enrolled in electrical engineering. After two semesters in the College of Engineering, during which time he failed several courses, he requested vocational counseling, during which the foregoing

---

* The cases of Warren F. and Marcella M. were contributed by Dr. George B. Strother from the Counseling Bureau at the University of Missouri.

facts were brought out. It was also found that he had been working about 40 hours weekly since re-entering school, leaving himself very little time or inclination for studies. He stated that he had always enjoyed courses that were practical and that dealt with techniques and materials but disliked theoretical courses and those that involved extensive reading. His work environment, home situation, and social contacts were adequate except for the unbalanced schedule produced by his heavy work load.

It was found that his English grammar and usage were substantially below average for college freshmen. In abstract verbal and quantitative reasoning he was low, and in a test of physical science aptitude he was in the lowest fifth of freshmen Engineering students. His vocabulary was also below average for college freshmen. In view of the fact that only about half of the students who start an engineering course actually receive their degrees, the probability of his success in this curriculum seemed small. However, he ranked high in tests of dexterity, mechanical comprehension, and space relations, and had an excellent background of mechanical interest and experience.

The possibilities of taking noncollegiate courses or on-the-job training were discussed, as well as the possibility of re-entering the College of Agriculture or remaining in Engineering. Significant interests in farming, engineering, and sales were considered. Warren mentioned the fact that a man in his home town had offered him work in the installation of refrigeration locker plants with an opportunity for advancement in installation work, sales, and management. He considered the possibility of taking a short noncollegiate course in refrigeration and small business management preparatory to accepting this offer. The counselor suggested that he discuss these possibilities and opportunities with his prospective employer.

After a trip home, during which he discussed these programs, he decided to take a nine-month course of training which would combine refrigeration and some small business management. On completion of this course he planned to accept employment with the refrigerator locker contractor.

Marcella M., age 29, requested counseling because she wished confirmation of her tentative plans to obtain a degree and teacher's certificate in the College of Education. She had completed the eighth grade in a rural school and seven weeks of high school when her father died. She left school after his death and for three years managed the family's farm. At the end of this time she took a five-month course in practical nursing and worked in this occupation for three years. She then joined the WAC and served for 21 months as practical nurse in an Army hospital.

After her discharge from the Army she returned to practical nursing for eight months before deciding to apply for admission to the university. She took special qualifying examinations for college entrance and ranked in the upper 10 per cent of entering college students in all areas tested: English usage, natural science, social science, mathematics, and English literature. In order to go to school, she supplemented her small income by working as relief nurse in a small girls' college.

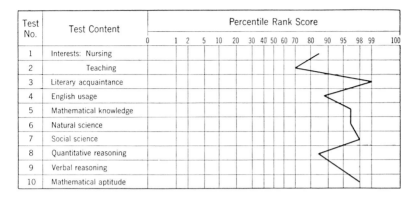

Test No.	Test Content	Percentile Rank Score

Figure 5. Profile of interests and aptitudes for Marcella M.

In addition to the high school level tests of general educational development, she took similar tests designed to measure college achievement, and
ranked in the upper brackets on these. A psychological examination to
determine general college aptitude placed her very high for college freshmen in linguistic ability and in quantitative reasoning. A test of mathe-
matical ability showed exceptional potentialities in this area, too.

Marcella has significant interests in nursing and in education but prefers
teaching. Since she has had considerable experience in nursing and is well
informed on occupational possibilities in both fields it seems that her
decision is sound.

Despite her lack of formal education, the vocational counselor agreed
that her plans were suitable. After two semesters in college, her grades
have been mostly excellent and she has received some superior marks.

General Intelligence in Vocations. We are now ready to turn
to some facts that develop from the laboratory, statistical, and clinical
study of intelligence, special aptitudes, interests, and social traits,
which will cast light on the relation of these traits to vocations.

GENERAL INTELLIGENCE. *Importance of intelligence in vocational
preparation.* There are vocations that will never be achieved by some
because their intellectual capacity makes improbable the attainment
of the education which is a prerequisite for that understanding.

Some state universities administer college aptitude tests while the
student is a senior in high school. The student's score on the test and
his high school rank are sometimes converted into a single *college
aptitude rating.* This is done because the scholastic rank of the
student in high school is one of the best indexes of college success.

The score obtained is a *percentile score*, that is, it indicates what percentage of all the students tested rate lower than the individual in question. For example, if the student's *college aptitude rating* is 56, 56 per cent of the students of the group made scores below his. On the basis of previous records and these scores, individuals below the 25 percentile have been advised at one period by the counselors in a college not to enter. Data show that 96.6 per cent of the freshmen with percentiles from 96 to 100 entering in a five-year period, were successful in college, whereas only 2.3 per cent of those with percentiles from 16 to 20 were successful. Studies in other institutions produce similar results (251). The judicious use of such bases for accepting or rejecting students prevents later unhappiness and maladjustment.

INTELLIGENCE REQUIREMENTS AT VARIOUS COLLEGES. All universities and colleges today do not offer students the same keen competition. The correlation between test scores and scholarship varies among universities (65). This fact is shown by authors of widely used college intelligence tests who have compiled the scores of students in the various colleges using the tests. Of some 300 colleges that used the same edition of the ACE Psychological Examination in one year, the lowest college had a median IQ of 94 (half of the freshmen obtained scores below this), and the highest ranking college had a median IQ of 122 (770). Students who are experiencing difficulty in meeting the requirements of their university should be aware of this wide *variation in the competition* afforded at different universities and colleges. Some colleges emphasize a certain type of work and select their students from a homogeneous background of high cultural status. Students who do not fit into this pattern probably should not subject themselves to competition which may result in unnecessary failure.

Arthur H. was from a small town in a Midwestern state. He had graduated first in his high school class and had migrated across several states to a university that selected its students very carefully and offered them exceedingly keen competition. The adjustments Arthur had to make were beyond any he had anticipated. Even though he was taken into a fraternity and put in contact with athletic activities in which he previously had excelled, the large school was so foreign to his high school experience, the situation required so much more initiative and so many new choices, that he was frequently in a quandary. He found the values of the men with whom he lived very different from those of his parents. Financial problems ensued, grades went down, and finally in desperation Arthur abandoned the idea of obtaining a college degree and returned home. Had Arthur gone to a state university or smaller college in his own vicinity, he might have been quite successful in competing with the same type of student he had encountered in high school and in having contact with former classmates.

INTELLIGENCE REQUIREMENTS FOR VARIOUS COURSES. The average intelligence scores patterns differ in the various divisions of the same university. For example, the scores on tests for verbal reasoning taken by students while in high school and now seeking degrees in the following fields are: science 81, business administration 72, miscellaneous including agriculture 64. For mechanical reasoning they are respectively 68, 60, 72 (63). These scores vary with institutions and decade. They are presented here merely to show that rather wide variations exist. Scores like these, or some estimate of the ability required by a specific college or professional school, can usually be obtained on the campus.

All these facts indicate that today a student should be able to know rather early the probability that he has the *ability to enter a field* and a specific school. He may first take appropriate tests administered by the school he wishes to enter, keeping in mind that universities and departments differ in the nature of student they select.

VOCATIONS IN WHICH INTELLIGENCE IS OR IS NOT OF MAJOR IMPORTANCE. Except for determining the minimum intellectual level for efficient work, the intelligence test is not of great value in predicting *who will do well and who will do poorly* in certain vocations, as shown on page 232. In general, the intelligence test is not diagnostic of the grade of performance in jobs of a mechanical type, such as metal worker. In those occupations, on the other hand, in which proficiency in dealing with symbols and ideas is stressed, rather than skill in dealing with things and people, intelligence test scores are correlated to achievement in the occupation. This is true of executives of certain types, technical salesmen, accountants, life insurance salesmen, secretaries, stenographers, and bookkeepers, to mention some vocations in which tests have been administered. Emphasis should be laid on the fact that there is no relation between business leadership and intelligence keeping in mind that a minimum level of intelligence is required for adequate functioning. Of a large group of businessmen tested, several of those who made lowest scores were presidents of their companies (367).

INTELLIGENCE TESTS MAY NOT REFLECT TRUE POTENTIALITY. In general, intelligence test scores indicate quite well the kind of academic work the student will do. However, it is assumed that the individual taking a certain test has lived under conditions that have favored his acquisition of the skills and materials tapped by the test. Favorable environmental conditions, particularly of a cultural nature, stimulate intelligence test performance, and unfavorable environments are associated with lower performance (16). There are some students who have never had favorable motivation or surroundings, and this is reflected somewhat in their scores. Studies show that scores are related to parental occupation. The higher scores in the professional group probably reflect superior opportunities (321). Scores improve as the student is exposed to the college environment (316).

INTELLIGENCE IS MERELY ONE ASPECT OF PERSONALITY. The results just discussed, particularly those which show that business leadership and intelligence are not correlated, illustrate the *limitations* of high intellectual ability unaccompanied by other factors. Follow-up studies of gifted children show that, even among this group, success is determined largely by factors such as social adjustment, emotional stability, and motivation (792). There are few occupations that demand the same ability as that required in more advanced school work and college, for in the classroom one deals with symbols and abstract matters. It is not unusual to have a student tell about a roommate who left school because of unsatisfactory work, and who has since achieved success in selling or in other work that calls for skill in dealing with people. Besides general intelligence there are specific aptitudes and general reaction tendencies that are important.

Special Aptitudes. Tests of special capacities. The last decade has witnessed extensive experimental work on the preparation of aptitude and personality tests. Some psychologists are quite enthusiastic about the possibility of using a *battery* of these tests for ascertaining vocational aptitude. Some of these tests have been built around a given profession or vocation, assembled in a single booklet, and labeled a medical, nursing, or law aptitude test. Other tests have been devised that are more *general* in nature and that purport to determine the individual's status in the *primary mental abilities*. Preparation for the various vocations and professions requires different degrees of these abilities. Functions in these vocational patterns can be discovered. The individual's profile, expressing his pattern of abilities, can then be compared with the requirements of the vocation or the courses leading to it (69). Seven of these primary abilities are labeled: N–numerical; V–verbal; W–word fluency; S–space or visualizing; P–perceptual speed; M–memorizing; and R–reasoning.

A test battery is available that gives scores on some of these abilities as well as such nonverbal factors as eye-hand coordination, motor speed, and finger and manual dexterity (195). Another well-used battery includes in addition to several primary abilities aptitudes labeled "clerical," "spelling," and "sentences" (63).

Another method of measuring aptitudes is to select from the whole array of specific aptitude tests those which seem appropriate for the vocations or curricula for which a given individual or group of individuals seems to have an inclination (112). This will be discussed later under "Special Academic Aptitude."

In most colleges now there are available to students testing and counseling services. A battery consisting of several kinds of aptitude and achievement tests together with interest and personality tests is usually given.*

Progress is being made on the prediction of the potentialities for success in other professional schools. Tests have been devised, for example, that are intended to predict success in law school (66). High prelaw grades, however, are found in some studies to be better indications of the students who have greater chances of succeeding in law school than the test (838). Investigations similar to the above are conducted on students in engineering and technology, nursing, pharmacy, dentistry, and teaching (148, 677, 551, 650, 461, 770).

MECHANICAL APTITUDE. Mechanical aptitude, to a certain degree, is independent of general intelligence. It seems to have these components: (a) manual dexterity; (b) mechanical comprehension; (c) spatial perception (62). A youth may be aware of such ability because of his skill in performing odd jobs around the house or shop, or he may learn of it through a mechanical aptitude test. A student who has high mechanical aptitude and intelligence for college work may be particularly fitted for some engineering fields or for an executive position in mechanical enterprises. The prospective surgeon, dentist, artist, architect, and sculptor should also exhibit manual dexterity.

---

* The Psychological Corporation, 304 East 45th St., New York 17, N. Y. has a number of research associates in various parts of the country offering tests and services at reasonable fees.

MUSICAL APTITUDE. A number of specific functions are included in this category, among which are singing; violin, piano, and organ aptitude; and ability to compose. At the college level many students who have ability along this line have already discovered it. If not, the counselor can administer laboratory tests of musical aptitude, or the student may be able to secure opinions regarding his potentialities from several reputable musicians who would have no reasons for over-estimating them.

Musical gifts reveal themselves early in childhood and are to a large extent independent of intelligence. It is doubtful, however, whether a person who is gifted in musical ability and low in general intelligence would give promise of becoming a superior musician, particularly in the creative aspect. One with slight or moderate musical aptitude and a flair for business has open to him related administrative and commercial positions, such as musician's manager, dealer in music, or manager of a symphony.

ART APTITUDE. Much that has been said of the general nature of musical capacity holds also for art. There are many types of art careers. They all require *craftsman skill*. For the creative types, in-telligence, aesthetic judgment, and creative imagination are indispensa-ble (530). The method of ascertaining ability here is the same as that suggested above for musical ability. Art aptitude is of importance in interior decorating, architecture, photography, landscape work, and clothing design.

SPECIAL ACADEMIC APTITUDE AND ACHIEVEMENT. With the exception of general intelligence, there is probably no aspect of mental func-tions that can be more accurately tested than academic ability. Edu-cational achievement tests in the various school subjects may be used to investigate aptitude in these realms (112). Students may also learn of these aptitudes from consistent good grades in certain subjects (680). Students who excel in English, spelling, reading, and foreign languages can consider the journalistic and linguistic fields, library work, the ministry, advertising, copywriting, and such; those who are proficient in mathematics might consider engineering, accounting, statistics, actuarial work, banking, etc.; those who are particularly apt in chem-istry or physics might turn to the engineering profession; and those who show ability in botany, zoology, and psychology might think of medicine, various laboratory techniques, nursing, veterinary sur-gery, medical social work, and related careers.

Journalism students who have been successful were found to have high achievement scores in linguistic and verbal silent reading, English, literary acquaintance, and contemporary affairs tests (767). Even mechanical and nonverbal tests have been promising in the prediction of success in college (333). In one study such tests were given to students in a college of dentistry and one of fine arts with some promise of value (796).

VOCATIONAL APTITUDE AND ACHIEVEMENT. Just as there is for school subjects an aptitude that is the result of general and specific native ability plus motivation, effective habits, and possibly some social factors, so are there aptitudes for certain vocations. The various stars, champions, and masters in different fields are the results of such patterns of ability. Some vocational aptitudes are acquired by early interest and activity in the field. It happens that occupational experiences, in addition to giving superior competency in a field, sharpen perception so that the individual is more alert in school and college to the applications of the subject pursued to his vocational province.

AVOCATIONAL APTITUDES. We hear now and then of clever or fortunate persons capitalizing on some ability that had its origin as an avocation or hobby, or an activity engaged in for self-amusement. These individuals usually possess native capacities and interests, which, combined with hard work, gain for them amateur status and later a professional position. The athlete who has merited considerable publicity while participating in collegiate sports finds his past of value, directly or indirectly, when he gets into the work-a-day world. The antique collector, the rare-book connoisseur, the poultry fancier, or the apiarist sometimes finds his avocation profitable and continues to devote more energy to it until it becomes his vocation. It has been found that college men who choose vocations because they are related to hobbies show a high degree of vocational stability (196).

It may be recalled that Charles Lamb was a petty clerk in London, Robert Burns a Scottish farmer, and Mark Twain a journeyman printer and river pilot. Writing, for each of these men, was originally an avocation. We are told that Welch, the grape juice manufacturer, was a dentist who made grape juice for the communion ceremonies of his church; Pemberton, who concocted Coca-Cola, was a physician; H. J. Heinz, famous for his 57 varieties of food, originally grew and peddled horseradish; Clicquot Club ginger ale was the discovery of a farmer who owned a spring famous for its good water (266). It has been suggested that a more fruitful method of learning the vocational inclinations of an individual is to study his avocations. Present-day interest blanks afford a means of investigating this aspect of the individual's preferences. A brief list of avocations is given on page 225. Avocational capacities may have a native basis, but certainly the experiential aspect is very important.

APTITUDES IN SOCIAL PROFICIENCY. Leadership, salesmanship, and public speaking are examples of this type of aptitude. Some personality tests indicate this ability (308), but the individual who is adept in handling his fellows is often made aware of it without the aid of a test. Certainly this aptitude is valuable in "contact" positions. It is a capacity which is believed to be largely acquired. Some of the personality traits to be mentioned later tap social proficiency.

Motivation. Autobiographies show that it is difficult to surpass in achievement a lad who from childhood has daydreamed about some one vocation, has read in terms of it, thought in terms of it, and lived toward its fulfillment. Such a person, granted the ability to meet his ambition, is headed toward success. Evidence has previously been presented, in Chapter 2, that persistence affects success in school. There are always rare individuals who succeed because they have a strong desire to achieve when most objective indexes point to failure.

Motivation without capacity, on the other hand, is an unfortunate condition; it breeds maladjustment. The sooner the individual realizes that his ambitions are directed into an area for which he has no bent, the sooner can he redecide in terms of a field for which he can prepare himself.

One may be guided by less specific motives, such as the urge to succeed, to do one's work well, or to gain recognition. Some authors claim that *strong motivation is largely a product of early problems*, deficiencies, and training or circumstances which have given the individual *the habit of striving for goals*. The youth whose father supplies him with all that he desires without allowing him to strive for it, and makes of him an inert, apathetic creature, is an example of the opposite.

CONSOLIDATING MOTIVATION. Commonly a student will ask how to increase motivation in connection with a vocation. We have discussed this in Chapter 5 under this heading. Before attempting to arouse motivation, it might be well for one to discover his present motives and work in terms of them. However, alert college students have found that the following increase interest and verve in a vocation: detailed knowledge of a field, knowledge of one's own possibilities in it, present success in preparing for it, acquaintance with successful men in the vocation, realization of the social value of the work, realization of the social position given to those affiliated with it, and the creative value of the vocation.

A man who is entering the ministry, the Army or Navy, the stock and bond market, the diplomatic service, government service, teaching, or other professional provinces will find it profitable to compare his attitudes on specific current issues with those commonly accepted by the professional groups, to learn if he is motivated like those who are successful in the field he plans to enter. There is an inventory which helps the student to explore his values. Results show that students differ markedly in the organization of their values. Values may be primarily social, Philistine or materialistic, theoretical, or religious (474).

It may be valuable for the student to write out his "philosophy of life" before making a final choice of a vocation and weigh his choice in terms of it. A student should ask himself what value he attaches to such goals as wealth, prestige, self-development, and service. The opportunities within a field for the satisfaction of a prime motive determine in a large part the happiness to be derived from one's professional life.

Interest. Intense interest is an aspect of motivation. Two methods may be used to ascertain the interests of an individual: the *longitudinal* or biographical method, and the *cross-sectional* or contemporary method. The individual, in using the first method, with the aid of a list of interests like those mentioned in the vocational interest blank below, recollects the interests that have dominated his behavior throughout his life. The use of this approach to one's interests, which involves recalling from one's personal development the various interests that have been dominant at different times, is shown in the case of Alfred L. on page 214, and also to some extent in the case of Barbara A. on page 257.

VOCATIONAL INTEREST BLANK. One blank, the Strong Vocational Interest Blank, contains 420 items and is an example of a cross-sectional approach to interests. It attempts to learn the individual's personal interests and to compare them with the interests of executives and professional men in various fields (764). Correction keys for these blanks have been devised for the following 38 vocations for men and 24 for women.

FOR MEN

Group I

Artist
Psychologist
Architect
Physician
Dentist

Group II

Mathematician
Engineer
Chemist

Group III

Production manager

Group IV

Aviator
Farmer
Carpenter
Printer
Mathematics—physical science
   teacher
Policeman
Forest service man

Group V

Y.M.C.A. physical director
Personnel manager
Public administrator
Y.M.C.A. secretary

Social science high school teacher
City school superintendent
Minister

Group VI

Musician

Group VII

Certified public accountant

Group VIII

Accountant
Office worker
Purchasing agent
Banker

Group IX

Sales manager
Real estate salesman
Life insurance salesman

Group X

Advertising man
Lawyer
Author-journalist

Group XI

President, manufacturing concern
Mortician
Osteopath

The keys for women in addition to many of the above also include:

Buyer
Dietitian
Home economics teacher
Housewife
Laboratory technician
Librarian

Nurse
Occupational therapist
Office worker
High school teacher of
   various subjects

It will be noted that the vocations for men are listed in groups that
are associated because of common interest patterns.

Samples of each type of interest investigated by the blank are:

Occupations. Actor, advertiser, architect, etc.

Amusements. Golf, fishing, boxing, poker, picnics, smokers, conventions, auctions, fortune tellers, *Life,* art galleries, musical comedy, pet canaries, poetry, *Atlantic Monthly,* cowboy movies, etc.

School subjects. Algebra, agriculture, arithmetic, etc.

Activities. Repairing a clock, arguments, handling horses, raising flowers and vegetables, interviewing clients, making a speech, calling friends by nicknames, taking responsibility, acting as yell-leader, writing reports, bargaining (swapping), being left to oneself, regular hours for work, continually changing activities, saving money, living in the city, etc.

Order of preference of activities. Develop the theory of operation of a new machine, operate the new machine, discover an improvement in the design of the machine, etc.

Comparison of interest between two items. Street-car motorman, street-car conductor; head waiter, light-house tender; physical activity, mental activity.

Rating of present abilities and characteristics. Usually start activities of my group, usually drive myself steadily (do not work by fits), win friends easily, usually get other people to do what I want done, usually liven up the group on a dull day, etc.

Another interest blank frequently used is entitled the Kuder Preference Record. Scores are obtained in the following nine general interest areas: 1, mechanical; 2, computational; 3, scientific; 4, persuasive; 5, artistic; 6, literary; 7, musical; 8, social service; 9, clerical. There is available a list of occupations which the student may consider in view of high ratings in any of these areas (430).

One worker in the field has given the Strong test to students in professional schools and to successful professional men. A few cases that illustrate how the test differentiated these individuals on the basis of interests follow (495).

A successful engineer. This man's grade was among the highest 20 per cent of each of the following vocational groups: engineer, chemist, physicist, scientific farmer, mathematician, architect, and doctor; whereas it was among the lowest 20 per cent of the professional group of teachers.

Pastor of a church. This man's grade was among the highest 20 per cent of each of the following vocational groups: teacher, Y.M.C.A. physical director, minister, lawyer, journalist, and life insurance salesman; whereas he was among the lowest 20 per cent of the following professional groups: engineer, chemist, physicist, scientific farmer, architect, and doctor.

A student who left an engineering school to enter law school. This man's grade was among the highest 20 per cent of each of the following vocational groups: certified public accountant, journalist, life insurance salesman; whereas it was among the lowest 20 per cent of the following professional groups: engineer, chemist, physicist, scientific farmer, mathematician, architect, doctor, psychologist, artist, teacher, and minister.

A student who is planning to enter the business side of engineering. This man's grade was among the highest 20 per cent of each of the following vocational groups: teacher, certified public accountant, personnel director, Y.M.C.A. physical director; whereas it was among the lowest 20 per cent of the following vocational groups: architect and artist.

There have been several statistical analyses of the factors present in vocational interests (293). One study reveals that four of them make up eighteen vocational interest patterns surveyed by this blank. If these factors were classified they would fall under such terms as *literary*, *social service*, *business*, and *scientific*. A common factor (scientific), for example, was present in the vocations of chemistry, engineering, psychology, architecture, agriculture, and medicine. A common factor (social service) was also found in the vocations: ministry, teaching, Y.M.C.A. work, and personnel work. Life insurance salesmen may be used as an example of the business group, and journalists of the literary (197). This knowledge is valuable in that it allows the individual to determine first his general type of interest and, later, to ascertain more specific vocational interests.

An individual will find value in taking this test, if it is available to him, and comparing it with a longitudinal study of his interests as made by himself (169).

THE STABILITY OF INTEREST. A review of the evidence on the question of the permanence of interests leads writers in this field to generalize: whereas changes of interest occur, changes from one broad category to another are somewhat rare even in young people, and in adulthood interests are rather well established. Surprising agreement is found between scores in college and in occupational situation twenty years later (765). At the college age interests, on the whole, have become fixed enough so that interest questionnaires have considerable prognostic significance (844, 808, 453).

INTERESTS AND ABILITY. The question is often asked, "Is the interested student the good student?" The teacher of some experience knows that such a relationship does not always exist, although it is frequently found. It has been suggested that the relationship between interests and ability is like that of stability of interest in that the two variables become more closely related to each other with increased age. At birth, neither interest nor ability has developed. Later, as success produces interest in an activity, or failure avoidance of it, the youth develops an interest for the field in which he is adept and shows greater achievement in that for which he has interest. There is some evidence that vocational interest is related to grades in some fields (201). Both interest and aptitude need to be considered separately so that the presence of one will not mask the absence of the other (297).

Social and Temperamental Traits. Previous mention has been made of individual social and emotional traits as crucial factors in determining one's vocational choice (743). Attempts have been made in recent years to discover the primary personality traits or factors found in persons of our culture (92–94). Inventories have been constructed to appraise individuals in relation to these traits. In addition, numerous individuals in given vocations have been studied to discern whether there are personality and temperamental patterns characteristic of that vocation. We shall discuss more fully sample studies of both traits and patterns that have significance for adjustment in vocations.

Questionnaire type inventories revealing traits mentioned in individuals may be misused. They are most valuable when they are applied

Tests are available today that can produce a profile chart . . .

Rollie McKenna

individually, accompanied by professional opinion (210, 583). The use of this test enables the counselor or psychiatrist to assist the individual in making an adjustment so that he will be at his most efficient in a vocation.

Basic Personality Traits. Today the man on the street uses the terms *extrovert* and *introvert* somewhat freely to distinguish the outgoing, gregarious, carefree person from the emotionally sensitive, shy, self-analytic individual. This reflects the early work of psychologists and the publicity it received. Early studies showed a relationship between introversion scores and interests in journalism, medicine, and literary work; and between extroversion scores and an interest in engineering, law, psychology, and architecture. On tests office workers, research engineers, accountants, and older teachers tended to be introverted whereas salesgirls, policemen, foremen, nurses in training, and executives extroverted (292). Likewise, the traits *ascendancy* and *submission*, which refer to dominance, confidence, social aggressiveness on the one hand and social passiveness and lack of sureness on the other hand, were studied and related to "limelight" vocations versus vocations requiring less responsibility. Questionnaires on neurotic symptoms constitute a third early attempt at personality testing. From this beginning twenty years of research devoted to an exploration of the primary factors underlying the structure of personality has resulted in twelve or fourteen factors which have been named and described. The list that follows is an example of the products of such research (295, 296). Tests are available today that can produce a profile chart indicating the test scores on such traits.

One such inventory has been successfully used to indicate emotional instability and its various expressions in an individual's behavior (319). Some research has been done on relationship of factors such as surgency and emotional stability in an individual and his potentialities in leadership situations (138).

You may find it interesting to read over the list of traits that follows and *check* (√) *those adjectives that definitely describe you in your opinion and place an* (x) *beside those that tend definitely not to describe you.**

| I. Cyclothymia | Schizothymia |
| Emotionally expressive, frank, placid | Reserved, close-mouthed, anxious |

* Modified from R. B. Cattell, *Description and Measurement of Personality*, Yonkers, N. Y., World, 1946.

II. General mental capacity
    Intelligent, smart, assertive

Mental defect
    Unintelligent, dull, submissive

III. Emotionally stable
    Free of neurotic symptoms,
    realistic about life

Neurotic emotionality
    Variety of neurotic symptoms,
    evasive, immature

IV. Dominance
    Self-assertive, confident,
    aggressive

Submissiveness
    Submissive, unsure, complaisant

V. Surgency
    Cheerful, joyous, humor-
    ous, witty

Desurgency
    Depressed, pessimistic, dull,
    phlegmatic

VI. Positive character
    Persevering, attentive to
    people

Dependent character
    Fickle, neglectful of social chores

VII. Adventurous cyclothymia
    Likes meeting people,
    strong interest in opposite
    sex

Withdrawn schizothymia
    Shy, little interest in opposite sex

VIII. Sensitive, infantile emotional-
    ity
    Dependent, immature, gre-
    garious, attention-seeking

Mature, tough poise
    Independent-minded, self-suffi-
    cient

IX. Socialized, cultured mind
    Polished, poised, composed,
    introspective, sensitive

Boorishness
    Awkward, socially clumsy, crude

X. Trustful cyclothymia
    Trustful, understanding

Paranoia
    Suspicious, jealous

XI. Bohemian unconcernedness
    Unconventional, eccentric,
    fitful, hysterical upsets

Conventional practicality
    Conventional, unemotional

XII. Sophistication
    Logical mind, cool, aloof

Simplicity
    Sentimental mind, attentive to
    people

Personality Patterns. Do certain vocations attract persons with describable needs and personality patterns? Research on this question is relatively new, but persons in certain vocations have been well studied, and some tentative conclusions are available. Some vocations it seems are such that the people working in them appear to be quite homogenous in personality. Scientists who study vertebrate paleontology, for example, tend to be low in creative imagination, like to work with concrete facts, show a lack of ability in dealing smoothly with other people. There is a suggestion possibly that their scientific work is an escape from people and intangible tasks (652). A study of artists show them to be high in intelligence, outgoing in seeking emotional satisfaction, more anxious than most people, and sufficiently different from the general population to merit the description "artistic personality" (653).

Biologists and physicists, like the artists, are not outstandingly masculine in attitudes and interests, but better adjusted to life. This better adjustment is attributed to their greater rational control and the more stable and supportive environment or social climate in which they live. Biological scientists and physicists tend to see things as a whole, but do not overlook details; they are objective in their thinking, and their relations with other people are smooth but not warm. They possess considerable general anxiety but do not tend to express it in aggression; stubbornness is more often their response. They tend to be neither dominant nor submissive (655, 654).

In looking at the lives of people who become successful as scientists, we see individuals placed on their own resources early in life who have developed deep interests, learned to think about things in a question-and-answer manner, and to work hard to find the answers. They learned early in life to satisfy their curiosity by their own efforts. Despite similarities among scientists we must cautiously say that the scientists described as a group merely *approach* a clear-cut homogeneous personality (656).

Studies of the American business executive show him to be an individual with *high motivation for achievement*, with many successive goals in sight. He *accepts authority* in his relationship with his superior with whom he strongly identifies. He is not frustrated by the presence of authority; he is *emancipated* from parental ties and is "on his own" (331). He has *learned to make decisions* about alternatives rather than have them continue as conflicts. He can *clarify his goals* and has acquired techniques to reach them.

With further research we may discover the extent to which other vocational groups or subgroups within a vocation have clear-cut personalities. As you come to know more persons in a vocation of your choice you may advance hypotheses of your own about the personality patterns that seem to reflect a good interaction with the roles and activities required in the profession. These hypotheses should then be tested by careful and continued observation and critical thinking.

Supplementary Readings

J. G. Darley and T. Hagenah, *Vocational Interest Measurement: Theory and Practice*, University of Minnesota Press, 1955.

D. C. McClelland, J. W. Atkinson, R. A. Clark, and E. L. Lowell, *The Achieve-ment Motive,* Appleton-Century-Crofts, 1953.

D. C. Miller and W. H. Form, *Industrial Sociology,* Harper, 1951.

D. E. Super, *The Psychology of Careers,* Harper, 1957.

In addition see the references cited by number in the chapter and appearing in the bibliography of an accompanying volume entitled *Teaching Personal Adjustment: An Instructor's Manual.*

Vocational Choice and Personal Adjustment

The thought of being a doctor, a business executive, an engineer, or an artist plays an important part in the personality development of the young person. A vocational goal is associated with one's *self-concept*. It may seem to the person to be a means of extending and enhancing himself. Vocations in our culture are associated with social status, personal values, and attitudes and style of living (480). They also may be an outlet for deep-seated creative tendencies and a means of satisfying many personal needs—a true source of *self-actualization* (263).

A vocational choice may be highly unrealistic, and one may need to go through a period of finding himself which may be fraught with disillusionment and readjustment. A young person may be so impressed with middle class cultural values that extol white collar and self-employed jobs over others that he may be in severe conflict as he is pulled toward a vocation less valued in the culture but which more truly satisfies his deep individual needs. Vocational selection

CHAPTER 9

VOCATIONAL CHOICE

involves *reality testing*, many trial-and-error choices, and *compromises*. Both in preparation and in later practice, if one is successful in a vocational role satisfying to him he can grow in confidence and self-assurance. If the vocation is not fully satisfying, if he feels himself in a rut, this influences his self-concept (263, 124, 270, 77, 773).

Concern over finding an appropriate vocation may reflect motivations, frustrations, and conflicts that go beyond merely finding an occupation for one's life. This concern may be rather a concern over oneself as a personality. Vocational adjustment then, in our culture, is an aspect of total self-understanding and creative development. It involves the satisfaction of as many personal motives as is possible. Although much of these two chapters deals with the details of self-discovery and vocational exploration, there is the constant implication that this adjustive process is related to matters discussed throughout the book. On the other hand, the vocational area—despite its relationship to deeper personal factors—seems less emotionally involved, easier to discuss than a nontangible avenue, through which the individual can explore himself and his world.

Occupational Analysis

After one has gained an objective impression of his own personality, he is ready to view extensively vocations as a whole, and intensively a few fields which attract him. A questionnaire administered to 533 college students revealed that less than 2 per cent had made any deliberate study of occupations. When their completed questionnaires were classified in three groups according to value, only 21 per cent of the students were unquestionably informed on the vocation selected, and 13.3 per cent submitted papers with obviously uninformed answers. When college students were divided on the basis of how well informed they were about vocations and what influenced them in their search it was found that the best informed were influenced by "work experience," "study of occupations," and "immediate opportunity"; the poorest were influenced by "advice of parents or family," "desire for a professional career," "social position," and "ambition"(165). These results emphasize the necessity for the following recommended program in addition to a thorough personality analysis.

The investigation of vocations may be viewed as consisting of four steps: (1) knowledge of all the vocations open to you; (2) thorough knowledge of the most suitable vocations; (3) comparison of personality and vocational analyses; (4) educational and vocational planning.

Knowledge of All Available Vocations. *Value of knowing many possible specific vocations.* We saw on pages 217–218 that collegians think in terms of very few vocations. The student who makes a choice after having considered every group of possible vocations and selected several for careful study is far more likely to choose wisely than the student who has not given the matter such systematized thought.

Colleges realize the need to relate the preparatory value of courses to the occupational world. Several helpful volumes have been prepared of which *Ohio State and Occupations* is an example (589, 538, 81). It presents brief descriptions of hundreds of vocations. These are classified under 69 departmental offerings such as accounting, advertising and sales, agricultural chemistry . . . veterinary medicine, welding engineering, and zoology and entomology.

John M. contemplated entering his father's oil business although he did not know specifically what aspect of the business to prepare for.   He was interested to learn, in his junior year, that the Physics Department offered a course in heat, the Accounting Department a course in business cycles, the Agricultural Economics Department a course in land economics, the Agricultural Engineering Department a course in drainage and erosion control, the Economics Department a course in business management. There were also several courses in geology, chemistry, and engineering, all of which would be of advantage to anyone engaged in the oil business. John's father had sent him to college to get an education.   The father felt that John's professors would give him what he ought to have, but John didn't inquire about his choice of courses in relation to his plans for the future until his junior year.   There were courses that could aid in the solution of numerous problems that he would encounter later if only he would decide where he wanted to work in the oil world.

Such a student is not rare.   Rare, rather, is the student who knows his specific role and the problems involved.   Consideration of a number of specific vocations is apt to force one to think in terms of definite problems while taking valuable general courses.   One is challenged and motivated by these problems and gains maximum information from the courses.

Lists of Vocations Suitable for College Graduates.   Following is listed a sample of many vocations that are open to college students (107–116).   Rather exhaustive lists of vocations are included in the Bureau of Census *Classified Index to Occupations*, Government Printing Office; in *Dictionary of Occupational Titles*, and in several other publications (181, 818, 125, 573).   Consultation of this list should have value for the student who thinks in terms of a small number of vocations.   The vocations mentioned on page 238 are not repeated here.

VOCATIONS SUITABLE FOR COLLEGE GRADUATES

Actor	Assessor	Columnist
Actuary	Astronomer	Conservationist,
Adjuster	Athlete	wild life
Advertising agent	Auctioneer	Consul
Agricultural specialist	Banker	Criminologist
Airport director	Buyer	Critic
Announcer	Camp director	Decorator
Anthropologist	Case worker	Designer
Architect	Chef	Detective
Archivist	City manager	Dietitian
Army officer	Civil service worker	Diplomat

Economist	Journalist	Physiologist
Educational director	Labor executive	Playwright
Exporter	Librarian	Purchasing agent,
Extension agent	Manufacturer	industrial
Exterminator, pest	Market researcher	Radio script writer
Federal police	Novelist	Representative, Congress
Financial adviser	Nurse	Research director
Forester	Nutritionist	Sociologist
Fruit grower	Occupational therapist	Statistician
Governess	Optometrist	Stewardess, air line
Gynecologist	Osteopath	Teacher
Historian	Penal and correctional	Technologist
Illumination	worker	Translator
specialist	Pharmacist	Undertaker
Insurance agent	Photographer	Veterinarian
Interpreter	Physicist	

Many of the mentioned vocations represent a whole area of different careers. For example, "designers" include those which plan automobiles, costumes, furs, furniture, industrial commodities, jewelry, millinery, stage sets and textiles.

Classification of Vocations. There have been several classifications of vocations published (657, 558). Here is one the student might find helpful as he thinks over his inclinations as related to the world of work:

Service	Outdoor
Business contact	Sciences
Business administration	Cultural
and control	Arts and entertainment
Technology	

Know the Most Suitable Vocations Well. An *occupational analysis* consists of a systematic, somewhat thorough, analysis of an occupation, in which an outline similar to the one presented below is used. An analysis of this type should be made for each vocation in which the individual feels a strong interest. The preparation of these analyses affords considerable pleasure and inspiration, aside from the valuable information obtained through them.

FACTORS TO CONSIDER IN STUDYING A VOCATION

1. *Activities and Duties*
Detailed survey of a typical day's work.

Types of activities—indoor or outdoor; with people, ideas, or things; involving responsibility or subordination; in limelight or background.

2. *Disadvantages*

Mental and physical hazards—effect on health, disposition, and mental, moral, and ethical standards.

Inconveniences—working hours, monotony, associates.

3. *Qualifications*

Education—general and specific; its cost, accessibility, duration.

Previous experience, or preparatory occupation.

Entrance—examination, influence, capital, or equipment.

Personal—physical traits, appearance, intelligence, and special abilities; interests and attitudes; emotional, volitional, and social traits.

4. *Income*

Minimum and range, opportunities for extra remuneration, bonuses, system of pay.

Special benefits—sick benefit, insurance, room and board, pension.

5. *Future*

Directions of promotion and extent possible in each direction.

Stability—through year, throughout life.

Supply and demand—possibility of radical change in vocation due to invention or industrial shift.

6. *Supplementary Advantages*

Social position.

Opportunity for service, creative work, and reputation.

Importance of position in community.

Miscellaneous—such as social contacts and travel.

This outline suggests items to be investigated. The more thoroughly these matters are investigated, the more valuable the analysis becomes. This outline may be copied or typed on a large sheet, and items of information supplied through methods presented below. A brief sample of an occupational analysis follows.

ABSTRACT OF JOB ANALYSIS OF FOREIGN SERVICE

Foreign Service, An Occupational Brief
Western Personnel Institute

1. *Activities and Duties*

The Foreign Service acts as the eyes, ears, and voice of the American Government. It has the responsibility for friendly relations with other governments; for protecting American citizens and promoting American interests; and for keeping our government informed on developments abroad.

The officer has fifty or more duties, among which are: the issuing of passports, registration of citizens, advising on questions relating to American citizenship, issuing bills of health to American vessels, submission of reports on health conditions, issuing of passport visas to foreign visitors and of visas to immigrants under immigration laws, promoting and protection of American shipping, certification of invoices of goods shipped under United States custody, administration and settlement of estates of American citizens and seamen who have died abroad, and extradition cases.

2. Disadvantages

The Foreign Service officer has hard, dull, routine work in a hierarchical organization, in which he is subject to superior officers at all times and limited in expression of his individual opinions. He is obligated to accept appointments as they are made, some to unhealthful lands where he is isolated without modern necessities. He is separated from his friends, family, and country. It is difficult to educate a family with his continuous moving about, and impossible to save with added expenses of schools and traveling.

3. Qualifications

To be eligible to take the written, oral, and physical examinations for the Foreign Service, the applicant must be from 25 to 35 years of age, a citizen for at least ten years, and, if he is married, his wife or husband must be a citizen. He must have a bachelor's degree, or he must have completed three-fourths of the requirements before entering the service. He must read with facility French, German, or Spanish. He must be loyal to the government, and attached to the principles of the Constitution.

He should have a taste for study, be keen mentally, have a stable and winning personality, be patient and tactful, have a sound business training, have technical knowledge, and inborn wit and shrewdness.

4. Income

[When this brief was written] the salary for the beginning (class 6) level was $3300 to $4400, class 3, $8000 to $9900, and class 1, $12,000, to $13,500. This gives only an approximate range which can change with economic conditions.

There is an extra allowance for living quarters and travel expenses. He is entitled to 60 days' vacation every year and 15 days of sick leave.

5. Future

The officers are given regular promotions until they are retired at the age of 60 or after 20 years of service. They receive benefits from the Retirement and Disability System.

6. Supplementary Advantages

In highly cultural surroundings, the Foreign Service officer is living and working with the most interesting and powerful people of all nations. Opportunities for personal growth and unfoldment are innumerable, as he may study history, languages, and customs firsthand. Engaged in useful work, he has security, adequate financial returns, and gains professional and social prestige.

Sources of Information Concerning Vocations. There are available numerous pamphlets prepared by reputable agencies that describe the better-known vocations. They follow an outline similar to the one given, in their description of the vocation. Practically every college today makes them available either in a counseling or vocational bureau or in some accessible place in the college library. Sometimes the persons or offices offering vocational counseling have placed them on shelves or in files. With their aid, students can run over in a relatively short time the characteristics of a rather large number of vocations (94).

There are many inexpensive pamphlets that give briefly the essential information (242). Some, such as *Occupational Briefs*, are published by the government (587). Another example of low cost booklets is *Occupational Abstracts* * (586). They are prepared by experts, the first being a condensation of the known literature in an easily available form. Some of the more popular, lengthier monographs which cover many of the better-known vocations are *Careers* (125) and *American Job Series Guidance Monographs* (793).

BOOKS ABOUT VOCATIONS. In addition to the technical monographs standardized and prepared by experts, there are numerous books written by persons in various fields about their vocations. Such books differ greatly. Some are popular, interesting, and inspiring. Others are technical and resemble a textbook on the field (815, 33, 252). You might ask a specialist or one of your teachers in the field for suggestions. There also are volumes that offer descriptions of a number of vocations; for example, one called *Five Hundred Post-War Jobs for Men*, is listed in the references (818). Women will find this useful (21).

The card catalog of your local or university library or the coun-

---

* The addresses of the publishers and approximate cost of the above listed pamphlets are:

Occupational Abstracts, Occupational Index, Inc., New York University, Washington Square, New York 3, N. Y., 25 cents.

Careers, The Institute for Research, 537 S. Dearborn St., Chicago 5, Ill., 75 cents.

The American Job Series Guidance Monographs, Science Research Associates, 228 S. Wabash Ave., Chicago 4, Ill., 60 cents.

seling service at your school or college will offer further sources of information. Look under "Vocations" or under the specific vocation concerning which you are seeking knowledge.

BIOGRAPHIES. Although biographies frequently supply relatively little current information about a vocation, they give what is equally important—inspirational verve. Reading the life of a great man who has expended his effort in a vocational area that interests you gives personal insight to the problems and satisfactions to be found in that occupation. It also elevates the occupation in your mind. It is well to know the greater men in the field you anticipate entering; learn how they entered it, how they rose and reached success; know their interests, motives, attitudes, and philosophies of life. A librarian will help you discover some of the better biographies on persons in the field of your interest.

INTERVIEWS OF SUCCESSFUL MEN IN VOCATIONS BEING CONSIDERED. The intimate side of vocations can be obtained from men in the field in your own community as well as from biographies. It is preferable to gather information from a *number of sources* in order to avoid an inaccurate slant that may reflect the experience of only one individual.

The student probably should talk first with friends of the family. If his family has no acquaintances in the field in which his interest lies, he should not be reluctant about interviewing a stranger. He should, of course, know beforehand just what information he is seeking, so that he will consume a minimum of the stranger's time.

In some cities the Y.M.C.A., Kiwanis Club, and the Business and Professional Women's Club have committees on vocational guidance to which a young man or woman might apply to obtain an interview with successful persons. This avenue should be investigated. If an introduction cannot possibly be arranged in this way, the student should not be reluctant to take the initiative in arranging a conference with a business or professional man who can furnish him with information. If he makes an appointment beforehand and announces his purpose, few men will refuse him an audience. A good approach if the student has not had an introduction may be made either by telephone or by letter as follows:

Mr. ———, I am John Smith, a student at ——— University, College of Arts and Science. I am attempting to make a vocational decision in order to make a wise selection of courses next year. I am interested in ——— work, and I understand you are one of the successful men in the field. I realize that you are busy, so I have carefully worked out the questions

I wish to ask you. May I have an appointment at any time that is convenient to you? I believe I can present most of my problems in a maximum time of ——— minutes. I shall be very grateful to you for an interview which, I know, will be valuable to me in planning my educational and vocational schedule.

You will find that most successful leaders will be friendly to a young man, and perhaps be flattered to be approached on such an important mission. It might lead to a very helpful contact in the future. A businessman cannot but be impressed by questions that have been carefully planned, or by a youth who seems to be going about his educational and occupational career systematically. He will undoubtedly find himself thinking of that youth and inquiring about his progress. Successful men take pleasure in guiding a young fellow who seems on his way to success.

These interviews will produce information with which the individual may fill out his occupational analysis. Items in the vocational analysis that require opinions can best be supplied through this method. Such items as the possibility of radical change in the field due to an invention, entrance qualifications, specific courses, or knowledge of aids to persons in the field might be obtained through the interview.

WORK IN THE FIELD.

A newspaper reporter came into the office the other day after having been away from the campus for several years. One of his first remarks was, "I wish I had enough money saved to come back to college for a year or two. I don't want to take graduate work, I just want to elect some fundamental courses I missed. When I entered ——— University I pledged ———, and the boys all told me, the little pledge, what to take. I came right from high school, was only 17, and thought surely they knew more about what I should take than I did. I took Spanish, Geology, Citizenship, and Botany. These courses were all right, but they were not selected on the basis of my need.

"If I had spent a day in a newspaper office previously, or a month anyhow, I would have learned that there are certain positions, not so easily filled, which offer the best opportunity financially and otherwise. I would have seen that a good knowledge of Economics would have prepared me for a financial editorship; knowledge of History and American Government would have helped to make me a good Washington correspondent. I should have had French or German, or Latin and Greek, instead of Spanish. Even my Geology and Botany would have been of greater value to me, had I known that they could later be used as feature material. But when I was a student here I took notes only to pass examinations, and subsequently forgot all of them. If I had seen some connection between each course and newspaper work, it would have meant more to me.

"There is a 16-year-old kid on the newspaper now. I'm trying to get him to come over here next year. That boy will know what he wants to take, and he'll also know that in every course here there is good future newspaper copy."

This case indicates the value of having some knowledge of one's chosen field, perhaps obtained by working in it, even if for only a short time. The man in the field sees, or can be made to see, the problems to be encountered. A youth could well spend a summer or part-time employment in a vocation he intends to enter, even if he has to work without pay, in order to test his aptitudes and interests for the field, and to know something about it before entering. During this working period he should keep the factors of his *vocational analysis* in mind. He should gather information through *observation* and *conversation* with experienced workers. If he considers real estate brokerage, for example, he should spend as much time as possible at the side of a real estate broker noting the duties, problems, and many daily details that confront the man engaged in this type of business. He should note further the *qualifications* the position requires, the mental and physical strains, the *disadvantages*, and, finally, the rewards and *advantages*. He should try to learn from the situation those positions in the vocation that offer the greatest opportunity, and ascertain the knowledge necessary to prepare himself for them.

VISITS TO INDUSTRIAL AND PROFESSIONAL CENTERS. If the individual finds it impossible to find temporary work in the field of his interests, he should substitute for this valuable experience visits to many offices or industrial plants. He should try, through extensive reading, to compensate for his inability to get direct contact with the vocations. Direct contact, however, is imperative if a knowledge of the field's problems is desired.

OTHER SOURCES OF INFORMATION. Frequently *lectures* that afford occupational information are given at universities by men of reputation in different fields. College professors who teach courses related to the student's field of interest provide another source of information. In some courses *term papers* are assigned on various subjects, and the students sometimes have the opportunity to choose their own titles. Vocational selection, job analysis, or self-analysis may serve as a good selection and give the student added motivation to attack these analyses systematically. Such projects satisfy school requirements and, in addition, supply valuable knowledge to the student. One summer camp group planned vocational guidance work including testing, conferences, and try-out activities to determine capacities and interests

(731).   A school group organized an *excursion club* for the study of vocations and industries.

Vocational Selection

Cases of Vocational Selection.   Now that we have discussed methods of analyzing oneself and methods of analyzing vocations, it might be well to read cases of individuals who, with the help of trained counselors, have made these analyses (119).   Although the case describes the vocational explorations of a woman student the same principles apply to men; they concern careers which are open also to men.*

When Barbara A. entered a junior college, she stated that she wanted to become a radio control board operator.   However, she enrolled in occupational planning in order that she might know whether or not there were other fields more challenging to her.   In addition, she included two radio courses in her schedule—one was an orientation course, directed toward giving her a picture of the field and its social implications; the second one was more specialized and was concerned with program types.

In high school, her favorite subjects had been mathematics and physics.   Her extraclass activities had centered around work in student government and membership in the school chorus and *a cappella* choir.   During summer vacations, she had had work experience as a switchboard operator, receptionist, file clerk, and general office work.

In the occupational planning class, she had an opportunity to see the profile of test results and, after a discussion of them with the counselor in an individual interview, the following interpretation was possible.

Interests.   Her major interest areas were mechanical, artistic, and clerical.

Aptitudes and abilities.   There was evidence of superior academic ability, and her high school grades seemed to support this evidence.   Her vocabulary scores and the test of reading speed were also superior.   Scores in reading comprehension were at the average level.   There was indication of superior ability in mathematics.   Although she grasped ideas readily, she felt, and the test results seemed to verify the assumption, that she tended to neglect details to some degree.   She seemed to have superior ability in perception of spatial relationships.

Personality patterns.   Barbara enjoyed association with all kinds of people, although she felt she needed to develop more skill and facility in working with them and a greater understanding of their attitudes.   She thought ideas through carefully and logically and preferred to take action

---

* The case of Barbara was contributed by Bernice L. Williamson, counselor in the Occupational Guidance Service, directed by Dr. Dorothy Pollock, formerly at Stephens College.

only after long deliberation. Her point of view was conservative, and she was finding it difficult to adjust to new ideas and to make her own decisions. She was almost overconscientious in regard to acceptance of responsibility and tended to worry about it. However, as she was becoming accustomed to college life and activities, she found herself "taking these responsibilities in her stride."

During the semester in occupational planning, she carefully investigated three fields: radio, aviation, and merchandising. As she compared them, she found herself becoming more and more interested in radio. Aviation interested her, but here again the mechanical and technical aspects of the field appealed to her. Through her work in the radio courses she was obtaining practical work experience in the college radio station. In class discussion in occupational planning, and in individual conferences with the counselor, Barbara indicated that the greatest stumbling block in relation to technical work in radio was the fact that she was attempting to compete in a man's field. She was beginning to wonder if she had narrowed her choice within the field too soon.

She lived in a metropolitan area, and as a Christmas vacation project she visited two large radio stations to find out about the work and to see how women were accepted in the phase of radio which she was considering. The interviews confirmed information she had previously gathered: (1) there were women in technical work, but the way was anything but easy; (2) she should have a knowledge of the entire field rather than limit herself to one phase of it.

In a conference shortly before the end of the semester, she discussed a questionnaire that she had prepared to send to a number of radio stations in order to have additional data on job opportunities. At this time she was finding work in radio production highly interesting. She said: "I feel sure that I want to go on in radio. I think I have the ability. My interests are in this field, and it presents a challenge to me."

In May she came in to talk with the counselor about the possibility of working toward a Certificate of Competence in radio. This program offered her an opportunity to work with specialists in the field, and if she achieved the standards of proficiency set by the Radio Department she would receive the certificate upon graduation. Even though she was going on to senior college, she felt that the additional counseling would prove of real value to her. At this time, her interests were not limited to the technical field but had broadened considerably. Since women often get their start in radio through secretarial positions, she planned to take shorthand and typing in the summer vacation.

Accordingly, she came in in October of her second year to complete admission requirements for the certification program. Her reasons for her choice were essentially the same: "Radio presents a challenge to all my abilities and interests. It is not a static or routine field. It is not a typed field—that is, radio includes every field which composes our culture." Her academic standing for the first year was in the top 7 per cent of the student body.

During her second year, in addition to maintaining the same high academic standards, she was a member of the staff of the radio station and also became a member of the honorary radio sorority. She served as a member of the governing board in her residence hall and was assistant treasurer of the Independents. She gave evidence of having developed poise and confidence in her own judgment and of being able to take action on problems with considerably less worry than she had previously. This growth was felt by the student and was observed by the counselor and other faculty members working with her. Upon graduation, she was awarded the Certificate of Competence and was considered one of the outstanding students in the Radio Department. She has been accepted as a transfer student at a university and plans to continue her work in radio with the idea of obtaining a broad background rather than limiting herself to the technical field.

Comparison of Personality and Vocational Analysis. A vocational decision is often a *compromise.* There is the circumstance of the individual who must forgo the inheritance of a well-developed and firmly established business in order to enter a field for which he has more interest and adequate qualifications. A man will find it advisable to take a position with smaller initial monetary returns for the sake of the greater future which it promises. Positions that entail serious inconveniences are taken under the same provisions. A man may be too ambitious for his mental equipment and may find it necessary to lower his aspirations for his greatest happiness.

The various factors to consider in studying a vocation were mentioned on pages 250 and 251. Different aspects of a position or vocation do not form equally *valid* bases for making a wise choice, and sometimes the less valid influences are the most pressing. For example: tradition, family desires, admiration of someone in a vocation, or immediate large income should certainly be subordinated in most cases to aptitudes, interest, future prospects, possibilities for personal growth, and happiness.

There are times when some outstanding talent can compensate for a deficiency. Such questions as whether strong outstanding interests can balance mediocrity in ability must be answered from an overall viewpoint.

How permanent will this conclusion be? The validity and permanence of a vocational decision depend upon how thoroughly the analysis has been developed.

Permanence is often spoken of as though it were desirable in and of itself. This is not always true in choice of vocation. A man may work as an engineer for ten years and then become the editor of an engineering journal. His original choice was good, so good that his outstanding success as an engineer directed other members of the profession to choose him as editor of one of their journals. The first choice, however, was not permanent. A certain flexibility, in such circumstances, proves to be wiser than a strict adherence to one's original plan. There is a tendency at present to classify vocations in *families* on the basis of the characteristics required by those vocations (700).

The fact that a vocational choice may not be permanent does not argue against vocational planning. If after ten years a man has an opportunity to change from a good vocation to a better, his initial study of vocations will be advantageous in the later decision, if only to suggest a method of analysis.

Permanence, on the whole, is desirable, but the necessity for change due to economic and industrial movements should be anticipated. The fluctuation in supply and demand of occupations can be observed by comparing the Census figures over ten years. From 1920 to 1930, for example, there was a great increase in insurance agents, stock brokers, college professors, and electrical engineers, and a great decrease in untrained nurses, stenographers, typists, and street railroad conductors. The postwar era has opened new fields such as electronics and plastics. Much emphasis is placed today on trends and new careers by vocational publications (818, 15). Information of this type should be utilized in making vocational decisions.

Planning. Nearly all the vocations selected by college students require *educational planning* and preparation. Selection of the school, therefore, is an important item and involves knowledge of the school's offerings, the *reputation of the school*, and the requirements for entrance and successful work in various courses. It is well known in legal circles that, under favorable economic conditions, the graduates in the upper ranks of their classes in certain law schools are in demand. Certain schools of commerce have a similar reputation among large firms. Holders of Ph.D. degrees from some graduate schools rarely win appointments in large universities, granting such positions are desirable. If the student feels he can compete with individuals at the university which has the best reputation in the field in which he is interested, it is well that he make all efforts to attend that school.

On the other hand, there are some students who do not have this kind of aspiration. It is a wise course under certain circumstances for those who plan to live in the region in which they have spent most of their lives to secure their education locally. In some respects, attending a distant school might prove to be disadvantageous, whereas building a common background (one's school) with men and women who are to be of influence in the community in which one intends to practice professionally is a wise step in one's preparation.

In any event, considerable thought on this matter will not be wasted. Several volumes as, for example, Lovejoy's *College Guide* (468), and *A Guide to Colleges and Universities* (277), contain valuable information. They may be augmented by catalogs describing courses offered by colleges and universities. Interested students may secure catalogs on request.

Some students will find that in the light of their aptitude and interest analyses they can best complete preparation for their vocation out of college. Such a student was described in the case study on page 227. A young woman may find a good commercial course following two years of college work excellent preparation for the position of secretary. A mechanically inclined, conscientious young man who is making inferior grades in college may realize his ambitions for success by taking a trade course to supplement his college work. There are public vocational schools, night courses, and reputable correspondence schools that may be used to complete an education when continuation in college is inadvisable and unprofitable.

VOCATIONAL PLANNING. Daydreaming is an interesting, fascinating pastime, but dreams that do not relate to reality are not desirable from the point of view of mental health. Daydreaming on paper is safer than the entirely subjective type, because it is more likely to lead to activity. The reader might daydream on paper, after deciding upon his vocation, as a means of ascertaining what aspect of it seems to lead to greatest achievement for him. He should ask, "What is possible for me to attain in a year, in five years, in ten years, in twenty years, in forty years? How many avenues are open to me for advancement? Where can I be in terms of each one of these pathways? Of the possible specific avenues I can traverse in a vocation, which seems best suited to my attributes?"

A note of warning is in order. Planning of this type should not be too *rigid* or be taken too seriously. Success depends in part upon *events* as well as individuals. The individual who plans within narrow limits and refuses to accept any goals but those determined by him in his daydreams will find adjustment difficult.

PLAN SPECIFICALLY BUT KEEP BROAD GOALS IN MIND. Some authors urge broad goals instead of concentration on specific vocations. They argue that changes in the occupational world due to inventions and economic and social changes require the worker to be versatile and to possess a background that will allow adjustment to changes.

Stress upon specific vocation need not be at the expense of broad training. It should rather enrich and vitalize it. Thinking in terms of the field of insurance should not detract from interest in a college education, but rather make more realistic the courses in general economics, mathematics, and statistics, recent history, and political science. If the vocational purpose of the student changes he retains the broad training and valuable specific knowledge which he would have missed without his motive. The *average* student can profit by those motives that enrich his curiosity and increase his perspective.

At this point the question of the standard of success to be used arises—money, creation, happiness, efficiency, or public esteem. Those standards given least publicity often prove to be the most desirable measures of success so far as the individual himself is concerned; for example, happiness, creation, and professional esteem.

Some other suggestions that will prove of value in *securing a position through an interview* follow. (1) Make contacts while in school with executives in the field you wish to enter, either through sincere, interested requests for advice or through summer work. (2) Merit sincere, valid letters of recommendation. (3) Ask for an appointment before trying to interview the executive. If you are not acquainted with him, it would be well to state briefly your mission, your hope for the possibility of an opening, and your qualifications. Some students who lacked contacts have been successful in securing employment by writing letters to twenty or more executives, stating their reasons for interest in the company, their qualifications, and the positions they feel they could fill. (See suggested letter on page 254.) (4) Plan the interview thoroughly; anticipate the questions you will be asked and the interviewer's reactions resulting from your behavior. Know how you will present your qualifications and your knowledge of the problems of the industrial situation. Have with you all data that may be helpful, such as references, samples of work, and school transcript. (5) When nervousness occurs upon entering the executive's office, realize that it is quite natural. All your fellow applicants feel the same way. (6) Put yourself in the place of the interviewer and realize that you would prefer to employ an *able, well-qualified, aggressive, yet somewhat modest individual who understands the problems of the position and is sincerely interested in serving the company.* (7) Remember that, on many employers, factors that may seem irrelevant to competency, such as clothes, grooming, and a cooperative attitude may exert a paramount influence (445).

Supplementary Readings

R. Callis, P. C. Polmantier, and E. C. Roeber, *A Case Book of Counseling,* Appleton-Century-Crofts, 1955.

E. Z. Ginzberg, S. W. Ginsburg, S. Axelrad, and J. L. Herma, *Occupational Choice; an Approach to a General Theory,* Columbia University Press, 1951.

R. Hoppock, *Occupational Information,* McGraw-Hill, 1957.

P. E. Meehl, *Clinical vs. Statistical Prediction,* University of Minnesota Press, 1954.

A. Roe, *The Psychology of Occupations,* Wiley, 1956.

In addition see the references cited by number in the chapter and appearing in the bibliography of an accompanying volume entitled *Teaching Personal Adjustment: An Instructor's Manual.*

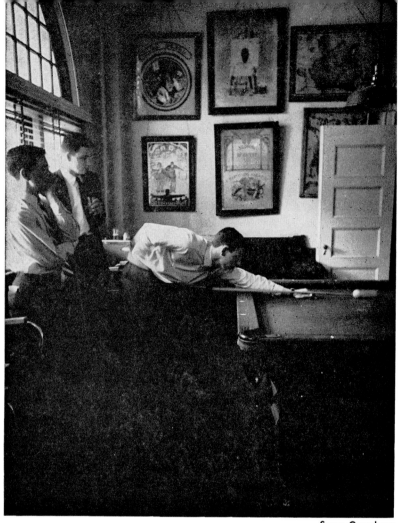

Sociality and Emotional Balance

During the teens and early twenties, adjustment to other people and the conventions they represent looms high. Jack feels that he is not one of the select group and desires strongly to be included; Mary prefers to remain alone in her room rather than experience awkwardness in a group; Bill thinks he is not the kind of fellow who is wanted by groups; Martin is in constant conflict with the fellows and seems to have a chip on his shoulder; Alice has never been sought by others but instead has been teased and has learned to fear and suspect most people. Whereas Jack, Mary, Bill, Martin, and Alice think about their social relationships, they do not see them in terms

264

CHAPTER 10

SOCIAL

ADJUSTMENT

of their background, their total adjustment, or their inner security. Whether an individual tends to be a lone wolf or a social butterfly is largely determined by the way experiences of the past have played on his basic temperament. There is a strong tendency for collegians to seek sociality in college (521). If a student is to improve his social adjustment to meet *his* standards and the group pressures more satisfactorily, it is necessary for him to understand his present social traits.

Circumstances in childhood may not have brought him among people, as shown in Chapter 4. Events in school and on the playground sometimes encourage seclusiveness. Not all children learn to play, to fight, to become toughened to rebuffs and teasing. Retirement to a world of hobbies, books, and inner adventure may lead to neglect of grooming and social interests. Some childhood and adolescent environments leave the individual unprepared for parties, kidding, ease with groups, and adoption of styles. With an understanding of his own development the individual may regard the different problems of *popularity, friendship, leadership,* or *social effectiveness* in perspective. The relationship of sociality to self-consciousness, feelings of inferiority, or emotional instability will become apparent. He may see that it is his emotional life that causes him to withdraw from people or to offend them.

Social adjustment is important in youth because at this age the "crowd" is supplanting the family as an influence. In early life, rejection by the mother or father and loss of their love is a very disturbing experience. In adolescence and youth, loss of the approval of the group is an equally disturbing experience, particularly for the individual who readily experiences anxiety, as, for example, one who is trying to move from the orbit of the family into the orbit of outer society. A sense of security in a group or the feeling that one is a wanted and integrated part of a valued society, on the other hand, is an aid to personality growth and adjustment. At first, in an attempt to adjust to social insecurity, a student may become meticulously conventional and conform to the behavior of his group. Any deviation from the pattern of the crowd is carefully avoided. He may become disconcerted too because his past training has not supplied him with the social habits and attitudes that he sees others using freely. He may think himself so far removed from the smooth, easy, social person that he surrenders and turns to solitary ventures or daydreams.

Understanding of one's social traits will be enhanced as one recognizes his basic *conflicts and frustrations,* mentioned in Chapter 3, and their origins, and moves toward inner security. He will then find it easier to select relevant suggestions on social relations and to put them into practice. It will be helpful also to see the various *social roles* he plays and the *expectations* he carries into a social situation. He may come into the group as a newcomer, a successful previous group member, a friend, an outsider, an antagonist. Some roles are fixed for him, and he may accept or reject them. For example, he is either a boy or a girl, has a specific age, is married or single, from a rural or an urban background, is classed specifically from freshman to senior (460).

Frequently, after an individual understands his basic problem and the causes of his insecurity, the desire for popularity or inordinate friendship is not so *compulsive*. Most important is that a feasible and realistic adjustment to others be made—not a mere imitation of their conventions, which sometimes have little lasting validity. More appropriately his adjustments to others should also do justice to his own potentialities and inclinations and thereby promote his growth as the kind of person he can best become. In this manner he will serve the group best in the long run. He should see, for example, the kind of leadership he can assume. Current social conventions and the means of achieving them may be considered with calm rather than with urgency. Furthermore, as he gains freedom from the tensions of his own personal problem, he may regard other people more objectively and come to appreciate the wide range of individual differences in social behavior. He will see that there are persons who are reserved, yet have made a good social adjustment; that there are others who are in the thick of social intercourse, yet have not achieved a good inner adjustment.

Case of Social Development.

Harry N., as a 20-year-old college sophomore, was only moderately friendly, *not at all popular, a poor strategist, but a leader of a small group* of liberal students on the campus. He was born on a farm near a town of 500. His parents were frugal farmers who were gradually paying off their debt and educating their children. They were strongly religious, conservative in politics, and somewhat intolerant of the more carefree persons with whom they occasionally came into contact. Harry had had few playmates. His mother taught him to read early in life, and he became an avid reader. Most of the books he read in later childhood and adolescence he obtained from a liberal doctor in the community who owned a good library. In high school he admired a social science teacher who was well on the left side of the political horizon. During this period he was rarely considered "one of the boys." He was also only moderately popular with the girls. He was not conscious of the styles. He did not participate in athletics except as he was brought into them by pressure. He was masculine in physique and general attitude, but his reading had given him more mature interests than most of the students with whom he associated. As the gap between him and the typical high school student widened he began to justify his own attitudes, to think of his fellow students as superficial, immature, and a block to social progress, and to look to his teacher and doctor friends for companionship. Unlike some of his associates he did not feel strongly inferior or depressed because he was not among the "upper crust" or the social crowd. They just did not interest him.

In college he found others of similar attitudes, although he was distinctly out of the class of the more urbane students. He met a girl in his sophomore year. She was far more sociable than he. She taught him to dance and prevailed upon him to improve his grooming and dress. It was through her eyes that he saw for the first time the more sociable type of student.

His values began to conflict. He and his roommate were very active in an organization composed of scholarly underclassmen who ignored all social functions on the campus. His leadership in this group conflicted with his newly acquired interest in social activities in which he was not skillful.

This was not the only conflict in his personality. The conservative attitudes with which his parents had imbued him were conflicting with the liberal attitudes he had acquired from his physician friend and his intimate college group. He felt that he was right to differ with his parents on political issues and with his girl on social matters. Nevertheless, he was dependent on them in many respects. He also, paradoxically, felt superior to the more sociable students because of his better vocabulary and comprehension of current events, and yet felt less at ease than they when they met socially.

Harry found, as he discussed this matter with an older friend, that he achieved a better integration of the two aspects of his life. He learned to accept his social ineptitude as well as the lack of understanding on the part of his new associates of his political and social views. He was beginning to accept coexistence of the two ways of life.

Harry's case illustrates the complexity of the development of social traits, and how in our growing up we may acquire or introject the social traits of several different people, thereby experiencing a conflict.

The Question of Conformity. To what extent must one conform to others at the expense of individual development in order to communicate well with a group and gain acceptance by them? What do we mean by conformity? Young adolescents, at first glance, seem blatant nonconformists with their colorful and faddish clothing, personalized cars, slang, and strenuous dances. On closer examination, they show slavish conformity to what is acceptable to their more vocal peers and their group (232). Though they may enjoy mildly shocking their parents' contemporaries, they are quite anxious lest they violate the pattern of their group or fail to "rate" with the influential groups. They are quite sensitive to what is in vogue, because they realize how ruthless some of their fellows can be in rejecting the "odd" person. They have a need to identify with someone who has value in their frame of reference, and their peers influence them more on casual matters than do those in authority (175, 232). On factual matters and in a serious context they will tend to follow those in authority (163). Some adults follow the same anxious conformity even to the point of being in conflict with their desire to out-distance their neighbor or fellow worker in some

Conformity
assumes
uniformity
and rigidity
of human
customs,
neither of
which
exists.

Susan Greenburg

respect. Some writers believe conformity is increasing in American culture to the extent of being stronger than competition as a cultural force. Many individuals, however, have learned the art of going their own way without alienating others too greatly.

In this book we have observed people who have difficulty in conforming because they had little contact with others earlier in life, and who suffer emotionally because of it so that it disturbs their personal growth. Some have been overprotected and have experienced so little frustration that they expect others to accede to their willfulness. Others, conversely, have not grown because they conform too carefully or withdraw from social contacts and smother their individuality (see Chapters 14 and 15).

From the individual's standpoint, knowing the accepted mode of behavior simplifies action for him. It removes conflict and insecurity

269

and gives him a feeling of belonging which, if he has been rejected previously, he will crave. However, since groups differ and there is no universal way of behaving, when an individual conforms slavishly to one group he will find himself differing from people of a different geographical location or social character. As the world becomes smaller because of rapid communication, he comes more often into contact with other groups that have different modes of behavior. Furthermore, because change is inevitable and constant, behavior that is acceptable at one time is not at another. Rigid adherence to one set of practices may cause the individual to be at odds with another group, or with his own group of a different generation. Conformity assumes uniformity and rigidity of human customs, neither of which exists. *Too strong an emphasis on conformity might impede one's adjustment*, which necessitates continuous adaptation to surrounding circumstances.

Some students have such strong inner purpose and are so successful in their nonsocial interests and accomplishments, such as hobbies, projects, or small interest groups, that they are not greatly disturbed if rejected by a social group of high status. Others gather with persons like themselves, form social movements, and espouse causes. Both worthwhile and impractical and socially disruptive organizations have grown out of the efforts of rejected groups and individuals. Persons who have outlets for their talents and interests may be quite oblivious of the latest grooming and etiquette and may not want to be included in the more social group. In their fearlessness toward the pressure of society, they sometimes bring about badly needed social changes. We have but to read biography to see how many of our greatest personages ignored that which was popularly exalted in their times. Van Gogh, Socrates, Jesus, Lincoln, Beethoven—all were true to an inner purpose and were not concerned about the minor conventionalities of their times, and some ignored them.

We are beginning to see in such individuals the answer to the question we raised in the beginning of this section. Conformity or nonconformity in behavior can best be evaluated for an individual or society in terms of the effect upon creativity, thinking, and human development. Both conformity and nonconformity may be motivated by strong anxiety and previous experience of relief or reward by behaving in a given way. When anxiety in the individual instead serves as motivation to think through plans and find outlets for personal development, he can decide to conform or to exert rational nonconformity to meet his valid goals.

Before we leave this subject, some mention should be made of the individual who makes a fetish of being popular, belonging to groups, and conforming to superficial pressures.   There are those who put their greatest emphasis on building traits which will provide them with the proper *front* so that they may be judged most popular by their contemporaries.   There are others who think of front as subordinate to integrity, inner convictions, devotion to ideals and truth.   The former exalt popularity, group memberships, and group activities for their own sake, without reference to what these groups do for society.

Popularity

Meaning of Popularity.   The dictionary tells us that to be popular is to be *pleasing to people* in general, to be beloved and approved by people.   One need not be a dynamic leader, however.   There are many college students who are popular, who run for offices successfully and become headmen of organizations, yet are not leaders in the sense of bringing about social change.   There is the "good fellow" who has a smile for everyone, who is known by his first name all over the campus, who knows many names and many faces, and who can play many of the popular games well.   He may not be a close friend to anyone, he may not be a leader, he may not even be socially proficient to any great extent, but he is popular.

Evaluation of Popularity.   In our teens and twenties we put a large premium on popularity.   Adults who lead somewhat superficial lives also emphasize it.   They want to be well known, they want to be seen in the right places, and they want to associate with well-known people.   In fact, the term "popularity" has a very pleasant connotation to most people.

ADVANTAGES OF POPULARITY.   The popular person receives numerous invitations, and he enjoys the give-and-take of pleasant social relationships.   He knows the latest songs, jokes, books, and games, and shines in social groups.   He may be envied by those who are not as flashy as he, but who aspire to be so.   They see him as a carefree and assured individual.   Many would consider the popular man happy and think that popularity has few undesirable aspects. But is this true?

WHEREIN THE POPULAR INDIVIDUAL FALLS SHORT. There is another side. The superficial individual *seldom gets beneath the surface of life*. The only classical music he listens to is that which has become popular. His inability to comprehend good literature never troubles him. He acquires only those athletic and social skills that are in vogue. The subtleties of history, international politics, and philosophy never arouse his interest. Nor is it often that the masters of the various arts, sciences, and skills come from this group. He cannot be counted on to help fight the battles for freedom of speech, civil liberties, or international understanding. Since he must be popular he must represent that which the masses can understand. He must condone their prejudices, agree with their attitudes, and become one of them. He is a "practical" individual. He usually adjusts to things as they are. Many dilettantes and extremely popular persons are too busy gaining the simple skills that are demanded of them by their audiences to make any serious contributions to their vocation or society or in some cases even be true to their own values and basic interests. Their evenings are taken up with social gatherings so that they have very little time to read, attend lectures, concerts, etc., or by other means improve themselves substantially.

The popular individual has *little private life*. His social engagements become a responsibility. Once he begins to refuse invitations he endangers his reputation of popularity. Furthermore, in order to be popular he sometimes finds that he must flatter certain people whom he does not like especially. It is hard for him to hew to the line of his convictions.

A COMMON-SENSE VIEW OF POPULARITY. Is there a middle course? The popular individual demonstrates the value of the free, pleasant attitude which we may assume during leisure. He shows that great personal satisfaction can be derived from *amiable social contacts and some superficial interests*. He stands as a contrast to the specialist who is not interested in people and who cannot relax with the commonplace. The specialist spends all his time acquiring a skill, sometimes becomes proficient in his field, sometimes makes a contribution to society. His own life, however, may be very shallow and bounded by the limits within which his skill lies. Can the attitudes producing popularity and personal integrity be combined or operate under different conditions?

FACTORS THAT AFFECT POPULARITY. At the senior high school and college age there are few factors that seem more important than appearance and conduct (715). Athletic skills and dominant behavior seem to win popularity for boys along with poise, balance, and maturity which is doubly important for girls (810). These are the results of habits of grooming and cleanliness, habits of carriage and posture, habits of speech and etiquette, and those personal habits that make us liked or disliked.

Habits of dress, neatness, and personal behavior have been acquired so gradually that the average person is *unaware* of the specific factors which enhance or mar his effect on others. It is for this reason that we shall deal in terms of specific items in the next few sections. The observations may seem trite to the student who has always been aware of the daily habits that affect appearance. However, he has but to look around him to find many others who fall short of the rigid standards of youth and do not know the precise reasons.

Grooming, Cleanliness, and Style.

Look over any group of one hundred college students. Many of the most attractive have enhanced their better physical qualities. Colors are chosen to flatter the particular type of complexion. Styles of hairdress are used to cover any defects and bring the proportions and shape of head and face closer to the current ideal. A girl who has large ears will dress her hair in such a fashion as to minimize their size. Her hair will be parted in a manner that will make her profile appear to advantage. She is aware of the fashions and fads of the moment. If it is fashionable for her hair to be curly, usually her hair is curled. If it is fashionable for fingernails to be tinted, hers are tinted in an inconspicuous, pleasing fashion. She lives in her time, and she dresses *in a manner that will enhance her natural beauty*. Lines of design in men's and women's clothing may be used to change the effect of certain physical features that are not very attractive, or to shift attention from them. Design may also correct minor physical disproportions.

Every college student can experiment with such simple matters as color and hairdress. Most of us fall into habits of dress. We tend to accept our habits of dressing and grooming as fixed and immutable parts of our personality. Furthermore, we sometimes are initially displeased by any experimental change in hairdress, in the use of color, or in type of clothes. We therefore should not depend entirely upon our own judgment in making such changes because we will be prejudiced in terms of previous practice. It is wise to get the opinion of friends regarding such changes.

Some college students acquire habits of dress that make them unattractive. A short person may wear clothes with horizontal lines which make him look even shorter than he is. A double-breasted suit or a wide hat accentuate lack of height. The opinion of store salesmen will be helpful in this respect. The woman who wants to dress attractively usually has more aids than the man, through fashion magazines, saleswomen, and beauty operators.

Beauty and its opposite are rarely intrinsic to the individual, although many believe that they are. What is considered beautiful varies quite widely in our own culture and within other cultures (479). What we like and how much we like it is largely acquired as a result of satisfying personal needs. The reactions of other people to us are largely affected by general appearance, habits of cleanliness, style, and aesthetic use of color, line, and symmetry. Changes in these are brought about by *trial and error, once a student realizes his goal.* It is often surprising what shoe polish, dye, home pressing, consistent use of soap and water, and effective combination of colors, all of which are inexpensive, will do to improve overall appearance. On every campus there are students who dress well and others who dress poorly on similar budgets. One of the biggest impediments some students must overcome is their belief that relative beauty cannot be achieved by them. Students have reported that others have helped them when their advice was solicited on matters of dress, deportment, and grooming. Sometimes merely being around others who have good habits of grooming and getting hints from them has value. Reference to the section on Changing Behavior in Chapter 5 will produce some specific suggestions regarding the building of new habits.

Habits of Carriage, Posture, and Speech. The manner in which an individual carries himself and the stiffness or relaxation that is characteristic of his posture influences how others perceive him. One's manner of sitting and of walking is likewise a factor. Some sway; others hop; others save the toes and wear out the heels of their shoes like persons twenty years their senior. Then there is the man who walks briskly, firmly, with an economy of bodily movement that speeds him on his way; and the woman who is characterized by walking in a coordinated feminine manner which is evaluated positively for a woman in our culture.

Some of these are habits that were acquired early in life and may be attempts to cover up certain personality traits. There is evidence that the various aspects of the expressions that are peculiar to us as individuals are interrelated. Posture, gait, and voice, for example, reflect our whole pattern of behavior (567, 12, 861). When individuals were asked to match descriptions of a number of different persons with heard samples of speech, they were able to make these matches with a considerable degree of accuracy (12). Our expressiveness, then, consists of more than mechanically acquired habits. It reflects inner attitudes, personality, and temperamental traits and states. It is well for us to understand the basis of our characteristic modes of expression before ruthlessly trying to change them. We should surely want to know what inner traits our expressive movements are reflecting. We should consider them first as a reflection of our real self. Then, if necessary, we should modify them in an intelligent manner. Walking and speech are often the reflection of total personality, but some minor mannerisms that are extreme may be changed through understanding of self and through habit training.

High-pitched wavering voices are usually judged undesirable in men. Nasal twangs and loud, coarse voices have negative value in women. Indistinct speech and affectedly precise speech are equally undesirable in the opinion of the average person. In your experience you will find that the speech that attracts you most is that which suggests naturalness and calm. It is smooth and well modulated. You will find members of the speech department in your college willing to assist you to overcome inappropriate speech habits.

In contrast to these characteristics, which are doubtlessly interpreted negatively because the person possessing them seems to ignore the attitudes and feelings of those around him, studies show that beginning in childhood we judge others as desirable if they are good-looking. Even children seem to prefer those who are active and alert, good-looking, cheerful and friendly, above average in intelligence, scholastic standing, and health (85, 868). Children low in popularity seem uninterested in their environment and in other people, are more often either quiet and shy or noisy, rebellious, and boastful (585, 379).

The emotional stability of the home and such factors as a sense of personal worth and a feeling of social belonging are also important in one's social adjustment (860, 827).

Habits That Make Us Disliked. A list of activities that annoy others has been compiled. Here are a few activities found on that list (134). Could some of these be among your habits?

Attracting attention to yourself
Gross noises such as belching and
    smacking
Sneezing and coughing openly
Grooming in public
Talking during public perform-
    ances
Sly allusions to sex
Unsolicited affection
Public love-making
Dirt on face, clothes or fingernails
Unpleasant odors
Gross and unpleasant table manners

Poor dental hygiene
Temper tantrums
A dictatorial manner
Extreme criticalness
Intoxication
A poor loser
Bragging
Petty lies
Prying curiosity
Touchiness
Tardiness
Inattention
Nagging

Etiquette. Other personality patterns that are evaluated highly in our society are the habits of etiquette. Etiquette is a combination of *good sense, good taste,* and a generous admixture of *kindliness.* The fearsome collection of rules which makes up the usual etiquette book may be boiled down to this. Many of these rules have been continued from another era. For example, in the time of unpaved, muddy city streets, passing vehicles threw large clods of mud on the sidewalk. It was necessary then for the gentleman to walk next to the roadway in order to protect his lady's clothing from such accidents. If one keeps this in mind, there ought to be no conjecture about the man's place when walking with one or more women.

One's conduct in public or private should be based on consideration of others, which precludes loud talk or annoying behavior. Self-sufficiency of women is a rather recent development, so rules governing conduct on dates require the man to take the initiative in most situations and treat the woman as if she really were a very helpless person. And the woman assists in the deceit.

A sample of questions regarding conventional practices follows. Test the above definition of etiquette by applying it to these questions. They have all been worded positively. The answer to each one is "Yes." Where there are alternatives the first is usually regarded correct.

QUESTIONS FOR COLLEGE MEN

1. Do you make your plans definite and never break a date except in unavoidable circumstances? When you must break a date, do you send flowers or candy as an apology or send a friend as a substitute?

2. Do you go to the door and ask for your date, or do you drive up in front of her house and honk for her to come out?

3. Do you assist her with her wraps whenever necessary and open doors for her to pass ahead of you?

4. At theaters, do you let her follow the usher and be seated first? If there is no usher, do you lead the way and stand aside for her to be seated?

QUESTIONS FOR COLLEGE WOMEN

1. Are you ready, or nearly so, when your date calls?

2. Are you considerate about expenses on dates?

3. Do you tell the boy you had a good time when he thanks you for a date, rather than thanking him?

4. Do you suggest that he call again, without being insistent about it?

5. Do you know that a hostess rises when someone is being presented to her; a lady never rises when a gentleman is being presented unless the gentleman is elderly or of unusual importance; a young lady always rises when she is being presented to an elderly lady?

QUESTIONS FOR COLLEGE MEN AND WOMEN

1. Do you break your bread first into small portions, and then butter each piece separately as you have need of it?

2. At a dinner party, do you follow your hostess's example with the array of forks, knives, and spoons? In case you can't see around the centerpiece, the theory is to work from the outside in.

3. Do you place your butter or steak knife securely across one corner of your plate after use, or do you let one end of the knife rest on the tablecloth?

4. At dinners with maid service, are you aware that things are always passed to you on your left side, or do you twist around and try to grab a roll over your right shoulder?

5. In introducing two persons do you always present men to women with the statement, "Miss Jones, may I present Mr. Mark?" Do you also present younger persons to older ones?

Service to the Group. Persons who make definite contributions to the group to which they belong are usually well-liked. They stand out because of their social ingenuity and resourcefulness and other qualities. What are these qualities? The following have been suggested (831).

Conversationalist—witty and interested in a variety of topics.
Willingness to assume responsibilities—to do the dirty work.
Repertoire of things to do—games, stories, entertainment.
Ability to handle the business of an organization.
Understanding of the personalities of the members.
Sincere desire to promote good relationship among the members.
Appreciation and applause of the efforts of other members.
Introduction of members of the group to interesting outsiders.
Common sense and good practical judgment about group affairs.
Keen awareness of the wishes and needs of the group.
A good, attentive listener.

Improving Social Adjustment. Individuals do improve over a period of months or a year in human relationships and in overcoming characteristics that previously were displeasing to associates. These improvements take place in the normal process of living with others, being influenced by group morale, and through trial and error developing behavior consistent both with the individual's own inner life and with the group. Personality inventories and guidance program follow-ups tend to show these changes (162, 7).

Difficulty in adjusting to a group may be due to the incompatibility between the behavior one has acquired in his development and the behavior and attitudes emphasized by that group. If this is the major factor and the individual wants to become a part of the group and is reasonably stable, the change is not hard. With time the student may perceive aspects of his grooming or deportment that produce an aversion in his contemporaries and gradually change them. He is more likely to *idealize someone* in his environment and alter his behavior in imitation of this model. This is the usual pattern with the adolescent who hangs around with the gang, notes minutely the details of their behavior and attitudes, and affects them himself.

Sometimes changing one's behavior is a more *deep-seated process* and does not entail merely adding new and different habits. In fact, some individuals, when they regard the behavior of others, find it grossly incompatible with their inner feelings and own way of life. We suggested in Chapter 5 that it is far more effective, when thinking of self-improvement, for the individual to seek to understand himself, his development, his inner traits and purposes, and the manner in which he expresses them. This understanding should develop in an environment that allows him to feel acceptable and in harmony with others. He may attempt to see the role that he can best play in relationships to others in his group. Some perspective may grow from this discovery and indicate to him that individuals differ widely, that they need not be stereotyped, but that certain common modes of behavior are desirable. With a calm evaluation of his likenesses and differences in terms of the behavior which is currently in vogue, he may accept and see reason for his strong basic traits. Furthermore, he can positively modify other traits, habits, or expressions without doing violence to his fundamental way of life and thereby make an adjustment both to his total personality and to his contemporaries.

The less masculine man or the girl who enjoys robust sports and has become more aggressive than passive in personality may likewise accept these basic, well-established traits with a view to utilizing them in a good, long-term adjustment.

John is below average in stature and physical attractiveness. At first he impulsively adjusted to this lack of height and good looks by a hostile, compensatory attitude, putting on a front of boldness and toughness. With more maturity and perspective, he came to say to himself, "I am one of the short and less handsome men in the world. I have many of the reactions that short men have had in our particular society, which puts a social premium on height and physical symmetry. There are certain things I can do about my physical features in terms of dress, but an intelligent, long-term evaluation should show me that this is a minor aspect of my personality. My aptitudes, philosophy of life, interests, and capability of making a contribution are far more important than my physique. I can play an effective role, and there are certain traits within my personality that will help me to play it."

Adjusting socially, then, involves *understanding oneself, accepting oneself as a worthy person capable of growing, and working out a program for integrating one's traits with some changes. This may involve conforming where it is deemed wise, or associating with others who have similar motivation, and opposing conformity* when conformity seems to mean the sacrifice of higher values for trivial gains.

The college student who fights all conventionality may find upon reflection that many of the traits listed above, which most people in our culture dislike, indicate essential insecurity and maladjustment. As he gains assistance through a counselor or through success in some field of accomplishment, he may find it easier to acquire some of the etiquette and behavior exhibited by his group.

Friendship

There are some people who, in the more profound meaning of the term, have no friends. They know many people well enough to call them by their first names, but there is not an intimate relationship or an affection that entails sacrifice and permanent ties. There are many persons, in contrast, who insist that they have many very good, staunch friends. They insist, too, that these friendships are not synonymous with acquaintanceships. The friends are persons in whom they would confide, to whom they would turn for help and find genuine understanding, and to whom they would in certain circumstances give their most cherished possessions.

In this discussion we shall distinguish acquaintanceship from friendship on the basis of the *depth* of the relationship. Acquaintances are individuals who are met and known superficially. Friends, on the other hand, are those for whom we have a *deeper affection*. We know them *intimately*, and the relationship is *lasting*. When college students are asked how many friends they have, their answers vary. The average for a group at one Midwestern university is 53 "friends" and 421 "acquaintances." The students who made these estimates no doubt used a broader definition than that used above. The acquisition of numerous acquaintances is a condition of popularity.

Patterns of Friendships. Below are some of the various relationships that exist between individual pairs of friends. As we discuss the patterns you will recognize some of them as existing among persons you know. In some cases there will be mixtures of several of these patterns. Not all patterns of friendship lead to the most stable or favorable relationships. Where we find friendship growing there is a perceived reciprocal attraction and frequent interaction (579), which modern methods enable us to study (234).

SIMILARITY OF PERSONALITY. First, there are those persons who are drawn together because of similarity of personality. They have similar interests, similar attitudes, similar motives, values, and ideals. They are drawn together because they are alike.

Here are two men who play on the football team, who room together, have classes together, discuss their problems with each other, and often have double dates. They are close friends; each enjoys the other's company and confidences. Neither of these men has an allowance from home, and both earn or borrow the money for their entire expenses. They are drawn together by a number of factors common to both of them. Both rate with the "select." They share a similar background of earlier hardships and experiences. They know each other's faults and accept them. There is relatively little rivalry between them so each adds to the other's security. When in social groups they enjoy the same games, topics of conversation, and interests. They depend upon each other for companionship in going places. They appreciate most the fact that they can let off steam in each other's presence without breaking their essentially warm and stable relationship.

COMPLEMENTARINESS OF PERSONALITY TRAITS. In addition to similarity there is another pattern that is important. You may find many individuals who are drawn together, not because they are of like temperament or personality but, conversely, because they *differ*. These individuals have personalities that are complementary. One satisfies motives of the other. One has traits which the other admires, wishes he might have, but knows he does not possess. He admires his friend's prestige, possessions, accomplishments, humor, poise, or social competency. Without knowing it necessarily, he may vicariously live through his friend. He can display strongly desired traits to others by incorporating his friend in his social life and routine. Sometimes he in turn is able to satisfy needs in the friend and thus bind the relationship. The friend may receive acceptance, sincerity, and warmth or some other satisfaction from him. However, as shown in the next section, the pattern may be strained because one of the pair becomes too possessive. An example of complementariness follows.

Two members of the same sorority are devoted to each other. One is pretty and vivacious and dates frequently. The other is not pretty, is somewhat shy, but is very unselfish and pleasant in disposition. The second girl has a large allowance and a car. She feels dissatisfied without her attractive friend because the friend makes her life more complete, makes her feel more secure. On the other hand, her car and the clothes she lends her friend add prestige to the friend. They invite each other home. Throughout three years of college they have become inseparable. Each gives to the other what she lacks. The pretty, pleasant, popular girl comes from a family that has practically no resources. The other girl's family can give her everything. The popular girl gets prestige from the money and the name of her less popular friend, whereas she lends some of her popularity to the other. The relationship is finally cemented by the understanding, acceptance, mutual respect, and need that each has for the other.

This type of complementariness is found in some semi-platonic *relationships between boys and girls*. A girl may need a date upon whom she can depend under all circumstances, although she may feel no affection for him. The boy, on the other hand, may be very fond of the girl and quite willing to take her places in order to be near her. One may serve the other as a confidant or trusted adviser. The relationship may be composed partly of the motherly or big brother element. If the satisfactions are too one-sided, however, the duration of the relationship will be short. Perhaps a boy and a girl will study together. The girl will enjoy being with the boy and may even help him with his work and do chores for him.

POSSESSIVENESS IN FRIENDSHIPS. Another pattern is frequently found which sometimes cuts across the two patterns previously described. Some individuals want friends whom they can possess and dominate. They become jealous if the friend is seen with other persons. Usually these possessive individuals have few friends. They expect much from their friends, but they also give much. They frequently obligate the friend through their many services; the friend begins to feel that he should reciprocate although he does not share the feeling of his companion. Sooner or later he begins to feel restricted. This so-called friendship demands too much. The friend begins to feel irritated, and the friendship usually ends at this point. An underlying hostility toward this friend may exist, although not too well recognized by the more possessive of the pair. He may have affection for his friend but he may also inwardly resent and dislike this friend who "has so much." He may be a person who feels he never has been loved and seeks affection so vigorously that his demands are insatiable. There are, however, individuals who want to be possessed, who want to be directed, and, if the friend is such a person, the friendship does not cease. In these friendships the more aggressive of the pair serves a purpose in the life of the less aggressive.

ACCEPTANCE AND WARMTH. There are friendships that are based mainly upon the mutual respect, mutual security, loyalty, and warmth experienced in each other's contacts. Some individuals have a real affection for others with whom they enjoy recreational and relaxational pursuits, with whom they release tensions and feel more serene and genuine (856). Differences and similarities of personality may both exist in these patterns of friendship. Members of the pair may give affection to each other without expecting too much or without limiting too greatly each other's freedom. This sort of friendship is not one of possessiveness. It is not marked by conspicuous competitiveness, and it is not demanding in nature. Many of the more basic processes of friendship discussed below are found in this pattern. There is, in short, an *absence of mutual frustration*. Mutual affection is one of life's greatest experiences probably second only to love as valued by mankind. It constitutes one of the best relationships for personal growth and self-realization.

Conditions for Development of Friendship.   Studies have been made of friendships at all age levels.

FRIENDSHIPS AMONG CHILDREN.   As children our friends usually are those who live in the *same neighborhood* or are in the same school grade and who are about the *same age*.   We choose friends who have developed to about the *same status* as we have (684, 639, 612).

FRIENDSHIPS IN HIGH SCHOOL.   In the city junior high school, we begin to see more of the bases found in adults in their selection of friends.   Children at this age tend to choose friends who have parents of the *same socio-economic* position as theirs.   Proximity of homes is not so important a factor at this period as it was earlier in life. Friendships are about equally divided between those made in school and those made in the neighborhood and through home contacts (639, 612, 603, 576, 723, 85).   Two boys become friendly not only because they play baseball together and have similar outdoor interests,

Susan Greenburg

but also because they meet certain *social standards* that are becoming important in their lives. Their friends must meet their standards of presentability and must have attitudes they approve or at least can accept.

FRIENDSHIPS IN COLLEGE. The emphasis on social traits and personal motives found in the high school period reaches its greatest strength in college. Whereas at the college period, as at all periods, *similarities* among friends are more pronounced than dissimilarities, the traits which are similar are more deep-seated (639, 820). The opinions of the friend are important. Likes and dislikes are also a major factor. Specifically, college men who are friends are similar in their desire for participation in sports, in possession of determination, and in the habit of church attendance. Both men and women who are friends tend to be alike in ideals, morals, standards, athletic interests, neatness in dress, and in such matters as reading tastes, hobbies, and grades (222). Physical appearance, such as color of hair, eyes, and skin, does not seem to be so important in friendship as the other traits. This observation substantiates the importance of *motivation* (desires, interests, and attitudes) rather than physical factors in promoting friendships. In the college period families seem relatively unimportant in influencing friendship.

English college men were also found to form friendships on similar bases. Friends of extroverts were characteristically extroverted. The friends of men who were rated as conscientious, persistent, and tactful had the same traits. Concerning the trait of perseverance and single-mindedness, the Englishmen were either almost identical with their friends or quite *dissimilar* (137). The dissimilar friends were probably examples of complementariness.

At college, although most students make some friends, those who make them most easily tend to be more extroverted, emotionally stable, vivacious, tolerant, generous, and capable in conversation than others (490).

Basic Processes in Friendship. What do the above descriptions and studies of friendship show? Friendships thrive and deepen as they (1) mutually satisfy, broaden the motives of the pair; (2) produce a minimum amount of conflict or frustration of the kind seen in possessiveness; (3) provide a conducive environment in which both can grow and develop satisfying human relations; (4) and in addition lead to a better understanding of each other's emotional outlets and inner potentialities.

The best friendships, as shown above, allow the satisfaction of most human motives: affection, recognition, security, adventure, and success. It is one of the most conducive relationships and allows much of the growth described in our discussion of counseling in Chapter 5.

Friends are a source of deep understanding and acceptance in times of trial or triumph. They can share intimate feelings with us. We can see ourselves most frankly in the warmth of our friend's acceptance of us despite our limitations. Friends can do that which we cannot do for ourselves with propriety. They recite our virtues, plead our case, and indirectly help us to see our faults. They furnish companionship as we learn to deal with the difficult social and emotional problems of life.

Friendlessness. What are the causes of friendlessness? Why are some individuals devoid of real friendship? In studies of children and in conferences with college students, a number of reasons for lack of friends may be observed (585). Some of the many patterns follow.

A student has grown up in a *family* that is not socially inclined. His parents have held themselves aloof from neighbors and associates. For some reason they have not built friendships. Their children lack the skills for building friendships.

Another student is *egocentric*. Since early in life he has been given the center of the stage. He received great attention as a child; now in adulthood he demands it. He resents any person who receives the attention he believes should be given him. As a result he has built many dislikes and few friendships.

A third individual is friendless because early experiences in his life have taught him to *enjoy being alone*. He grew up on a farm where he saw few people. When he first came into contact with others he experienced difficulty in getting along with them. This failure to become social has caused him to turn to solitary tasks and amusements in which he satisfies most of his motives and finds his greatest pleasure.

Another person does not acquire friends because he refuses to become close to others. He is afraid others will find out too much about him. He does not want *others to know his inner life*. He holds others at a distance. He does not become intimate with them. He is somewhat stiff and formal in their presence. He is not "one of the gang." He is sensitive to their real or imagined gibes and cannot banter with them.

Here is a student who feels that she is not wanted in the group. It is true that she is *different*. She dresses peculiarly. She spends many hours alone. Her ideas differ from those of most students. She is bright, but she has never become socialized. She feels inferior in social groups although she knows that she is superior otherwise. She knows that she is not popular, that she is not sought, but she does not know the reason. She has never made an attempt to become acquainted with others. Since she is not typical, they make no effort to know her. Therefore she remains friendless.

Finally, there is the student who was *teased* and persecuted in childhood. He has a misanthropic attitude, and he expects other people to be antagonistic toward him. He has a warped attitude toward people in general. He hates and fears them. He thinks they dislike him, and he feels that he is not wanted by groups.

Acquiring Friends. No one need be without friends. The preceding discussion should provide *understanding* to those who have had difficulty establishing friendships. A few questions may further enrich this understanding. Why are you who are without friends not closer to those with *simliar interests, background* and *attitudes?* What about those with *needs you can satisfy* as you also satisfy your own needs? Has *possessiveness* toward friends been a problem? Has your background been such that getting closer to people will be a slow growth rather than a *quick solution in one cherished friend?* Is your difficulty because you reject yourself and thereby reject people like you? If this is true you are depriving yourself of the deep satisfaction of friendship. Do you tend to express your hostilities toward those around you? Do you in other ways fail to attract others because of *personal traits* mentioned in the early part of the chapter? Do you bring earlier, *inappropriate childhood attitudes* into relationships with present acquaintances? Do you *anticipate rejections* which may not take place and by so doing strain relationships? An answer to some of these questions may bring insight and suggestions that may result in better relations with others.

Social Groups and Creative Activity

Finding or Organizing a Congenial Group. Some students have friends and acquaintances but for some reason or other do not belong actively to any organizations. The reasons for this are numerous. They may have expected the group to seek them. Motivation to become a member of a given organization may never have been strong enough to produce the initiative to investigate the nature of groups and the methods of affiliating with them. Some unfortunate experiences in groups encountered earlier, or the feeling that one does not rate well enough to associate freely with members of a group, may be among the ideas which prevent affiliation. In addition, there are persons who have been with others so infrequently that they prefer hobby activities that are best performed alone. They thereby avoid the discomfort which they experience in trying to be a desirable member of a group.

SEEKING A CONGENIAL GROUP. In Chapter 5 we showed that a congenial group or a conducive environment does much to help the individual develop, project his inner traits outward, and come to understand himself. It affords opportunity for personality release and growth. Many of the individuals just described have well-developed attitudes and skills, but these traits are not associated with group activities and have not been stimulated by responses from others. In a sense they are cooped up within the individuals. Frequently such individuals will discover one or more persons of similar temperament, interests, or traits, band together with them, and their interests and activities become socialized. This may lead to the formation of a warm group that takes the place of a warm family, so important in childhood development. As an individual expands in such a group, however small, the sense of his own worthiness usually increases, as shown by cases on pages 8 and 121. There are many hobby clubs, subject matter clubs, and organizations built around indoor athletics and skills encountered in colleges. These are purposive and meaningful groups that have grown out of common interests. In many academic departments, there exist clubs such as chemistry, education, journalism, music, forestry, and home economics clubs. Special interest groups include fencing, aviation, dancing, and photography. Eating, living, racial, political, and hobby groups are also found (309). These have value particularly for students who feel self-conscious in the groups that depend upon social intercourse for their reason. These students will find that, as they place their attention on the activities that the group espouses, they will become less self-conscious. In a group of this type they may grow in intellect and in skills. Social adroitness and acceptance by others and oneself will be a by-product. The interest of a group like this does not wane with time as is found to happen with members of social fraternities who drift apart after graduation. There is a substantial purpose that holds the members together. They are adult in character.

A professional or interest group of the type described above is exclusive, but this exclusiveness is based upon *merit* or *interests*. The members need not worry lest they cause nonmembers to be unhappy.

There is no need for fear of being inferior in such a group. The club has its avowed purpose: growth in some area of experience.

The neophyte who has just arrived on the campus must expect a period of readjustment. It is well for him to realize that the students whom he sees assuming leadership and behaving with confidence at group meetings probably felt and acted, when they were freshmen, as he does now. For this reason he should look about him for other newcomers who feel just as uncomfortable as he does and strike up relationships with them. The sponsor of any group can cite numerous examples of the green newcomer who seemed awkward, ill at ease, and friendless on arrival on the campus, and who, with time, expanded, took responsibility, made contributions, and grew personally.

HARMONY AND TENSION IN GROUPS. Working together with a group especially against external obstacles builds a relationship among the members. An experiment in a camp showed that individuals who had not known each other well could gain a stronger feeling for each other when playing against former "friends." Conversely, when it was contrived that in group competition against these former "friends" they would lose to them, the losers became hostile toward the former friends. This experiment shows that harmony and disharmony can be achieved by relationship and events between and within groups.

One of the most serious social hazards between individuals and groups is an impasse that *breaks harmonious communication* or leads to no communication at all. When this happens we are likely to become anxious and unrealistic in our thoughts about the other person. For fear of losing face or status we remain aloof instead of discussing our differences and seeing ourselves and others in perspective (839). Accurate understanding of the other person's motives and attitudes, sometimes called *social perception,* is associated with competency in dealing with them. When this is lost in personal interaction, the group represented also suffers in its effectiveness (744).

Athletics and Play in Social Adjustment. Play has always been regarded by theorists as a great *socializer.* It brings persons together under pleasant circumstances. It is *cooperative.* It is a source of facility in handling people. In addition, it is recreative and relaxing. It allows the player to assume social responsibilities with a less tense and a more pleasant attitude. It broadens his interests. It gives him additional goals and keeps him from being single-tracked.

In athletic and other games, individuals must cooperate with or

Susan Greenburg

pleasantly oppose one another. The players fuse purposes; they become absorbed in a common pleasure. They lose self-consciousness, social tensions, and inhibitions. Sports are a great leveler in a democracy. Those who participate are found also in other organizations (718).

In life, the penalties for errors are heavy and inescapable. However, winning and losing are events that occur several times in a play period. They are all taken with the game. The game is the main interest, not winning it or losing it. No doubt people differ in the extent to which they carry over this wholesome attitude into the serious, work-a-day world, but certainly all of it is not entirely lost when the person leaves the game.

There are several lines of evidence that those who have grown up with limited play and companions and little interest in games are less *well adjusted* than if they had experienced a normal play life

289

(522, 36, 140). All of us have noticed the difference between the carriage, mannerisms, and attitudes of the student who has been one of the group most of his life and those of the student who has been "out of it." The former contributes his opinions surely and without embarrassment; the latter offers his hesitantly and self-consciously. The former expects to be accepted, expects his opinions to carry weight, and they do. The matter of getting along with people is nothing new to him. The latter is dubious of his reception in a group and advances his opinions with little hope of their acceptance.

Play has been described as *integrating*. We are completely absorbed in the game when we play it well. Every sense organ and muscle acts toward the single end. Integration is a desirable goal. The more often we can display integrated behavior in everyday life, the more unified and consistent we are and the better we handle our problems.

Play is also a *means of satisfying motives* that cannot be satisfied elsewhere. Children play house or school and in the process act as their parents and teachers will not allow them to act in the living room or schoolroom. They enjoy the thrills of the gangster or G-man even though they would be punished severely if they should pilfer at the neighborhood store. Similarly, the adult removes inhibitions as well as clothes when he goes for a swim. Dancing is a sublimation of certain human motives. Games like gin rummy and bridge enable the players to compensate for a humdrum existence in the office, factory, or salesroom. Much adult play takes the player back to the memories of childhood or adolescent freedom.

There are numerous studies to show that delinquency is reduced when the older child is engaged in supervised play (634, 274). This seems true for the college period. The athlete has reason to keep himself *physically and morally fit*. His extra time is consumed by a pleasant activity, and he should have little time for the dissipation in which some of his nonathletic friends indulge. In addition, he is in the limelight. His reputation must be clear because gossip that concerns him has extra news value. To be sure, not all students who are active in athletics achieve these results. Play is only one influence in the development of a complex personality (548). Some writers make more claims for athletics than are given above. Traits such as courage, determination, decisiveness, enthusiasm, loyalty, self-initiative, perseverance, self-reliance, self-control, aggressiveness, fairness, good sportsmanship, and ambition are among them (150). Surely most of these are elicited by many athletic games. We cannot say that athletics alone can establish all these traits until there is empirical evidence to substantiate the claim.

Other Extracurricular Activities in Social Adjustment. Many of the advantages of athletics apply to other extracurricular activities (864, 26). Since they also are a form of recreation, they integrate, socialize, and satisfy motives many of which would not otherwise be satisfied. They, too, release tension, enhance the reputation of the individual, give him experience in dealing with his fellow students, and provide an avenue for projecting outward his inner life and testing his potentialities for development, as indicated in Chapter 5.

Many educators have written on the value of extracurricular activities. Below are lists of advantages and the number of writers that emphasize each (425). Directors of extracurricular activities in college mention that their aims are similar to the advantages listed by educators. These include socialization, leadership, and discipline (26, 864, 759). They also stress the happiness and zest that arise from these activities, the self-confidence they produce, the feeling that the student has "a place in the sun," and the opportunity students have *to lose themselves in causes outside themselves* (309, 537). Students, too, value these activities highly. They mention advantages in social conduct, ability to meet others, friendliness, and poise. Participants show evidence of better grades and ratings (97, 733, 546, 846). There is evidence that students who engage in such activities in college carry them into life after college.

One reason that extracurricular programs sometimes fall short of the ideal is that a minority of the students participate too extensively, become overactive, and assume more than their share of the responsibility. The result is that the student cannot do justice to the office, the organization is not representative enough, and many students who need the opportunities for personal growth that the group would give them are not brought into the organization (150). The activity in turn also suffers by being less effective than it might be and neglecting talent it might otherwise exploit.

DRAMATICS. If one has ever been charged with being an "exhibitionist" one should try dramatics as a social means of expressing the urge for attention. Many of the motives mentioned in connection with athletics are also satisfied by dramatics.

In addition to the prestige that grows from ability to command the attention of an audience, dramatics may provide an outlet for strong traits not otherwise expressed. When one participates in a play, he lives a role that he has not experienced in real life. He can be the inner self he feels. The timid individual may find himself in an ascendant role, and he enjoys the experience. The loud, aggressive individual may be told in jest by his friends that, if he were really the quiet, mild type of person he played in the dramatic production, he would be more popular.

Dramatics may give the participant *perspective* of himself and his role in society. It may *suggest new traits* in new roles and allow him practice in these roles. He may learn the value of grooming, posture, facial expressions, and attitudes. If he can gradually add to or subtract from his own characteristic actions without self-consciousness, he will have achieved a valuable accomplishment.

The following were mentioned as aims by dramatics sponsors in American colleges (309): appreciation of plays, development of avocational interest, poise, self-confidence and cooperation, a means of self-expression, fellowship, leadership, initiative, and responsibility. A study gives some evidence that social changes within the individual grow out of participation in dramatics (804). Students of psychodrama and play therapy emphasize the value of drama in permitting spontaneity and creativity in personality. It provides an opportunity for some tensions to be resolved and for new personality patterns to emerge (30, 553). This is discussed on pages 142 to 144. There is some evidence that dramatics, and activities connected with publications, draw students from high ability and grade ranges (719, 182).

FORENSICS. Forensics are similar to dramatics except that they probably are not so extensive in their contribution. There is a great premium upon ability as a public speaker. People gain confidence and a feeling of ascendancy when they are able to hold the attention of an audience or handle a group. The speaking situation is one in which the individual can gain realistic experience in dealing with problems of self-consciousness, as discussed on pages 447 to 448. Debate gives direct practice in this skill that is so valuable in modern society. There is, in addition, the *research* experience that the average debater gains. He is given an opportunity to enhance his knowledge on numerous topics that he would not otherwise have probed.

STUDENT JOURNALISM. The student who writes for the school paper or magazine usually puts forth effort far in excess of that which he displays in his English classes. He feels that he is doing something real. It is a lifelike situation. It gives him direct practice in the organization and expression of his ideas in writing. It extends his interest in current affairs and gives him prestige and association with other students. This, too, is a source for spontaneous expression of inner feelings, an avenue for the projection of one's subterranean emotional life, discussed on page 144.

STUDENT OFFICES. The student who holds offices in college organizations gains executive experience. All the functions performed by the business and professional leader he must carry out in a more limited field. As treasurer, he plans or meets a budget. As secretary, he organizes the agenda of the association. He carries on correspondence and sometimes assumes an aggressive role in making social contacts. As president, he assumes responsibility for the successful operation of the organization for a period of time. He secures the cooperation of the members. He appoints committees. He handles resignations and acquires an impersonal attitude toward them. He becomes able to see his policies criticized and to deal with opposition. He acquires ability to manipulate people and win them to his point of view when necessary. He is prepared to meet deep disappointment occasionally when a plan or policy he has fostered fails.

Membership in a Fraternity, Sorority, or Social Club. Membership in high school or college fraternities, sororities, and social clubs is widely regarded as a badge of popularity. It is also looked upon by some as a means for the attainment of social poise.

"Is membership in a fraternity worth while?" is the question that faces many students. The fraternity man may need to justify the institution when its value is questioned or charges are brought against it. The student who remains unaffiliated with such a group throughout his college years may also need to clarify his reasons and attitudes. So let us consider very briefly the pros and cons of membership in a fraternity (464, 387, 449, 523).

Fraternities differ greatly in every aspect. The best fraternities are those that offer to their members most of the advantages listed and few or none of the disadvantages. Not only do individual fraternities differ, but also the roles of fraternities as a group differ in their influence on different campuses.

ADVANTAGES OF A FRATERNITY. Stimulates or provides for:

1. Forming friendships.
2. Self-government and leadership.
3. Group loyalty.
4. A bond between students in different parts of the country.
5. Extracurricular successes.

   6. Thinking about the welfare of group.
   7. Acquisition of manners, etiquette, grooming and social skills.
   8. Supervision of study.
   9. Social relationship with faculty.
   10. Discouragement of socially undesirable behavior.
   11. Cooperation and group living.
   12. Rivalry for grades and group honors.
   13. A home to entertain friends.
   14. Prestige of a national group.
   15. Contacts with mature and successful alumni.
   16. School spirit and tradition; cooperation with the administration.
   17. Belonging.
   18. A colorful existence.
   19. Freshman orientation.
   20. Group discipline and conformity.
   21. Taking orders as a pledge; giving them as an active.

For many a student, fraternity membership is a "social necessity." His friends and associates are members, and the force of the group opinion seems too strong to ignore. If you are a member of a fraternity or are considering becoming one, measure the fraternity of your choice by this ideal fraternity. As a member you can be instrumental in raising the standards of your fraternity so that it will fulfill these functions.

DISADVANTAGES OF THE FRATERNITY. The critics of fraternities would first claim that the so-called ideal accomplishments mentioned are rarely a reality, particularly items number 8, 15, and 16. They would also challenge as advantages items 12, 19, and 20 as carried out by a fraternity when viewed from a standpoint of broad social individual growth. Furthermore they would argue that under a well-equipped and well-operated dormitory system that employs trained personnel many of the listed advantages occur without these disadvantages (797). Fraternities invoke or encourage in too many cases:

   1. High cost—pins, rushing, parties, national fees and luxuries.
   2. Snobbishness, provinciality, prejudices and undemocratic pressures.
   3. "Selling the house bill" during financial stress.
   4. Group thinking rather than development of individuals who have their own convictions.
   5. Cribbing, misappropriation of examinations, sex irregularities.
   6. Interfraternity bitterness over pledges.
   7. Division of campus into "have" and "have nots."
   8. Superficial and materialistic standards rather than an emphasis on

those compatible with a cultural and humanistic goal of a college education.

9. A disillusioned and mildly interested alumni.
10. Loyalty to the fraternity rather than to the college.
11. Listing of groups within which members may date.
12. Selection of members based on veneer and similarity in personality rather than on character, integrity and individuality.
13. An easy-going social life rather than a stimulating liberal and intellectual life.

With the claims and complaints clearly stated you should be better able to evaluate fraternities with which you come in contact and possibly have a better basis for action be it choice, rejection or attempted improvement.

Supplementary Readings

E. F. Gardner and G. G. Thompson, *Social Relations and Morale in Small Groups,* Appleton-Century-Crofts, 1956.

L. Festinger and D. Katz, *Research Methods in the Behavioral Sciences,* Dryden, 1953.

H. C. McKown, *Extracurricular Activities,* Macmillan, 1952.

W. C. Menninger, *Recreation and Mental Health,* Austin, Texas: Hogg Foundation, 1949.

M. Sherif and C. W. Sherif, *Groups in Harmony and Tension: An Integration of Studies of Intergroup Relations,* Harper, 1953.

In addition see the references cited by number in the chapter and appearing in the bibliography of an accompanying volume entitled *Teaching Personal Adjustment: An Instructor's Manual.*

Culture and Social Roles

Practically no one today lives by himself. Besides being a member of a family and neighborhood he is also likely to be a member of a work or recreation group, church, club or some informal clique. At such times, as we saw inferentially in the previous chapter, he assumes certain roles—friend, popular acquaintance, rejected because he fails to show the behavior cherished by the group, or fellow member in a special interest group such as sports or dramatics. He might assume some form of leadership. To a certain extent he is a product of the *culture and subcultures* in which he has lived, but usually he is not clearly aware of these determinants of his personality.* In this chapter we will examine critically some of the roles we assume, certain of the social forces influencing us, and describe the behavior mutually satisfying in the relationships between interacting individuals. This behavior is sometimes referred to as social strategy and leadership.

---

* *Culture* is the term applied to the customs, attitudes, and beliefs of a group. Within the culture of the Western World there are numerous subcultures representing nationality, religion, and racial backgrounds.

296

CHAPTER 11

LEADERSHIP AND GROUP ROLES

Social Forces in American Culture. Among the social forces present in midtwentieth century America, particularly amid the middle class which is in the focus of our culture, is an emphasis on *individual competition* in striving to "improve" our social status. This is sometimes called an emphasis on *upward social mobility*. Progress in this direction is largely measured by money and symbols of social prestige and power. Thus material things, action, technology or "know-how" are idealized. Education, special skills, personal presentability and inoffensive initiative are placed in high value. Other patterns and values that are found to permeate American society include a tendency to rebel against authority, a conscious quest for pleasure, a preference for rationality, a glorification of science, and a dream that the common man's life will be made easier and enriched (152, 841, 421).

Social Class Characteristics. Each of us is also a part of a subculture represented by our family and neighborhood. From there we acquire attitudes and values (see Chapter 4 dealing with personality development). Sometimes these values that are acquired early in our lives either on the farm, in a small community, which has a given ethnic nationality or religious flavor, or in the suburbs, come in conflict with the values we subsequently acquire. Such a conflict was shown in the case of Harry N. (see pages 267–268). These conflicts may not be conscious but are nevertheless influential.

The social classes in America have been studied and differences in values and attitudes between the classes have been noted.* We indicated above some of the attitudes of the middle class: an emphasis on upward mobility, a high value on education, special skills, cleanliness, and decency. The individual in this class learns to repress and suppress impulses, particularly those toward aggression or sex behavior. He learns to express his aggression in competition and ambition, or experiences a conflict between the ideal of the virile male and the need to be a well-mannered gentleman (171, 418). The family group is important in his early years; he is closely supervised, and loyalty to his family is instilled. This is in contrast, to a certain extent, to the early influences in the lower classes in which the family is less closely knit, the mother perhaps working outside the home, discipline less consistent, and the neighborhood disorganized. The child in this economic group gets many of his values from his fellows as he plays in the streets. He is found to be more impulsive, aggressive, and more emotional than his fellows from the middle class (172, 171, 348).

These forces of class are quiet determinants of personality. At the present time, individuals from various classes probably have more interaction than in previous eras. Universal military service is partially responsible for this as well as the better opportunities for individuals with special abilities to attend college. Individuals from various American subcultures find themselves to be profoundly different in their attitudes and habitual way of behaving. Those from the middle economic subculture may envy the emotional openness and freedom of the lower economic subculture; on the other hand, there are some individuals from the lower economic group who might wish they had the well-ingrained ambition, reserve, and capacity to postpone present gratification for future success found in the middle economic subculture.

Individual Roles in Social Interaction. The various attitudes found in American subcultures are associated with roles that are in

---

* By *class* we mean the groupings of people in a community or culture on a scale of prestige, which gives them a certain status. Occupation, neighborhood, family background, and social membership are some of the criteria of class status.

part an expression of the subcultures and in part entirely individual. We often regard our culturally acquired attitudes as universal or innate until we discover foreign cultures idealizing attitudes and roles that are highly different from ours. For example, the Arapesh, a tribe in New Guinea, emphasize cooperation; both men and women are nonaggressive, permissive, and maternal in the roles they play. Another tribe in the area, the Mundugumor are aggressive, jealous, competitive, and vengeful. In the Tchambuli tribe, the sex roles we know are reversed. Women control the power and economic life of the group, a role our males perform. The men are dependent, sensitive, aesthetic—a role that we regard in our culture as feminine (526).

In a complex modern industrial society such as ours there are many functions to be performed and many roles to be played.* Different vocations call for different roles. Ideally, the individual plays, at least during the hours he devotes to his vocation, those roles he can best play to reach his greatest personal fulfillment and make a contribution to society. The roles he plays during avocational pursuits again bring out those traits that are most satisfying to him. Ideally in a democracy that emphasizes individuality, many roles are permitted and encouraged. To a certain extent this is true also in reality. We mentioned in the chapter on Social Adjustment on page 277 some functions the individual may perform for the group. The individuals differ in the satisfaction they gain out of playing different roles.

In our society, mass production and distribution of goods is a highly important function, along with professional services, to better the welfare of the individual. Supervisors, salesmen, and professional people have high prestige. The socially ascendant role that allows one to influence others without offending them has become, at least in the past few decades, a role that many have assumed whether or not it was compatible with their inner personal organization. That this assumption of an incompatible role raised questions and conflicts in the individual is illustrated by the popularity of the book called "How to Win Friends and Influence People." It became the most popular nonfiction book of its time, selling four million copies. Let us examine this role, which is represented in the individual by traits we shall call social proficiency.

---

* By *role* we usually mean the pattern of behavior a person in a particular social status is expected to exhibit.

Social Proficiency

Social Proficiency in Our Culture. The able, serious student who lacks outstanding charm or social presence sometimes questions whether his talents will be lost because he has not developed along with them a pleasing personal manner or a convincing line of chatter. How important is this social proficiency? Can these social skills be used insincerely to the later detriment of the user? We shall use the term "social proficiency" to refer to that behavior which stimulates many others to evaluate one positively. *It utilizes conventionality*. No matter what our cultural group, we are subjected to numerous strong social forces. These forces *produce group behavior* known as customs, fads, and fashions. If we are cognizant of them we understand our own attitudes and are better able to communicate with and lead others. The man who is ignorant of or ignores customs, fashions, and the generalized ways in which the group behaves comes into conflict with its members and certain of its leaders. This kind of conventionality is in many respects similar to etiquette, discussed in the preceding chapter.

To be more specific, a college graduate who seeks a position in the office of a stock broker would be considered at least peculiar if not definitely abnormal if he should enter the office of the broker with an arrogant manner and wearing a collegiate sweater, an open-collared shirt, and campus slacks. He may have more knowledge about stocks and bonds than anyone else of his age. It is doubtful, however, that the broker will bother to penetrate the unconventional *exterior* to learn the applicant's true nature. It behooves this individual to understand why he has ignored the conventions of brokerage offices if he intends to affiliate with them.

Inoffensive Social Initiative as a Cultural Role. If we analyze those who seem most effective in public relations, they seem first to have prestige either as a result of their own personal traits, their social or vocational position, or their associations. Secondly, the individual in his relationships with others seems in some way (usually indirectly) to *acknowledge their personal worth*.

In describing the attitudes and behavior of such an individual in social situations the following are to a greater or less extent observed about him:

Has memory for names and faces.
Is good-natured and pleasant-mannered.
Approaches others through their needs, problems, and interests.
Is modest about his own achievements.
Is judiciously complimentary.
Has sense of humor and may direct it toward himself.
Can accept graciously the complimentary overtures of others.
Anticipates objections and resistances to his behavior.
Listens to others, including their objections to his views.
Is not rigid in thought, may concede on minor points.
Respects the feelings of others, is not latently hostile.
Is successful in getting attention and vividly presenting his views.

Observe a socially effective person and notice to what extent the above items characterize him. *You might be interested in checking yourself on this list if you feel this role is appropriate for you.*

Social Prestige.   Personal prestige is the influence or respect which certain attributes give to an individual. These attributes may be previous success, position, personal charm, power, appearance, or the like. Studies of successful salesmen show that prestige elements such as these are often related to their success (308).

Prestige in our culture is enhanced by friends, prominent and interesting relatives, past achievements, appearance, possessions and various personal potentialities as mentioned in Chapter 10 under popularity. Latent possibilities may be developed as elements of prestige. An individual may develop his abilities in athletics, hobbies, or the arts. In fact, the *most enduring prestige is that which emerges from the development of aptitudes and potentialities through creative activity.* The individual who through his efforts creates objects of value to the group, or makes a contribution to an organization and thereby receives acclaim, has discovered a real basis for his own satisfactions and prestige within the group.

Acknowledgment of the Personal Worth of Individuals.   A very important factor in smooth social relationships is recognition of the value of the other individual. Habits of good manners and of appreciation of others are automatic with the person who has a genuine interest in and *sincere and warm appreciation of his fellow men.* To be most effective this appreciation of others must come from one with *prestige.* The effective person avails himself of all the prestige he possesses and integrates it in order that his appreciative recognition of others will seem important to them. The following is a case which emphasizes gracious recognition of another.

Manuel attended a banquet recently. He was seated beside the wife of a faculty member who has attained widespread recognition in his field. On his other side was seated a young authoress of no mean ability.

The young authoress spoke only when spoken to and obviously felt that she should have been seated beside a more important person. Her long silences were spent in gazing across the room of tables toward some of her big-wig acquaintances. Manuel's occasional remarks elicited slight response from her, and this was given with condescension.

On the other hand, the wife of the faculty member introduced herself, repeated Manuel's name as he mentioned it, asked if he were related to another Marco whom she knows. Manuel found himself telling her the name of his home town. She spoke of persons she knew there. Before long Manuel had told her his interests, previous successes and plans. When he told her his plan to go into medicine as a vocation and to practice in rural areas she spent some time talking of the needs in such areas. She told him how much she admires a person who gives up the chances of a more lucrative practice in order to serve a greater need. All this was said with a genuineness that was completely convincing.

When Manuel mentioned his home town, instead of saying "Oh!" she recalled that two of the most interesting old homes she had ever seen are there. She also added a few items of state history that are associated with his town. Manuel appreciated the fact that there are many adverse matters she might have mentioned, but avoided.

Manuel was greatly impressed with her *interest* in him, her appreciation of his assets. He was conscious of the fact that she was a person of importance, but at no time did she force this upon him.

Throughout the meal she was as *considerate* of Manuel's needs as of her own. She offered the relishes when she thought he would like more. She set the sugar and cream beside his place when she finished with them, rather than placing them where she had found them as the writer next to him had done. She did all of this with graciousness. Several times during the conversation she referred to his opinions: "As you say, Mr. Marco . . ." and, "I agree with you in your opinion regarding . . ." She used his choice of words rather than others that might have been no more suitable but whose use by a person of superior prestige might have seemed like a correction. Occasionally she asked his opinion on minor matters.

Effective Factors in the Presentation of Ideas. Regardless of the means by which the idea is presented by lecture, press, or dramatization, it should be presented vividly and frequently to be effective. The vehicle should *vary* from time to time. If at all possible, attempts should be made to get individuals *ego-involved* in the idea presented, as shown below.

Should you as city health officer want to launch an educational program in hygiene you would first name your program. You would set aside a month in which to educate your group. It would be called "Health Month." You would have eight or ten outstanding persons in the community (*prestige*) write ten rules of health. These would be flashed on the screen of the local theater. They would appear several times in the local newspapers. Health buttons would be issued to the school children. There would be health pageants at the schools (*vivid presentation*). The merchants would dress their windows with the health motif, with special emphasis on the theme in the drug stores. Radio programs with pleasant music would be planned. Case histories of healthy and unhealthy individuals would be presented. Over and over you would repeat through various media "Health Habits Pay," and you would give your public ten specific suggestions for attaining these health habits. You might even conduct a health contest, might include a series of lectures with a prize for the best essay on the material covered in the lectures (*ego-involvement*). You would have students in school check daily the extent to which they practice the ten health rules which you are trying to publicize. You might even have them engage their parents in building these practices also.

Effectiveness in Opposition to Ideas. For years politicians, debaters, essayists and others have practiced effective social strategy. Their specific approach has varied with their own personality, the situation at the time, and the person they are trying to convince (374). They have exhibited most of the characteristics mentioned on page 301. The same methods that have been successfully used by some persons have resulted in complete failure for others. The inoffensive approach to opponents usually consists of paying tribute to them and their ideas in some way and then proceeding to show fallacies in their views. This technique is shown in a statement such as, "There are some things to be said for this view but . . ." A more aggressive technique usually consists of a strong challenge of the opponent's viewpoint, his motivation, of his associates in the name of some higher principles or the welfare of the challenger's constituents.

This hostile approach when successful is calculated. It is *not* an impulsive explosion from a habitually antagonistic, aggressive, egocentric, arrogant, or dominant person who not only alienates his opponent but arouses anxiety and distaste in those who might support the view he espouses. Individuals who are themselves highly insecure and anxious, who possess some of the socially alienating traits mentioned above, and who have not clearly integrated their own position have great difficulty in convincing others effectively. This was discussed in Chapter 10 in connection with "friendliness" and "habits that make us disliked."

Critique of Social Proficiency. Compliments, smiles, and feigned friendship may be very impressive at first. They do not, however, wear well with time, especially if we find that the person is deceiving others by these methods. We label him a fraud or a hypocrite. A sincere person who is really interested in people, in social situations, and in a more *effective compromise*, which will better his lot as well as that of the average man, may profit by these suggestions. One whose social motives are highly questionable will not profit long by learning social proficiency. He will soon be labeled in terms of his true basic motives.

PROFICIENCY AND ONE'S INNER FEELINGS AND CONVICTIONS. If we heed the advice of the popular books on acquiring friends and winning influence over associates through compliments, pandering always to their interests, putting emphasis on externalities, we may find ourselves putting greater value on the superficial in our culture than on the expression of our inner convictions. Students of human nature who are cognizant of the force of inner motivation raise the question: "What happens to the real self and the impulses that are perforce inhibited in order to conform to the wishes, attitudes, and interests of those with whom we come in contact?" The degree to which one is to become a shell of conformity and social niceties at the expense of his convictions and self-respect, in order to avoid the outer (and possibly amicable) conflict which is inevitable, is a question that must be weighed.

SOCIAL PROFICIENCY MASKS ISSUES; IT IS NOT A FRANK APPROACH. Certainly the critics who make this statement do so with some justice. In a sense, however, a discussion of social proficiency is at the same time an exposé. Once we have learned the art of persuading others, we are more capable of recognizing a persuasive technique when it is directed toward us. A frank discussion of it brings it into the open, allows students to learn it as well as to detect its use. Social proficiency will always be employed. It is doubtful whether we will ever attain the objectivity that will allow us to reason without having emotional factors complicate our thinking.

Leadership

Leaders and Their Roles in Groups. Groups, as well as individuals, differ from each other and have describable characteristics. Groups, if they are to survive, must satisfy the needs of their members, and various individuals assume various roles to meet these needs. A college fraternity or social club, for example, must pledge, recruit new members, provide parties, decorate and maintain the house or meeting rooms, keep up the members' scholastic average and social status. Some may have more idealistic goals such as personal growth, development of emotional maturity or leadership of the members, or pursuit of some common interests. Various students are elected to offices or chairmanship of committees to satisfy these needs. Many members serve as leaders in some activity or other. They must be able to *facilitate the roles that various members play in the group toward the accepted goals of the group.*

Who and What Are Leaders? Most of you who read these pages are members of one or more groups. You recognize people in these groups who influence the whole group or segments of the group. They are showing leadership. Of what does this leadership consist? Is it of a different nature for different people or for different groups? What kind of leadership role can you play now? Does this differ from the kind you idealize?

SOME DIFFERENT LEADERS IN HISTORY. Let us look at a brief sketch of the lives of three well-known leaders who differed greatly in the roles they played.

Warren G. Harding came to the presidency of the United States after a political career that started early in life. He attained a college education, and in his youth taught in a country school, studied law, and worked in a newspaper office. At 19 he became editor and owner of the *Marion* (Ohio) *Star.*

He is said to have had a kindly and genial nature and to have reposed too much trust in his friends, who at times took advantage of it. He presented an excellent appearance and was the kind of man to whom the populace as a whole was attracted. He was the "head-man" kind of leader. In politics he belonged to the stand-pat element but frequently favored popular legislation. His administration was conservative and won its greatest support from the more affluent portion of the country.

Nikolai Lenin was the son of a government official in Czarist Russia. He studied law but gave up its practice to carry on propaganda work. This step was taken in spite of the fact that he had been banished to Siberia during his student days for participation in prohibited gatherings. He studied Karl Marx's work during his early years, became a devoted disciple, and took an active part in the Social Democrat movement.

Throughout his career he was arrested on numerous occasions and spent a great deal of his life outside of Russia either as fugitive or exile. He did not deviate from his original purpose despite these experiences. He continued to write and lead movements which favored the liberation of the working classes. He wrote much of his *Development of Capitalism in Russia* while in exile.

He had the capacity to formulate policies, maintain his position in regard to them, gain followers, and carry his policies into action when the appropriate time arrived. He founded the Soviet Republics and the Communist International. He formulated policies for the workers of his own and other countries. He took a definite stand against the First World War and in 1914 organized the proletariat for attacks on capitalists. He carried his country through many crises, and it gained strength under his leadership. He was an active leader even after he lost the power of speech toward the end of his life.

Louis Pasteur was the son of a tanner. He received a thorough grounding in chemistry and graduated from the Ecole Normale of Paris. As a young man he held professorships in physics and chemistry in universities in France and achieved distinction through his research on beverages.

At 35 he was appointed Director of the Ecole Normale Supérieure. This did not interfere with his experimental work. Many of his friends believed that his research was fruitless, but their attitude did not influence him and he was soon able to show that his researches had great practical value.

As a result of his reputation he was sought to aid in the eradication of a silkworm disease. He attacked the problem without previous experience in this field and in a short time discovered the origin and suggested a means for its cure. He later developed a method of inoculating cattle against anthrax, and dogs and humans against hydrophobia. His work in these fields has resulted in saving many thousands of human and animal lives.

Pasteur led a rather simple life. He is an example of a leader who influences others through his discoveries. He had a brilliant mind, strong drive, and good work habits. He attacked problems of great importance to the welfare of the human race.

How do these leaders differ in personal characteristics and in the roles they serve for the group?

Examples of College Leaders. Campus leaders in a large Midwestern university were questioned and given personality tests in an attempt to learn the characteristics of the variety of leader who functions in extracurricular activities. The results indicate a division of the leaders into four groups that have value in this discussion.

Student editors. These leaders belong to the group that we shall call the *expert.* They lead indirectly through their creations (writing in this case) rather than through direct contact with other people.

Debaters (men) were of superior intelligence, markedly introverted (shy and emotional), and had fairly extreme inferiority feelings in terms of their own ratings. The women debaters, on the other hand, were found to be extroverted (sociable and active) in terms of their own and their associates' ratings, though they admitted mild inferiority feelings. They too exemplify the *expert* variety of leader.

Campus politicians were found to be strongly extroverted, in their own and their associates' opinions, moderately good in general ability, but to have poor school records. The women in politics professed extreme feelings of inferiority. These leaders represent the group named the *executive* variety.

Leaders in *university dramatics* were able intellectually and did slightly superior work in school. The women were mildly extroverted, according to their own and their associates' ratings. Feelings of inferiority had more than average frequency among the male actors. These leaders are another example of the *expert* type of leader in that they lead through a creation or skill (774).

Definition and Kinds of Leaders. The first question that must be answered is, "What is the definition of a leader from the viewpoint of the following discussion?" The word "leader" will be used below in its broadest sense. A leader is one who *influences consistently the behavior of a given group of individuals.* This definition includes all the kinds of leaders discussed herein.

Classifications of Leaders. An exhaustive study of great men who lived between 1450 and 1850 shows us that there is *no single leader type.* Instead, there are varieties of leaders. Any classification of leaders will show much overlapping of traits between groups. As one observes individuals who are in a position of leadership, one sees those who are simply holding an executive office, others who are seeking to play a role that will serve the needs of the group even if drastic changes are necessary. There are those leaders who influence others mainly through their background activity and their creations. Leaders may combine in various degrees each of these traits and tendencies: *executive* or titular leadership, *dynamic* leadership or one who shows initiative, and *expert* or creative leadership.

LEADERS WHO ARE PREDOMINANTLY EXECUTIVE. Executive leaders are usually selected by the group they represent. They speak for the group, preside at meetings, and in a democratic group guide and coordinate the thought and actions of individual members of the group. These leaders vary from the "stuffed shirt," head man, or office holder to the one who is able and willing to coordinate efficiently the major contributions of the more talented members of the group. Some are institution-minded—are more loyal to the organization than to the ideas it represents. They may be so bound to the *status quo* that they are insensitive to new forces and developments.

The amount of prestige attached to this type of leader varies from a moderate amount to placing the leader on a pedestal and clothing him in many ideal human qualities.

LEADERS WHO ARE PREDOMINANTLY DYNAMIC.   The *dynamic* leader, the leader with initiative, has certain plans and directs the activity of the group along the line of these plans. It is conceivable that such a person may not possess many qualities that make him popular and, consequently, may need to execute his plans through a head man or executive. He may be a background leader, a power behind the throne. His direction may be of the dominant type rather than the persuasive. Some leaders emerge as a result of interaction in the group and assume an authoritative leadership (132). Regardless of the methods used, this individual is forceful. The group looks to him for guidance and throws upon him the responsibility for its welfare.

An example of the dynamic leader in college is the student who desires to change the existing form of student government. Another example is the student who tries to start a weekly student forum on the campus, or who sets in motion a plan to combine two or three ineffectual service groups into one effective organization. These individuals are more likely to favor the ideas or the spirit of the organization rather than the particular form it takes as an institution. Revolutionary statesmen and some soldier-statesmen, as Napoleon and Cromwell, represent one form of this kind of leadership. Student leaders of the liberal to radical cast were found on a personality inventory to show more unstable and neurotic tendencies than fraternity and sorority leaders who were "just students" (853).

In both executive and dynamic leadership a distinction may be made between domination and integration. The integrative leader is not the rigid, inflexible man who has made up his mind about what he wants and is now imposing it upon his followers. He *realizes that others differ*, that there is *value in the viewpoint and purposes of others,* and he attempts to find a *common but vital purpose among differences.* This kind of leadership is spontaneous, flexible, and changing (133). Its growth is through cooperative activity and survival of the best ideas and actions. The leader is aided by an intellectual constituency or following. Such a leader is found to be more objective, more controlled emotionally, and broader in his world view (146). He is successful in estimating group opinion (144). This is more characteristic of ideal democratic leadership and in contrast to the authoritarian leader who is inwardly insecure and who must dominate the group. The authoritarian leader may get superior performance from the group, but usually builds poor morale. His followers are dependent on him; they themselves may show frustration and aggression toward weaker individuals (345, 702, 463).

LEADERS WHO ARE EXPERTS. The third variety of leader is the *expert* or creative leader. This individual usually is so superior in abilities to the average person that he may or may not be popular, and he often does not try to be. He acquires, however, certain skills that help him to utilize his talents to full advantage and so makes a contribution to society in the form of invention, works of art or of literature.

The inventor and creative artist, like the social leader, are products of the group and express what the group has impressed upon them. The expert continues to live in the group, is a follower in other groups, and has acquired and makes use of the contributions of the past. Every inventive step depends upon the steps that have preceded it. Inventions that occur today were impossible a hundred years ago because of the inventions in the interim that had to precede them.

CHARACTERISTICS OF EXECUTIVE AND DYNAMIC LEADERS. In view of the many forms that leadership takes, dictated by the needs and characteristics of the group, the personality characteristics of leaders vary greatly. The popular view that certain personal characteristics in the individual produce a leader type person is not completely substantiated by the findings. Leadership is too varied and too intimately tied up with group activity to have a universal character (698, 280).

A survey of traits found in twenty different studies of leaders showed that leaders of different kinds of groups have different traits. It has been suggested that the only characteristics common to all leaders is that they reflect the *membership* characteristics of the group to which they belong. They are definitely representative of the group they lead. Second, they are *superior in one or more personal characteristics*, usually valuable to the group (580). When personal characteristics such as age, size and physical make-up, energy, intelligence, knowledge and skill, social status, and social and emotional traits are considered, they are found to be associated with some forms of leadership and not with others (377, 580, 462, 443, 281, 751). Often the one or more traits in which the leader is above the average are relevant to the needs and function of the group. The lack of agreement of studies on personal characteristics is understood when we see leadership as being determined by the character of the group in which it occurs (178, 580).

Since leadership is a group phenomenon it is not surprising to see certain personality traits continually appearing in lists of traits seemingly important for leadership. Such traits are popularity, verbal facility, and sociability. Because *executive and directional* functions are also very frequently demanded, traits such as initiative, persistence, self-confidence, adaptability, and responsibility appear as important (751, 50, 279, 640, 699).

Members of groups can usually describe in their own language what they want from a leader, and these activities suggest personal characteristics of the individual who takes the leadership role. When the responses of 500 individuals are classified these general characteristics constitute the list:

1. Ability to advance the purposes of the group.
2. Administrative competence.
3. Activity that is pace-setting and motivating.
4. Contribution to the member's feeling of security about his place in group.
5. Freedom from activity serving only his own interests (329).

Another way of looking at this resulted from a factorial analysis of the behavior of leaders. Three factors emerged as essential in describing the leader's behavior or its consequences in the group.

1. Behavior increasing his *acceptability* to the group.
2. High production and organization.
3. Effective *interaction* of group members.

Here we see the leader functions as *inspiration* and an *executive*.

Gifted Children as Potential Expert Leaders. Besides participation in as many extracurricular activities and holding about twice the number of offices as average children achieve, gifted children furnish us with our potential expert leaders (237, 788). We consider as gifted children those who have intelligence quotients above approximately 140. They represent about 1 per cent of the population, the average of which has an IQ ranging from 90 to 110. These children are very outstanding in school work and are noticeably bright even to casual observers. They have the mental equipment to master and to create in the most complex vocations. They maintain, on the whole, their general superiority over the periods of years they have been studied (792).

Extensive studies show that the gifted child is from a good family background, has good health, good intellectual ability, wide interest and motivation, and pleasing personality traits (788). With this combination of traits these individuals are capable of success in the more difficult fields, such as the professions and the arts and sciences, and can contribute to society the knowledge and skills that are necessary for progress. Some of them will become our executive and dynamic leaders.

A follow-up of the children in the study above after 25 years showed that as a group they did make unusual use of their superior ability. However, some failed to reach their potential and some even got into trouble with the law. The less successful were not outstandingly different in intelligence but rather in their *social and emotional adjustment, their family background and rating on the traits of perseverance, self-confidence, and integrity was lower* (792).

The Leadership Role. Individuals need the group for better satisfaction of their needs. The group gives them a feeling of security and confidence (517). Within the group there will be personality differences particularly in attitudes. If individual needs are paramount the effectiveness of the group may be greatly disrupted (663). However, what is common in the group can be used to form the basis for the group's unity and *cohesiveness*—a very valuable property of the well-functioning and productive group (32). Cohesiveness is also more satisfying to the participants (499). The effective leader symbolizes this group unit—he is a common stimulus and if he functions well all the many activities that make the group a working organization can operate well with the minimum of stifling conflict.

The group, as well as the individual, can use frustration and conflict as a source of growth or disintegration. These conditions can weaken the cohesiveness and integration of the group, hamper activity, and cause the group to wane in its capacity to satisfy individual needs, or they can serve as motivation. The leader is important here. His relationship with the group should be such, as pointed out previously, that he can unify it and enable each member to play his own role best. In this way the group accomplishes its purpose without too greatly stifling the creativity of the individual. If the group frustrates the members too much, the energies of the members can be dissipated by conflicts within the group. On the other hand if the group can mobilize against outside threats or toward exciting goals it will gain greater solidarity and effectiveness (707).

The participating leader who is actively aware of the attitudes and feelings of the members as well as the functions the group can perform, behaves in a way to influence the attitudes of the members toward unanimity and appropriate actions as shown in the examples on page 301 to 303 (312, 621, 233).

The Leader and the Needs of the Group. The leader must be clearly conscious of the strongest attitudes and wishes of the group, and to a certain extent he must be a symbol of their satisfaction.

Herbert Hoover has all the requisites of a leader, according to some textbook discussions of characteristics of leaders. He has excellent appearance, experience in handling men, and ascendancy. At the time of his election he was extremely popular, owing to some extent to his past successes during World War I. His victory over a very strong opposing candidate, Governor Alfred Smith, was overwhelming. At the time of his election he represented to "prosperous America" the symbol of their desires: success in business; a handsome, rich businessman who had numberless influential contacts; a symbol of that which every American would like to attain.

Then there occurred a change in the character of the group, brought on by the financial depression. Instead of a group which was unified by a common loyalty to "prosperous America" they were divided in a class struggle. The wealthy were desirous of retaining as much of the paper success they had attained during the boom period and therefore made drastic financial retrenchments. The poverty-stricken, who lacked sufficient food and clothing, clamored for jobs and physical security and were envious of those who had plenty in comparison. This divided the group. Mr. Hoover represented the "better" of these factions and therefore antagonized the other. He lost sight of the change in the character of his group, did not adequately represent them as a whole, and he did not represent the majority. He favored the minority and lost his position as leader in spite of the fact that he retained all the individual traits he possessed when he entered office.

Franklin D. Roosevelt was conscious of the sentiment of his group, particularly in view of his re-elections. His speeches and recommended legislation faced a need which had been vocal for some time in America— economic readjustment and social security. He assumed the role of the champion for the satisfaction of these needs and acted in a fashion compatible with the strong attitudes they aroused. Later he comprehended the international crisis and its implications and marshaled public opinion in the direction of action. He retained his position as leader despite errors on his part and vehement criticism from a powerful minority.

Hitler's rise to power can be understood by a similar realization of the stronger wishes and attitudes of the members of the group. He realized the desire of the German people for a strong Germany, the repudiation of an unjust treaty, the re-establishment of the country as a world power, and a bold and confident attitude toward foreign and domestic enemies. He provided an outlet for strong emotion through the discovery of a scapegoat. He convinced the people that the pernicious influences were responsible for their plight. The frustrated masses hungry for satisfaction of their common needs readily accepted his simple solution. When he gained power he retained his supporters and forcibly crushed any change in sentiment.

When Boy Scouts were allowed to choose their own leaders for numerous small groups, the characteristics associated with their choice of leader varied with the character of the group. For example, if the accepted thing in the group was for the leader to have been with the group for two years, the tradition colored materially the choice of the group. The correlation between leadership and factors such as appearance varied with the group from 0.60 to 0.91, depending upon the attitudes of the group (596).

Does the Leader Mold Events or Do Events Mold Him? A realization that the leader is the symbol of satisfaction of the needs of the group throws light on the perennial questions: Does the individual leader shape the course of history, or is there a general tendency independent of particular persons? Do individuals merely act as vehicles for the expression of this general tendency? Would history be the same if our famous or infamous men had died in infancy, or has the course of history been influenced by Cromwell, Hitler, Jesus, Mohammed, Clive, Caesar, Roosevelt, Alexander, Darwin, Newton, Galileo, Beethoven, Goethe, Rousseau, Nietzsche, and others?

Certainly there are general trends in history and particular individuals are the vehicles, but these general trends have been influenced by specific individuals. The trends can only impress themselves on the minds of the specific individuals. The freedom of individual leaders is limited greatly by the social forces in the group. Likewise, the attitudes most evident in the group are limited in terms of the adroit maneuvers of the individual leader. The group and the individual are two aspects of a single process, and to separate from the individual all that he has gained from the group is just as impossible as to separate from the group that which can be attributed to certain individuals.

The Prestige Factor. Most positions of responsibility and leadership lend *prestige* to the holder. Some persons, however, possess *personal* prestige which adds to the office. They are persons who seem to draw other human beings toward them and influence them through inspiration or fear. Certainly Buddha, Jesus, Mohammed, and Napoleon had this characteristic, and it is found to some extent in many executive leaders of today. Theodore Roosevelt possessed this personal charm which drew persons to him, as undoubtedly did Franklin D. Roosevelt, Mussolini, Gandhi, Lawrence of Arabia, and Huey P. Long.

The Leader Is a Good Follower. There is no clear-cut distinction between a leader and a follower. We cannot set up two classes with leaders representing one mode and followers the other. Every leader is a follower, usually a follower in many groups, and some followers are leaders in other groups. Furthermore, the best leader, as we have shown above, must be a good follower. He must follow the group as a whole in his attitudes and wishes. These generalizations can be supported by reference to some of the studies already cited.

Boy Scouts who were divided into groups at random on several occasions were allowed to choose their leaders for the group. Their choices did not divide the group into leaders and nonleaders. Instead, there was a continuous distribution of degrees of leadership ability which ranged from those who were seldom, if ever, chosen as leaders of their group to those who were chosen as leaders in almost every group in which they found themselves. Most of the individuals were sometimes leaders and sometimes followers (596).

The Development of Leadership. Leadership develops through experience as do the many related traits, such as friendship, ascendancy, and extroversion. The child through his playground and school experiences may be developing traits and learning group skills and attitudes that he may later use in some kind of leadership role.

Graduates of a Midwestern high school who had been out of school from 10 to 15 years were studied. They were divided into three groups in terms of their activities in school: leaders, 25; scholars, 32; and random control group, 32. The criterion of leadership was based on consultation of the school annual and teachers' opinions. Scholars' names were taken from the honor roll. The remaining group was selected at random. All the students were interviewed if possible. The leaders were easiest to find in later life. Success was measured in terms of income and special honors and awards. The leaders had acquired the most money, the scholars the least; the leaders and the random group had more Ph.D.'s among them; the leaders were ahead in evidences of community service. The random group and scholars were about equal in evidences of community service. The author states that there is evidence that the person who does not stand out in high school may attain some leadership in later life. The high school leader, however, seems to have a better chance of doing so (696).

An example of transfer of leadership to a new situation is shown in a study of boys in camp. Boys whose standing as leaders was definitely established in their own groups were taken before groups of boys who had never seen them before. The new group was asked to rate the visitors on their leadership ability on the basis of hearing their voices behind a screen; later seeing them, hearing them, and speaking to them at the same time. The leader stood out from the other boys in the votes received. Even on the basis of voice alone there was a relationship between the votes from strangers and from his own group. The votes he received in the strange group were not related to his height or weight. They were somewhat related to his age but were related mostly to the rating he received as a leader in his own group. There was apparently certain behavior which the boy had shown or developed in his own group that was recognized by the strange group as indicative of leadership (596).

A similar study was carried on in the Air Force. Eleven selected leaders entered new groups successfully and continued to emerge in top positions in these groups even though the composition of the group changed (88). It is because members of a group recognize traits in certain persons that enable them to exert leadership that ratings by peers ("buddy ratings") have been so effective in forecasting platoon leaders in the service. They are superior to officer ratings or individual tests (290).

These findings do not negate our position that there are many varieties of leadership, but merely show that there is overlapping of certain leadership functions when different specific leadership positions are compared, and that leaders transfer to related tasks.

The evidence to date, then, would argue for transfer of leadership from one period in life to another. Leaders in grade school are more often leaders in high school and in extraschool activities. Those who have developed skills which are important in the group are more likely to be leaders than others. This justifies the school systems' emphasis on training in leadership by practice in beneficial extracurricular activities compatible with the student's interests and talents. Students who take responsibilities well sometimes tend to hold too many offices, to their own detriment and to the deprivation of others who need this experience (849).

Can One Train for Leadership?   A project which set out to train leaders by means of lectures and conferences resulted in only slight increases in leadership ability in the subjects after the training interval (202).   It is doubtful whether precepts which concern leadership can be compared with *actual practice*.   No doubt an individual can, while practicing leadership, profit by reading what is known about it.   But the knowledge must be converted into overt reaction patterns of leadership to be of value (51, 485).   More and more industry is planning group sessions for their supervisors in which they can discuss the problems and skills involved in supervision of employees (238).

A group of 4-year-old children was trained in ascendant behavior.   This type of behavior is found in certain kinds of leadership.   The children were put through an experimental training period.   The five least ascendant children were selected and submitted to three training situations in which they were given information regarding, and opportunity to use, toys and materials that were used during play with other children.   After the training situation they were paired with other children.   Four out of the five children made a gain in absolute score, and all made a relative gain (370).

Discovering One's Potentiality as a Leader.   An effective group requires many individuals who can take leadership responsibility.   The individual's problem is to discover how he can make his greatest contribution and still preserve his integrity and creativeness as an individual.   Because leadership consists of activities that influence the behavior of others in a group situation, these are illustrated by chairmanships and subchairmanship, study groups, and power groups that introduce motions from the floor.   Some individuals contribute to the larger groups and cultures to which they belong by inventing the gadgets used, writing reports, articles, scripts, novels, essays, songs, poetry, making talks, and leading discussions.

The college student must first discover his own abilities and interests and the groups that can best utilize them.   Our schools are so organized into extracurricular interest groups that he has opportunity to make discoveries about his possible services in and to groups in his culture.   This was discussed in Chapter 10.   If an individual sees a need in society he is wise to gather with others of similar inclination with the hope of integrated action toward satisfying that need in a way that will give him personal fulfillment.   Few activities in life are more satisfying to the individual than identifying himself with a movement in society that will deeply satisfy its members. The opportunities are unlimited even if the path toward the goal is tortuous.

As a student learns to work with one or more groups he acquires the social skills and the emotional and cognitive adjustments that are involved in the compromises that he must decide upon as a member of a group. It is clear from the preceding discussion that leadership involves superiority in some traits—usually those that allow the individual to serve the group. Leadership also involves a broad perspective, which usually grows from experience. This is seen in a study of 100 Officer Candidate School students by psychiatric examination and tests. Results showed that leadership in that type of situation is related to *emotional maturity* and a *sense of reality* (204).

Usually the leader knows much more about the group than the average member knows. His knowledge may be the skill represented by the group. The captain of the team is usually a good player, the president of the dramatics society usually knows much about play production and acting. The leader usually has skill in obtaining the viewpoints of all the group members and in formulating the most popular policies. He may find it easy to form forceful movements within the group. Finally, the leader's knowledge may be in terms of the business of the organization. He may be best acquainted with its bylaws, budget, or history and therefore be capable of guiding the other members at meetings. All these functions must be performed by someone.

Group Dynamics. Many of the conditions presented as operating in effective democratic leadership reflect recent research in small group operation. These studies and the methods growing from them are referred to as "group dynamics." These conditions may well be utilized by students in their class and extracurricular discussions and in work groups. By and large, the methods help to produce a free, nonanxious environment that allows each member to have a *feeling of belonging* and to contribute in his own way to the activity of the group. Larger groups are therefore often broken into smaller, and the setting is arranged to promote participation. The group is also so structured that the members retain awareness of its goals and are *flexible* in their efforts to satisfy mutual needs. Such discussion groups have been found effective in changing attitudes and behavior (452). The composition of the group and the degree to which the leader understands what various members can contribute and helps them to utilize their skills is important (374). Sometimes the group is so informal that there is no fixed leader, but leaders emerge as they serve a function (49).

Supplementary Readings

B. M. Bass, "The Leaderless Group Discussion," *Psychological Bulletin*, 1954, Volume 51, pages 465–492.

D. Cartwright and A. Zander (Eds.), *Group Dynamics*, Evanston, Ill., Row, Peterson, 1953.

A. Davis, *Social Class Influences upon Learning*, Harvard University Press, 1948.

H. Guetzkow (Ed.), *Groups, Leadership and Men*, Rutgers University Press, 1951.

T. M. Newcomb, *Social Psychology*, Dryden, 1950.

C. L. Shartle, *Executive Performance and Leadership*, Prentice-Hall, 1956.

In addition see the references cited by number in the chapter and appearing in the bibliography of an accompanying volume entitled *Teaching Personal Adjustment: An Instructor's Manual*.

CHAPTER 12

There is probably no question which we in America have evaded more consistently than that of sex. Well-meaning parents have refused to instruct their children about natural biological phenomena. The well-bred girl of a generation or two past was "sheltered" from any such knowledge, and her ignorance of these matters was regarded as a mark of refinement. The result has been a heightening of children's curiosity so that they have sought their information in less desirable quarters. American parents have acted either as though there is no problem or as though any problem of sex is in itself unwholesome. This blind attitude has been especially culpable since movies, current literature, conversation, and other influences constantly stimulate the curiosity of those for whom the problem is unsolved.

Rather than to ignore sex, it is far more sensible to admit that there are vital problems in this important realm of life and that these problems influence our most cherished and exalted sentiments, those built

CHAPTER **12**

AFFECTIONS* AND CONVENTIONS

around love, home, children, and family. It is necessary, then, that we face these problems frankly, understand their origins, and attempt to solve them effectively in our culture.

We shall first deal with the *factors that mold* and direct these original and vague urges. Then we shall discuss *conventional standards*, youth's *attempt to meet them*, and the *problems involved*. Most of the problems—masturbation, crushes, unachieved heterosexuality, and petting and unstable love life—arise because of the disturbances in the development of one's personality, affections, and difficulties in meeting standards. We shall in each case discuss these problems and attempt to give insight into them so that solutions may be discovered. In conclusion, in Chapter 13 we shall deal with factors affecting the climax of affections, marriage.

---

* The term affections is used here for those complex emotions which develop from amorous and sexual motives.

321

Development of Affections

Affections and sex adjustments are based in part upon the love one receives as a child. They fuse in later life, the one unconsciously affecting the other. We cannot, therefore, separate them in discussing their influences on the growing personality. Nor can we separate the development of affection from the development of the total personality, the atmosphere in the family, the relationship to each parent, and the traits these influence. The attitudes and behavior we show in our love and sexual relationships are not unrelated to tendencies, such as passivity, confidence, acceptance of ourselves, inferiority, hostility toward people, self-esteem, anxiety, and security. These are the result of development discussed in Chapter 4.

We differ in the expression of affections in our sex attitudes. John always has a new "steady girl." Bill is indifferent to girls. Joan is "boy crazy." Elsie is surrounded by boys and does not seem to let it affect her greatly. Anne, although pretty, does not attract boys at all and is sensitive about the whole matter. For Bob, girls are an aspect of a busy life with athletics and school competing for top priority. What causes these differences? Are they the results of inborn temperament, the accumulation of experiences, or both? What are the experiential factors that mold our love life? A discussion of the development of affections should throw light upon each individual's present sex tendencies and problems. You may want to consider each topic with the intent of understanding how this factor influences your life.

Basis for Affection. We begin life with certain constitutional tendencies which are the raw materials of temperamental traits—passiveness, general pleasant manner, activeness, or irritability (12). In addition there are both the natural tendencies to respond positively to caressing, loving, and mothering (638) and the learned positive response first to the mother who satisfies our needs and motives—hunger, warmth, dryness, thirst—then to other individuals who play with us and satisfy our other motives.

In order for love to develop in a wholesome way, one must be loved adequately but not excessively by one's parents; one must feel that one is lovable, have self-esteem, a feeling of worthiness, and show a capacity to adjust to the desires of others. Ideally, this, together with the absence of excessive frustration, should lead to security, emotional stability, and capacity to love (777, 106, 790).

Stages of Development of Affection.   Our affections for others have a history. The baby becomes interested in various parts of his body, particularly those that yield pleasure from manipulation. The child is most strongly attached to his parents before his interest in other children develops. The boy, just before puberty, derives greatest pleasure from boys' games and "other fellows." Of over 300 collegians, 54 per cent could immediately recall a period just prior to puberty during which they felt a distaste for the opposite sex (154). Strong friendships sometimes develop in this period. Later, there is attraction to the opposite sex, and, finally, to one member of the opposite sex in particular.

At puberty we experience restlessness and expansiveness. We become more keenly aware of the world about us. Sex urges mature and increase in strength at this time. Glandular secretions bring about bodily changes, growth in sex organs and pubic hair. Previously formed sex attitudes and impulses are intensified. There is no conclusive evidence that glands determine specifically *how* we shall act. The vague cravings we experience are associated with thoughts or experiences of caressing. These conditions and our *previously developed* personalities determine how we behave. We associate our inner feeling with our friends as well as with the beauties of nature. We are then building the sentiment of love. We are living in a highly heterosexual culture that teaches us that intimacies and tender feelings occur only between persons of opposite sex. Our friends impress that fact upon us by their allusions to the opposite sex and by their behavior on dates and at parties.

This heterosexual attitude is not well established before puberty. In early adolescence mildly amorous relations to other members of the same sex may be observed. Boys put their arms around their buddy's shoulder, tickle, wrestle, and exhibit other activities involving physical contact. Girls at this period experience "crushes" on other girls and, sometimes, on older women. Such behavior is rarer in late adolescence, and usually it is unpleasant to the individual who has definitely established heterosexual attitudes. One may fixate at any of the levels described above before he reaches the heterosexual as a result of events in his development. A youth may show more interest in himself, his parents, or his own sex than in attractive members of the opposite sex of his age. This usually creates a problem, which he may or may not see frankly. Natural tendencies toward affection, then, are modified, elaborated, and conditioned by the many specific experiences we meet during our development. The child and youth learn to experience a certain type of love in certain situations just as they learn to fear, dislike, or hate specific conditions. Romantic affections follow the same learning process that governs other personality traits. Experiences are associated with the various urges and guide their future expression.

The importance of some of these factors has been shown through the studies on adjustment in marriage and will therefore also be discussed in Chapter 13. Since the nature of one's affections and attitudes toward sex are influenced also by one's total personality development, a review of Chapter 4 at this time would be pertinent. Trends such as jealousy, antagonism toward or lack of interest in the opposite sex, antisocial attitudes, immaturity, anxiety, lack of confidence in oneself and one's attraction for the opposite sex, tendency to play an active or passive role—all are developed in one's life history.

The Family. Studies dealing with marriage indicate that probably the major factor influencing the love life of a youth or adult is his *relationship to his parents.* The parents create an atmosphere which may be accepting and warm or may be critical, dominative, neglectful, or rejecting. In the former instance, the child emulates the parent and introjects his traits. In the latter, he turns elsewhere for a model and retains hostility which may show itself as late as marriage (106, 790). A boy may grow up in a family which is dominated by the mother. He may build up hostility for her, select his father as a model, develop masculine traits, but retain the hostility and resentment which he directed toward his mother, even into marriage. All during his youth in relationships with girls, he may have resented suggestions from them or any attempts on their part to influence him. The climax may come in marriage when he shows open hostility toward his wife, develops countless complaints about her, or refuses to cooperate in any venture in which he is not dominant.

The various roles the boy or girl learns to play in love or hostility are numerous and can be related to the family constellation. An older brother or sister who has been loved or resented can influence later relationships. Overprotective grandparents or aunts may enter the picture. The absence of one parent through death or separation may be influential.

There is a well-known pattern of lack of interest on the part of the father for a child, perhaps a boy. As this son becomes rebuffed he turns to the mother for affection and recognition, introjects her feminine traits, and, for the period during which she remains his most influential model, he acquires attitudes and behavior of a feminine nature. A girl may withdraw from a dominating or neglectful mother to a warm, sympathetic father or older brother, become his pal, and introject masculine traits for a period.

Sex Education Influences Affections. Sex instruction of some kind was mentioned more often in personal histories by people who were adjusting in marriage than by those whose marriage was less stable (106, 790). A good, confidential relationship with parents is known to produce a better adjustment in adolescence. When sex is regarded as shameful, tabooed in discussions, and is a subject for anxiety, there is a strong likelihood that the child will not develop the proper attitudes toward it or obtain from wholesome sources the information that he should acquire. He is forced to gather his knowledge from the street, where reproduction and associated processes will not be presented as related to love, the home, and the family. One study of neurotic women shows that they did not differ from the normal in terms of what they had done or what had happened to them sexually in childhood, but their attitude toward the experiences was a more anxious one, toned with guilt and strong emotion (435).

The necessity of sex education is being more widely accepted (174). Writers concerned with child guidance recommend that instruction be given early in a somewhat *natural*, pleasant fashion so that early superficial *curiosities* may be *satisfied*. Later, as opportunities present themselves, more technical information may be furnished. Facts must be coupled with the proper emotional attitude as well as with the accepted conventions and attitudes.

The older child should be taught to become sensibly conscious of persons of both sexes who have a lewd and perverted attitude toward sex. He probably also should understand the person who is struggling between the acceptance of sex ideals and a self-stimulated sex urge, these attitudes alternating in their occurrence. Certainly, in the attempt to guide sex impulses rationally, it is unwise to inculcate ideals of sex without giving information about pitfalls.

Too often passion and love are separated so that neither is complete. Unless the parent consciously guides the thinking of the child an unwholesome view of sex may be gained. The adolescent should appreciate the *naturalness of sex* on the one hand, and the *importance of social standards* on the other. Knowledge of these emotions, the modes of controlling them, and their role in enriching our affective life is important for future happiness.

Studies have been made on the extent of sex education. Students were classified as (1) serious students, (2) socially well-adjusted students, (3) students who were badly adjusted, depressed, and confused, and (4) those who were poor in social adjustment. The percentage of men who had sex instruction in each of these groups were 74, 72, 27, and 36. The differences among the women were similar but not so great. One cannot say that sex education or the absence of it caused the difference in adjustment in college, but it probably reflected parental attitudes that differed in these groups (19).

Playmates and Friends. The individual may have difficulty in overcoming an aversion to the opposite sex resulting from early teasing by them or jealousy of them. This, together with some factors, such as shyness or segregation, which block the natural interest in them at adolescence, may prevent a growth in interest in the opposite sex (791).

Sex attitudes cannot be separated from social life and self-impressions. If a child's sex experiences, or the experiences he acquires in associating with his playmates, cause him to *think himself inferior* to others, he is disturbed. Inability to play the games that other boys play, shortness of stature, being the butt of jokes or raillery, physical unattractiveness and its attendant kidding, "insufficient" stylish clothes or possessions—all affect the individual's impression of himself. They make him feel less the average boy and, in late adolescence, less the man. The same sort of experience occurs in the girl who is less attractive, different in some way, obese, of a minority race or religion, or more shy and less sociable.

On a background of inferiority feelings, the problem of masturbation, improper sex proposals, sex play, vivid sex thoughts, sex dreams, teasing by others about one's sex life, or any similar experience may be magnified until it reaches disturbing proportions. Of a group of college students who were studied, 33 per cent say that they have been afraid that they were inferior to most people sexually and 18 per cent admit strong feelings of sinfulness and guilt (522). The specific nature of these fears is probably that the individual feels that he differs from others in organic structure, strength of sex drive, sex habits, development, fertility, or morality; he may believe himself intrinsically very unattractive, or from inferior social stock, or believe that no one of the opposite sex could love him.

Sometimes these fears arise from *parents who frighten* the child when masturbation or sex sophistication is discovered. Sometimes they are implanted in young minds by older children or by quacks. Such feelings are thwarting to the individual, cause him to worry, or sometimes to overcompensate in either undesirable or desirable ways in order to redeem himself as pointed out later in the chapter.

Attitudes toward oneself as an object of love and affection are also influenced by experiences with the opposite sex on dates, at dances, and at social gatherings. Factors which *enhance the social value* of the individual, such as clothes, luxuries, generous allowance, car, family wealth or influence, are all effective in causing one to believe that he or she is worthy of the attention of certain members of the opposite sex, or able to attract them. Undue shyness, acne, beliefs that one is not attractive or likeable influence negatively one's attitudes toward the opposite sex. They also affect attitudes toward one's personal sex nature.

ROMANTIC EXPERIENCES AS THEY INFLUENCE AFFECTIONS. The child learns to expect romance from casual remarks, the movies, the fiction he reads, and from adolescent companions and bull sessions. He realizes that as a human being it is the normal thing for him to fall in love and to be loved by another. Many children in grade school talk of sweethearts and are jokingly encouraged or teased about attention from a member of the opposite sex of their own age. Forty-five per cent of college students say they had the experience of "puppy love" in grade school (522). There were probably more who had it but did not wish to admit it on a questionnaire. These experiences include a strong affection for the opposite sex. Sometimes it involves the showering of gifts and favors or compliments on the loved one, sometimes kisses and caresses, and usually considerable daydreaming. Sometimes, however, they include merely observation and admiration from afar, supplemented by young hopes.

Personal Inner Life—Sex Experiences. A considerable percentage of persons pass through childhood and adolescence without any actual sex experience other than occasional petting and possibly masturbation. A certain percentage of individuals, more than is usually suspected, some of whom are prepared and others unprepared for the events by their elders, have various types of experiences with differing results (411, 412, 212). These experiences are sometimes the curious experimentations of children who have been uninformed of sex matters or of those who have gained information from lewd sources. The child may be initiated into masturbation or some other form of sex play by an older child or, in rarer cases, by an adult. Some idea of the extent to which this type of initiation exists among the upper classes is seen from a questioning of 1000 married women before 1931. Twenty-five per cent admitted sex play before they reached fourteen years of age. *Of these*, 15.7 per cent admitted to emotional relationships with other women, with physical expression, 39 per cent to spooning, and 7 per cent to intimate sex relationships with men. Except for the spooning, which varies from mild kissing to less frequently occurring but extensive intimacies, these percentages are not large (180).

Sometimes, as case studies show, such experiences color the attitude of the individual toward sexual relationship even into adult life. Other times the effects of these experiences are "outgrown" (187). They are covered by more acceptable and conventional expressions of emotion that influence the individual so that he has neither a strong aversion for nor an unwholesome attraction to specific sex acts. All these experiences influence our affections for others to some extent and fuse to make up the adult's sex attitudes, urges, and practices.

PECULIAR SEX TENDENCIES OFTEN GROW FROM SEX EXPERIENCES. The various aberrations of sex may be traced usually to childhood or adolescent experiences. The compulsion toward peeping, exhibition of self, and various fetishes, such as excitement at the sight of certain types of hair, of certain facial features, of objects of clothing either in the opposite or same sex, are examples. A normal case taken from a college student's autobiography might be used as an example:

"I was just fourteen, a somewhat lonely fellow, and girls interested me little. My father and I were vacationing at a resort, an experience which in itself was very pleasant. There sat at a table near ours a beautiful girl about my age, blonde, blue-eyed, demure, and reticent. I watched her for several days and thought of her when I was lonely at night. One beautiful moonlit night we were introduced. I shall never forget how she looked at me with those large, modest, blue eyes. We talked on the large veranda and then strolled through the thickly wooded grounds of the hotel. At about three hundred yards from the building we sat on a bench and talked. I have a picture of that spot yet, a cool, wooded area, lit here and there by the moon. I remember how the pine needles felt under my feet. We sat close and soon I had my arm about her, but she objected and I had to be content with fondling her hand. It was the first time I had ever felt passion, and I was as emotionally wrought up as I have ever been. I held her hand, caressed it, idolized it in the moonlight, became eloquent over its beautiful shape and lines. To this day women's hands fascinate me; I become emotional and have an urge to hold them, caress them, follow the lines in them. Sometimes this urge is so great that I want to hold the hand of the girl next to me in class. I trace my compulsion to hold hands to this experience which I daydreamed about for months. I became as conscious of girls' hands after that as most men are of their faces."

Just as this normal compulsion can be explained in terms of past, vivid experiences, usually on an unstable background, so can the abnormal. The individual with perverted sex tendencies usually has had early sex outlets during a period of emotional upheaval that influenced the direction of his present perversion. The peeper, for example, was aroused early in life by some event he saw through a window. This may be followed by an orgasm (the emotional sex excitement) and sometimes frequent repetition of the experience in actuality or imagination. A boy who had exhibited his genitals in public places before girls discovered in conference that the practice grew originally, in part at least, from childhood experiences during a very unhappy and unstable part of his life. The act then shocked a friend of his sister of whom he was jealous. His exhibitions were aggressive as well as sexual in nature.

DAYDREAMS. Daydreams occur and influence the life of the individual. This influence is much greater if the normal outlets of the individual are *blocked*, that is, if he does not live a full life which involves creative work and contacts with other persons, particularly those of the opposite sex. Even when a youth has a healthy outlet for his affections for the opposite sex, daydreams occur. He supplements his experiences with his loved object by dreams of experiences with her, of later life, and by dreams of what he would like to do for her. Dreams of possible accomplishments and their impression upon one's fiancé are common.

Unhealthy daydreams are those that concern happenings which are grossly *incompatible* with the dreamer's *ideal*. These dreams may consist of the elaboration of a childhood sex experience which he condemns some of the time and yet enjoys in dreams at other times. They may also consist of unpleasant worries over the consequences of early behavior which the individual has never discussed with anyone. Such dreams often color the conception the individual has of himself as a possible lover.

Background of Courtship. We in America take for granted romance in relation to marriage. In many places in the world today romance in marriage is nonexistent. A romantic attachment between mates is foreign to many primitive peoples. Marriages in some European and Asiatic countries are arranged by the families of the individuals concerned. These decisions are made on the basis of similar cultural, social, and class interests rather than personal attraction between the principals. Our practice of dating is foreign to them and somewhat puzzling. Some sociologists decry our tendency to *over-romanticize* marital relationships and to ignore those traits which lead to a more stable home life.

Some American youths think that they have been destined to meet, that their bliss will continue through all the problems of living together. Under the influence of this blind attraction all the incompatibilities of temperament, habit, attitude, and station in life are overlooked. We shall see evidence in Chapter 13 that the ideal marriage is probably a fusion of a *practical* and *romantic* match—*harmony of psychological make-up* plus *mutual emotional attraction* and discovery of psychological compatibility. This can be achieved through a sensible courtship, a custom that has arisen in complex civilization, in which the average age of marriage is postponed.

If a boy and girl find themselves congenial and affection develops between them, they will be found together quite often. This relationship culminates in some sort of public declaration that they are not dating other members of the opposite sex. In college this is done usually by the acceptance and wearing of the boy's school pin or ring. They are "going steady." Afterward, and sometimes before this time, the pair engage in much work and play together, such as dining, attending classes, movies and concerts, and studying. Many of the pleasant experiences that are available they enjoy together. Together they appreciate the change of seasons, the beauty of the surrounding country, the latest music, jokes, books, and gossip. From the experiential viewpoint, the emotional attraction, which may be based at first on a few physical features, later is embellished by many commonly shared, emotionally pleasant experiences. All these pleasant experiences become fused and associated with *her* or *him*. Caressing is under the control of the ideals of the pair. As shown on page 373 courtship allows the couple to test their compatibility in terms of attitudes, habits, roles and motivations.

There has been some criticism of "going steady," particularly when it occurs on an immature level. It may prevent the individual from knowing well enough many members of the opposite sex. It may also lead to physical intimacies which get out of control and produce

guilt. Adolescent "love" is a serious problem to many young people.
It has been called a normal hazard in a competitive culture like ours
(727).

BASES FOR SEX ATTRACTION. Adolescents' answers to questionnaires
indicate that in attraction to the opposite sex physical beauty, especially of the face, is the most potent stimulus. Some find other
anatomical patterns more important—beautiful hands and feet, bodily
contours and build, specific details such as eyebrows, ankles, and
mouth, and others refer to clothes rather than to the person. Intelligence (education), personality, honesty, affection, and good manners
follow good looks in the order named as qualities which adolescent
boys think their ideal girl should possess.

Whatever is in vogue with regard to costume, hairdress, cosmetics,
manners, and speech constitutes sex appeal for the generation then on
the scene. The truth of this generalization can be casually noted by
the conformity in style in high school and college of the boys or girls
who are the most popular.

"Disposition and personality" is voted first place and "health"
second place by college students. Parents, however, place "health"
and "same religious faith and moral standards" high in the list of desirable qualities in the prospective in-laws (31).

Despite the relative importance of these factors, the person who
attracts us is usually one who lives near us. He has been subjected
to influences similar to those that have molded our behavior. He is
selected to some extent because he has been available and it has been
possible to know him well. This propinquity factor is particularly
important in the lower economic group (408). The factors of *novelty*
and *uncertainty* are in the background of sex attraction. Those young
people who are not easily figured out or who are new on the scene
are at first very attractive to others. No doubt these factors are important in flirtations.

Sometimes a specific social structure restricts the choice of an
eligible mate. A boy feels that he must marry within certain families,
date persons from certain sororities. It is alleged that in some groups
fines are levied against members who do not bring girls from certain
rating sororities to the fraternity dances. It might be well *to raise
the question as to the effect of this "rating and dating complex" on
the choice for a stable marriage* (823). It certainly weights heavily
such superficial and immature factors as prestige-bearing relatives,
membership in certain organizations, and stigmatizes externalities
which fall short of the social ideal.

Conventions

Emphasis on Chastity. In America we emphasize chastity as an ideal. The church requires a chaste life of its members; society penalizes obvious deviations.* Youth is told that chastity offers the greatest happiness and allows the most favorable later sex adjustment. Psychologists are unable at present to offer conclusive objective data to substantiate or disparage the chaste life in a society which regards it as ideal. However, there are some data regarding the attempts of people in our culture to control sex and the desirability of certain kinds of control in achieving marital adjustment and happiness.

Sex Control. Before we discuss sex control, let us point out what is conventionally meant by it in this country. Few would recommend for the average man complete, lifelong celibacy. Similarly, few would deny celibacy to those who wish it and who demonstrate their ability to adjust to it by living a sane, stable life. History is replete with the names of persons who have professed celibacy and who have helped in the direction of man's destiny. These personalities are not limited to monastics but include many who live beyond the cloisters in an active, social world with human problems impinging daily upon their consciousness. Among the rolls of influential well-balanced teachers, religionists, social workers, statesmen, and writers will be found the names of many who ostensibly lead a celibate life.

The average young person in America today wants a deeply satisfying, happy life. Love is part of it. The wish for a happy marriage is widespread. The goal, then, in sex control is the enrichment of love life and the prevention of an unfortunate marriage, sex perversion, promiscuity, mental disease, crime, venereal disease, and the abject misery that may grow from ostracism and guilt due to sex irregularity.

To reach these goals there is no need to deny our basic biological urges or sex impulses or to attempt to build sentiments of pure love devoid of an organic background. An individual who is technically pure

---

* Judaeo-Christian clergymen are not unanimous in their views on the physical aspects of love. The viewpoint presented in this book is essentially in agreement with a nonrigid and nonlegalistic Judaeo-Christian view which places an emphasis on the context of the act as well as the act itself.

but seething with repression, conflict, and fanatical hostility toward his fellow man is not the model of the chaste individual. Nor should we hypocritically put the total blame for sex irregularity when it occurs on the offending individual and allow the rest of us (society) to feel self-righteous.

Our early life and our emotional stability in general determines, in part, the ease with which sex control and maturity can be attained. Excessive occurrence of erotic night dreams, petting, masturbation, crushes, and sentimentality toward the same sex are usually due to the blocking of the sex urge. They represent some compromises in the conflict between biological urges and the pressures of the social structure which the individual has accepted. There are times when some of these make-shift solutions for sex tension have been directly learned and are accompanied by a disavowal of the ideal of sex control. However, many times the individual who is searching for satisfactions for deep affection and recognition has been blocked in his efforts to find them, and he turns to these compulsive acts as an inadequate solution to what seems an insolvable problem.

Sex control for the average man or woman who plans to marry, rear a family, and lead a conventional American life refers to *sex continence before marriage and limitation of experiences to the mate.* This is an ideal condition which is not easily attainable or universally existent. There is evidence that sex output is rarely curbed entirely (411, 412, 785).

TRADITIONAL MOTIVES FOR CONTINENCE. *Fear alone has negative value.* Disease, disgrace over illegitimate pregnancy, and undesirable marriages are sources of deep unhappiness and of distorted personalities, and although they are negative means for guiding behavior, they cannot be disregarded.

Fear is one of the strongest negative motives. The study of abnormal individuals has shown us the dangers of inciting strong fear. It causes a withdrawal reaction and paralysis of behavior rather than redirection of it along wholesome channels. Fear is a frustrating experience. At times it may be necessary to appeal to it in order to break sex compulsion. However, since anxiety may be associated with repressed hostility, we might raise the question whether it is compatible with the development of love and the direction of sex impulses toward a satisfying, creative experience.

POSITIVE MOTIVES AND SELF-CONTROL. The positive appeals or motives for conventional behavior have been less effectively presented than the negative. Too frequently these positive motives have been advocated by highly sentimental persons whom virile youth does not respect. Briefly stated, *sex control as an ideal is presented as a code that integrates the personality, enhances self-esteem, promotes love and attractiveness as a person, and points to a full, happy life.*

Ideals integrate personality. Conventions provide an attitude to govern our relations with the opposite sex. When ideals are effectively built up, they facilitate the behavior compatible with them and tend to prevent behavior that will be followed by regrets. They define what we should and what we should not do. With effective ideals the relationship between us and the opposite sex is normally one which is very pleasant. The whole force of one's personality is behind these satisfactory acts. We can associate them with all the other pleasant aspects of our experience rather than suppress them from association with that which we approve (see the case of Jack on page 337).

SELF-ESTEEM AND DISCREET CHOICE OF SEX PARTNER. Mating or sex intimacy, as one author has brought out, involves the choice of a sex partner and all the consequences thereof, regardless of the circumstances under which it occurs (601). The sex act is most intimate. It consists in setting aside all barriers, a move that the individual who has self-control and respect makes only when he has found a true mate. Intimacy that is the exploitation of another person through the arousal in that person of feelings that are not reciprocated is crass. The choice of a partner who is greatly different in social, cultural, and personal status involves conflict.

In our culture, sex intimacy to the average person with standards constitutes a major psychological step which involves all the partner's values, strongest attitudes, and innermost feelings. These inner experiences are the most sensitive aspects of the personality. They have been built up over a period of years and are not changed by single events. It must be remembered always that strong attitudes, values, and sentiments are stable aspects of the organism.

SEX CONTROL ENHANCES LOVE. Impulsive young people frequently feel bitter disappointment with the premarital experimentation, which must occur under extremely undesirable conditions. *The physical act of sex expression is not in itself the basis for the rich experience* that accompanies sex relations under the best of circumstances. Rather, the mental component is the more important aspect. This is particularly true of women, whose attitude toward this aspect of life is more sentimental. Too frequently individuals do not find in compulsive sex behavior satisfaction of the deep motivation that impels them. More simply, they don't get what they go after.

The most enduring happiness, it is conceded, grows from a relationship of this type rather than from the sexual fling or orgy. The orgy results in momentary physical gratification without all these other psychological satisfactions. It may be followed by guilt and depression. Few persons can experience the physical gratification divorced from the psychological without being keenly conscious of shallowness and sometimes sordidness and cheapness. Physical gratification may establish a strong sex habit, but this experience may be a compulsion rather than a rich emotion.

It has often been said by those who argue for sex control that an early sex experience may prevent later emotional development on a higher level. It is to be expected that the adolescent who has been subjected to unsavory adult sex experiences will establish his sex life on the physical level. He is impatient with the "romantic stuff." He may never know the rich emotion from such slight events as the touch of the hand of a member of the opposite sex, a smile, a letter, a walk through the park. Many of the other symbols that are associated with sex and which occur before marriage and sex intimacy will remain outside his experience. Those who so short-circuit their sex life usually do not allow the many intervening stages to occur before sex intimacy. As one writer has stated, *"The best insurance of chastity is the love of a high-type member of the opposite sex"* (601).

LOVE DIFFERS FROM LUST. Love and lust are not synonymous. There seem to be two basic motives in this realm of behavior and experience. They may be called (1) genital and (2) amorous (283). The amorous motive is the one most predominant in the experience we call love. Love is *more complex* and *less impulsive and intense* than lust. Love *involves the sentiments* mentioned above; it is a *pervasive, integrating* experience. Love is selective and unselfish; lust promiscuous and selfish. Love is probably the most valued experience known to man. It does not develop naturally in all people. It must grow from physical attractions, ideals, and sentiments. Genuine love goes further than this. It involves the enrichment of the physical with sentimental values. It is enhanced by reciprocal emotions from the loved one. Sex control, then, results in delayed satisfaction. It allows these sentiments to develop. *The enhancement of one's love experiences is indeed a powerful argument for controlled sex behavior* (252, 633).

Incontinence is neither a masculine necessity nor a necessity for feminine popularity. There is a common belief, almost a superstition, which appears mainly among the lower economic urban groups, that continence is effeminate. Those who hold this belief usually say that certain overt sexual expression is necessary for health. They regard it as a biological necessity for men and regard suppression (often control is meant) of sex as ill-advised. Accompanying this view is the thought that nocturnal seminal emissions or "wet dreams" are unhealthy. All these beliefs are false. A specific overt sex expression is not a biological necessity in man. True, in the male human, some sort of sex outlet seems to occur periodically (411). However, individuals differ greatly in frequency and kinds of sex outlet. Nocturnal seminal emission, if it occurs naturally at intervals, is normal and is a means of achieving the release of tensions. Usually, those who hold these beliefs regarding the necessity for certain outlets lead lives uncolored by interests, hobbies, or creative ventures. In-

Susan Greenburg

stead there is constant stimulation of sex impulses through conversation and stories. It is highly possible that this verbal stimulation rather than physiological factors are major causes for the tension and the desire for expression. Furthermore, these individuals usually have not acquired the highest moral standards and are not much affected by the guilt and social stigma of sex scandals. These males with their emphasis on physical stimulation may not make the best adjustment in marriage—particularly when most women are aroused by tenderness and affection rather than by a direct sexual approach (412).

Sometimes a young woman may entertain the idea that submission to the demands of her date will make her more desirable. This argument is the "line" of the roué who threatens to reject the girl who does not accede to his demands. She may be sure that rejection will probably be more certain should she surrender completely to him. No one has ever produced evidence that promiscuity leads to *popularity*. It yields notoriety and solicits the lustful but does not benefit one's reputation or produce popularity.

Sex control requires in the realm of sex behavior qualities demanded of men and women in other realms of living. Self-respect, conscientiousness, idealism, honesty, and responsibility are qualities that are demanded of the individual of superior caliber in vocations, sports, and other avocations. The standards of behavior in the realm of sex are not different from those in other relationships.

Individual Differences in Attitudes toward Sex Control. *Examples of individual differences.* As in other traits, individuals differ widely in their desire and capacity to lead a chaste life. These differences seem to be a result of the type of early sex education the individual has received, his ideals, associates, recreation—often represented by social class and religion (411). An individual in the lower socio-economic class, for example, more often accepts sexual intercourse prior to marriage as natural and petting as unnatural. The reverse attitude is more likely in the upper middle class. These attitudes seem to be formed early by contact with associates and to exert a force throughout youth and early maturity. A person who expects to lead a chaste life must have a wide range of stimulating and absorbing interests and live in a situation that does not continually stimulate him sexually. We might look at the attitudes of three different students.

Jack has had a wholesome early development, had good relationships with his parents, and was given sex education by them throughout his development. He has sex urges but believes sex control the best basis for stable romantic love. He is strongly attracted to girls, but his relationships with them consist of dances, discussions and study, hikes, outdoor games, and coke dates. Once or twice he has thought himself in love. His physical relationship to these girls consisted of caressing compatible with his and her standards. Each time, after a longer acquaintance with the girl, he has realized that they were not compatible.

Paul's sex life has developed without systematic guidance. He has always lived in neighborhoods of low economic class. He was exposed to sex experiences early in life and has come to view the opposite sex almost entirely as a source of physical satisfaction. He asserts that there is no difference between lust and love. He has never acquired ideals of sex control. He regards continence as unhealthy and unnatural. He has an unsavory reputation on the campus. Up to the present he has avoided scandal by choosing equally indiscreet and "sophisticated" partners.

Henry's attitudes are the result of a puritanical rearing. He inhibits all thought of sex, considers disgusting anything that is physical, and limits his discussion of the opposite sex to empty, sentimental symbols which are divorced from anticipation of later physical contact.

These three examples represent only a few of the many sex attitudes and behavior patterns found in society. Although all three cases are young men, similar attitudes are found in young women (98). There are other reasons for incontinence besides those shown in these cases. Impulsiveness, curiosity, fear of being sexually abnormal, influence of alcohol, desire for inordinate attention from the opposite sex, and social pressure from associates are a few other factors related to incontinence.

Adjustment to Differences in Standards in Associates. A college student might expect some of his associates to differ from him in sex behavior as they differ in eating habits, neatness, conscientiousness, speech, and use of money. Some have few sex inhibitions, others are strongly inhibited, but most are balanced in this respect. A study shows individuals maintain surprising constancy in sex behavior throughout certain periods of their lives (411). The acceptance of differences in sex behavior in one's associates, along with some understanding of why these differences occur as suggested by the factors stated above, will prove helpful to one who is attempting to reconcile his own attitudes and behavior with those of his associates.

Chastity is an *ideal* state and as such it is not reached by all persons or attained easily by those who do. It requires parental and educational foresight as well as individual effort. Nevertheless, there is no doubt that it is attained, along with personality adjustment, by a large group of persons of high standards. Fifty per cent of male and 75 per cent of female college students stated on an anonymous questionnaire that was circulated that they had never experienced sexual intercourse (98). Statistics of this kind vary with groups and are influenced by the methods used to collect them. Some groups show frequencies above and below these (411).

To be sure, chaste or unchaste behavior usually is not deliberately chosen in a cool, rational mood. Instead, unchaste behavior is usually the consequence of impulsive acts. If we are made vividly conscious of all that the two courses of action mean, if the events of the moment are not too compulsive, and if we have a fairly stable background, most of us no doubt will choose the chaste course.

Mary's ideals of behavior are gradually being altered by a boy of whom she is very fond and whom she dates frequently. Her opinion of what constitutes permissible petting has broadened considerably from her original standards. She is one of a group one day when the conversation turns toward a girl they all know. The gossip concerns the girl's furtive affair. Each one has some detail to add until Mary is appalled by the picture of sordid meeting places, use of fictitious names, and distasteful and shocking details which the whole story presents. As a fastidious person, she is deeply shocked when she realizes she has been considering the same climax to her own affair.

It cannot be too strongly emphasized that the sex ideal and all that ideal represents must be associated with the *specific acts* leading to chaste or unchaste consequences. For this reason it is argued that an attitude, mental set, or ideal of chastity must be built up before adolescent sex experience. This ideal should be *realistic*—one based on events as they will probably occur in our lives. An ideal which does not prepare one for real experience will be easily discarded.

To be more specific, it is argued that if the boy (or girl) realizes the subsequent attitudes that he and his partner will have toward their behavior and toward each other, and the remorse and anxiety that will remain in their minds for some time to come, he will be less impulsive at the critical moment. If he realizes at the initial surge of passion that after the excitement has subsided there will follow a depression during which many of the following questions will rush through his mind with their unpleasant trail, his conduct will tend to be affected:

Does she behave like this with all boys? Does she think I behave like this with all girls? What attitude shall I take when I see her next time? Will she be disgusted with me? Have I contracted any disease? Does she love me, or was she merely swept off balance by emotion? Will she discuss this with parents or confidants? Do I love her enough to have justified my behavior? Have I started something that I am not willing to continue? Have I broken any of her strong ideals? Will she expect affections that I do not feel? How can I have done what I did, when I am so disgusted by it now? Do I have little will power and poor character? Have I been blinded by lust to other personal qualities that I could never learn to love? Will I have the character to meet any responsibilities that result from this? Does the behavior that I have shown fit in with the rest of my personality? What would my mother, father, sister, and best friends think of what I have done?

Chastity Does Not Assure the Development of Love.   Love develops in part from a balanced attitude toward physical intimacies. Early physical intimacies may jeopardize the development of enriched love experiences.   On the other hand, complete lack of interest in physical intimacies with the opposite sex does not give promise of later enduring love.   There are some individuals who have developed an abhorrence of the physical side of sex because of some early training or experience.   In compensation for this they build up a wealth of sentiment.   They talk of pure, beautiful relationships untouched by the crassness of the physical side of love.   Love has an experienced or *anticipated* physical aspect regardless of how mild or implicit it may be.   It is doubtful whether true love for the opposite sex ever exists without a biological foundation.   A marriage based on sentiments dissociated from sensory experiences will rarely satisfy both partners.

There is some evidence that, when a physical interest in the opposite sex does not develop during youth and early maturity, it seldom develops later.   It is well then for the individual who is totally uninterested in the opposite sex to place himself in an environment, and through counseling gain insight and release, that will be conducive to the development of such interest.   This subject is discussed in detail on pages 355 to 356.

Ambivalence towards Sex in Our Culture.   Several surveys of students' attitudes indicate that they as a group are not more tolerant than the population as a whole, at least when expressing themselves on attitude blanks.   Different studies among college and high school students show sex irregularities to be rated first among the primary "crimes," "sins," and bad practices.   Certain sex offenses are rated more serious by both sexes than jeopardy of human life.

The people of our culture continue a strong defense of conventionality in sex life (651).   On the other hand, as has been shown recently in an interesting study of contemporary songs, conversations, magazines and light literature in America, there are many stimuli in these which are sexual in nature. The conventions on the one hand, and the constant sexual stimuli in mass media on the other, constitute a conflict in our culture, as well as a diversity in attitudes toward sex (206). Some individuals exaggerate the frequency of unconventionality in order to support their own wishes for it. The studies of marriage, however, show prevalence of the desire of others for the conventional based on moral reasons and the wish for marital happiness. Others, however, view sex as a ". . . nasty and tasty, a vicious and delicious business" (209).

Realize That Most Young People Have the Same Problem in the Main as You. One helpful attitude for the young person who is trying to live up to standards which he has rationally accepted is the realization that *many others whom he admires have similar problems.* This attitude is helpful regardless of the conventions he is trying to meet or the problems with which he is battling. He will find that there is a certain percentage of the persons whom he knows who are either striving with identical or similar problems at present or have in the past. Furthermore, in addition to those fighting the problem, be it masturbation, incontinence, crushes, or some peculiar sex tendency, there is a *greater number on the fringe of the problem.* They are not actively disturbed by the problem all the time, but they have mild forms of the difficulty or are troubled by it some of the time. The civilized human being, particularly the idealistic male, is besieged by the biological urgency of sex, however vague, on the one hand, and by the social pressure of standards on the other hand. The result is a compromise, with some resultant emotional upheaval.

The Question of Petting

Meaning of Petting. To some the term means *lust* practices— "play-at-love," promiscuous and selfish, with little thought of the partner as a personality. The relationships in such cases are ephemeral. The individual holds no great enduring respect for the other. The relationship tends to increase in sexual intimacy and to be followed often by remorse or disgust. In such cases all other attitudes, motives, and personality traits of oneself and the other personality are ignored.

To others, the term means caressing that involves the *association of the higher ideals* that usually occur in the courting stage. Sometimes a stable relationship has preceded the petting, and the individuals show consistent deep affection for one another. They give all public indication that they are sincere and compatible in interest and attitudes as well as affections. Their love-making is controlled, as much as strong emotions can be controlled, by their ideals.

These represent two extreme relationships, but there are numerous variations between the extremes. All the physical components of these widely different relationships are usually called petting.

Consideration of "Arguments for Petting." Booklets on petting addressed to young people usually point out the tendency to justify or rationalize petting as a release of sex tension or as an aspect of natural boy-girl relations. These authors maintain there is a fallacy in these arguments in terms of some of the considerations mentioned previously. (See pages 335 to 337.) They state that often petting becomes a preparation for mating rather than a substitute for sexual relations and is associated with the emotion of lust rather than love (223).

Opinions of a Group of Young People Regarding Petting. A group of adolescent girls who admitted having experienced light caressing give "reasons" such as "infatuation," "curiosity," "others do it," and "fear of unpopularity" for their behavior. Reasons given by men for *refraining* were: lack of opportunity, fear of response, common decency. Girls refrained because of common decency, physical repugnance, social disapproval.

Another questionnaire filled out by several hundred girls indicated that only 23 per cent of them thought it part of a girl's routine in her relations with boys and practiced it. Of these girls, however, 92 per cent classed sex relation outside of marriage as immoral (496). The majority (60 per cent) of young male college graduates in one study asserted that petting *increased* the sexual impulse, and 51 per cent said that it was a quickly passing enjoyment (602).

It is obvious from these replies that some of the sex play is *unsatisfied curiosity* that may be curtailed through education. Some is of a social nature, since both sexes believe it is *expected of them.* If other interesting activities were planned the petting would probably decline.

Stability in Affections

Impulsiveness in Affections. The question is often asked, "Is there such a thing as love at first sight?" If it is not answered immediately, the questioner will go on to relate his personal experience which may run as follows:

"I saw the most beautiful girl today that I have ever met. She has everything I think a girl needs. She is beautiful, sweet, well-groomed, knows just how to act—she has everything!"

This emotional experience did not develop fully on the spur of the moment. The boy's present experience is the emergence of a *long, subterranean growth*. The present experience merely ignited a flame, the fuel for which had been stored for a long time. He had read fiction about girls, seen movies, daydreamed, and admired girls from afar. All this was superimposed upon emotions previously experienced with members of the opposite sex. The sentimental background was established. Furthermore, at this time no doubt he was "in the mood" for affection. Biochemical processes probably had *lowered the threshold* of the appreciation of sentimental and affectionate objects. Finally, the admired person seemed *compatible with more* of these *sentiments* than anyone he had met previously. The qualities she did not have he supplied with his imagination. He does not stop at this point but continues to embellish his memory of her with imaginary traits and attributes whenever he thinks of her. If the kind of courtship previously discussed ensues, he will be able to *test* his original impression. The more realistic the situations are, the better the testing process. If he continues to daydream and reinforce his conception of her *without really knowing her* his delusions will be increased. Although we have used the boy as an example here, girls go through the same experience as frequently as, if not more often than, boys.

"Love at first sight" is highly impulsive. It is bound to be an intense *emotional reaction* to very *fragmentary impressions*. It must be tested to prevent the emotional experience from blinding the attracted one to the real traits of the person.

Fickleness in Affections. *Nature of fickleness.* Why are some girls "boy crazy"? Why do some boys always have "girls on the mind"? Can we explain the member of either sex who seems to be highly stimulated by the presence of *any* member of the opposite sex? He will be swept off his feet by one individual today and be equally enthusiastic about an entirely different one tomorrow.

This kind of fickleness is a typical phenomenon of early adolescence. It shows *emotional immaturity* or *lack of breadth of experience* with the opposite sex. The mature individual has made many associations with the opposite sex and has learned to like those who seem to satisfy or reinforce the sentiments he has built up as a love pattern. Others he learns to regard differently. Some are "just another person," "another girl," "not bad," or "a good sport." He comes to enjoy the presence of girls, but he is not inordinately emotional when they are around. He has become adapted to them. It is true that some older adolescents and chronologically mature persons show fickleness, but it is doubtful if they are emotionally mature. Some have been secluded from the opposite sex as love objects.

Fickleness is another example of impulsive affections. The individual is responding to the *emotional* side of his experience rather than to the cognitive or intellectual. He does not regard members of the opposite sex as *individuals* with many personality traits, some likeable and others wearing. He instead regards them solely as objects of emotional excitement. The emotion may become so intense for a time that he can think of nothing else. His only desire is to see the object of this emotion. Then, when a new personality appears and he again responds to the emotional aspect of his impressions, the first person's attraction wanes.

The promiscuous man who cannot be satisfied with one love object but must find many temporary ones has been called a "Don Juan." Case studies have given evidence that such an individual is not what he might seem—a virile, secure lover. Instead he is compelled to prove his attractiveness by having many women respond to him. Other motivations that have been given for this fickleness are his fear of losing his loved one and an inner hostility that shows itself by the breaking of many hearts. As his hostility produces insecurity, he must have many loves to compensate for it. Some of this anxiety has been traced to a childhood in which family relationships and love have been of an unstable kind. So far as the individual is still being influenced by these early experiences, he is immature (777).

Disillusionment in Affections. All of us have heard of the "broken-hearted." The victim has built strong emotional attitudes around some member of the opposite sex. He may be one of the inexperienced persons we discussed above. He may have had few dates and few experiences previously with the opposite sex. On the other hand, he may have chosen his girl because he thought she was different from the others he had known—she was perfect—to find out later that she was not so angelic. When he discovers how things really are, he has already fallen for her. She means everything to him, and she *must* fit his expectations!

This individual has deceived himself. When he finally reaches reality, he finds it extremely unpleasant. Since this happens most frequently to people who react emotionally to many aspects of life, it is hard for such a person to look at the matter objectively. He broods over his loss. He has fixated on this object of his affections, built up vivid emotional attitudes toward her, and now they are blocked. In extreme cases the individual loses his appetite, his zest for life, and his interest in his work.

This individual may have had limited experience supplemented with a vivid life of daydreams. He may have magnified the importance of the relationship. For some reason, this relationship *had to be* exceptional. No doubt there is much more to the matter than his affection for the girl. There may be involved a personal problem which he believed this relationship would solve.

Tim's father was a Prussian autocrat, his mother a submissive, hardworking farm wife. He had one sister whom he idolized and in whom the parental training had produced immaturity and repression of amorous interest in boys.

An officer's uniform brought out more manly attractiveness than even Tim realized he had. The family's rigid moral training was actively disregarded now as Tim went from conquest to conquest. He tried not to face the conflict between his training and present behavior. He wanted to marry a good girl who combined the coquetry and glamour of those he had known in his flirtations with the qualities necessary to build a family life similar to that he had known on the farm.

Isabelle was the answer. She had everything that the other girls had, he believed, and yet she was good. But he had to be sure of this, so the inquisition began. Finally she admitted that she had once loved another fellow, and what had happened between them was quite similar to the relations Tim had had with several girls in the preceding year. Tim was beside himself, first with rage, then with a general emotional disturbance. He discussed his problem excitedly with a counselor and received some relief and some insight in the discussion. The following questions should suggest the conflict Tim was experiencing:

To what extent was Tim fighting his own guilt? How much of the real difficulty was due to the conflict between extremely repressive, rigid home standards and the standardless life he later led? To what extent did his sister enter the problem? He was sure *she* was different too—but maybe she had dated fellows like himself? Did he dare raise this question? Can Tim's emotional upheaval, which was out of character for a strong, confident ex-officer, be explained better in terms of his own conflicts or in terms of his disillusionment by the girl?

Sometimes emotionality over the loss of a loved one can be better understood in terms of the threat it represents to the individual's ability to attract the opposite sex. It may touch off a feeling of inferiority over one's immaturity in this area, one's falling short of a masculine or feminine goal.

SUGGESTIONS FOR THE DISILLUSIONED. To talk over such matters with someone else always helps one's thinking about them, as shown in Chapter 5. As illustrated with Tim, the individual obtains release and sometimes gains insight into his inner life and the circumstances that created the problem. He is then better able to turn to his normal routine, which gives him opportunities to meet new people, possibly some with similar problems, and to satisfy his basic motives. Time and new experiences will do much to give him more perspective. Insight from conferences and new experiences may help him to change some of the circumstances of his living and some of his attitudes.

Controlling Masturbation

Meaning, Significance, and Origin. There are few habits that have caused more personal unhappiness than masturbation. The practice itself is not the cause of mental and physical problems; it is the *attitude* held by most people toward the habit that is the major cause of emotional difficulties (488, 763).

Masturbation is usually a form of autoeroticism (literally, self-love). It includes all kinds of self-induced sex activities, from sexual daydreams to manual stimulation. The term is usually applied, however, to the manipulation of genitals. Masturbation occurs in small children almost universally. Parental censorship usually terminates the practice in this period, but it is rediscovered in adolescence. This discovery is made either accidentally, or through another child or an adult.

The experience which results from masturbation undergoes a change at the time of adolescent physical changes. It becomes a more intense and vivid experience with many of the physiological concomitants of a strong emotion. This is known as an orgasm.

Frequency of Practice. Masturbation is a part of the experience of a large number of persons at different times in their lives. The reaction to the habit and its duration vary greatly with the individual's emotional background. Questionnaires answered by various groups of men and women in college and elsewhere indicate the practice of masturbation at some time in their lives in 62 to 98 per cent of the men and 40 to 64 per cent of the women (628). The frequency falls in college. These percentages are given because so often those who continue the practice in college believe their behavior to be so unusual as to make them abnormal. This view, as we shall show shortly, is erroneous.

False Notions Regarding Masturbation. Several generations ago, it was generally believed that masturbation caused insanity, sterility, feeble-mindedness, "loss of manhood," ill health, physical weakness, and other intimidating consequences. The young adolescent still picks up beliefs of this type. Sometimes he retains them and broods over them. Even if he later learns that these beliefs are false, he may continue to be influenced by them subconsciously (624).

Examples of the manner in which the habit of masturbation influences the individual in his teens and early maturity are numerous. Some young people believe that there are "tell-tale" characteristics that indicate to the world that they have been or are guilty of the practice. Different individuals isolate different aspects of their physical make-up as "giving them away." Some believe that they are betrayed by their thinness, nature of their genitals, the expression of their eyes, others by a facial blemish or peculiarity such as acne, pimples, jaw curvature, or length or shape of nose. One college coed feared she would become epileptic in class—a fear that was caused by a childhood belief that masturbation causes epilepsy. These ideas, of course, have no foundation in fact. These beliefs and the personality pattern that allows them to perpetuate and disturb the individual no doubt have an effect upon the continuation of the habit.

Frequently bodily sensations occur after an orgasm. Some individuals center their attention on these sensations. They are anxious about them later in that day or the next day, and before long they have developed a real complaint. The quiet, introverted, reclusive young person may become so emotional over the effect of masturbation on his *health* that he mistakes for illness the natural changes which occur during emotion.

Since masturbation is an autoerotic practice, the attention and affection of the individual is expended upon himself rather than upon an individual of the opposite sex. The most successful adjustment in marriage is associated with absorption in the interests of one's mate rather than preoccupation with oneself. Although there is evidence that many who have strong habits of masturbation adjust to marriage relationships later, it is no doubt more difficult, because the individual has become satisfied with one type of sex habit and then must learn to be satisfied by an entirely different type.

The eradication of masturbation is sometimes a goal that *assumes great importance* in the individual's existence.

A conscientious youth builds up, on the one hand, all the ideals and sentiments associated with his ideal conception of himself. We might label this, as he often does, his "better self." With this ideal self he fights the sex impulses that lead to masturbation. He stakes his whole reputation on his "better self's" winning the battle. He puts great faith in this "better self." He may even tell himself that in the past he has been a weakling but now he will be strong. During the time when he wishes to prove that this "better self" is stronger, he is afraid it is not. This fear holds him. He continues to struggle. He may struggle successfully for days and fight all the events which arouse sex. Then one day the urge overpowers him— he falls in defeat. He meets again his disgust for the practice and his fear of its consequences.

Suggestions for Dealing with the Problem of Masturbation. Individuals differ, statistics show, with regard to the continuation of the practice. The suggestions and insights below should be helpful.

SEE THE HABIT IN PERSPECTIVE. Realize that masturbation is not a practice limited to queer, abnormal persons. Instead, it is a habit that many normal persons acquire and overcome. Its physical consequences are negligible. It does not lead to insanity or other formidable results. The effects on personality, however, particularly in persons who are falsely informed about masturbation, are undesirable.

Furthermore, one should clearly recognize that any habit system like this is merely *one aspect of personality*. The practice may assume great importance in personality if the individual emphasizes it unnecessarily through worry, disgust, and feelings of guilt. The depression that occurs after the act is partially a contrast to the highly emotional experience of the orgasm and partially a result of the mental conflict between one's ideal and one's action (89).

Do not expect to change any habit or attitude, particularly one associated with as strong an urge as sex, in one or two days or even one or two weeks. Also *expect regressions* or back-sliding. In all curves of human progress in the laboratory or in nature there are falls in the curves as well as rises.

Participate in social and physical activity with your own sex. A frequently reported result of masturbation is a lowering of self-respect. It is doubtful, however, whether masturbation is the sole cause of this.

Masturbation, it seems from study of individual cases, is resorted to most frequently by individuals in moments when they are lonesome, depressed, blue, and not enjoying the company of their fellows. It is a vivid source of transient pleasure for the depressed individual. It seems to decrease in frequency when the individual is satisfying dominant motives for affection and recognition. Dejection because of masturbation, then, can lead to anxiety and stronger tendencies toward more masturbation.

College extracurricular activities are excellent outlets. They *satisfy most of the dominant human motives.* They allow the individual to gain mastery over some skill, which is important at this time in life, and to gain social recognition, new experience, and, sometimes, affection. They take the individual's *attention off himself.* Athletics offer another outlet for the satisfaction of these motives and in addition provide an avenue for expending physical energy. In boys they act as a symbol of masculinity and physical fitness which enhances self-respect and greatly lessens the problem.

PARTICIPATE IN SOCIAL ACTIVITY WITH THE OPPOSITE SEX. The individual should learn some social skills that allow contact with the opposite sex, such as dancing, bridge, and other activities. Pleasant associations with members of the opposite sex detract our attention from ourselves and allow us to fixate our affections normally and to increase heterosexuality. Courtship and the reciprocation of affection from the opposite sex are also *symbols of status* for both sexes. The man is considered more manly if he deserves the affection and interest of members of the opposite sex, and the woman is considered more attractive when she receives attention of this sort.

Successful participation in activities with members of the same or opposite sex often results in the individual becoming *more like the average* individual in superficial factors, such as dress, grooming, speech, sports and interests. This also aids self-esteem. Our appearance to ourselves is a stimulus that affects our attitudes toward ourselves. It is not necessary for us to alter our personalities profoundly. We need merely add those superficialities which are in vogue at the time and help us better communicate more satisfyingly with our generation.

UNDERSTAND THE SOURCE OF INSECURITY AS A MEANS OF CONTROLLING THE SYMPTOM. Since masturbation may be a sign of insecurity, the important problem is to understand the source of this feeling of inadequacy, which probably originated early in life. When the real causes of the tension are understood and relived in memory with a new attitude toward them, the individual is relieved.   One may have a need to feel that he is accepted by others, or that he is not so inadequate as the events of his childhood made him fear.   As he sees himself and his development more clearly he may feel freer to pursue the social activities suggested.   These activities may bring more success, acceptance by others, and greater self-esteem.   Presumably all this will help one to plunge into other activities and release some of the tensions that contributed to the need to masturbate.   He will then be better able to avoid events leading up to the act.   The events that lead to masturbation differ with individuals.   Most persons know what these are in their own case.   Sometimes reorganization of one's routine can remove or change the nature of these situations.

Redirecting Crushes

Characteristics of Crush.   The development of affection does not always run in the course indicated in the first section of this chapter. An individual may not meet members of the opposite sex frequently enough or under the proper conditions during puberty (period of adolescent changes) when heterosexual attitudes usually develop.   He may have established some definite aversions to them in early life through conflict, jealousy, or hints from adults.   On the other hand, close contact with members of the same sex at adolescence when sex expansiveness occurs may cause *one to gain strong affection for them.*

Some individuals find they are attracted to a person of the same sex who has traits they admire but lack themselves.   Others have failed to gain the affection and recognition they desire from the same sex parent.   When this occurs among girls it is known as a "crush." The taboo against affection for the same sex in women is not so strong as it is among men, and for this reason the crush is more apparent among girls and is often thought of as characteristic of them alone. Boys, however, also have crushes.   They are probably less frequent and usually of the hero-worship variety.   Crushes are reported in approximately 30 to 50 per cent of the cases in a study of unmarried women recalling adolescence (154).   Twelve per cent of male college graduates admit they have experienced "feelings of affection" for the same sex in the teens (602).

Among girls it appears that in many cases the attraction is for an older woman, very often a woman who has achieved some distinction. The older individual may reciprocate.   She may merely be flattered by the adulation. She may be disturbed by it and may discourage it. The attraction may also be toward one of the same age or toward a younger person.

The behavior of the girl or boy who has the crush may differ little from that of one who holds an affection for someone of the opposite sex. There may be a desire to be with the adored person, a demand for constant attention, a display of jealousy if someone else seems interested in the same person, a desire to caress, and unhappiness in the absence of the object of affection.

Sometimes the boy or girl has an affection for an older person similar to the affection he has or might have had for one of his own parents. He may write affectionate letters, go see them often, caress their hands, say "mushy" things, and tell others how "wonderful" the older person is. He or she may plan his life to be like the life of the admired one and build an elaborate dream world about him.

Daydreams in Crushes. A crush may greatly influence the dream life of the youth. The crush may be entirely secret, the relationships with the adored one occurring only in a dream world. He or she may secretly have a crush on another individual, worship him or her from afar, and dream about relationships with that individual.

An adolescent told her counselor in confidence of her behavior during the period of a secret crush. She said she would watch the object of her affection from the window as she passed several times daily. She would go out of her way to get a glimpse of this person. She looked forward to these moments. After seeing the other girl she would improvise elaborate daydreams involving detailed activities with her.

A college man who was having difficulties in adjustment told of having crushes on younger boys. Apparently he had not developed well in athletic activities and got most of his attention from younger boys. His affections for them were intensified through a sex experience with a child when he was in high school. Several later attempts to shed affection had failed because of their repulsion. He therefore turned to the movies and had secret crushes on young actors. He would see their movies two and three times. After the show he would daydream about the actor and himself in elaborate plots.

He was counseled psychologically over a period longer than a year. After graduation he achieved success in his profession, married, now has several children and apparently is a good father.

Criteria of Normal Friendships. What is the distinction between crushes and friendships? We discussed in Chapter 10 the factors that give rise to friendship. They consist of similar economic and social environment, similar intellectual and nonintellectual interests, and compatible supplementary motives. We usually like those individuals who best satisfy our motives, whether they be our interests, our attitudes, or our wishes. Whereas all friendships involve an emotional element, in the normal friendship this emotional element is not of the tender, sentimental, or sexual kind. The motives satisfied are *not so intimate*. In normal friendly contact our emphasis is on the *activity* in which we and our friends are engaged, rather than on the *friend himself* and his intimate relationship to us. We normally enjoy our friends, prefer to have them around us, but we do not show a strongly *possessive* attitude toward them. There is more *realistic interaction* and less phantasy in normal friendship. Our whole life does not revolve around the friend. To be sure, we like to help them and even to make sacrifices for them, but these sacrifices are not the result of our desire to have this friend intimately dependent upon us (633, 777). One may realize that an intense friendship borders on a crush and become frightened.

A 22-year-old college student states that for two years he has prevented himself from forming *any* strong friendships. This attitude is the result of his realization that the last friendship that he formed was in the nature of a crush. He was frightened. He thought himself abnormal, and instead of guiding future friendships and seeking to make himself independent of them he systematically prevented himself from becoming too friendly with any of his male acquaintances.

This type of behavior, of course, is almost as abnormal as the crush itself. No doubt he needed to become more mature in his relationships with his fellows, considering the description of his latest relationship with a fellow student, but growth was necessary—not complete prohibition of all friendship. Possibly he could have broadened his scope of affection. No doubt there were numerous individuals on the campus who had similar interests, attitudes, and motives. A number of friends would prevent him from becoming too intimately attached to any one. Furthermore, he could plan double dates, parties, and participation in "bull sessions." The latter would bring out the typical man's attitudes toward the opposite sex. Staying away from the person one finds attractive has been suggested, but this may not keep him or her "out of mind." Very close contact often produces quarrels and breaks the relationship.

Crushes—Bisexuality and Homosexuality. Whereas many normal individuals idealize members of their own sex in their development, or are more attracted to activities with their own sex than with the opposite, there is a small percentage of both sexes who for various reasons continually satisfy their tender emotions or sex urges in physical relationships with their own sex. These individuals are inveterate, overt homosexuals (158). They face the problem of adjusting in a society hostile to their way of life. Sometimes they make a partial adjustment in a society of other homosexuals. There are and have been homosexuals who have made fine contributions in their fields of endeavor, but many fail to find full happiness because of their conflicts.

Not all individuals who have had homosexual experiences in childhood or youth fall into this category, because about 30 to 50 per cent of men have had some sort of experience with their own sex (411, 434), and the percentage of persons confirmed in a homosexual life is very much smaller. Furthermore, there is a difference between the confirmed homosexual and the adolescent or young adult who is struggling with bisexual tendencies—attraction to both sexes—or who is striving to develop toward heterosexuality. Many individuals of both sexes who have achieved public or private recognition and success, and who have represented idealistic and socially desirable causes, have had such struggles in their development. Others have made adjustments in marriage. A study of marriage shows that lack of male dominance or a history of sex shock in the wife are not crucial in marital happiness (790).

Too frequently the realization of some homosexual tendencies causes the individual to identify himself with persons who make public advances or seduce children. He comes to reject himself, feel unworthy, and anticipate rejection from others. He cannot accept some of his most intimate experiences and impulses, and this undermines his self-esteem. This rejection of his inner self does not result in control of emotion, and it often creates new, more serious problems.

Although there are instances of homosexuality that seem to be the result of a biological or glandular factor, and research in the chemical or endocrinological aspects of sex may later establish definitely that this operates in some cases, it probably is *only one factor* (572, 352). Homosexual traits, like most human traits, are the development resulting from an interaction of certain temperamental factors and learned attitudes and habits. The bulk of the studies and opinions favor the explanation that homosexuality is acquired in development (411, 552, 216, 434, 208, 8), and there is evidence that it may be redirected if the individual has strong motivation and a full life otherwise.

Homosexuality may be related to the fact that the individual has been alienated by the parent of the same sex and thereby gains the habits and attitudes of the parent of the opposite sex. If a boy, his father may have been excessively stern, or uninterested in him. He may have been reared as a child of the opposite sex and prevented from taking part in the typical childhood play of his own sex. Many times emotional attachment to the same sex occurs before puberty (212). He or she may, finally, have been seduced or aroused in early life by an older person of the same sex (719, 216, 58), as well as blocked in some way in his tendency to have tender or passionate feelings toward the opposite sex.

Attitudes toward Parents Affect Sexuality. An attitude which seems to prevent the acquisition of heterosexuality is that of *over-idealization of a parent*. This attitude is illustrated by the fixation of a son upon his mother, of the identification of all women with his mother. The youth may build an ideal girl and find that none of his dates comes up to the ideal he holds. They are always being compared disadvantageously with an ideal which they cannot rival because it is composed of traits that no person in reality possesses.

A parent of the opposite sex, a mother for example, may, without full realization of what she is doing, enourage tender affections in her child. She may also, through constant association and confidences, together with the rejection by the father, cause the son to introject her attitudes and habits rather than those of his father. This boy has a more feminine outlook, and the girl who holds her father as a model a more masculine outlook, than the typical person of their own age and sex.

A parent may warn the child or adolescent about the wiles and deceptiveness of the opposite sex, point toward the pitfalls of love and sex contact, and encourage him to delay his amours. Over a period of years heterosexuality may be discouraged, traits of the opposite sex may be acquired, and friendships and tender feelings toward the same sex may be developed.

Segregation of Sexes Affects Sexuality. A discussion of the need for the mingling of the sexes on a pleasant, healthy level is not complete without pointing out another source of unhealthy attitudes, namely, the *strict segregation* of sexes such as was found in the boarding and military schools of previous years. In the laboratory, experimental animals become homosexual if segregated from the opposite sex before puberty (376). In the young human who is placed in a segregated group, puberty arrives, and the individual develops, extending his affections to those around him, connecting romantic ideas with those persons, and indulging in slight, casual physical contacts such as kissing among girls and playful bodily contact among boys. As such institutions were conducted years ago, the opposite sex was carefully eliminated from the scene, and the only objects of affection were ideal, imaginary sweethearts or individuals of the same sex. Today the inadvisability of this practice is realized, and military and boarding schools and girls' colleges provide opportunities for dates, mixed parties, and entertainment of the opposite sex. It is interesting to note that crushes seem to develop in certain kinds of societies. They are not found at all in the more primitive cultures (580). It has been suggested that crushes don't appear in those cultures where no clear-cut distinction is made between the sexes, but do appear where this distinction is so rigid that some feel inadequate in the sex role they must play.

Suggestions for Achieving Heterosexuality. Heterosexuality or strong attraction to the opposite sex is not established at birth. We become heterosexual through a normal development of the personality traits of our own sex. As has been shown, some events prevent or delay its growth.

UNDERSTAND THE BASIS FOR PRESENT ATTITUDES. If one realizes that he has developed some of the traits of the opposite sex and along with them some attraction to his own, he should not give way to panic. This development is no doubt an orderly one in terms of the conditions that surrounded the individual in early life. His status is not different from that of many others who are admired and who are fine persons. One can create more problems than he solves by ruthlessly denying, fighting, or attempting to obliterate this aspect of his personality. A more sensible approach is to understand and accept himself. This should *better enable* him to guide the traits of his personality into creative avenues and through the learning process acquire the heterosexual attitudes that will enable him to make a better adjustment.

EXPLOIT PRESENT TALENTS THROUGH ACTIVITIES. Many of the suggestions for dealing with the problem of masturbation on pages 348 to 350 are appropriate here. They consist of the indirect approach arising after the individual has explored the needs that caused him to develop crushes. These needs for security, recognition from his own sex, feelings of status and self-esteem may be satisfied through the talents he possesses. For example, a student can gain recognition, status, self-esteem, and the respect of his fellows through success and wide recognition in forensics, offices in an organization, music, or art just as well as through prowess on the football field or basketball court. Moreover, the tough, muscular, well-built man is not the only kind whom women select, or the submissive, sweetly feminine girl the only kind men prefer. The frailer, neat, shorter man who may be more gentle and more compatible with women, who has a real attraction toward them and is capable of playing an active role with them, will win favor in some instances in which the more "masculine" man would fail. This is true also in the opposite situation—the attractiveness of the large, athletic kind of girl for many men who prefer her to her more feminine sisters.

Most men and women are a combination of masculine and feminine traits. In most cases adjustment is a matter of strengthening certain traits without disparaging or fighting others too vigorously.

Few circumstances can compare in efficacy with a warm friendship between a secure individual who has the attitudes and habits of his own sex and one who needs to develop in that direction. There is no doubt that losing oneself in group activities and in relationships with other people in an effort to become less self-centered and brooding is an aid to this whole problem. Part of the solution of the problem is the development of security and self-esteem.

Summary. Before leaving this topic let us again emphasize that changing behavior is a slow process with many reverses. The attitude that one assumes toward a habit is important. One should not hate himself because of the course his sex life has taken. Rather, he should seek to understand himself and accept sex urges as natural functions that require direction. Finally, any problem is merely one aspect of a total personality. Some writers in this field view masturbation as a symptom of an incomplete life. From this standpoint, the indirect approach to the eradication of the habit is most effective. It is well to understand the early bases for the feeling of insecurity, unworthiness, or being "left out" of the group that is one of the major causes of atypical sex tendencies. Satisfy dominant motives, pursue social adventures and hobbies, and seek other satisfying experiences with the same and opposite sex as a means of gaining security and social acceptance.

Supplementary Readings

A. Ellis, "Psychosexual and Marital Problems," in L. A. Pennington and I. A. Berg, *An Introduction to Clinical Psychology*, Ronald, 1954.

V. W. Grant, *The Psychology of Sexual Emotions: The Basis of Selective Attraction*, Longmans, Green, 1957.

A. C. Kinsey, W. B. Pomeroy, C. E. Martin, and P. H. Gebhard, *Sexual Behavior in the Human Female*, Saunders, 1953.

G. H. Seward, *Sex and the Social Order*, McGraw-Hill, 1946.

In addition see the references cited by number in the chapter and appearing in the bibliography of an accompanying volume entitled *Teaching Personal Adjustment: An Instructor's Manual*.

Ted Russell

Marriage in Our Culture

Marriage has different meanings for different individuals. Monogamous marriage does not exist in all societies. In Samoa, a husband or wife may tire of the mate, withdraw from the household, and the marriage has "passed away" (525). In our culture we regard the ideal marriage as a high stage in personal-social development—a sacrament from the religious standpoint; yet in our own society we also find people in wedlock who show no great fusion of feelings, attitudes or motives and many marriages that end in divorce.

Marriage in its best form usually is the culmination of romantic love and courtship, with some sublimation of the sex impulses. It is a fusion of the relationships existent in friendship, companionship, and sexual attraction. Ideally, it seems to occur after numerous friendships with the opposite sex, and after a courtship that has tested the social and temperamental compatibility of the pair. It is a public declaration of affection and fidelity and is approved by society. Logically, therefore, it should be discussed at this point, immediately after our consideration of the development of affections.

358

CHAPTER 13

MARITAL

ADJUSTMENT

Evaluation of Marriage. Marriage is held in high regard in our culture. Studies show married older students judge themselves happier than the unmarried (828). Certain statistics seem to indicate that it is a healthier state than the single (494). Students in high majorities intend to marry and respect the institution, women choosing it over a career. People over 65 mention the period between 25 and 40 as being the most happy, and attribute it to marriage and the family (437). The institution is defended even among unhappily married couples; few say they would not marry again, and only about half had even considered divorce (789). Our tendency to idealize and romanticize marriage also creates problems when there is no preparation for the realities of marital adjustment.

A YOUNG MARRIED COUPLE HAVING DIFFICULTIES. Let us begin our study of marital adjustment with a case that might have its counterpart on any American campus. An analysis and class discussion of it will open the way for the relationships and facts to be presented later.

Clay Clark had washed out from the Naval Air Corps, returned to school and to an old girl with whom he had broken relations while he was in the service. They dated and soon were going steady again. Alice, his fiancée and later his wife, belonged to a sorority which was high in the social hierarchy on campus, lived pretty closely within the pattern found in city suburbs, looked forward to a stable marriage that would allow her status, social contact with her friends of both sexes, and membership in a country club. She was very much in love with Clay and was pleased that the relationship had been resumed. She was willing to wait until they could have a church wedding to follow the usual prenuptial parties. Her folks were also enthusiastic about Clay and about their daughter's prospects.

Their relationship at college appeared quite romantic. They were seen together a lot, had classes together, went to dances, and participated actively in the campus social life. Clay seemed to grow in confidence and spontaneity. The counselor hardly recognized him as the ex-Navy cadet who had come into the office at the beginning of the year. Clay's separation from the Navy was a bitter experience. At that time the counselor had the impression that, though a good-looking, well-proportioned young man with a pleasant smile, he was immature, had apparently been overprotected by his mother, lacked confidence, and was emotionally disturbed and sensitive about the *rejection* that his separation from the service meant to him. No doubt Alice's sweet, stable personality was a solace then.

Clay postponed the marriage several times, much to Alice's embarrassment, and, as the date finally agreed upon drew near, he became uneasy over his ability to assume the responsibility, although he did not analyze his reluctance until after marriage. Just a few days before the wedding, he was in a state bordering on panic, and he frankly told Alice that he thought it would be best for them to postpone the wedding until he felt more sure about himself. This brought on hysterics from her, and her parents thought that it was unwise to postpone again. There was the usual attitude of "What will people say and think?" so they went through with the wedding. It was lovely, and, as the result of Alice's taste, her mother's assistance, and the wedding gifts, she and Clay were able to set up a very attractive apartment in the college town.

Alice got a position doing secretarial work with a law firm, and things ran smoothly for a few months. Then Clay began to enjoy his visits to the fraternity house more thoroughly. He had a job which took him out of town on week ends with a group of boys. He looked forward to these trips and to the drinking they did after work. When at home with Alice he became morose, stared into space, lost sleep, his appetite, and interest in school. He realized that week by week the marriage meant less to him. He did not enjoy the bridge parties, the evenings at home, or even the coke sessions together that had been so pleasant during their engagement. He became irritable and hostile toward her. He knew Alice was not entirely happy living below the standard she had anticipated, but he also knew that if he really loved her this would not be important.

Finally he talked the matter over with his parents who were disturbed over the prospect of a divorce but told him he would have to do what he thought best. Alice was deeply disturbed when he broached the subject of a divorce, but she had gone through months of sullenness and heartache and had begun to wonder too if their marriage could work out. Their sexual adjustment had seemed good to them at first, but now Clay found it increasingly more difficult to approach her.

What roles was each playing, and what roles did each expect of the other? How were these roles conditioned by the early family relationships of Clay and Alice?

Clay had had his way most of his life. Although not very much could be gleaned from him about the family life, it undoubtedly was the kind that kept him immature. He grew up to be essentially a passive man without much interest in the opposite sex except as he was pushed into dating and conventional romance in college. He had never become the ardent suitor, and although ambitious in intention he did not have much initiative. His mother or his parents were indubitably responsible for the fact that he was essentially narcissistic, more concerned with himself than with anyone else. Failures were disturbing to him. He repeatedly said that the marriage had disturbed his career. He was unready for it. He wanted more freedom. He wanted to go to graduate school. He did not know that he ever wanted to marry again, but he knew he wanted to meet more people before he married. He was getting along better with the fellows than he had earlier, and he wanted to enjoy these relationships more thoroughly.

Although his own desire to dissolve the marriage was uppermost, the conflict that the consequences of a divorce produced was very disturbing. He realized that he would wreck Alice's life and would be regarded as a heel. He had no grounds for a divorce. Everything was in favor of a trial for a year or two except the fact that he was becoming more repelled by the relationship. For a time he saw no solution.

Alice had come from an upper-middle-class family. Her mother was very aggressive and, from the information gained, was not too happy with her husband and devoted most of her energies to social climbing. Alice's attainments were the culmination of a successful career. She had joined one of the "best" sororities, had a lovely wedding which was a social event in their community, had a presentable husband, and, apparently, until the facts became known, was on her way to achieving a lovely suburban life. Neither she nor her mother saw or allowed herself to see beneath the veneer of the man she was marrying.

Alice had quite a bit of affection for her father, who remained in the background, but her rearing had been such that she was unprepared to play the aggressive or mother role to Clay. She was unable to take any responsibility in this crisis. She, like her husband, became depressed and emotionally disturbed.

Investigating Marital Success and Failure. Today facts concerning marital success and failure are available from *psychological tests* given to happily and unhappily married persons to ascertain how they differ. The husband fills out one blank and the wife another. *Systematic interviews* with married persons of various degrees of happiness also tell us some of the causes of marital unhappiness. *Case studies* supply us with a story of how this unhappiness developed.

Statistical computations of marital desertions and divorces add other facts. From these sources we hope to derive factors and processes in marital adjustment and formulate generalizations that may be considered by college students who seek to make a happy marriage. Most of these studies are of persons of a high cultural status with above-average or superior education. This must be kept in mind when the results are read because they may not apply to persons in the lower economic group.

Extent of Marital Failure. Some figure *between 15 and 30 per cent* represents the proportion of obviously unhappy marriages as shown from studies of married couples and from questions answered by students about their parents' marriage (306, 522). In addition, the ratio of divorce to marriage is roughly one divorce for every three marriages! (107) This does not include separations and desertions. These studies also imply that a great number of marriages are *happy*. Studies show that about 40 per cent of the couples involved describe their marriage as "very happy" (106). Thorough study of 792 married couples shows that there is little tendency for marital happiness to decrease with the passage of years (790).

It is not difficult to see, however, why so many who wed with infinite faith in matrimony and with a sincere desire for its success fail to achieve happiness. Remember how often the decision to marry is made without any knowledge of the factors that lead to happiness in marriage, the pitfalls that must be guarded against, and the relationships that must prevail. This ignorance of the circumstances leading to matrimonial felicity is so general, and emotional behavior is so characteristically impulsive, that it is amazing that the proportion of unhappy marriages, as stated above, is no greater.

The Unmarried Individual. A certain percentage of our population, either through choice or circumstance, will not marry. Another percentage will marry and then conclude that they can live a more harmonious life as a single person, and a third group will not marry but not through their own choice. In our culture in which marriage is the prevailing pattern, these people may feel the sting of minority status. Many unmarried individuals in our society have lived very full lives, rewarding to themselves and their fellows, as mentioned in the last chapter. Some of the circumstances which lead to the single state include the fact that in our culture there is a larger number of women than men of marriageable age who want to marry. It is estimated that there are 6 million females in the United States over 14 years old, many of whom would choose to marry who will not marry. Who these will be depends on many factors, some of which are not directly associated with personality (1). Let us just consider three of several factors. Marriage in our culture usually occurs for women more often in certain vocations and in certain geographic areas. For example, teachers and city-dwelling women meet less acceptable mates than do business women and women in the rural areas. Also, the more education the woman has the less likely she is to marry. Seventy-two per cent of college women marry as compared to 90 per cent for the population as a whole. Some individuals who want to marry perceive these patterns in our culture and plan their lives so that they will operate to favor their plans (440).

The widow has her problems, she feels that society disregards her or takes advantage of her, resulting sometimes in resentment and bitterness. One widow, a sociologist, has written a book for counselors of her fellows in bereavement and loss (441).

Factors in Marital Adjustment

Not all people who want to marry have a background that will make them good marital partners. The conditions discussed below are those that have been found to be *associated with* a happy marriage. They may be in part *causal,* or some deeper, more important factor associated with these factors may be the actual cause. As in all complex social relationships, there are many factors that produce a desirable equilibrium. Not all these factors need be present to produce a satisfactorily happy marriage. One or two conditions may be so important that their presence will be more effective than a combination of six or eight other factors. The presence of these conditions may make amends for the absence of a number of other factors that usually lead to marital bliss.

Marital happiness is an *individual* matter. It differs with the personalities of the individuals considered. We are dealing here merely with those factors found to be important in *most* marriages. The evaluation of the various factors in any individual case is a matter for the marriage counselor. When the individual does this for himself he must guard against wishful thinking. Certainly most divorcés believed that they were properly mated on their wedding day. Many knew at that time that a certain circumstance in their relationship was an undesirable one. They no doubt reasoned that the many desirable factors would compensate for this undesirable one and that their marital relationship would not be jeopardized by it.

Similarity of Interests and Attitudes. Consider for a minute those roommates whom you have had at school who have been most congenial. You realize you liked best, other things being equal, those fellow students who had similar interests and attitudes. This allowed you to enjoy many activities with them and to associate many pleasant experiences with them. Practically all the studies on marriage and friendship to date support the above generalization and disprove the belief that "opposites attract" (639, 109, 406).

When we compare the personality tests of happily married husband and wife with those of unhappily married couples we find that the happy pair agree more often in such matters as *recreation, religion, table manners, conventionality, philosophy of life, friends, care of children,* and *family finances.* Happy couples mention a community of outside interests considerably more frequently than unhappy couples. The unhappily married disagree on more things. The unhappily married men mention a total of almost three times as many things as "sources of disagreement" as do the happily married men. The women mention almost twice as many (789).

Before going on to other bases for happiness let us make it clear that it is not superficial but profound similarity that is important in marriage.

Two persons may be Methodists and yet be very different in religious attitudes. A young man and woman from the same economic stratum of society may marry, and yet the man may be very frugal and thrifty in habit and the woman a spendthrift. The husband and wife may have grown up in large families; the husband may be convinced that large families are very desirable, and the wife may be of the opposite view.

It is well for those who anticipate marriage, in addition to working and playing together, to discuss fields of religion, and their attitudes toward children and a family of their own. It has been found from the results of one study that agreement in the desire for children bears a slight relationship to happiness. The number of children, on the other hand, has not been found to be an important factor affecting happiness. *Agreement* was the crucial matter (789).

THE HALO TENDENCY AND ITS EFFECT ON ATTITUDES. One author suggests that it is possible that married couples are not so much alike or so dissimilar as the studies of happily or unhappily married couples indicate. It is possible that the "halo" effects operate. Happily married couples, because of their happiness and pleasant attitude toward each other, might see pleasant traits and agreement in characteristics when they do not actually exist. Unhappily married couples, on the other hand, might grow to dislike attitudes and interests that are characteristic of the spouse (789).

Financial Attitudes. Most college students believe that the size of income itself is highly important to a happy marriage. This is not a fact. On the whole, the economic factors, as such, are comparatively unimportant in marital happiness (106), despite the fact that indebtedness and unemployment will be found along with other factors in cases of marital difficulties (854). Economic conflicts usually arise because of *dissimilar attitudes* on the part of husband and wife regarding the use of income. Further conflict arises when previous standards of living conflict with present income (790). Apparently, if couples fuse their aims in the spending of money, all is well. If, instead, they become competitors, friction results. Engaged couples might well work out together as an interesting project, an individual budget and a family budget for their future home. They might find it interesting to save and buy home furnishings together and then after marriage to make an active attempt to live within the budget. Security and stability, shown in regularity and steadiness of employment, rather than *income level,* are important in marital happiness (106).

Similarity in Personal Characteristics. *Age and age differences.* Not all personal characteristics need be similar in order for the marriage to be happy. Age differences between the partners are *not highly important* factors affecting happiness. There is no evidence that the husband must be older than the wife for an effective adjustment (559, 790). Age differences are found to vary both between couples with no prior marriage and those who had been married before (347). There are, on the other hand, *temperamental factors* that should be similar for the best marital adjustment.

There is some evidence to show that marriages contracted between very young people under 20 lead to more unhappiness (307, 106, 790). On the other hand analyses of divorce statistics showed the shortest marriage duration for women who married at age 30 and older and for men 35 or older (783). Possibly then, there is an optimal chronological age. Age itself may or may not indicate *emotional maturity,* a very important underlying factor. To be sure, practically all men and women are physically ready to become parents at the age of 18.

Furthermore, postponement of marriage does reduce the number of children which a couple may have. Finally, it should be pointed out that the prospects of marrying decline as the years increase. These three reasons, then, may prompt young people to plan early marriages. There are always questions that must be raised when individuals marry young. Will she or he be the person I want to live with ten years from now? Will events in life change one of us and not the other? When one matures will the other seem undeveloped?

AGREEMENT IN BASIC PERSONAL TRAITS. How can the man who loves costly adventures be happily married to a woman who is insistent on saving for security? The radically inclined woman will be thwarted by a conservative husband. The man who loves opera, literary classics, few visitors, and a large home will bore a wife who has gay, superficial interests.

We have already emphasized the desirability of similarity in interests and attitudes. In our later discussion of studies of marital disharmony we shall again refer to the importance of *similar deep-seated personal characteristics*.

It is interesting that some happily married individuals are found to possess mutually certain attitudes and traits that are usually considered undesirable (205). In the studies of some couples, for example, both reported in a questionnaire that they were "often in a state of excitement" and that they lacked "self-confidence." The important factor here is that the couple *agree* (789). Similar results were found in the study of friends. Human beings are often brought together by similar handicaps. It seems that, when two individuals experience the same emotions together, they feel more intimate.

COMPLEMENTARY PERSONALITY TRAITS. Everyone has known couples who have been dissimilar rather than similar in personality. For example, two dominant persons will clash unless they are in agreement regarding the area of life which each plans to dominate. On the other hand, one of the marital pair may be a submissive person with a disinclination to assume the dominant role. The other dominates most of the situations that arise in marriage. Each partner may feel the need of the other and thus find harmony in their differences. The following specific instance is illustrative.

An ambitious, well-appearing man of mediocre intelligence and emotional immaturity was attracted to a very brilliant girl of great drive and stability. After marriage he frequently solicited his wife's judgment concerning business matters. In fact, she was the major partner though a silent one. She made most of his major decisions, bolstered him, and assumed the role which his parents previously played. She in turn was very proud of her husband's appearance and of the ultimate outcome of his activity. She did not lack insight into her husband's character, but she loved his handsome boyishness.

Happy Family Background. *Importance of affection for parents.* When questionnaire answers of happily and unhappily married persons are compared, the happy people report more attachment for and less conflict with both of their parents. In fact, of all the factors that affect marital happiness, *happiness of parents, attachment to parents,* and *lack of conflict with them* are among the most important (789, 106). Along the same line, it is found that wives who rate their fathers as physically unattractive, and husbands who rate their wives as physically unlike their mothers, tend to be less satisfied in marriage (106, 790). Furthermore, there is evidence that happiness is significantly associated with marriages in which husbands resemble the wife's father and wives resemble the husband's mother. A psychiatrist who interviewed 100 married women and 100 married men reports as one of his findings that the happily married husband shows reasonable affection for his mother and, similarly, the wife for her father (306).

Studies show that being one of a family of several children is favorable for a matrimonial adjustment, especially among husbands. Case histories showed patterns of behavior found in the husband and the wife to be related to *patterns* found in the marital life of their parents. An individual builds up a *relationship to the parent of the opposite sex* that influences his selection and treatment of a love object in later life. In other words, he learns to play a *role* in childhood and he tends to play a similar role in some relationships as a spouse. He finds himself favoring one who is similar in characteristics to his parent when the relationship with the parent has been a pleasant one. If the relationship has been unpleasant, he is more likely to fall in love with a person whose behavior is antithetical to the parent's. Exceptions to this pattern occur when the child has been in some way frustrated in seeking the love of this parent and consequently idealizes the parent. In such cases he will persistently seek the affection of a personality type of the parent of the opposite sex. For example, if a boy loves his mother deeply and a second son is born to whom the mother gives a great deal of attention so that the first son feels rejected, he may idealize the mother and seek more strongly a person similar in characteristics to her.

If the attitude toward the parent of opposite sex is ambivalent—

compounded of both love and hate—the individual may alternate in marriage between kindness and hostility toward the spouse. Under some conditions, too, the child may idealize the parent of the same sex or a brother or sister (106).

Even the discipline in the parental home has been found related to later marital happiness. It appears that firm but not harsh discipline is more conducive to happy marriages than either exceedingly strict standards or extreme freedom in which the child has his own way. The absence of punishment rather than the use of severe or frequent punishment likewise appears conducive to later happiness in marriage (790).

AGREEMENT IN ATTITUDES OF COUPLES TOWARD PARENTS. Not only is the marriage affected by early relationship to one's own parents, but it is also affected by the couple's attitudes toward both pairs of parents.

"But I won't be marrying her parents," said one undergraduate to a counselor when it was indicated that he would have a difficult time getting along with a girl since he disliked her parents so greatly. The answer to this is that the student will probably (almost certainly) marry her parents. One study shows that similarity of family background of the couple and approval of both families is important (106, 498). Very few individuals can or will sever all previous ties when they marry. It must be remembered that our parents are our first love. Most of us spend at least 20 years being dependent upon the service and the affection of our parents. Furthermore, studies show we frequently select a partner because he or she resembles a parent (762). Frequently one will tend to break with one's parents when they oppose a loved one, but this break is often superficial and the memory of the division may come between the pair. In other cases in which the antagonism between spouse and parents is not very great, there can be an unpleasant undercurrent which mars marital felicity. It is safe to say that, when the marital partner likes the parents of his spouse, marriage is enhanced by this attitude. To be sure, *agreement* in attitude, *whether it is one of pleasantness or antagonism*, has been shown to be important (789). This is true regardless of the educational or economic status of the couple. "Family interference" was named as a factor in 13 per cent of the cases studied by social service bureaus (559).

NORMAL PARENTAL AFFECTION. To be sure, there are individual cases in which the mother shows practically the same type of affection for her son as she would for her husband were he living or responsive to her. There are also cases in which the father feels similarly towards his daughter.

These attitudes frequently result in a reciprocal emotion on the part of the child. There are cases in which the child has responded to domination or excessive affection for a number of years and then at *adolescence*, when he tries to make an *adjustment for himself*, a conflict ensues. At this time, the boy dislikes the affection which he previously accepted or enjoyed. The girl may fight excessive interference from her parent with her dating, which she considers as perfectly normal. These are not examples of reasonable affection or normal affection, but rather they show us what a relationship between the parent and child that hampers his emotional growth can do. These incidents are due usually to a blocking of the parent's normal affection. One of the parents may not respond emotionally to the other. He may never have deeply loved the other, or have grown tired of her. Frequently, when conflict arises between marital partners, one of them will turn to the child for the response that is lacking in the other. This creates a real problem, called by Freud the *Oedipus complex*. The child is strongly attracted to the opposite-sex parent and hostile to his parent of the same sex.

Here is an illustrative case:

Margot endows her husband with qualities that neither he nor any other man has ever possessed. When her husband turns out to be an ordinary man she is disappointed. He has fallen short of her ideal. She no longer finds him attractive. But there is one hope in the relationship. They have a son, Cyril, and he will be the perfect man. She will make him the type of man she hoped she had married. She sets out to do this, and at 20 years of age the boy is perfect, but is neither attractive to nor attracted by girls of his own age. His mother loves him dearly, and his whole life is shaped around the life of his mother. He views his father critically and has never held him up as one to emulate or one with whom he can identify. Unless an entire re-education takes place over a period of time, he will have difficulty adjusting as a husband or may never desire to marry (791). If the change does occur his mother will have difficulty adjusting to his marriage —a real conflict.*

The marriage that runs smoothly is one in which there has been a *transfer of certain emotional reactions* from the parent to the husband

---

* The same sort of development can occur in the girl who identifies with her father and is hostile to her mother.

or wife. The wife learns to depend on the husband for security and affection. The husband turns to his wife for feminine attention and affection. The parents, then, by a wholesome affection, can prepare the ground for a happy marital growth or, by undue affection, can prevent the child from ever looking for a mate to satisfy affections on the adult level.

Similarity in Educational and Cultural Background. The psychiatrists who interviewed 100 married men and 100 married women found that *equal education* was an important factor in encouraging marital bliss (306). There is some evidence that higher education leads to greater marital happiness (106, 790, 174). Higher education, at least of the wife, is probably a reflection of superior intelligence (790).

Nationality and *religious differences* should likewise be minimal. A study of marriages in Germany made before 1929 showed more divorces in marriages between Protestants and Catholics and Jews and non-Jews than in marriages between persons of similar background (506). An American study failed to show that religious preference made that much difference, but the author indicates that many of the individuals studied were emancipated from religious controls (106). Sometimes couples themselves may feel that marriage, in spite of different cultures, is workable. Their friends and parents, however, will feel differently and cause unhappiness (91, 139). The heiress, for example, who marries the family chauffeur may later find herself unwilling to lose former friends and unable to endure the snubs from her acquaintances. Social class differences among the spouses is related to difficulties in marital adjustment (665).

When these cultural factors in the background run deep into the personality of the individual, and when they represent his fundamental attitudes, similar attitudes in the mate are important. Sometimes persons of two different religions are more similar in attitude than are two persons of the same religion. A non-orthodox Jew and a liberal Protestant will be much more similar in attitude than an orthodox and a non-orthodox Jew, particularly if all the cultural attitudes of Judaism have not been emphasized in the development of the non-orthodox Jew. It is hard to see how a literal-minded Roman Catholic and a Baptist Fundamentalist could be happily married. Usually, however, the individual discovers these discrepancies and attitudes if his courtship is long enough and if these matters are frankly discussed (497).

Adequate Sex Direction and Normal Romantic Interests. Continence until marriage and sex relations within wedlock is the convention we verbally emphasize in America. Deviations from this may cause mental and social conflict and often disturb marital felicity. Several studies point out that reported *premarital virginity* in both partners tends to lead toward the most happily married life (306, 174). They also emphasize the importance of a *normal romantic attitude* involving some caressing as the seriousness of the relationship increases. There is some evidence to indicate that those wives are most happy whose "first love" occurred between 12 and 16 years of age rather than earlier or later. Husbands, on the other hand, who had experienced their "first love" after 15 years of age rather than earlier seemed most happy (306).

Oversexed mates were found to be unhappy in marriage. The happiest couples are those who are *similar in strength of sex drive*. Attachment for individuals other than the mate was found to be a negative factor. *Adultery* represents one extreme that produces unhappiness. At the other extreme is found the woman who is incapable of experiencing an orgasm. This seems to be related to the temperament and general responsiveness of the individual, most of which is determined by early basic development or native constitution. It does not seem to be related to early affection or sex experiences (790).

An extensive study of almost 1000 marriages indicates that, whereas sex habits before marriage affect marriages to some extent, details of sex life during marriage are not related to marital happiness, as many sensational books on this subject indicate. For example, fear of pregnancy, pain during first intimacy, wife's history of sex shock, rhythm of wife's sex desire, and details of intimacies are not related to happiness in marriage and therefore need not worry the engaged couple (790).

One study indicates that admitted petting before marriage was a factor significantly associated with unhappily married persons of an earlier generation. *Masturbation* and *sex practices* and recollection of sex feeling in childhood are mentioned more frequently in the histories of the unhappily married person but are not significant in differentiating the happily and unhappily married groups (174).

It seems the preferred attitude prior to marriage is one that directs affection so that it does not lead to unconventional and guilt-producing physical intimacies.

Similarity of Emotional Experiences Is Important. In sex as in all other areas of marital life we again find the factor of *compatibility* important. When personality tests of couples were compared, the happily married couples agreed to the demonstrations of affection much more often than the unhappily married (6). A goal that young married couples can strive for is *similarity of feeling and emotion on both the physical and the psychological levels.* This is a theme that runs throughout the discussion of marriage. It is well-illustrated on the physical level. The greatest satisfaction from intimacies results when both partners rise to a climax of emotion together. But this sympathy should *not remain only on the physical level.* One of the most disconcerting experiences in marriage is for a husband or wife to become enthusiastic over a matter while the spouse is apathetic or antagonistic. Couples can often enjoy books, poetry, sunsets, games or symphonies together and share in a common emotion. The more frequently and vividly the individuals experience these common emotions the more secure is the marital bond.

Sex Education. The studies likewise point to sex education as having some value in the solution of marital problems (306, 790, 174). The form that this should take was discussed on pages 325 to 326.

Premarital Medical Examination and Counseling. In one study a thousand married women were given a questionnaire regarding relationships in their married life. One hundred and sixteen of the most happily married and 116 of the least happily married women were compared. The happier women were *healthier* before and after marriage. One medical investigator found adjustment in marriage to be related to medical and psychological instruction about relationships in marriage and to anatomical corrections (180). Out of the physical examination there can grow a discussion of some of the problems that they will meet in marriage if the physician consulted is one who is a specialist in this field. Some of this premarital information falls into the categories of psychology and sociology. Well-planned *college courses and counseling bureaus* are now functioning in various institutions and communities (92, 156, 269, 31, 466, 108, 396, 440, 194). The studies of marriage have produced marriage adjustment scales that, when used by qualified counselors, will furnish the young couple with realistic information about their prospective adjustment (766, 786).

Normal Premarital Testing of Compatibility. *Value of conventional courtship.* The traditional way of learning whether two people are compatible in their viewpoints and many habits in our culture is courtship. We have discussed the value and activities during courtship in the previous chapter. (See pages 329–331.)

An adequate courtship may enhance a more realistic choice. Some people have romantic ideas of an ideal husband or wife, a synthesis of twenty-four-hour beauty, brilliance, charm, perfect health, a never-sinking bank account, poise, versatility, and vivaciousness. Since there probably is no such living person, the one whom they marry, no matter who he or she may be, is a disappointment. Likewise, married existence is real and lifelike; if faced and responded to, it challenges one's adaptability to life. If viewed, however, from a standpoint of false idealism it may be imperfect and ugly. There are meals to be prepared, laundry to be done, messy children, broken china, and tense moments contrasted to the more romantic episodes that are more apt to be the theme of daydreams.

INADVISABILITY OF HASTY MARRIAGE. There is no excuse whatsoever for failing to test many daily habits, attitudes, ideals, and temperamental traits that will be elicited by the marriage experience. Young married couples should have gone through a period of courtship long enough to have learned whether they are irritated or pleased by the behavior of their "loved one." They should have seen each other in many situations and compared each other with many others of the opposite sex. A study of many marriage relationships showed the more happily married had not met in a "place of public or private recreation." Happier marriages, studies show, are based on longer periods of acquaintance and engagement as contrasted with an acquaintance of a few months (790, 106). A marriage that is contracted *too early* or *too impulsively*, as many war marriages are, does not allow a sufficient period for work and play together, an ideal test of compatibility.

Arguments and Alienating Affections. Two outstanding symptoms of the stormy marriage often mentioned as "causes" of marital difficulties are: *arguments* and *jealousy* caused by affections for others than the fiancée or wife. Statistics based upon 1500 cases coming before the attention of social service bureaus also indicate that jealousy (9 per cent of cases), immorality (30 per cent of cases), and abuse

(41 per cent of cases) are factors in marital discord (559, 862). Arguments and alienating affections merely mean that there are incompatibilities in the roles expected and played by the members of the pair or that one or both of the pair do not have a good background for marriage. Many of the frustrating factors mentioned by couples in their bickerings, like money matters, in-laws, manners, grooming, spouse's friends and standards, are merely focal points for discussion and displacement of emotion. If some of the underlying conflicts were smoothed out, these factors would be less disturbing.

During courtship, it would be well to try to determine what we expect of the mate and what he or she expects of us, how we feel inclined to treat him, and how they habitually and naturally treat us. *Do these personal traits make for affection and a happy relationship, or are they irritating and disturbing?*

Stable Environment. Divorce statistics show that the divorce rate is closely related to the *cultural background* of the community, in respect to emphasis on home and family life. For example, in a large city like Chicago, certain occupational groups, religious groups, and urban areas yield higher divorce and unhappiness rates than others (106, 118). Upon analysis it is usually found that the predominant attitudes of the individuals composing the groups with high divorce rates do not favor stable home life. Marriages contracted without religious ceremonies were more than twice as likely to end in divorce (556). Marriages contracted in an unstable period following war resulted in more divorces than marriages contracted in other periods (302).

Certainly an environment which encourages extensive use of alcohol, drugs, freedom in sex standards as well as in general values, continued exciting and ephemeral activities, small space for living quarters, necessitating that the dweller spend most of his time away from "home," are not conducive to a stable, enduring home life (761). On the other hand, it has been found that church attendance, religious background, small town or country rearing, social tendencies reflected in friendships and organization membership, and good health are all associated with good marital adjustment. It seems that good advice to the newlywed is: *Live in a community in which there are good examples of happy home life.*

Almost two-thirds of divorces occur among childless married couples. Of the childless marriages 71 per cent end in divorce, whereas only 8 per cent of married couples with children eventually are divorced (118). The presence of children does not appreciably increase marital happiness, according to one extensive study (790), and whether it aids marital adjustment or not depends in part upon the desire for children (145).

Happy and Unhappy Couples

Personality characteristics that are associated with happiness or unhappiness in marriage usually develop long before the wedding day. They are often individual characteristics that can be recognized and possibly modified over a period of time. The characteristics of a relatively large sample of people follow.

Characteristics of Happily Married Women. Women who are happily married are kind in attitude toward others, and they anticipate kind attitudes in return. They are not unduly concerned about the impression they make on others, and they do not look upon social relationships as rivalry situations. They assume subordinate roles if necessary, accept advice from others, and are in general cooperative. In their work they are painstaking and methodical. They attend to details and are careful in regard to money. They are conservative and conventional in religion, morals, and politics. They show a quiet self-assurance and optimism (790). In short, studies show that in our culture and at this time in our history it is the wife who makes the major adjustments in marriage (106).

Characteristics of Unhappily Married and Divorced Women. Women who had been divorced were found to be more *self-sufficient* and more *masculine* in interest than women of unbroken marriages. The interest of the divorced woman does not correspond to the interest of the average woman office worker. Possibly the divorced woman lacks the *docility* and *love of detail* that we might expect the office worker to have. The divorced woman's interests are also unlike those of the woman engaged in insurance and real estate selling. The divorced woman lacks interests in *handling and convincing* people (789).

It is interesting to find that the *happily married woman* and the *unhappily married woman* are not very different in interests and attitudes. On the other hand, the divorced woman differs from both of them. We shall notice later that divorced men, unlike divorced women, are more like the unhappily married men than the happily married.

A study of factors in the affections of 2200 women, 1000 of whom were married, indicated that employment before marriage, as well as employment outside of the home after marriage, was more frequently associated with unhappily married individuals. Although our attitudes are changing regarding the importance of a dependent attitude in women, apparently society still causes a very *independent* and aggressive woman to suffer a conflict that makes marriage more difficult (174). There is even a tendency in college for the more practical and more aggressive girl to find herself less popular than her effeminate and dependent sister.

Unhappily married women tend to be emotionally tense and moody, to feel inferior, and as a result to become aggressive. They are inclined to be irritable and rather dictatorial. They are more often the "joiners" who strive for *extensive circles of acquaintances*, but they are more concerned about being important than about being well-liked. Their social life expresses an overanxious and egocentric attitude. They seek romance and are more conciliatory toward men than toward women. They show little sex antagonism. In their work they are impatient and fitful. They dislike cautious and methodical people. They are more radical in politics, religion, and social ethics than are the happily married women.

Characteristics of Happily Married Men. Happily married men seem to have an even and *stable emotional life* and have many characteristics previously discussed as attributed to happily married women. They tend to look upon women as equals. They show initiative superior to that of unhappily married men. They have a greater tendency to take responsibility and evidence a greater willingness to give close attention to details in their daily work. They show a preference for methodical people and methodical procedures in work. Regarding financial matters, they are saving and cautious. Their attitudes are much more conservative than those of the unhappily married men. They are usually favorable toward religion and strongly support the sex mores and other social conventions.

Happily married men's interests are not extreme in masculinity or femininity. The happily married man is unlike the divorced man and the unhappily married man in interests. The unhappily married man's interests seem to be of a pronouncedly masculine variety. The divorced man tends to have interests resembling the feminine type.

The happily married man's interests lie midway between the unhappily married and the divorced. This might be expected. The truly feminine woman and highly masculine man differ considerably in their interests and attitudes. For a number of years the feminine girl is taught to enjoy perfume, pretty clothes, colors, art, music, sewing, and little children. These interests represent fundamental trends in her personality that have been established with years of practice. Extremely masculine men, conversely, have been interested in athletics, mechanics, business, outdoor life, and have never warmed up to some of the pretty things that mean so much in the life of the girl.

In certain groups and levels of society the man who is able to break many hearts and who is willing to boast of his conquests is viewed from these standards as the most potent male. This viewpoint is without doubt inimical to marital happiness. It is difficult for some men to believe in and practice promiscuity during their early years and then suddenly become monogamous in attitude and practice. There are cases in which the individual does this successfully, but there are many other cases in which the individual never makes the adjustment.

Attitudes of promiscuity toward the opposite sex are usually not associated with a regard for an individual member of the sex as a personality. In several respects this self-centered attitude, if carried over into marriage, makes it difficult for one to fuse his own feelings and ideals with those of his mate. He is less disposed to lose himself in her motives, wishes, and plans. Bearing upon the view discussed above are some facts found in the statistics from over 1500 cases that came to the attention of two large social service bureaus. Drunkenness was found in 31 per cent of the marriages that were about to go on the rocks. Irregular habits, such as gambling and laziness, were found in 18 per cent of the cases. These may be viewed as highly masculine traits and are often associated with the more promiscuous type of man (564).

Characteristics of Unhappily Married Men. Unhappily married men tend to be *moody and somewhat neurotic*. They show a tendency to feel socially inferior. They dislike being conspicuous in public. They are strongly influenced by public opinion. The unhappily married men who have a sense of social insecurity usually compensate for this. They *dominate* those situations in which they do feel superior and make those beneath them very unhappy. They take pleasure, for example, in dominating business dependents and women. They also tend to evade any situations in which they must play an inferior role or compete with someone of equal or superior caliber. Unhappily married men compensate for this retreat from superiors through daydreams of themselves in superior roles in which they wield great power. They tend to be sporadic and somewhat irregular in their habits of work. They do not like detail and are not so methodical as the happily married individual. The unhappy husbands are not the ones who carefully save money; rather they like to wager. They tend to be less religious in attitude and somewhat more radical in sex morals and politics (790).

Relationships in Marriage

Roles and Marital Happiness. What do we see basic to happiness or unhappiness in the day-to-day marital interactions? These interactions are associated with the roles we learn to play with other individuals close to us from childhood on. They vary with the individual. They include, for example, a dominant role we may have learned toward a younger sister, a submissive dependent role toward opposite-sex parent, or a cooperative or rivalry role toward a sibling. In addition we have seen the roles our parents have played with each other in their marital drama—jealous, responsible, complementary, nagging, immature, loving, cooperative, stubborn, or adjustive.

What are some of the roles associated with happiness and unhappiness in marriage? *Cooperation, agreement, complementariness, adjustiveness and nonperfectionism,* all of which reflect love are clearly related to happiness. Contrariwise, *self-centeredness, narcissism,* * *immaturity shown in nagging, jealousy, stubbornness and dominance* tend to lead to unhappiness.

Studies of sex attitudes indicate that some adaptation in attitudes of the man and woman must take place. Men and women in our culture differ in the stimuli that are most effective in arousing them sexually. Men have a history of easy arousal to sex thoughts and impulses prior to marriage by various stimuli referring to the physical aspect of the woman and sex activity. Women often have aversions

---

* This is an *immature* state of self-centeredness in which the individual seems to be absorbed with self-admiration involving his appearance or activities. He subordinates others to his needs and demands (776).

to the crudities of physical approaches and reflect a life history of inhibition; they reach a stage of readiness through a tender, personal, love attitude (411). With frankness, understanding, patience, and time partners make a more effective mutual adjustment (592). Often marital partners do not expect these intimate relationships to be learned, and early frustrations and disappointments lead to recrimination of themselves, their spouses or both. Studies show these adjustments do improve over a period of time (194). When they do not the mentioned roles leading to unhappiness are among the causes.

The Married Student. An impressive percentage of university students are married. In 1957 about 25 per cent of the men on some campuses were married. These students live in campus villages, trailer communities, or housing projects. They represent a relatively homogeneous group with similar purposes and problems. Most of the data presented earlier in this chapter are roughly relevant to them. The wives differ in the roles they play such as contributing to the support of the family, attending school themselves, or playing a more traditional wife-mother role. These students impress many observers as they go about their work and play as being realistic on the whole, responsible, supported emotionally by each other and by the awareness of their common problems, and above the average of their age group in marital adjustment.

One group of veterans studied had a mean age of 26.5. Both husbands and wives had 4 years of college education, 80 per cent had 1 or 2 children. The husband was usually headed toward a profession; he had part-time employment and assisted with the housework. Their most difficult current problem was economic, and both husbands and wives rated their marriage as very happy (716). Another study indicated that student fathers range widely in the time spent with their children, with an average of over 8 hours a week. Whether their activities met the ideals or not, their concept of their role was compatible with the concepts indicated in developmental courses (814).

Cases Illustrating Marital Relationships. Let us look at the realities in some present-day marital relationships. In reading these cases it may be well to do two things: (1) see which factors that affect marriage are present, such as good relationship toward parents, superior and similar background and long acquaintance; and (2) try to decide the role each of the spouses expects to play and whether these roles are compatible. *You might find it profitable to discuss these cases in small groups.**

Carrie Long came to the counselor with this story. She had been married for six months and admitted upon interrogation that some periods of this time had been the happiest in her life. Fred had been recently discharged from the Army after several uneventful years spent in this country. He was back in school, and they were living in a trailer village at a Midwestern university. Her visit to the counselor occurred after an Easter vacation spent at home and a separation from Fred. Fred stayed alone in the trailer while she was with her parents.

Carrie had been a career girl in college and had shown a great deal of leadership during the years when boys were a rarity on campus. She had met Fred when he and fifty other soldiers attended a college dance. The romance developed mostly through letters. Apparently Fred never received the full approval of her parents. Carrie's family was closely knit. No member was interviewed, and their characteristics must be largely pieced together from conjecture. Her parents appeared to be people who dominated their children and planned their lives for them. Carrie had never thought of questioning her parents' judgment. In fact, as she related these events she referred to her husband as "him" and to herself and her family as "us" without realizing it, and at no time had she thought of Fred and herself as "we." She had accepted her mother's suggestion that the two families should meet in order to settle the domestic affairs of the young couple.

When Carrie's mother visited the trailer, she was disturbed because Carrie was working too hard and had lost weight. She berated Carrie for getting up before her husband, fixing the breakfast, packing the laundry into the car herself and taking it to the self-service laundry. The mother's whole attitude was that "her little girl wasn't brought up to be someone else's servant."

The crisis occurred at the vacation period over a number of little incidents (all written down) that her parents regarded as indicative of Fred's lack of character. The mother's attitude toward Fred was shown the day before the marriage when *she* was of a mind to call the whole affair off because Fred had bought her teen-age sons beer and told them off-color stories. Now during the vacation crisis the mother and father presented Fred with a bill of particulars, telling him that he would have to mend his ways if he wanted to live with their daughter. When he became hostile they sent him to his home 500 miles away to talk the affair over with his father.

Fred respected her parents and felt that they had some of the culture his parents lacked. He had been indiscreet and hostile in their home. He continued his critical negative attitude that had been a repressed sore spot in the trailer. He made remarks about his father-in-law's driving and his mother-in-law's supremacy in the home. Undoubtedly some of his verbal

---

* The case of Clay and his wife, found on pages 359 to 361, might well be reviewed along with those presented here.

aggression and mildly shocking behavior was a hostile response to his feeling of frustration and inferiority. Carrie had learned to play the submissive role which she carried with her into the marriage, so much so that his aggressions were crushing to her. His mild verbal hostility seemed like abuse to her. At no time did she tell him how much he had hurt her but merely stored the incidents in her memory to be regurgitated for her family after he had left.

Fred apparently had felt rejected when his younger brother arrived in the family, and other events in his early life had given him a feeling of inferiority. His father apparently was a mild man, a minister, and Fred's whole attitude toward his own family was not too good. He was glad to get away from them and did not enjoy very much their visit to his home on the campus. Although the facts are not known, it might be conjectured that Fred resented his brother and was punished for his jealousy. His mother dealt firmly with his stubbornness, and some of the aggression that was intended for his mother was directed toward Carrie and his mother-in-law. He had never been too much of a success. His marriage to this girl from a socially superior family, who had been an obvious success on the campus and who already had a degree while he was struggling for his, were all frustrating and produced the aggression that he showed.

There is no doubt that he loved Carrie despite occasional critical remarks. He was ambivalent toward her family, showing alternate love and hate. When she left he phoned her continually, wired and wrote her, but found it very difficult to apologize to her mother. It so happened that, as Carrie was having a conference about the marriage at one university, he was simultaneously and independently seeking advice from a psychologist at another. Her family was counseled, and all of them entered a new period with more insight than they had before. Fred and Carrie both loved each other very much. However, Fred's ambivalence toward her and the clash with her varying submission and ascendance toward him and toward her family were causes of disturbance. Whether the insight alone will keep the parents out and affect the roles that Fred and Carrie play toward each other, time will reveal.

Oliver and Virginia Y. were attending college together, enjoying particularly their courses in the Humanities. They both had strong interests in literature and tne arts and had a pleasurable year amid atrocious housekeeping conditions in two substandard rooms. They had grown up in the same neighborhood. Both had dated other people, and although they had known each other for years they discovered only when he returned from the Army how much they had in common and how much they enjoyed each other's companionship.

Virginia's relationship to her father was ambivalent. They both loved each other, but there were violent scenes when she failed to meet his expectations. Oliver's father had died young, and Oliver had become a father to the younger children in the family. He reared them, and when catapulted into the Army he became the parent-substitute sergeant for a number of immature rookies. He is a massive, calm, but colorful individual, liberal, with an almost Bohemian veneer over his stable traits. She, too, is bright but submissive and nervous and strongly desirous of someone upon whom she can lean. Unlike her father, Oliver is understanding, tolerant, and helpful. Their marriage seemed to be happy.

They came to the counselor after a hysterical evening when Oliver had an unprecedented verbal battle in their rooms with a friend of his. This brought back to Virginia's mind the parental scenes, and she went to bed trembling and sobbing. She feared that Oliver might some day direct this side of his personality toward her. Her behavior puzzled them both so much that they sought a counselor next day to discuss the episode.

Nettie and Zach had been married for several years and had a baby girl. They were living on the campus. He had been deferred from service during the war. Whereas they had planned to go to school together, the baby's arrival and low finances had interfered with that plan, and Nettie remained in the apartment all day, washing diapers and dishes.

They had been married in their teens and had come from an isolated, fundamentalistic southern community. Zach was intelligent, had initiative, and he and Nettie planned to have a teaching career together. They left their home state. Zach got a job, worked hard at it, and at this time his career was not far off. He was slow to discern what was going on in his wife's mind. After the baby's birth he noticed that she no longer responded to him physically as she had previously. She vacillated in her attitude toward the baby from love to hostility. She complained that the pregnancy had ruined her figure and that she had missed her youth.

Her childhood had been stormy. Her mother had deserted her and her brother, and she was reared by a repressive foster family. An older boy in this family had made incomplete sexual advances to her as a child and probably aroused her more than she would admit. This ran along beneath extensive lip service to purity and ideals. The reasons why she was attracted to Zach were that he was idealistic and that he was a "clean" fellow. After the baby arrived her daydreams continued and she admitted in conference that she had crushes on most of the fellows her husband brought to the house as well as on the heroes in pulp and movie magazines. She longed to have a couple of years of freedom in which she could meet other men. She felt guilty about these fantasies. Although she did not realize it, she was actually reliving the life of her mother because later she told her husband that she was going to leave him and the baby for a few years. At first he was shocked and sought advice. He felt that he must have failed in some respect and was willing to do anything to make his wife happy. He rearranged his schedule, allowed his wife time to take courses and become a co-ed, took care of the baby himself, but this apparently was not entirely satisfying to her. She said that she and Zach were too different. He was "in love with words and learning which I do not understand, and he cannot give me the romance that I crave more than life itself." Before leaving she went through a period of extreme conflict between her desire to fulfill her duty as a mother and to satisfy urges that were aroused early in adolescence and had been repressed since then.

Kirk M. was reared by his mother after his father deserted her. His father was an alcoholic and a roué. Kirk's attitude toward his mother was affectionate and acquiescent. Her attitude toward Kirk was not revealed directly in the interviews. However, it was partially instrumental in producing this extremely masculine, headstrong youth who had been quite a successful athlete during his high school days in the East. He had taken advantage of these successes to the extent of acquiring an enviable wardrobe, a car, and a good supply of money.

Kirk had never been popular with his contemporaries. Although he despises his father, his own behavior, except for alcoholism, is not very different.

Margaret left him a month after she became pregnant, and no pleadings would bring her back. She had changed her religion, had agreed to have the child brought up in his, and had apparently worshipped him early in marriage. However, before she left she would not let him come near her. She apparently was afraid of him and had learned to dislike him very strongly. She told him the last time he visited her that he would have to leave her alone if she were to get over her aversion to him. Although he gave her the car a great deal of the time and provided her with an allowance, in other matters he dictated her every move. He said, "I have treated her better than any other girl I have ever gone with, but this has taught me a lesson. Next time I'll get what I want and leave them." He came for consultation when his academic record, his sleep, and his appetite were affected. During the interview he raved and ranted, pounded the desk, and said that he should have "beat the hell out of her" for the way she treated him.

The nature of her parents had to be discovered through him. Her father was a successful salesman who provided the girl with a good allowance. She apparently had had the most superficial interests, such as clothes and a good time. The pregnancy was a shock to her. She greatly feared the birth and blamed Kirk and his religion for her condition. Her mother seemed to be a calm, understanding person who gave the girl a great deal of solace when she returned home, and listened sympathetically to Kirk. Margaret apparently wanted tenderness, understanding, and affection which Kirk had never learned to give. She undoubtedly found his advances devoid of anything but lust, and they were not satisfying to her. It may be conjectured that Kirk felt guilty after the relations. It is not known whether he identified the girl with his mother. At any rate, his dominant egocentric attitude over a period of several months produced such a revulsion that she could hardly bear to see him.

Kirk admitted that the main reason he wanted her back was because of the child, particularly if the child were a boy—and his attitude was "it had better be a boy." He had plans all made about the kind of athlete he would make out of the boy. He was completely baffled by Margaret's departure and wondered why she left when he had "done so much for her." The counselor had the feeling that the blow to his ego and the separation from his unborn child constituted the major loss to him. He had already consulted a lawyer and had learned his "rights in the case." One of the things that disturbed him was that he could not go out with other girls without placing his case in jeopardy.

Supplementary Readings

E. W. Burgess and P. Wallin, *Engagement and Marriage*, Lippincott, 1953.

H. J. Locke, *Predicting Adjustment in Marriage*, Holt, 1951.

J. T. Landis and M. G. Landis, *Building a Successful Marriage*, Prentice-Hall 1953.

J. A. Peterson, *Education for Marriage*, Scribners, 1956.

In addition see the references cited by number in the chapter and appearing in the bibliography of an accompanying volume entitled *Teaching Personal Adjustment: An Instructor's Manual.*

CHAPTER 14

W e gain greater stability as we learn to deal with the typical problems of life. Feelings of depression, loneliness, hysterics, somatic complaints, anxieties and worries all have their causes, which when understood can be more effectively controlled.

We shall review the symptoms of some of the common patterns of instability that we all experience to some extent. We will see not only *examples* of these nonadjustive reactions, the kind of personality structure that forms the background for the disturbance, but also we will review again the *causes* as applied to each disturbance. Then we will be in a better position to suggest some *preventive* conditions and finally to repeat some suggestions about the *process of readjustment*, which was presented generally in Chapter 5 and will be applied briefly to the various patterns of instability discussed here.

The meaning of stability will become clearer and more personal as we see these specific examples of instability within and outside the range of normality.

386

CHAPTER 14

EMOTIONAL

STABILITY

Emerging From Feelings of Depression

Let us read about some individuals who have experienced rather strong feelings of depression before we examine the bases for the feelings.

Thelma A. accepted the suggestion of her sorority sisters to see a counselor. They had previously talked with the counselor of their concern over Thelma's crying spells and temper tantrums. "When she is given a job she does it well. But she is peculiar, and the girls just don't include her. We don't seem to be able to teach her to groom well. She is always eating, particularly fattening foods like candy." (The counselor explained that this too might be a symptom, that sweets might be a substitution for the affection which she avidly craves.)

Thelma is the younger of two girls. Her sister, who is prettier and more popular, is now married. Thelma was pledged to the sorority because of her sister's membership, and no doubt some of the girls resent her as an obligation. During her first semester at school she clung to one girl who befriended her, and she developed a crush that continued after the girl

387

graduated. Thelma wrote her frequent long letters and waited weeks in eager anticipation for the few replies.

When the girls who showed the initial interest in her left the house, the rejection by the others became severe. She became more childish and more shut-in. She was frequently found sitting in her room, lonely, or playing with her dolls, which gave her more response than people. She could live an interesting life through her dolls!

Thelma's grades were good. She worked hard. She enjoyed athletics and was a good basketball player. She received little encouragement for this in the house and, because of her aloofness, failed to be absorbed emotionally by the girls with similar interests at the gym. She belonged to a church which had an active, effective young people's group, but because of her sorority affiliations she spurned this opportunity for companionship. These two potentially *congenial* and satisfying social groups under other circumstances might have changed the course of Thelma's life.

She received considerable relief and some minor insights into her self through the conferences with the clinical psychologist. In conference she complained of the cheating done by the girls in her house. Their emphasis on prestige rather than on character traits were the opposite of the teachings of her parents. She knew she was a disappointment to the sorority, and their relegation of her to inconspicuous duties when guests appeared was significant to her and disturbing. She admitted that she did not have the traits of her sister. Evidently her parents had overprotected her at home. Her actions were much like those of a 12-year-old. She was able to discuss in conference her crush and her fear of homosexuality. Her home life had been repressed, but she thought of her parents as happy. She regarded herself as unfeminine, uninteresting to boys, and constantly played the role of a pre-adolescent girl in her manner and her interests. She thought she was a disappointment to her parents at birth because they had wanted a son.

She did not return to the counselor the second year because she probably thought she was unworthy of the time he was spending and the progress was slow. With more frequent conferences and an accepting environment the first year and possibly with a counselor who took greater responsibility in her life, Thelma might have gained more self-understanding and might have been more willing to accept her traits and find the best way to use them.

It might be well at this point to read the cases of Leonard on page 442 and Steve on page 126. *You might find it valuable to discuss in small groups possible causes and remedies in each of these cases. You will find the analyses in Chapters 3 and 5 helpful.*

Basic Nature of Depressions.   Depressions result from frustrated or conflicting motives. "Low" feelings, like all other unpleasant and disturbing emotional states, are *symptoms*. It is sometimes difficult to distinguish a depression from an anxiety condition or a feeling of inferiority. Basically, we do not need to distinguish them. The emotional pattern that we feel when we have failed to achieve our goals is not the most significant factor. The most important consideration is the *cause* of the failure.

Most emotional depressions are due to *conflicts* between strong motives or the frustration of strong motives or human needs, as we saw in Chapter 3. The individual has fallen short of cherished goals or ideals for himself; or he may want to reach two goals that are incompatible. He is tense and unhappy. He must seek a means of releasing tension and effectively satisfying his motives.

DEPRESSIONS AS DEFENSES AND SOURCES OF PUNISHMENT. If the depressed individual does not realize the source of his conflict, his predicament is usually greater. Under these circumstances he is blindly seeking a goal that he will recognize only after it has been found and identified. He may, however, know the source of his conflict and be so anxious because of his believed failure or guilt that he cannot fully face it and find a solution. He may have some inkling of the source of his trouble, but it is too painful to examine, analyze, and meet effectively. Then the depression acts as a *defense*, a smoke screen. It is *satisfying to deeper motives of self-protection* even though it is unpleasant.

Those of us who tend to experience depressions often have felt we were not loved as children or were rejected by parents or by early playmates. We may feel alone, unwanted, abandoned by others, and left to our own insecurities. This produces as much sense of unworthiness as do feelings of guilt from wrong-doing. Sometimes the conflict is due to our opposition to the wishes of loved ones or to being disappointed by them. Individuals may compensate for and protect themselves from this insecurity by rigid ideals and habits of perfection. This complicates the problem rather than solving it, for then there are more standards to violate and more opportunities for failure and depression. The *perfectionist* whose physical beauty must be flawless, whose grades must be perfect, who can make no social errors is never satisfied in a real world. He has set the stage for depression and self-punishment. Perfectionism and an acute "conscience" may have been encouraged by an early rigid environment.

This kind of individual is often mild and passive, not very capable of directing his hostilities outward toward others. Instead there is much self-hatred. The depression, from one standpoint, acts as a potent source of *punishment*. As such, *the depression is partially satisfying*. If one feels unworthy or feels that his wrong-doing needs punishment, a depression may *reduce the tensions* that are built up in anticipation of punishment.   To put it simply, the individual may have unconsciously found a way to give himself the punishment he feels he needs and thereby prepare himself for further punishment from others or, by administering it to himself, avert punishment from them. He, too, may get more attention from those around him while depressed than at other times (540).

Normal Moods.   It is *normal* for everyone to experience occasional "low moods" when some cherished goal is lost. During "low moods" our actions become slower and less spontaneous, thoughts are unpleasant and frequently about childhood events. Depression tends to take from us our daytime expansiveness and the deep sleep of night (390). Normal moods have been studied. They seem in general to be lowest in the first and last half-hours of the day, on Mondays, in January, February, and March (738). They differ, too, for different individuals and seem to run along at a given level in cycles irrespective of environmental influences (870). They are most related to motive satisfaction as illustrated by accomplishment and social recognition (199). One study showed no relationship between moodiness and popularity (390).

Suggestions for Dealing with Feelings of Depression.   Our eventual goal is to understand the basis for our own depressive episodes. We wish to *gain deeper insights into the frustrations, conflicts, or earlier experiences* that give rise to feelings of unworthiness and guilt and that cause us at present to belittle and punish ourselves. We may also come to see the depression as satisfying certain motives, as preventing us from coming to grips with the problem, or working out a new plan of life; it might give us motivation toward action. *Repression* of unpleasant mistakes is usually a part of the pattern. The depression is the return of a memory touched off by some recent event. The individual punishes himself now through sorrow and remorse, rather than face frankly his shortcomings in perspective, talk them over with a confidant, see that anything he might do now must be done in the future, and realize that past events are closed issues (459, 812).

AIDS DURING DEPRESSION.   In addition to searching for causes of his low feelings while he is under emotionally secure conditions, certain *symptomatic treatment* seems to be helpful. Students report that, if they turn to certain activities and environments that to them represent sources of recognition and afford an effective outlet, feelings of depression abate.

Students mention events that lift them when they are low in mood. These vary in different students.

A walk or a drive	Read a favorite book
"Cuss it out"	Sleep
A funny or gay show	Sports, dancing, music
Dress up and go out	Reason it out
Get with carefree people	Talk with a friend
Pretend happiness	"Tomorrow is another day"

Susan Greenburg

Below is a sample of the responses checked by the student who is subject to emotional depressions (294).

Often has the "blues"	Introspective; analyzes himself
Worries over possible misfortunes	Cannot relax easily when lying or
Frequently in a meditative state	sitting down
Not carefree	Concerned about the future
Ponders over his past	Analyzes the motives of others
Not happy-go-lucky	Overconscientious

Similar traits are found in the more extremely depressed people, together with emotional immaturity and insecurity in life situations. Usually those who have depressions have high ethical standards and attachments to parents. They blame themselves for their mistakes (540).

"NERVOUS BREAKDOWNS." When the individual in conflict finds an escape that lessens the extreme unpleasantness he experiences, it is usually termed by doctors and laymen a "nervous breakdown." The exact nature of the events that allow him to "save face" varies. He may become ill. To be sure, his illness will be of a vague nature and may be evidenced by the loss of weight, numerous unlocalized pains, a heavy, tired feeling, or extreme lassitude. Sometimes depressions lead to hysterics or persistent periods of crying and emotional effusiveness. Behavior of this sort attracts very active attention from those who are close to the person, even though the attention is not entirely pleasant. They become convinced that some change of environment or circumstances is imperative.

The change may consist in leaving school and refusing to return. The remainder of the semester may be spent at home "resting up." Relief comes with the relinquishment of responsibilities for a time and with acceptance by others of this course as permissible or wise. He or his physician may prevail upon his parents to take him on a trip or to a new environment for a change of scene and to get away from the circumstances that plague him. He may quit his job, resign from an office, or in some other way acceptably resolve the present conflict. The curative element is that both he and the world accept his solution. Although our western world does not make so open a practice of face-saving as the oriental, we are equally desirous of it.

Far more beneficial than the break from routine is a conscious examination of the present problem and a plan for solution. Sometimes traits and personality trends formed earlier are scrutinized, understood, accepted, and redirected.

Some of these events appear to be substituted *defenses* and *escapes*, and they may be just that. However, as we have shown in our discussion of creative adjustment in Chapter 5, when one succeeds in a secure environment in a task that has the possibility of satisfying many of his basic motives, he is more willing to face without guilt his mistakes and shortcomings and thereby make discoveries. In this sense these activities do not serve as an escape but eventually lead to a frank examination of some of one's conflicts. In other cases, used as escapes, they break the previous pattern of depression and withdrawal from reality. Old interests are stimulated. The intrinsic value of reality as a source for complete satisfaction of needs and wishes is realized.

Numerous writers suggest *doing something for someone else* during low periods. Keeping up the daily necessary routine has been stressed. This does not mean pepping oneself up, but realizing that the show must go on despite our own feelings. An active fighting attitude—even anger seems to change the mood. Inactivity and surrender have never improved a depression. However, true relaxation as in deep sleep or after exercise or hard physical work is beneficial.

In deep, persistent depressions in which one's efficiency and health are impaired and suicidal impulses arise, it is imperative that the individual seek professional advice. He should consult a psychiatrist, a qualified clinical psychologist, or a qualified physician. The profoundly despondent individual may not see much hope, but he can be assured that with modern drugs and treatments the darkness will clear (166). The existence of such deeper depressions is indicated when all other previously stimulating sources fail to bring about improved morale and only depress further. In general, depressions are not removed by the cheering activities of those around us. The rise in mood grows out of what we do by way of ventilating our inner feelings or seeking satisfying environment, people, or activity. Experiments show that on repeating tasks that are not preferred, under typical laboratory conditions our aversions to them change (607).

Prevention of Depression. Individuals with emotional problems differ to some extent from those who are relatively free of them in their way of life (520). In Chapter 16, under "The Meaning of Adjustment," we discuss the difference between the adjustive and the unstable individual and make suggestions for a more wholesome way of life. This consists mainly of working out the kind of life pattern that satisfies basic needs and personal motivation, discovering conflicting needs, and finding means of resolving them for personal growth. The best prevention begins early in life and involves the encouragement of traits that allow the individual to deal with the causes of his emotional disturbances before they gain great intensity and when they can still lead to trial-and-error behavior rather than withdrawal.

There is no fixed, absolute solution to most personal problems. There are social as well as asocial means of satisfying most of our needs and urges. Sometimes we become preoccupied with the asocial tendencies, assuming that they provide the only satisfaction of given needs.

Many a person who has said to himself, "I would never be satisfied with that," finds when he is in the midst of doing "that" he is challenged to put forth greater effort.

The student who is eliminated from the school of medicine is positive on the day of his elimination that dentistry or social work are not substitutes he can accept. His rigid standards dictate that he must succeed as a physician or life will not be worth living. When he finally enters the school of social work and is allowed to begin assisting with cases, the daily problems that must be met, the prestige that his position gives him, and the realization of the human needs he is satisfying may make him see in social work a highly desirable career. Before long he may work out a whole system of thought to convince himself and others (probably rightly) that elimination from medical school was one of the best things that could have happened to him.

Depression and Insights for New Life. Recovery from depression can be a valuable experience, particularly as it involves knowing oneself more thoroughly and *accepting one's weaknesses and present status*, no matter how negative they may seem. If it amounts to clearing the air, of assuming the attitude "this is what I have and this is what I must live with and life can be interesting despite it," then the depression has achieved much for the individual. It will possibly give rise to changes in routine and to realization that certain activities and attitudes are more suitable than others. One may see some of the causes of his ideas of failures and inadequacy, his feelings of inferiority, the conflicts between old and new standards, the disillusionments, and the cherished but false dreams. He may see that his failure involves *only one aspect* of personality or that *many others have the same problem he is experiencing*.

Recovery from depression may even stimulate a richer life. The individual may come to learn the importance for him of friends, wider interests and hobbies, more realistic goals, sources of play, and more physical activity.

Homesickness and Loneliness. Homesickness is a term applied to one's apparent *inability to adjust in a new environment*. It frequently is accompanied by feelings of depression. A complex of factors such as feelings of inadequacy, conflict between the standards of the group and of one's parents, feelings of failure, and inability to maintain the level of success to which one is accustomed is frequently found. The individual longs for home or a loved one because home represents to him an escape from his present situation, which may be insecure, cold, and frustrating. Home may be an environment that has held in check feared impulses within himself. His reputation at home kept him in line, but now he *has new freedoms that may produce anxiety*. Such conflicts are often the crux of the problem, and the other failures are merely contributory. For this reason adults, even apparently tough soldiers, may feel quite insecure in new environments (90). (See the section "Reducing Anxieties and Fears" in this chapter.) Frequently when he returns home, home is not too pleasant, either, because his feeling of inadequacy may persist. A study has shown that those who experience homesickness do not differ from others primarily because of the nature of their home, but because of factors within themselves, such as emotional instability and lack of confidence (509).

Typically the homesick individual is one who has received a great amount of affection and protection from parents and other members of the family. He usually has failed to revise his habits progressively as age advanced. He is emotionally immature and lacks the characteristics discussed more fully in Chapter 16 in the section on the mature individual. He has been away from home seldom in the past. Much is expected of him by parents and friends. He is usually sensitive, and his feelings are easily hurt. He does not make friends readily. He may be so interested in his own success and inner feelings that, if he does associate with other students, he is not very attractive to them. He also either lacks initiative or is easily discouraged. He usually feels that he *has failed in some respect in college in contrast to his previous success.*

Almost invariably he finds the customs and emphases at the college very different from those at home. He may fall short in the skills that are emphasized, such as dancing, light conversation, dating, colorful dress, and other social activities. He feels *insecure* in the new environment. He soon begins to associate his feelings of lonesomeness and failure with his new surroundings so that as he goes from class to class the sight of the buildings brings depressing thoughts. He has not built up positive habits of success and pleasure in association with the many sights in this new environment. Often he cannot break through this depression to do the things that are recommended to him by other students and counselors. He feels failure before he starts.

He sometimes thinks of the sacrifices his parents are making for him. He perhaps feels that they would be displeased with him if he accepted the habits and attitudes of the typical student at the university. This feeling may be aggravated by letters from home that express anxiety for him or confidence that he will in no way depart from the rigid code acquired in childhood. Sometimes he exaggerates the immorality of his new comrades because they seem so free on the surface. This new world may *stimulate adventures and exploits of which he fears the consequences.* Home and everything it represents seem right to him, and everything else wrong. New friends do not have the force that his parents and other close friends have, and their suggestions are not accepted.

He may either disregard his successes in high school or wonder if they were not accidental. He thinks possibly he has overestimated his powers. The present failure, he is often convinced, is prophetic of what the future holds for him. The contrast of being important in high school and totally unknown at college is disturbing to his morale.

The homesick student may be said to be undergoing conflict between the desire to grow and adjust in a new situation and the difficulties encountered. Continued failure creates in him the desire to withdraw (509).

ADJUSTING TO A NEW ENVIRONMENT. Because homesickness is merely a symptom of instability or anxiety, adjusting to a new environment involves most of the factors mentioned in a preceding section, "Suggestions for Dealing with Feelings of Depression," and a following section, "Suggestions for Dealing with Fears and Worries." Briefly, this adjustment consists in discovering elements within oneself, developing a more tolerant attitude toward them, and *finding resources in one's new environment for satisfying basic personal needs.* Any steps that enable one to become emotionally a part of a new environment—to belong to a larger family—assists adjustment. Affiliation with extracurricular or campus groups of persons with similar interests has been an opening wedge for many. If the new environment tends to jeopardize old attitudes and values and to suggest new ones, the individual will need to reconcile the two. This is discussed in the section "Personal Philosophy of Life," Chapter 7.

Directing Unstable Behavior

Meaning of Unstable Behavior. We are using this term for several widely different nonadjustive behavioral expressions. They include temper tantrums, extreme impulsiveness, irritability, hysterical phenomena, psychosomatic symptoms, alcoholism, irresponsibility, and unpredictable or asocial behavior. How much of this instability is due to *basic temperament* and how much to *learned habits* or responses probably varies with individuals. There are some individuals who have had difficulty directing their behavior as long as they can remember. Other individuals have learned disturbing traits or habits during their development that have satisfied some motives and have been retained. Traits of this nature may also be learned directly from parents and associates, or they may be the result of the frustration and conflicts of early life. Under favorable conditions undesirable traits and habits may be eradicated and more serviceable ones learned.

Kinds of Unstable Behavior. At the college age, the *temper tantrum* may take many forms (534). The student may merely speak very strongly to the person who angers him, or he may refuse to speak to him for several days. He may, however, have a childish seizure similar to a hysterical fit. Crying, trembling, shouting, throwing objects, stomping, and banging tables are not unusual in the college population. Fellow students usually are highly intolerant of this type of behavior and sometimes help to eradicate it by not allowing the temper display to get results. Girls, it seems, show more of this extreme type of emotional behavior than boys show. This is readily understood because there is a strong taboo among boys regarding emotional explosions. Fights alone are condoned, and even these are frowned upon in more gentlemanly circles. They may occur, however, when the individual is under the influence of alcohol and inhibitions tend to be removed.

HYSTERICAL PHENOMENA. Some adults behave like children. They are accustomed to having their own way. They express their emotions in the presence of others. Much of their behavior is aimed to *secure attention.* Such an individual may like and dislike strongly, be impulsive and *suggestible.* His attitudes and habits may be poorly integrated, and he becomes a creature of the moment. Furthermore, he *represses* that which disturbs him. Because of his *egocentricity,* he refuses to face problems or situations distasteful to him.

Individuals with traits similar to these sometimes develop hysterical symptoms in crises, symptoms which win for them attention, which get for them what they want, and which save face. Such a person has been known to faint readily, to suffer paralysis of limbs and muscles, and to develop anaesthesias in various parts of the body. A successful animal trainer who depended upon her "inability to experience pain" for her recognition in the show said she felt no pain on the occasions when the animals had attacked her. She reported differences between pin pricks and other stimuli upon being subjected to laboratory examination. She had developed hysterical anaesthesia as a means of adjusting to her strongest motive—to be the bravest of trainers. Blindness and deafness have been shown to be hysterical in some instances. More extreme symptoms are illustrated by functional amnesias and the fugue, in which the individual leaves his environment and afterward is not thoroughly conscious of everything that transpired. Individuals have been known to forget their own names, their facial appearance, or that of their parents, to remember them only later, after the emotional crisis has passed. There is hysterical vomiting, hysterical somnambulism or sleep-walking, and hysterical fainting. The college physician is acquainted with all these symptoms. He usually finds very little cause for them in terms of pathological conditions in the individual. Instead, in order to obtain more clues, he examines the motives of these students and the extent to which they have been frustrated in their present modes of life.

The vomiting, fainting, headache, or other vague and hysterical pains or complaints *satisfy strong unconscious needs*—they are an *escape from some more unpleasant situation*. They sometimes represent symbolically a substitute for more direct hostility, disgust, or anxiety (695).

IMPULSIVENESS, BIDS FOR RECOGNITION, VIOLENCE, AND PSYCHOPATHY. Other anxious and egocentric persons may be dissatisfied with the usual laborious methods of gaining recognition. They want to be conspicuous, so they use bold methods to achieve a place in the limelight. They may wear peculiar clothes, affect a conspicuous hairdress, or be loud or ostentatious in manner. They may collect one or more peculiar appurtenances.

One student acquires an old car and paints it in very striking and unusual colors, even for a campus. Another gets a dog and takes it around with him to all classes. A third may wear a ten-gallon hat and boots. One student rode 300 miles on a mule to school. Another recited poetry on the main street of the town. A third carried a gun around the campus. A fourth grew the only very thick black beard on the campus. A very pretty girl from a farm background of which she was ashamed wore a fake bandage and concocted a hair-raising story to explain her wound. She also had the highest dating count in the dormitory because of her flirting habits but the boys rarely returned for a second date. All these students were relatively unknown on the campus and were seeking recognition in a nonadaptive manner.

Braggadocio, prevarication, and even pranks are other means used by the unstable individual to gain recognition. It is interesting what a small quantity of alcohol does to such a student. It is sometimes his excuse for grossly violating the standards of propriety.

How can this behavior be explained? Usually the individual feels inferior or very insecure, as shown in Chapter 15. He has a strong desire for recognition that is not achieved. Means of gaining attention present themselves to him. He does not think such matters through. Under the force of emotion the suggestion issues forth into action. Before he realizes it, he is doing absurd things, which he must substantiate by rationalization. This he may do. He may rationalize "I am different. I believe in being colorful." or "I am superior to the average student," and claim that the same standards of conduct do not hold for him. He may delude himself into a belief that this is a legitimate means of attaining prestige for later projects. His arrogance and indiscretion win for him the ridicule of his fellows. This may or may not depress him. It may spur him on to even more ridiculous action.

Sometimes an emotional outburst issues from a person quite unlike those described above. In fact, the individual may be an exemplary character on the surface. For months he may show good working habits or appear to be a mild, pleasant, submissive individual. Then suddenly some unpleasant emotional explosion may astonish his friends, as in the case of Mason V. that follows. Other examples of instability are found in the person who vacillates from kindness and pleasantness to irritability and harshness.

Instability exhibits itself in miscellaneous other ways. There is the individual who must always be on the go, is constantly changing his residence or his job, or must go from one bar to the next or from one source of amusement to another. Instability is found in the person who must project his difficulties on others, who thinks that others dislike him, find fault with him, and are trying to harm him. This he may fight in his various ways of dealing with them.

Mason V. is of average height, well-proportioned, dark, and very handsome. He grew up in the submarginal economic area of a large city. He had the superficial appearance of a "regular" fellow. He came to the attention of the counselor through his wife, who had been one of the counselor's outstanding students. Mason, too, had received very good grades and had a great respect for most of his teachers. He had a good attitude about the conference.

His wife had complained that he beat her. He said he was as much puzzled about his wife-beating as was anyone. He thought he loved her and he certainly appreciated all that she meant to him, but his jealousy at times was overpowering. After he had beaten her he felt like whipping himself.

He was extremely chagrined that the neighbors had inadvertently been aware of the fracas because of the thin walls between their apartments. He responded quite well to the opportunity to discover his difficulties and, because he was highly motivated, to write professionally. He was encouraged to do this by the counselor. He submitted his short stories and writings to the counselor. Mason found his writing a satisfying outlet and source of self-discovery. He also found that by talking his feelings over periodically with his understanding but similarly unstable wife, his tendency to become violent was sharply reduced.

The outline of his history runs somewhat as follows. He had been overprotected by his mother even up to the time of his entrance into the Navy. His father was not companionable. He was extremely jealous of a younger sister, whom he frequently beat in childhood. He had always been attractive to girls and women of his own age. He was regarded as cute and likeable, but because of his sensitive and sheltered childhood he never felt that he played the role the girls expected of him. Though not outwardly impotent and certainly craving the affection they could give him, he still felt inadequate. He described himself as lonely, friendless, fearful, shy, unhappy and self-conscious in childhood. He was prone to violent temper tantrums which usually obtained the desired results. He swung from these characteristics to those of a kind, sympathetic, idealistic person interested in reforms and a better world. Some of the boys kidded him. He had not learned to play the traditional games, and he felt that his outer masculinity and toughness was a sham.

During his years in the Navy he had many love affairs and almost invariably deeply hurt the girl after a few weeks. He became engaged to one but jilted her to marry his wife. He suppressed all this guilt but soon after he was married demanded that his wife tell him all about her previous love affairs. He embroidered upon them in daydreams, adding lurid and stimulating details. It was after indulging in some of these, at the end of a day spent in frustrated effort at school and in trying to make ends meet financially that he had the urge to beat her. He had some reason to be envious of her ability to assume responsibilities and her social capabilities.

In his writing and during the conferences in which he was very frank, he came to see some connection between his childhood jealousies, his demand for unswerving feminine loyalty, and his desire to punish by temper tantrums and violence any attention that his loved objects gave to others. He wondered if he had not been unconsciously punishing the girls who had fallen for him and if this strong suppressed guilt was not at the basis of some of the difficulties between him and his wife. With this insight the relationships in the home improved greatly, although they were not completely resolved. The fiction he wrote before the conferences showed an unusual amount of violence, a disparagement of women, and a reliving of many of his own disturbing experiences through the characters. He felt toward the end of the conferences that he was discovering the source of some of his motivation and finding some outlets and methods of self-control. He also knew that, with a history like his, he could not expect everything to clear up within a week.

The pattern of instability shown by Tim's story is found every now and then. In a more antisocial form such individuals may have brushes with the law, go AWOL in the services, or exploit people who become interested in them. The term *psychopath* is frequently applied to such individuals. A study of forty psychopathic personalities showed that among important factors in their early environments was an indulgent and solicitous mother and a highly successful, driving, but distant father (326). Other studies show them to be individuals hungering for affection but who on the surface appear unmotivated and calm. They show an attitude of futility, are constantly getting into difficulties, and are often regarded as amoral and hopeless by people who come in contact with them. Recently, some psychologists and therapists especially interested in psychopaths are more hopeful about the rehabilitation of some of them (604).

Tim I. impresses you with his outgoing manner. He is not relaxed or carefree but seems quite purposive even in his social behavior. Some of his friends call him a "big operator." He is always planning some maneuver or some big deal. In his 20 years he has had a great deal of experience, including a period in the Army. He has held jobs since he was a small boy and has been quite successful for a time in each of them. He is an excellent salesman but soon tires of each job.

Both of his parents are highly emotional and apparently love him and indulge him very much. His folks do little planning and spend most of their income for display. He admits that he is moody, not too happy, was "all fouled up" when he came into the conference, and is not very consistent in his plans and purposes. He enjoys people, glamour, interesting jobs, and his hobbies. He has found little time for such outlets as Boy Scouts, athletics, team, or cooperative activities. Apparently his energies must be diverted through channels that bring him outstanding audience response.

He thinks most of the courses he is taking are time-wasters. He does not want to worry himself with prelaw courses. Why can't he begin taking law courses immediately? His concept of the lawyer is the Hollywood version. He wants most events to bend to his will and, if they do not, he quickly leaves them without qualms. He can nonchalantly break appointments and forget responsibility. He has few inhibitions in class and will bring up any subject. In spite of all this, he is a rather delightful person. People like him, and he has evaded through charm the consequences of too many situations for which he should have suffered. His appearance, pleasant manner, and sense of humor have won much for him, and he thinks he will always be able to trade on them. His values are highly superficial—they hinge on money, clothes, travel, and fashion.

He is quite restless. Although he wants security, he cannot face the fact that it must be earned or that his life must be planned. That would take the fun out of it. So he continues to vacillate between high moments and deep disappointments, moving out of the disappointment into another frantic and sometimes successful bid for adventure. It is doubtful whether he will ever accumulate enough credit for a college degree or build a reputation for dependability and responsible conduct. How much of Tim's personality is due to basic temperament, overindulgence throughout his life, and the charm which has heretofore extricated him from embarrassing situations has not been fully determined. It seems that only the accumulation of experience and circumstance will bring him stability, because he is not at present in a mood to foster self-direction.

Juvenile Delinquency. When antisocial behavior as described in this chapter occurs in individuals who have not reached their majority, it is called juvenile delinquency. It has many causes, including emotional instability (604). In Chapter 4 we showed the important effect on personality development of poor and overcrowded housing conditions, neighborhoods that do not have recreational facilities, parents who do not and cannot take the responsibility for guiding the behavior of their children, and social institutions that do not fill the gap. A query of college students shows that all college students can recall some delinquencies in their earlier life for which some children are brought before the juvenile court (616). Delinquency in youth is a symptom of conditions both in the surroundings and in the motivation and perspective of the individual. Misbehavior is almost universal, but when personal or environmental conditions allow it to persist, it calls for professional attention.

Alcoholism as Unstable Behavior. The emotionally unstable individual who habitually uses alcohol as a form of escape, and despite good intentions finds himself addicted to it, has been studied rather extensively. Although alcoholics are not an entirely homogeneous group and no one particular factor is characteristic of them (859), it is rather well-established today that there are certain unstable trends within their personalities that cause this small percentage of the drinking population to be dominated by the drug (334). The wise alcoholic frankly faces these unstable trends and plans his life around them. The Alcoholics Anonymous movement is based on this frank approach. The solution goes much further than forced cessation of drinking. The chronic alcoholic has been found to be immature, self-centered in motivation, weak in emotional control, and anxious about his physical make-up. He has rather high ambitions but achieves comparatively little. There is a better chance of his dealing with his addiction if he retains a close relationship with everyday reality instead of withdrawing from his usual environment, as he is prone to do (72), or if he recognizes his inadequacies (305).

Alcoholics are found to differ as a group from nonalcoholics in showing these developmental factors more frequently: a stern, over-critical father who was feared; strict, unquestioning obedience demanded in family life, with little freedom; a domineering but idealized and preferred mother; a strong feeling of sin and guilt; marked interest in the opposite sex with many love affairs but poor marital adjustment; outstanding ability to get along with and be socially acceptable to others; lack of self-consciousness; and a tendency to work under high tension (859). Women alcoholics showed a strong attachment to their mothers, as did many male alcoholics, intense narcissism or self-love, inner tensions that make social contact difficult, and experience of sexual inferiority. One author finds women's alcoholic tendencies more individual and more closely associated with life situations than they are in men (821). When two neighborhood areas that differed in the rate of alcoholism were studied, it was found that among the residents of the higher-rate area there was greater mobility (more moving about), less likelihood of normal family relationships, and a greater tendency for individuals to be socially isolated (560).

Alcoholism has been called a suicidal compromise. Many writers regard it as a form of self-punishment. There is an element of self-punishment in much of the behavior discussed in this section. Many of these individuals seem unconcerned about the consequences of their acts. They plunge recklessly into this or that activity, which sometimes results in mutilation and accidents (855).

Psychosomatic Symptoms. We have already shown in our discussion of hysterical phenomena that some physical complaints have a psychological origin. Later, when we discuss fear, the various physiological changes that occur with strong emotion will be outlined. Almost any reader can recall from his own experience instances when his appetite, sleep, digestion, relaxation, steadiness (to mention a few processes) were disturbed as a result of attitudes, feelings, and shocking experiences. It is easy to understand how the individual who is constantly influenced by an unsavory environment, who is frequently bombarded by disturbing experiences, or who is always within a conflict might develop a chronic physical condition as the direct result of abnormal physiological processes (560). It is only in relatively recent times that these unconscious aspects have been studied.

A few of the more common examples of psychosomatic symptoms are reviewed here. Our discussion of hysteria indicates that when these symptoms become an escape from unpleasant events or a defense from anxiety, they may readily be perpetuated, particularly in persons with certain personality patterns (191). Excessive appetite has been associated with desire for care, attention, and love and has been suggested as a substitute for affection. One study of obese children showed that their mothers overprotected them and restricted their participation in normal childhood activities (101).

It has been suggested that nervous vomiting is sometimes symbolic of the rejection of certain impulses that are associated with shame and guilt. Excessive drive, worry, and tensions are known to be important in peptic ulcer. High blood pressure that occurs without evidence of the diseases usually associated with it is known as essential hypertension. Such patients experience inner hostile and resentful feelings for which they provide no outlet. The patient may seem on the surface to be very gentle. The hostility and conflict is repressed so that inner tension and raised blood pressure develop as the unsatisfactory outlets (191).

Accident Proneness. Accidents may reflect emotional instability. Accidents do occur to an alarming extent in automobiles, homes, and games. Data show that bad luck is not the sole cause. About 98 per cent of accidents are preventable, and of these 90 per cent are due to human causes. Only two diseases kill more people yearly than accidents. There is some evidence that some individuals are more prone to accidents than others in a given situation. Among taxi drivers, for example, 20 per cent of the drivers in one study caused 50 per cent of the accidents, and 25 per cent of them never have an accident. Many of the factors that produce inefficiency cause accidents. If you can prevent by caution and stability the injury that may occur to you and to those around you, you will save yourself much remorse, many dollars, and many hours of useful work. A tendency to have more than one's share of accidents in a given situation is sometimes a symptom of deeper emotional problems that produce "faulty attitudes." These include: ignorance of potential hazards, impulsiveness, irresponsibility, inattention, nervousness, and fear (484, 721).

Suggestions for Attaining Emotional Stability. The behavior or symptoms of persons discussed in this section differ greatly from those described in the section on depression. The basic *causes* of the two disturbances are not very unlike. In both patterns there is inner insecurity. In depression the individual withdraws; in the miscellaneous unstable behavior discussed here, the individual *escapes from his* *anxieties and conflicts into some more or less frantic activity.* He may defend himself from his problem by violence, moving about, imbibing alcohol, or developing a hysterical or psychosomatic disorder. The need here does not differ from that expressed in the "Suggestions for Dealing with Feelings of Depression." The disorganized individual, thrashing about, trying to find a solution to his problem that will not entail facing it, must do the very thing he least desires: calmly and slowly *face difficulties, accept them as a natural consequence of his background,* and slowly, over a period of time, move toward a more stable, effective environment and way of life. This solution may come about through hard knocks. The failures and jolts that cause him to search for a new avenue of vivid experience may temper his impulsiveness. Insights and self-understanding may occur during some of his experiences. Amid disappointments he may find persons with whom he can talk out his difficulties or to whom he can write about himself. Sometimes he will go beyond the difficulties themselves and point to causes and events within himself that give rise to them. Through trial and error he may find more stable and satisfactory ways to fulfill his urges and needs.

This process, mentioned above and treated more fully in Chapter 5, occurs over a period of years in the lives of many individuals, but it can certainly be implemented by professional service. Many unstable individuals will get inklings on numerous occasions that they are unstable. Strong anxiety itself will not lead to the acquisition of the most effective new behavior (358). This is the time to seek a counselor and discuss the difficulties. This is the opportunity to associate with someone for whom one has affection and who is stable, to accept a position that will give one greater stability and yet not eliminate from his life some of the more vivid experiences and satisfactions that mean so much to him (207, 678, 800).

Should you come in contact with a person of one of the various kinds described above try to understand him but do not completely shelter him. Rather, let him experience the consequences of his poor judgments. Much of his behavior is nonadjustive, and it should not win for him false success or satisfaction. These individuals should learn what they must sometime acknowledge—that their conduct is essentially inadequate. Their more charming and desirable traits should not act as a shield to prevent them from experiencing the realities of life. It is not usually necessary to punish impulsive people or to plan a program of discipline for them. Circumstances will take care of that. To be sure, many of them cannot face abruptly or alone all their inadequacies and the jolts they receive. For the best effect, they should not be catapulted into some other vivid escape. The hysterical individual will be less prone to perpetuate his hysterical symptoms if they fail to win him attention or do not permit him to escape from an undesirable responsibility. On the other hand, friends of unstable individuals may render them a service by rewarding and complimenting those acts that are realistic, that give them basic security, and that contribute toward their assumption of further responsibilities.

Dealing with Alcoholism—a Form of Instability. Because much is written about the rehabilitation of the alcoholic and because there is some similarity between this individual and those who escape through other means, we shall concentrate on him with the hope of providing suggestions for others.

Most psychiatrists view alcoholism as a *symptom* and attempt to deal with its *causes* rather than directly with it. Their aim is to assist the individual to achieve self-understanding, a more socially satisfactory means of relieving the tensions that he has unconsciously relaxed through alcohol.

Among the least effective methods are the compulsory and punitive methods that involve the control of alcohol consumption alone. One group of scientists has used a more direct attack on the symptoms with considerable reported success. Their method consists in *conditioning the individual physiologically* to become disgusted when he imbibes alcohol by combining it with an emetic that makes him sick. Fifty-nine per cent of the individuals observed over five years had abstained, a high percentage for alcoholics who so often have a poor prognosis and frequently do not want to be cured (819).

The Alcoholics Anonymous program is discussed in Chapter 5 (page 150). It tries to *satisfy in a wholesome manner the individual's needs* for social recognition and approval, for dependence and protection, and for a frank admission of and attack upon his instability. It gives him a *means of compensating effectively* for his feelings of inadequacy through good works. Identification with a group assists him in relieving his anxieties. Alcoholics, many of whom have some marks of prestige, band together as a nonsectarian religious group who acknowledge their dependence upon and the reality of spiritual aid, and who work together to reinforce each other's morale and to find and rehabilitate other alcoholics. There are an estimated 50,000 of them, and they give tangible evidence that the very unstable individual can be aided. This success, considering their lay status, has been phenomenal. There is evidence that indicates some cases of alcoholism are at least partially nutritional, and nutritional therapy has been helpful in these cases (848).

Psychiatric methods vary in effectiveness with circumstances. These consist largely in helping the alcoholic to understand some of his basic personality traits and the influences of his past history as outlined above. They depend to a great extent on the individual's desire for and faith in rehabilitation. Through an understanding of his inner self he obtains relief, insight, and new attitudes. He learns also to face his anxieties gradually and to build up positive ways of dealing with them.

Drug Addiction. This differs from alcoholic problems in that morphine and heroin addiction involve a physiological condition and the problem is less related to personal maladjustment and more to the subculture of the individual. Youths comprise a very small percentage of the group. Sometimes drug addiction is preceded by marijuana smoking and the use of alcohol. Rehabilitation involves medical care and social readjustment (539).

Reducing Anxieties and Fears

Anxiety is a symptom, but we saw in Chapter 3 that anxiety is also a basic psychological state associated with conflict and capable of producing many other symptoms. Mild anxiety, when directed, may motivate us to learn habits to reduce it. Severe anxiety often leads to escapes and defenses and when these fail it is a highly unpleasant state of mind. Let us look at anxiety operating in the life of several individuals.

Examples of Adult Fears and Anxiety.

Beatrice B. is a bright, attractive, married student who was attending college with her hubsand. She is an only child and lived close to her loving parents until she entered school. She had always been a shy, serious, conscientious girl, somewhat aloof from others. Her contemporaries usually regarded her as conceited and conscious of superiority. If they had known her well they would have seen readily that this opinion was far from the truth. Her home was always a solace after she had ventured from it. Being overprotected by her parents and insecure regarding the variable world outside of the home, she was concerned during childhood lest her parents be taken from her. This fear and insecurity assumed a religious complexion when exposed to rural fundamentalism. Further she learned from these sin-conscious sermons the dire consequence of evil thoughts and activities. A black-clouded thunderstorm could throw her into a panic for fear that it meant the end of the world and that she would be separated from her parents and punished.

During high school and her early married life around Army camps, she learned to get along with others better. However, she was never equal to the social give-and-take, and any remarks from her contemporaries that were at all derogatory were not refuted but plunged her into tears and sadness. At no time did she fight back with repartee. She only felt crushed. Apparently any hostility that she felt was directed toward herself rather than toward others. Her whole life reflected anxiety. Her standards were very high, her conscience or super-ego acute. Everything she did had to be exact and perfect. She allowed herself few mistakes. She received very high grades throughout school. Her life was rigidly conducted so that mistakes could not occur and so that she might gain the approval of others.

Apparently her father was a mild, sympathetic, understanding person. Her teen-age dating gravitated toward a boy with similar traits. In many respects he was an ideal substitution for the family pattern, but his imminent departure for military service aroused her old panics. They were married and she followed him around the camps. The old fear of losing her parents was now associated with her husband.

At the end of the war she attended school with her husband, and things moved well until she entered a course that she felt was essential for her teacher training. It was taught by a stern, critical professor. Her mildly low records were defined as a crisis in her mind, and anxiety resulted. Racing heart, consciousness of breathing, feelings of coldness in various parts of the body, indigestion, tremor, fear of being called on in class—in short, all the typical physiological concomitants of fear appeared. Forgetting her early history, she regarded them as serious and as indicative of future difficulties.

She came to the student clinic and was referred to a psychologist who allowed her to describe her symptoms in detail. She talked quite readily, and before an hour had passed she had given her history and had seen some of the trends in it. She realized with little assistance that the anxiety pattern was one which had been established early in life and had shown itself whenever a crisis had occurred. She realized how much she had been helped by discussing these things with her husband. She saw the role of her high standards and repressed *hostilities* against the people who seemed so much better than she and whom she thought did not accept her, and the consequential *guilt*. She told of the outlets that she had used in the past for relief of accumulated tension—music, walks, and writing. She left the first interview with understanding, assurance, and a plan that included talking little matters over with her husband and settling them rather than repressing them, writing out some of her experiences for better perspective, and satisfying basic motives through hobby outlets. Subsequent interviews proved the efficacy of the counseling and emotional outlets.

Sid Q. came from a small town. At 19 he was a friendly, dynamic, red-haired boy of average ability. Like many students of his background, he found the first month in college very difficult. Despite this his participation in dances and bull sessions was above average. He had a strong interest in the outdoors and wanted to go into wild-life conservation. His father was a tense, irritable, insecure individual with a superior education who felt that he had never been very successful. His mother seemed stable, even-tempered, and slightly protective. He remembered fearing storms and his father's wrath as a child. He also recalled being upset by noises and by the confusion of cities, and preferring to roam around in the woods. He stated that at an early age he was attracted to girls and had been ever since, but his interest in each was transitory.

He was referred first to the counselor because of psychosomatic symptoms, chronic digestive upsets and concern about his health. After several interviews he came in one day pale, perspiring, and trembling. His voice quavered and there were tears in his eyes. He stated that he was terribly upset and was experiencing great fears. At times he felt alone in the world, he said. Discussion with his father did not help, because his father said he, too, had been that way in his early life.

Sid then related the fear that he would jump from a moving bus, regurgitate his food in public, that he might slit his throat while shaving or jump from a window. He said this fear of himself and what he might do had become most acute recently while he was attending a meeting in a large nearby city. His excitement had subsided a little when he began to talk to a woman near him who undoubtedly reminded him of his mother, and her soothing effect upon him. He stated that this fear was associated with urination, that he was sure the boys in his house thought him peculiar because as soon as one of them entered the washroom his normal functions were inhibited and he had to leave the room. Until recently he had kept most of these feelings to himself and it was very relieving to him to discuss them.

Despite his fears, his friendly, pleasant manner, his vocational objective and his quiet, unassuming social skills carried him along and made many friends for him. His four years of college were punctuated by occasional visits to the clinic as the result of anxiety episodes. He found that writing out his symptoms was helpful, and in his senior year he began to gain some insight into some of his anxieties. One day he discussed quite freely with the counselor his fear of being different sexually because of masturbation and because of his attraction to feminine body odors. He said he felt very much like an animal because such odors attracted him. For a time he associated his behavior with homosexuality but later doubted that that was his problem because he evidently could make a good adjustment to girls. The feeling of *difference* and *peculiarity* worried him, produced a vague anxiety, and caused him some concern lest he go berserk and break the conventions his family valued so highly, thereby *disgracing* himself and his family. The disturbances over his impulses and inner life were increased because he knew he was regarded by many adults as an ideal boy.

He was advised upon leaving school to make contact with a psychiatrist and continue this professional relationship. Further insight and understanding of himself resulted, and he later married, secured a position teaching in a small town, and eight years after the first contact with the counselor was making a good adjustment despite occasional tense periods. He has had continual promotions and holds an outstanding position in the area of his state to which he has moved.

Development of Fears and Anxiety States. All of us acquire fears through the conditioning process. We associate some object that ordinarily does not frighten people with situations or a background that does. We learn to adjust to these isolated fears particularly if our ongoing activity in later life causes us to associate desirable results with those situations we formerly feared. The child who fears the dark loses this fear by playing games in the dark or by going on walks and overnight hikes. The fears that are most disturbing to us are cumulative and acquired on a background of general insecurity. In the cases described above, the individuals were not disturbed by isolated, single, intense fears, but by anxiety states growing out of a certain temperamental background and through acquired traits built in early life conditions that represented insecurity and imagined punishment. A child will respond differently to a loud noise when he is alone in a strange room than he will when he is sitting in the lap of his reassuring mother. Then, too, children differ greatly in their susceptibility to fear situations (380).

Interesting aspects of fear have grown out of war-time bombings. Children showed a more remarkable ability to take the bombings during warfare than had been anticipated. With the passage of time, fear seemed to lessen. The crucial factor was the emotional excitement exhibited by people around the child rather than the severity of the bombing. The child readily followed his parents' good or poor example. The high similarity of the fears of mothers and of children of preschool age has been demonstrated. There is evidence also that fears in children are associated with and probably intensified by *feelings of guilt and apprehension* concerning future punishment and displeasure from their parents.

The fear that we find, then, in the youth or adult is a complex phenomenon associated with general anxiety, insecurity, guilt, and impending but improbable punishment. It is rarely the result of a simple, single, intense, disturbing situation. We bring our past and background into new fear situations and make them much more disturbing than they would be if stripped of these trimmings. Studies of the many service men with anxiety states during service showed the importance of family and personal history (775). Also there is a disparity between the fears of older children and the "worst happenings" in their lives (384). Whereas a large percentage of the worst happenings reported by children from 5 to 12 fall under the headings of bodily injury, illness, accidents, and operations, only 13 per cent of these children feared such experiences. About half of the children feared nonpromotion; only 1 per cent of them were "left back" in school. Some of this fear is due to threats from adults, reminders of fears, and general disparagement. Most of us in the period of our growth learn to fear a number of situations which, so far as our lives are concerned, will be harmless.

There are those who hold the belief that fear is a good deterrent and that if one worries he is sure to lead a better life than if he is carefree. Parents sometimes learn that the easiest way to repress the child is to frighten him. Instilling fear is a much simpler process than building positive habits. So the child is told that the harmless ragged hobo he once saw will "get him."

MULTIPLICATION OF FEARS. Fears multiply by *generalization*. A man may never again see the former boss who embarrassed him before his fellow employees, and whom he feared very much. There are, nevertheless, many men who resemble this boss and whose faces bring back the sensations of a quickened pulse, a change in facial expression, and thermal sensations in various parts of the body. The curve in the road that occasioned a traffic accident may not be traversed again, but there are other similar curves that recall the experience of seeing a dangerously close precipice.

ANXIETY AS A DEVELOPED PERSONALITY TRAIT. It is not difficult to comprehend how a child who has been frightened into conforming many times daily throughout his development may grow up to be very submissive and easily frightened. When we are frightened or are made to feel continually that we have done the wrong thing and deserve punishment we acquire a mental set that causes us to be anxious even when there is no immediate danger. Anxiety, then, becomes a personality trait. Anxieties, unlike specific fears, are vague. The object of them often cannot be named. They frequently arise *when deeply buried impulses to actions forbidden or censored in childhood are stirred and seek expression.* The individual in such cases puts emphasis on the anxiety or on the behavior alleviating it and avoids the underlying tabooed impulse.

Conflicts and suppression are the bases of fear and anxiety states. The cases discussed illustrate this. In many, the fear or symptoms mentioned were not those of prime importance. The effective cause was a *suppressed conflict*. This is found in disguised, vague and unrealistic fears. They cannot be taken at their face value. The thing or event feared is substituted for the real fear or suppressed experience.

In the cases of guilt, the individuals were not guilty of serious offenses, but the fact that they *believed* their misdemeanors were serious caused the conflict. It is interesting and important that often those who suffer most from guilt are not individuals with low ideals but with relatively high ideals that conflict with fundamental desires. Repression of sex impulses or worry over the effects of masturbation or sex play may be the cause of anxiety. Also hostility toward persons they feel they should love produces anxiety and guilt. Feelings of guilt and fear of sin are frequently the indications of a conflict between the desire to carry on the act and the standards preventing the act. The real fear in these cases is the fear of self, fear of violating standards, on the one hand, and fear of not satisfying the desires on the other. The solution is to discover the conflict; to resolve it by strengthening one drive and weakening the other through learning, as pointed out in Chapter 5. The strong fear of the unimportant event will frequently disappear.

Unreality and Anxiety. The adult, much as the child, has many fears of conditions that are not imminent (380, 527). His *imagination* is active in suggesting endangering situations that are quite improbable and unreal. The feared ills that befall him are seldom as intense in actuality as in dread anticipation. He fears losing the job that he continues to retain, robberies and accidents which never occur, and embarrassments and failures that, compared with the fears which precede them, are trivial. Dreaded medical, dental, and legal appointments that prove later to be of minor difficulty are numerous among the experiences of all of us.

Narrow escapes have special potency in inducing imaginative fears of what might have been. Often the situations that cause our fears can be *avoided*. Very few of us who are afraid of high places are forced to climb mountains or cross a wide gap between two precipices on a small plank. There are some fears, however, which cannot be avoided. Fears of failure, death, loss of or injury to loved ones, accidental injury, economic insecurity, disease, social insecurity, superior officers, audiences, criticism, gossip, and criminals are among the inevitable fears. These should be dealt with as suggested later in this section.

Most of us *separate possibilities from probabilities* and dismiss from the category of worry the possible but highly improbable events.

EVALUATION OF FEARS.   Apparently a certain degree of fear of possible dangers is stabilizing. We seldom elect to a responsible position a man who has no fears, whose action is not bridled in some way by the major conventions and by the fear of consequences of impulsive, careless action. Most of us regard the daredevil who tempts fate as unbalanced and dangerous to himself and others. We expect an adult to have some fear of physical danger or social ostracism. Caution, deliberation, and wisdom all include an element of fear.

Strong fears, particularly of imaginary, improbable occurrences or of events over which we have no control, not only lack utility but are also destructive in nature. In fear blood pressure is raised, breathing is quickened, and sugar and red corpuscles are increased in the blood stream. These are accompanied by other changes that *energize the individual* and prepare him for forceful action. Primitive man had use for this great energy in escape or in combat. In our modern civilized world there is seldom an outlet for this much energy. In most situations today we need carefully controlled, discreet, fine movements—not gross, highly energized activity. We have difficulty in controlling so much energy. Thinking is handicapped by the strong impulse to action.

Worry. *The nature of worry.* Worry is associated with fear and anxiety. When we review fears mentally, magnify them, and continue to think of them as impending, we are worrying. Worry has been called a "circular reaction" (695). The thought of the dangerous situation arouses fear, and fear perpetuates the thought. The circle is broken only by an adaptive act. Worry and the accompanying anxiety are unpleasant and can be relieved by an adjustive attack on the problem at hand. Otherwise, the individual will remain in an emotional state for hours and sometimes for days. His digestion and sleep may be upset, and he may become irritable and inefficient.

Frequently it is not an objective situation over which we worry. It is often a *subjective problem,* a condition in our personality. We usually meet real situations or events in a trial-and-error manner and often stumble on a solution, but inner problems are not so easily handled. Very often the person feels he cannot discuss that which worries him. If it is his health he worries about, he may be afraid to find the truth, fearing that it will make him unhappy. He may be afraid to discuss it with others, believing they will think less of him.

He may even think that the condition of his health reflects upon his previous habits or inner life. The same sort of reasoning usually takes place with other problems—sex problems, problems of ability, of efficiency or of quiet shame. Both Peter below and Sid on page 409 illustrate this. Worry is the opposite of a frank attack or of a plan. It is an *escape* from the real problem.

Psychasthenia, a milder mental disorder, includes as one of its outstanding symptoms a chronic tendency to worry. The psychasthenic individual is illustrated in the following case.

Peter C. had a relatively minor heart condition with good prognosis. He was referred to the counselor by a physician when he began staying awake nights worrying about his heart. Peter was 20 years old, tall and thin. He had returned to school after several years of work in a brokerage office. Although essentially immature, he had a strong desire to appear mature and sophisticated. In language and manner he was quite successful in playing the role of the fellow who had been around and who had a great deal of confidence and know-how. It was not until after he had talked for ten or fifteen minutes, mainly about his health, insomnia, class cutting, and disgust with his recent behavior, that he stated the real problem. He said discussing this matter with a clinical psychologist was the last thing he wanted to do. He was doing it only on the strong recommendation of his physician.

Once he decided to talk about his personal life, what he mentioned seemed quite significant. His mother died when he was quite young. His father became Peter's main source of emotional solace but before long married a woman whom he loved deeply. Peter felt that he was rejected and that he had been chivalrous not to jeopardize his father's happiness, even though he felt very hostile toward his step-mother. He idealized in imagination his dead mother and longed for her in his many brooding periods in childhood. He now realized that his childhood had been warped, and he undoubtedly saw some similarity between his step-mother's bid for attention through ill health and his own.

Peter tended to become very serious with girls and he frankly stated that his present condition could undoubtedly be traced to a recent love affair. He said he gave this girl everything—his whole inner self. He told her things he felt he should never have admitted to anyone about himself, about his inner feelings. He trusted her, and he feels now that he can never trust another girl. Apparently he had demanded a great deal from her and had felt that if she became physically intimate with him he could hold her better. Intimacies, however, stirred up guilt in her, and this guilt was probably one of the factors which caused her to leave him and to air the confidences he had given her.

Peter had an inordinate desire for attention and affection, no doubt related to the loss of it in early life. Probably the jealousy he felt toward his step-mother was related to his present desire to possess completely any girl he went with and to restrict her activities to his own selfish satisfactions. It bothered him that any girl he loved should find interest in anyone else, man or woman.

As he related events in his early and later life, he was unable to restrain his tears and sobs. These and other evidences of immaturity were very disturbing to him in view of his strong desire to be independent and self-confident, and tended to break the relationship between him and the counselor.

During later interviews he related that he no longer worried about his heart, that he recognized his real problem. It was his inability to trust people, to become close to them, and his fear of being hurt. His tendency to worry he saw as a smoke screen, and his concern over his heart as a bid for attention that was not too effective. His real anxiety and worry were related to his inability to satisfy immediately a very deep urge for affection from someone whom he could love and possess. He felt that his life would not be as long as the average, and for that reason he could not wait for this love, yet his own behavior seemed in the past to thwart all good intentions.

THE ATTITUDE THAT WORRY IS NECESSARY. Some who have the worry habit believe it is their duty to worry in the presence of the possibility of danger. They feel that, if they have worried over the matter, they have done all they can. They fail to distinguish the nervous, emotional, nonadaptive nature of worry from the adjustive, constructive nature of planning.

Some persons have frankly said that they worry about events that seem disastrous in prospect and are then greatly relieved when the actuality is not so bad. Others have a conviction that, if they do not worry when relatives or friends are facing danger, they are disloyal. They think that others expect them to worry and will consider them inhuman if they do not. They are not motivated by the advice: Do all you can about that which worries you, then assure yourself you have done all *you* can and turn your attention to more pleasant pursuits.

The worries of college women in one school were found to be more often about their personality, school work, and social life than about home, physical condition, or finances (500). Worries of children and youth apparently have not changed in frequency in the past twenty years, but there has been a tendency for them to worry less about natural events like storms and more about matters like popularity (620). The things we worry about often change with our age. Appearance and morality may worry us as young people, whereas economic matters and marital difficulty are concerns in middle life.

Suggestions for Dealing with Fears and Worries. Seek to understand your fears, anxieties, and worries. The effective methods for dealing with anxieties and fears do not differ greatly from those suggested earlier in this chapter in our discussion of depressions and instability. When an individual can talk about his anxieties and fears or even write them out and gain perspective and objectivity toward them, they lose some of their disturbing aspects. He may even discover the role of *guilt* in the fear. He may see how these fears make him feel inadequate and how they have been accentuated by their association with other aspects of his personality. He will see how early events in his development have prepared the way for these fears. Chapter 4 showed how the many circumstances of our lives influence our total organization. The individual may find the childhood origins of his fears. He may see how they have served to punish him or how they have enabled him to escape responsibilities or how they have protected him in some way or other.

Repression, distraction, ridicule, and palliatives are ineffective methods. Some of the insights mentioned can emerge in time as one progressively sees the fear in perspective. It is the antithesis of repressing the fear, or trying to forget it, to wipe it out—a very difficult process sometimes, especially when a fear has strong physiological components. There are other commonly used strong-arm methods that have been found ineffective and sometimes harmful. They include trying to talk the person out of his fears, ridiculing him, forcing him physically or verbally to face the intimidating object against his will, staying away from a common but feared object (383).

For milder fears and anxieties the frank, calm writing out process can be recommended. In such cases one might seek a confidant or an understanding listener. For fears and anxieties that are not alleviated by some of the suggestions that follow, a *professional counselor* should be sought. A psychiatrist or clinical psychologist is recommended for the individual who has been anxious all his life and finds the anxiety growing with years. He can be assured from the outset that many others have been greatly assisted by seeking professional counsel. In fact, the first interview will be reassuring because he will undoubtedly feel much relieved by unburdening himself.

Knowledge about the event feared and the physiology of fear helps. Ignorance or lack of knowledge greatly accentuates fears. We fear the unknown and unfamiliar. We fear situations to which we are unable to react positively and in an adaptive manner. This was shown in warfare. Seasoned troops exhibited much less fear than inexperienced men because they knew what happened in conflict and had more knowledge of what they could expect and what they could do about events. For this reason any valid, constructive *knowledge* about illnesses or future events that intimidate us lessens the fear.

One of the annoying aspects of fear is that it produces such violent *physiological changes*, changes which, as mentioned before, helped primitive man either fight or run. Today during fright we are put into a physiological state for violent, overt behavior even though the situations we fear now do not require this type of response. We cannot run away from problems within ourselves, insecurity, sensitiveness to censure and gossip, or illness. The vigorous bodily state of primordial life does not prepare us for the intangible fears of our day. All of us need to learn the appropriate reaction to fears in civilized society. Blood pressure increases and the heart accelerates in any fearful experience. We are aware of the quickened heartbeat. Breathing is accelerated and we become conscious of a choking sensation. Digestion is impaired; some people report feeling a lump in the stomach. The change in blood circulation from the interior of the body to the limbs is accompanied by changes in temperature which we feel. The tremor and stirred-up state continues because adrenalin is automatically poured into the blood stream and perpetuates the physiological states.

In modern life, as indicated in the next chapter, these changes, instead of helping one, merely call attention to the body. The individual who tends to be preoccupied with his health anyway is sure there is something physiologically wrong with him, and he centers his attention on these changes. The anxious patient then comes to the doctor reporting what are *natural fear changes*. The preoccupation with the physical, besides being disturbing, *takes attention from the real issues*—the insecurities, the shame, the little repressed experiences. If the individual can remain absorbed by these physical aspects of fear, he does not have to deal with the other unpleasant and embarrassing events in his background. On the other hand, when he learns that all the bodily sensations that have concerned him are normal, that when he is extremely anxious and terrified he should *expect* tumultuous inner states, he is moving toward an attack of the real problem. It was the inability to see the real nature of this problem that started the vicious cycle of preoccupation with the physical changes in fear, further fear that these changes are serious health conditions, continued and accentuated physiological processes, more fear.

Positive methods of dealing with situations reduce fear. Many times, as we develop skills in a situation, we have been better able to cope with it, and the initial withdrawal behavior or fear has disappeared. This is shown very clearly by the reaction of many children to school. For example, at nursery school, children show uneasiness and signs of fear, but with time they habituate to the situation and develop interests and skills which cause them to enjoy school. Sometimes the change of environment, particularly one in which the individual can feel free to start anew, has a desirable effect. New situations stimulate new interests and habits, and the individual learns means of adjusting to it, particularly if it is warm and hospitable. Camp is found to have this effect upon children with personal difficulties (470).

AN EXAMPLE IN ATHLETICS. A psychologist describes a football player who had lost his confidence and his ability to catch punts because of a fear situation, and presents a method of restoring confidence.

The boy in the case had just caught a punt with his usual deftness when two ends crashed into him, hurling him to the ground. The impact resulted in a slight concussion. When he resumed play he had lost confidence in his ability to catch punts. He seems now to fear the ball. He flinches as it comes down to him. He tightens his muscles and allows the ball to fall to the ground. He may be benched for a while in the hope that this will allow him to "come to his senses." Despite this, he does not improve. The sight of the ball is a fear stimulus. He must be re-educated or reconditioned. The association, ball-confidence, must be built again.

The re-education process consists of the following: first, this football player is asked to play "catch" with another man. He catches the football thrown to him with ease. This situation does not arouse the fear. It is too foreign to the other situation of catching a kicked ball in a competitive game. After several days of catching the ball, two new men are introduced into the game with him. They stand at a distance at first. One is stationed on the right and the other at the left. The "yellow" player continues to play "catch" in the presence of these two men until he does it calmly and smoothly. Later, the two men move toward our subject, who is catching the ball. At first they move slowly. As the man catching the ball continues to catch with ease and confidence the men at the side run toward him with greater speed until he has "licked the situation." Later they run at full speed toward the player just as he is catching the ball, and continue this until it has no effect on him. Finally they tackle him mildly. This situation produced fear before he had gone through hours of practice with men moving around him. It is now continued until he can perform with confidence instead of fear. A new response has been built gradually to replace the former fear reaction. The player has been *re-educated* (285).

MILITARY EXPERIENCE. Military experts have trained soldiers so thoroughly in the details of behavior during combat that in a terrifying situation the combatant can turn to these automatized acts, keep busy, and be relieved (272). When several hundred American veterans of the Spanish Civil War were questioned, 71 per cent mentioned experiencing greater fear before going into action, and only 15 per cent could recall fear during the action. During action, they had something to do. They were responding adaptively (184, 89). If the action is appropriate to remove the situation, real or imagined, that caused the fear, then the action has two effects—putting the individual into motion to utilize the available energy, and removing the disturbing situation.

OTHER CASES OF RE-EDUCATION. Fear of water, of climbing high places, of people, or of any other objects or situations can be supplanted by success and confidence in the situation. To achieve this we must build positive, pleasant, and confident reactions in the place of fearful ones. It should be noted that in the case cited the recon-

Susan Greenburg

. . . as we develop skills in a situation . . . the initial withdrawal behavior or fear has disappeared . . .

ditioning was scheduled over a number of periods. If fear should enter at any time the learner should be brought back to an operation, in the case of a skill, to which he is able to respond with confidence and pleasure. This operation should be repeated until he can proceed to a more difficult one without fear. By daily exercise of this type, any fear can be replaced by learned confidence.

You should not expect to perform well in a situation you fear. No doubt part of your fear is worry that your performance will not be smooth or will be full of mistakes. This is inevitable, and most persons have gone through similar experiences. You may be sure that the embarrassment caused by this positive though possibly crude action will be far less troublesome than a continuation of the fear, anxiety, and worry. Great relief accompanies bringing a situation to a climax, even though it is not done smoothly.

Many times we fear situations that cannot be subjected to experimental control. Suppose you fear meeting people or attending parties. How can you build up a positive attitude toward them? The same paradigm may be used. Attend smaller, less important gatherings or functions in which you feel pleasant and ascendant. You may want to decline all invitations to the more pretentious and awe-inspiring affairs for a while. Continue to attend the other congenial parties until action at them becomes freer and easier. Then you may want to try other kinds of gatherings. Look at the whole process as a game.

Try to utilize the energy produced by the fear situation. It is far better to use the energy produced by the fear situation to combat it than to sit and suffer the terror. See what caused the noise upstairs; get right up and talk to the fellow who can get you into real trouble with his idle chatter about you, even if he does overpower you; see your teacher, your coach, your father, or your boss, and get at the basic issue that is worrying you and involves them. Life is full of these conflicts and anxious moments. The individual who has developed methods of meeting them has acquired a real strength. The individual who escapes from them by withdrawal lives with himself in a veritable hell.

Rehearse feared activities in situations that normally do not arouse the fear. We saw previously in the section on building habits that if an individual who stutters is drilled in stuttering voluntarily he tends to gain control over the process and the stuttering is lessened. He is brought into the clinic and told to practice stuttering. This method of practicing an act which he previously dreaded tends to

eliminate the act (193). The technique may be applied to the eradication of fear.

A college coed feared examinations. She had average ability but had
always been subdued by the school situation. Even in grade school, teachers frightened her. In her freshman year in college, her school work was
complicated by a job that consumed much of her time and energy. Time
was precious, and she never quite finished her preparation for class. This
caused her to fear that questions would be asked on material she had not
covered. She walked into her classes trembling.

She talked over her fears with a counselor and saw some of the attitudes
that were producing them. Since the time factor in taking the quizzes
was her greatest concern, it was suggested that she take a number of trial
quizzes planned by her roommate and performed under as nearly the same
conditions as obtained in the classroom as possible. She was to have the
same number of questions, to be completed in the same amount of time.
She was to do this a number of times. It was suggested that it might
also be well for her to curtail her program to have more time to cover
the material of the other courses and thereby assure her of thorough coverage and remove one of the causes of her fears.

Associates who experience fear but are outwardly calm help in
crises. We saw previously that children did not experience excessive
fear during bombings if their parents were calm. The same sort of
calming effect grows out of talking out our fears with some understanding person. Calm associates only have a disturbing effect when
they make us feel inferior by contrast. Soldiers were told that humor
helps. All of us have had some experience in which the sense of
humor that produced a good laugh helped us through some terrifying
situation. Likewise, companionship or fellow victims have some
value at these times. The higher the *morale*, loyalty, and personal
relationships between men during battle, the less they seem to go to
pieces. Certainly repressing the presence of fear, being reluctant to
admit its existence, being afraid or ashamed of fear and its implications does not help. An inner calm that has been associated with
faith and religion and the belief that there is some order in the universe has been mentioned as important, and many people report that
it has meant a great deal to them (89).

Emotional Stability. We saw that we become more stable emotionally as we understand and reduce our mental conflicts, as we know
where we stand on matters that are vital to us, and as we strive for
goals that we can reach. We grow in emotional stability as we build
valuable habits and attitudes and prepare to meet the situations that
the world presents to us. We gain more stability as we learn not to

use escapes into emotional depressions nor to ignore our problems by effusiveness. Stability shows itself on the positive side in a *confident* attitude and behavior to which we now turn. A more complete discussion of the adjusted individual is given in Chapter 16.

Supplementary Readings

N. Cameron and A. Magaret, *Behavior Pathology*, Houghton Mifflin, 1951.

L. A. Pennington, "Psychopathic and Criminal Behavior," in L. A. Pennington and I. A. Berg, *Introduction to Clinical Psychology*, Ronald, 1954.

P. M. Symonds, *Dynamic Psychology*, Appleton-Century-Crofts, 1949.

In addition see the references cited by number in the chapter and appearing in the bibliography of an accompanying volume entitled *Teaching Personal Adjustment: An Instructor's Manual.*

CHAPTER 15

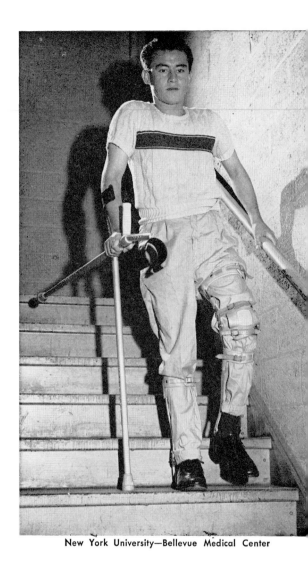

New York University—Bellevue Medical Center

Redirecting Feelings of Inferiority

F eelings of inferiority and self-consciousness are symptoms similar
  to depressions and other signs of emotional disturbance. Like
depressions, they are the result of frustration of needs. They are less
cyclical than depressions and unstable behavior and are related more
to inadequacies in skills and social endeavors rather than to moral and
ethical standards. Such feelings are found very frequently in varying
degrees among peoples in our culture. The causes of and the effective
424

CHAPTER 15
_____

SELF-CONFIDENCE

modes of dealing with these states are not dissimilar to those found in the behavior discussed in the previous chapter.

We have arbitrarily grouped the material in this and in the preceding chapter on the basis of the severity and frequency of the symptoms. In Chapter 14 we have dealt with symptoms and patterns of personality that are found in all people but which in their extreme form constitute disturbing emotional disorders. To some extent feelings of inferiority and self-consciousness have the same effect. However, they vary in degree and appear to be less disorganizing and more readily harnessed as motivation for accomplishment than the phenomena discussed in the preceding chapter.

The Paradox of the Inferiority Feeling. It is arresting to realize how many people in our culture have feelings of inferiority. It is even more astonishing to learn that feelings of inferiority are quite often found in people with talents and superior aptitudes, interests, and accomplishments. Biographies and autobiographies bear testimony to the existence of handicaps and experienced difficulties in the development of outstanding personages.

Lord Byron, we are told, was extremely sensitive about his clubfoot. He was considered a dullard in school. He was socially ostracized because of moral indiscretions. Because of these many factors which blighted his daily existence he turned to poetry and with his excellent style created lines which will live forever.

Charles Darwin was reared by a stern father. Mr. Darwin wanted his son to study medicine. Charles was so fond of his father and so submissive to his wishes that he pursued the study of medicine even though he realized that it was unsuited to his taste. He finally turned to the career of naturalist over the protests of his father. He felt that since his father did not agree with him on the choice of career he must succeed. We are told that, although he formulated his evolutionary theory at the age of 30, he waited until he was 56 before he published it for fear of offending his father.

Poe suffered from sensitiveness to slander caused by the other boys at the aristocratic school that he attended. He was also embarrassed when reference was made to his mother, who had been an actress and whom he idealized. It is recorded that he had "weak lungs," and this probably added to his feeling of inferiority.

Biographies bring to readers' minds the many handicaps encountered by the leaders in every realm of our culture. Andrew Jackson was descended from Irish immigrants. Martin Luther was from peasant stock. Daniel Defoe was the son of a London butcher. The adroit Cardinal Richelieu's ancestors lived in provincial obscurity. George Eliot was the daughter of a carpenter. These are only a few of the thousands who started with severe handicaps that may have been much of the motivational source of their success.

It is interesting that many great men and women were shadowed by feelings of inferiority *even after they had achieved* wide recognition.

Lord Curzon, Viceroy of India, was so conscious of his behavior that the slightest error or defeat humiliated him greatly. When he failed to achieve the highest honors at Oxford he was so chagrined that he resolved to compensate through later success. He spent hours night and day working on an essay that won him the Lowthian prize. He was a person who had few physical assets but his memory was remarkable, his powers of concentration unusual, and his range of interest wide (817).

Persons of superior ability and ideals may be unable to deal with the emotional conflicts in their own lives. Their concepts of themselves may have been colored by early, vivid, emotional experiences. If they ever gain a better concept of themselves they are well along in life, and habits are established.

Cases of Students Who Feel Inferior. Earlier in the book we have seen cases of individuals who have felt inferior. We began with Larry on page 9 who so compensated for the feelings of inferiority, which he never faced in his early life, that he became quite well known on the campus and gave the impression of having a high degree of adjustiveness. Later he had serious emotional repercussions, which he eventually learned to handle with professional assistance.

Edward, on page 121, felt inferior because of the attitudes that grew out of his physical condition and background. Betty's case, on page 127, shows a struggle by an able and attractive girl with feelings of inferiority. John's desire to be an outstanding public speaker, on page 149, was related to his feeling of inferiority. Irwin, on page 123, came from a superior economic and cultural background, yet he experienced marked insecurity and inferiority, in part related to supposed rejection by his peers. These cases illustrate that, although feelings of inadequacy, unworthiness, and inferiority may be the major symptoms, individuals who experience them deeply may also show the symptoms discussed in the previous chapters, such as depressions and disorganized behavior. Individuals who have difficulties in adjusting tend to derogate themselves more than those who have been more successful in adjusting to life (120, 14).

Harry T.'s mother died when he was a junior in high school. Shortly afterward, his father remarried and moved to a different part of the city. Harry decided at this time that he would be happier on his own, so he found a job and roomed near the high school. He was graduated and entered the university. He was a student of superior ability and rather good work habits, but he missed the affection he formerly received. Furthermore, his below-average height motivated him. At the university he earned practically all his expenses. He was a good worker and was praised by most of his bosses. When he was interviewed as a freshman, he appeared to be very ambitious. He inquired searchingly about courses that would qualify him for the vocation he wished to enter. He made an active effort to orient himself to college and found several odd jobs for himself. He planned his own curriculum. As soon as he was financially able, he subscribed to a professional journal so that he could learn more about the field into which he was going. He joined several extracurricular activities. His ear was always close to the ground for an opportunity to give him experience in writing, the field he was planning to enter. As a senior, he wrote 25 letters to various newspapers and succeeded in finding a position superior to those that many of his fellow students found.

Harry is an example of a "self-made" person, and now, ten years after graduation, has been unusually successful in his chosen field, is married, has several children and apparently has a happy family life. His feeling of inferiority was a strong influence toward development throughout his high school and university years. Underneath his pleasant, obliging manner, one could sometimes detect a nervousness and feeling of inadequacy which found compensation in his aggression and accomplishment. The counselor saw that his great restlessness and drive for success grew out of earlier experiences which Harry never discussed with anyone. Rather than reflect on his feelings of insecurity, he plunged feverishly into opportunities to distinguish himself; he will probably always be above average in initiative and accomplishment.

Nature of Inferiority Feeling. *It is an emotional reaction to believed failure.* Some of us realize that we are inferior in some ways, admit it, and turn our attention to something else. If we are able to do this with calm, we do not have an inferiority complex. One who has never aspired to be a singer may know that he cannot sing and therefore at no time becomes emotional over his poor musical aptitude. A young lady is well aware that she cannot compete in efficiency with some of her contemporaries in the commercial world. In fact she often jokes about her incompetence. She realizes, however, that she is markedly superior to any of them in her ability to get along with others and to handle social situations, which to her is more important.

There is a difference, then, between *knowledge* of inferiority and a *feeling* of inferiority. The inferiority feeling is an emotional state of mind. The individual who is bothered by it feels inadequate or insecure, usually because of events early in his life. In compensation he unconsciously sets his goal high, often unreasonably high. He often *fails to reach this high goal,* and his inadequacy is exaggerated. As a result he feels inferior and inadequate. He is not the free, stable personality that he might be.

It Varies with the Individual. The area of believed failure, the intensity of feelings and the manner in which the person reacts to it all vary with the individual (12). He may feel that he is of poorer stock or quality than most people. He may feel that he has sinned. In all cases, however, he falls short of a goal which he accepts as important.

Frequently the individual is not *clearly conscious* of the nature of his inadequacy. All he experiences is a vague unpleasantness, a dissatisfaction with himself, an irritability, or an unwholesome aggressiveness. He may feel thus for years and not analyze the reason. Others continually dodge the realization that underneath they feel inferior. Still others know exactly what causes them to feel inferior. They can trace the origin of this feeling. It is highly conscious in nature.

We differ also in the way in which we *react* to feelings of inferiority largely because of early habits. Some react to such feelings by aggressiveness, others by retirement, others by substitution of hard work in another field.

Symptoms of an Inferiority Personality Pattern. How does the person with an inferiority complex seem to his acquaintances? How does he feel? Some of the major symptoms of the person who feels inferior follow (327).

Self-conscious	Given to self-criticism
Daydreams	Given to remorse
Dissatisfied	Compares himself to others
Easily embarrassed	Hesitates to test himself
Sensitive to praise and blame	Has a secret ambition
Lives in the future	Analyzes his own motives
Worries about little mistakes	

The symptoms of the inferiority complex cannot be fully described in a check list of this type. It is difficult also to separate the inferiority complex from feelings of self-consciousness, emotional instability in general, chronic emotional depressions, and other personality problems.

The listed symptoms are mainly of the withdrawal kind reflected in external behavior by timidity, a disinclination to compete with others, a need to be perfect, noncooperative behavior, and sometimes irritability. In addition, there are aggressive symptoms shown by extreme self-assertiveness, loudness, boldness, flashy clothes, and an overbearing artificial manner. When men with tattoo marks on their bodies were studied they were found to be less stable than those without such marks (433).

COMPENSATORY ACTIVITY. Perfectionism or the desire to be perfect in all or most ventures may show itself in an uncompromising and highly dissatisfied person. However, it sometimes leads to superior accomplishment. This is particularly true if it finds its major assertion through the talents of the individual. Such an individual works many hours in order that his achievements may be perfect. His compensations may be in any channel. They may be of a social type. He may become a champion for the underdog, may enter the field of art, music, science, or commerce and achieve above-average success as a result of his hard work. He may enter the field of athletics and with his high motivation win fame. In every case, however, this person puts forth an unusual amount of effort in his attempt to be successful. Harry, on page 427, illustrates compensation. *Many great men owe a portion of their achievement to the fact that they experienced marked feelings of inferiority when they were younger.* It is through compensation that the feeling of inferiority often becomes one of the greatest assets the individual possesses.

Not all compensation that leads to success is wholesome. Rabid compensation is rarely a planned attack. It is usually an impulsive struggle to protect one's ego and achieve recognition. The resultant behavior is sometimes similar to that discussed in Chapter 14 as unstable behavior. We do not have to go far afield to find a little dictator who has run roughshod over lives of others in order to amass a reputation or fortune for himself. Such a person is rarely well balanced or happy, but is satisfying his own neurotic motivation.

ABNORMAL OR DELINQUENT BEHAVIOR. Childhood thefts and other antisocial behavior have been traced in some instances to the desire on the part of the child to be superior. The child may steal money in order that he may buy candy for the other children and win their approval. He may steal to show them that he is a real boy and can do daring things. He may steal a bicycle, for example, in order to possess such a symbol of prestige. Sometimes the adolescent desires superiority so strongly that he may violate rules and break laws to achieve it. Disobedience, insubordination and wild driving are found among persons who feel inferior. Pathological lying may be an attempt to gain superiority. Extreme jealousy may be the result of a believed or actual preference by the parent for another child in the family. When this asocial behavior is continued and the individual's personality seems disorganized as a result, when he does not respond to treatment and does not profit by experience, he is considered psychopathic.

Inferiority conflicts may lead to the *hysterical* behavior to which other conflicts lead. The individual may gain recognition through illness. He may project his mental difficulties into physical symptoms. In extreme cases he may even build up *delusions*, think that others are persecuting him, and organize an elaborate system of thinking in order to defend himself from the persecution. He may believe that he possesses some greatness, or that he is an adopted child and his real parents were famous. Frenzied compensation that grows from a piercing feeling of inferiority may take any of these undesirable asocial forms.

Cases Illustrating Various Inferiority Symptoms

A 20-year-old college student had been called a sissy in high school and had failed to rate with some of the other boys. As a result he built himself a trapeze in his back yard, acquired some gymnasium weights, and spent a half-hour every day building up his body until he had developed massive shoulders.

A sophomore coed had realized in high school that she was not as pretty as the average girl. At that time she made a systematic effort to be pleasant. She was very kind to the other girls and helpful to the boys. She groomed very well. She was very conscious of styles and selected materials to blend with her hair, eyes, and complexion. At the present time she is considered a college leader, and she possesses a charming personality as a result of her efforts to compensate.

A 21-year-old college student was born and reared in the slums. He carries the mark of his early days with him in his speech. In his attempt to better his social status he has suffered a number of rebuffs. He realizes he is not accepted as readily in social gatherings as other students. As a result he has a "chip-on-the-shoulder" attitude. He continually tries to put others at a disadvantage and to point to his own accomplishments. At every meeting he rises and gives his opinion.

A pretty, capable, extremely modest, and self-effacing young girl tells the counselor confidentially that she feels inferior. She recalls that her step-mother resented every minute of attention her father gave her. She was criticized constantly as a small child. She took this attitude of inferiority to school. She cringed and shook every time a teacher raised her voice. In spite of the fact that she receives good grades in school, is well liked by the few who know her, and is pretty, she still thinks herself very inadequate. She does not appreciate her physical charm or intellectual ability.

SUMMARY. From an explanation of the symptoms and a review of some of the preceding cases it is clear that previous experience leads to these attitudes of inferiority and that the individual may, on the one hand, react to these attitudes by withdrawing, surrendering, and regarding himself as incapable of meeting a responsibility or, on the other hand, he may become aggressive, flighty, bumptious, and in some cases hard-working in the field of some talent. Now let us trace some of the foci and factors in the feeling of inferiority.

Causes of Feelings of Inferiority. Almost every part of the body has been a source of worry to someone. Children and adolescents have worried about big ears, a long neck, crooked teeth, a receding chin, a large nose, complexion, shortness, tallness, large hips, size of sex organs or mammary glands, and hair color or pattern (41).

Any difference a child may notice in himself as he compares himself with the majority may become a *focus* for feelings of inferiority, especially if he feels insecure otherwise. Almost all children in our culture feel themselves *physically* inferior in some respect (454). Sixty per cent of students report they have experienced feelings of inferiority at one time because of physical factors. *Social* factors are named by 60 per cent of the group (227). Social factors include economic status, vocation, nationality or religion, parents, place of residence, clothes and requirements of parents (such as early curfew or forbidding the use of cosmetics)—anything that makes the child feel he is different from his age mates (12, 737, 724, 825). *Moral* matters are mentioned in 37 per cent of cases (227). Physical factors once thought to be the major cause of feelings of inferiority, probably gain any great importance they assume through their social significance. Less than 10 per cent of students report no personal experience with inferiority feelings (227).

It is interesting that the person who *feels* inferior need not actually *be* inferior in terms of objective indexes, such as measures of physical, mental, social, or economic conditions (170). Seldom is the *minority* group of an inferior character at all (724). It may merely be different in its behavior. "Majority" and "minority" in America varies from one community to another. A Protestant, usually a member of the majority, becomes one of a minority in a Catholic university. Similarly, an "A" student in a fraternity in which grades are not considered important may feel out of his element, whereas a "D" student will feel very ill at ease in a group of Phi Beta Kappas. Our strongly competitive attitude certainly does not help. Some children, because of neglect or lack of parental affection, compete with brothers and sisters.

Children are often encouraged to compete in fields in which they are inferior in constitution and background. The new movement in education that individualizes the teaching and guidance of the child so that he may find the activities that afford him greater success and satisfaction should do much to prevent the stereotyping that has occurred in the past. Certain communities are more culpable than others in encouraging the "keeping up with the Joneses" attitude in setting fictitious cultural ideals. Our American democracy and present interfaith religious movements emphasize the principle of the acceptance of people of all patterns and background, and if our community cultures were true to these ideals they would reward interesting, colorful differences in behavior, physique, and background rather than to stigmatize them.

A mother with a definite class-consciousness may imbue her daughter with the idea that she is *superior* to everyone else in a town of 1500 inhabitants. She may forbid her daughter to date the boys in that town. She may send her away to school and keep her close within the home during the two or three months she is not at school. The daughter will feel a mental conflict when she is eventually introduced to other persons in this town. This conflict will be accentuated if other persons react unpleasantly to her. If she has to spend much time at home or if she has attended school in this town and has been prohibited from associating with her schoolmates after school hours, it is not difficult to see that she will develop a strong *feeling of inferiority* resulting, not from inferior qualities, but rather from an allegedly superior background. It is also interesting to note that, with this type of regime planned by the mother, the girl will actually become inferior in dealing with people. She may even carry the attitudes of superiority and aloofness from the people in her home town to other groups and appear inferior in those circles, because her attitudes will actually lead to inferiority in social adroitness.

CLASSIFICATION OF CONDITIONS FOR INFERIORITY FEELINGS. All the specific factors that give rise to a feeling of inferiority may be classified in these groups:

1. Any type of *physical defect* or any physical factor different from the average that has been a source of embarrassment.

2. Real or imagined *disadvantages* due to race, family, or economic conditions.

3. Lack of social, professional, or economic *opportunities*.

4. Particular *experiences*, such as shock, disappointment, humiliation, and unfavorable comparisons.

5. *Defects, real or imagined*, in intelligence, appearance, moral character, and social attractiveness.

6. *Deviation* from local pattern in religion, custom, and conventions.

HOW PREVIOUS EVENTS PRODUCE INFERIORITY. It should be clear by this time that it is not the external factor itself that gives rise to the inferiority complex or conflict. It is, rather, the relationship of this cause to the *background* of the individual. If he has been reared by sensitive parents, or if he has been allowed to become sensitive over matters in his early history, he will react more strongly to minor matters at adolescence or in later life. Furthermore, if an individual feels that he has failed in an area of life that he considers very important, this failure will have a serious effect upon his personality.

The fact that Sam is of Jewish parentage will not greatly disturb him since he has been reared among Jews. His best friends are Jews, he strongly believes in his religion, and most of his ideals are Jewish ideals. He is proud of the fact that he is a Jew. He will fight all prejudices or ignore them. If, on the other hand, he had been reared in a predominantly Gentile community, had many times felt unique because he is a Jew, and had at times wished he were a Gentile, he might experience a conflict because of his origin and feel inferior because of it.

Feeling of inferiority is related to the disparity between one's *level of aspiration* and one's *accomplishment*. If one aspires to a certain goal and his daily behavior fails to attain this goal for him or makes him more realistic about his chances of attaining it, he feels inferior. If he has no aspiration for this goal, then if he does fall short of it he does not feel inferior and is not frustrated. A factor that may plunge one youth into deep despair may not affect another at all. We can explain this on the basis of the goal or motive to which the individual is responding. Fiery red hair may not bother a good athlete whose goals and level of aspiration are high in terms of athletics and gymnasium contacts rather than in terms of his physiognomy. Laboratory techniques have been developed for studying discrepancies between aspirations and accomplishments. Attempts are being made to relate these to personality traits and background (667, 685, 258).

Inferiority Complexes as Cultural Conflicts.   Many who feel inferior do so because they are experiencing a cultural conflict.

A college student may have adjusted excellently to a town of 200. He may have acquired all the prevalent habits and attitudes. When he arrives on the campus of a small college and finds himself one of a very few rural students he finds he does not "fit in" well.

A playboy collegian who receives his major income from bond coupons may feel at odds with a group of liberal, serious-minded newspapermen who have little sympathy for the wealthy absentee landlord or the nonproductive consumer. He may find that his social badges carry little prestige with them.

In both of these cases the individual has acquired a culture (customs, mannerisms, etc.) which is respected by his old group and not by the new group into which he has moved.

Inferiority Complexes as Traits. We have already brought out that the attitudes the individual learns early in life are important. It should be clear by this time also that the inferiority feeling is a learned trait, a way of thinking, and once it is aroused many minor matters that ordinarily would not affect the individual develop into major factors. If the child as he starts to school has a mental set that he is inferior, he may become more sensitive about minor embarrassments, about his clothes, about his possibilities as an athlete, and other accomplishments. He has a set of caution, of withdrawal, or of aggressiveness as the case may be. We have seen this tendency in many of the cases described. Often the individual feels left out of the family or an important social group, and considers himself unwanted and inadequate. This was seen in the cases of Ivan and particularly of Marie.

The individual may assume a posture and a manner consistent with his inferior attitude. In fact he may even associate this unpleasant attitude with his own mirrored image. Sometimes an individual like Harry will continue to plod in any area he has success. These accomplishments are oases on a desert of unpleasant consciousness. In general these individuals report that the attitude of inferiority is an intrinsic part of their personalities, which they feel they will never lose. They are convinced that they are inferior. They are positive that this inferiority is not something that they have acquired but that it is something they have always had. Many think it is innate.

A student with a physical defect in one of his legs, which causes him to walk with a limp, insists when the counselor talks with him that he is from inferior stock. His evidence for this point is that he has always failed; people have always disliked him; his work has never come up to par. A heavy, unpleasant attitude surrounds all his achievements, all the concepts he has of himself, and all his actions.

Alleviating Feelings of Inferiority. *Understanding of your feelings of inadequacy should bring perspective.* Like all other symptoms, feelings of inferiority are relieved when the individual sees himself in perspective as pointed out both in Chapter 5 and Chapter 14. Ventilation of one's feelings by talking over his traits with an understanding confidant usually brings relief and some perspective. With discussion we often come to accept the reality that *all people have feelings of inadequacy* at some time or other. We therefore with time may come to feel that we are not too different.

Even if one avoids a counselor one should certainly feel free to write out his present attitudes toward himself and trace their origins. The Pre-interview Blank presented in the accompanying volume entitled *Teaching Personal Adjustment: An Instructor's Manual* may be duplicated and may serve as a point of departure. This blank may be used to help the individual explore his present tendencies and the many factors in his past that have made him the sort of person he is today. Or he may write his *autobiography* and a *review of his contemporary activities*, using the blank as a point of departure. Some students who are in each other's confidence have found it profitable to work out this information together and discuss the results.

EXAMPLE OF VENTILATION PRODUCING PERSPECTIVE. Sometimes, after a student has discussed or written freely (see pages 144 to 147) about his own inadequacies and begins to feel better about them, he finds that he is more free emotionally to look around him and observe other lives not very unlike his own.

The following excerpts from a letter indicate what free discussion of oneself can do to release tensions and produce perspective.

". . . This is Christmas Eve, a festive day, yet I feel like the loneliest of men, troubled, burdened, unable to see my way or to relax, unable to catch a spark of the atmosphere of happiness. It is a hellova feeling to experience. Sometimes I believe that all this isn't happening to me but to someone else. . . . Maybe I should get to the point. I just seem to get more wound up the more I try to determine what's bothering me . . . I need help, counseling, and guidance. . . . Right now, at this very moment, I want to close my eyes to the whole thing. I want to shut the door on reality. A person who wants to quit and give up as I do has to face himself eventually. The picture isn't very pleasant . . . I felt inferior to the boys that had the least . . . I let others dominate the scene and the conversation completely just as I do at home and everywhere. I suppose that is the outgrowth of my dependency on Mother. I came to accept the fact that she would always be there, that I would always have refuge in her but, as a counselor told me, she won't always be here, I have my life to live and my way to make. Of course he is right . . .

"I really trumped up all these things in an effort to escape responsibility that was entirely foreign to me. Looking at these things in their true perspective, I accused school in the first place of causing me emotional disturbance. It wasn't. Then idleness, then school again. Every time I was unwilling to play a man's role in accepting the responsibiity that others accepted readily. By the same token, the first part of this letter was a prop that allowed me to be lazy. I haven't ever really pitched into anything in my life. School couldn't really disturb me because I never have really worked hard at it. I usually did enough to get by. For that reason I have a tremendous potential on hand. As my sister once told me, if I ever get rid of my inertia I'll be hard to stop. I have a job but I spend too much time on it introspecting. I've got to get to the point where I can work, laugh, and joke and be good company for others, get along well with them, and do this kind of thinking on paper and in interviews as you have suggested. Now that I've gone into my case rather thoroughly, I must plan a course of action that will give me these responsibilities a few at a time so that I can gradually put away the crutches I've been in the habit of inventing.

"I feel a good deal better now, Doctor. I hope you won't mind my writing you often. It certainly helps."

You may find that you have centered your attention on details of your physique, some social aspect of your life, or upon your family background. Unpleasant or embarrassing experiences may have caused you to brood over the details. They may have become *isolated in your own thinking* and have produced this psychological myopia. In attending to your large ears, the skinny body, your relative "poverty," your family's minority status, your lack of athletic ability or pulchritude, you have selected one aspect from literally thousands of details about yourself and have assumed that it is of inordinate importance in your life and of an extremely negative character. You assume that this aspect has no desirable connotations. You may ignore the fact, for example, that large features are an integral part of a strong, masculine face and might be highly compatible with a forceful personality. You may realize that you would not disparage all persons who have large features just as you have disparaged yourself. Other items that are isolated and thought to be the cause of one's feeling of inadequacy are also viewed quite differently when considered in perspective. You may realize, if you are concerned about your family background, that many very successful and worthy individuals owe their drive to what you have been regarding as a poor family background.

Very often some aspect of personality which is regarded as negative is also thought to be unalterable and to leave a lasting stigma. This is illustrated by the disparity between the attitude toward themselves of many who wear glasses and the impressions they make on others. There are some students who will accept poor vision rather than wear glasses in public. It is interesting that in an experiment designed to ascertain attitudes toward persons who wear glasses, it was found that the persons wearing glasses were judged from their photographs to be more intelligent, more industrious, more honest, and more dependable than others (801).

As you discuss and think through those aspects of your life that make you feel inadequate, you may discover that these minor features of physique or behavior are merely the *scapegoats* and that your present negative attitude toward yourself may have grown from *circumstances that have been operative over a period of years.* You may find that in the past you have been *unfavorably compared* with a brother, sister, or cousin. You may have lived with a highly critical or punishing parent or relatives. The lower economic status or reputation of your family may have produced early and persistent shame and embarrassment. You may have been *trying to excel in a field in which you do not possess any special talent.* Your preoccupation with failure here may have kept you from developing freely in an area in which you have ability. You may fail to accept some negative traits in physique, family background or social life, as events which are all a part of the complexities of life, as *realities which must be faced and dealt with effectively.* Inferiority feelings are attitudes that have been acquired originally through the accretion of events and may be unlearned under favorable conditions. An individual may regard a negative trait as a calamity and stigma and as a consequence reject his entire personality, become embittered, and thereby overlook other avenues for growth.

Superstitions and misinformation about physique, sex, heredity, physiology, or mental functions may be influential in producing disturbing attitudes about oneself. You may not be comparing yourself with others of similar background, advantages, and disadvantages. You may be expecting unrealistic accomplishments.

OBSERVATION OF OTHERS HELPS ACHIEVE PERSPECTIVE. Preoccupation with our own negative traits also often prevents our seeing *others who experience feelings of inferiority,* or who have some odd physical feature or other inadequacy. Poor perspective also shows itself when we imagine ourselves to be inferior *merely because we are not superior or excellent.* Persons with unusually high aspirations may fail to hit the mark of perfection and be unhappy although they are average or well above average. This person may be quite acceptable or even superior in other traits that others consider as important as the one that is disturbing him. Discussion and free writing about oneself very often produces perspective, which allows one to see oneself as a total individual with some faults and short-comings but with *assets and potentials for adventurous development.*

The incident from Arthur's experience as given below indicates the effect of identifying oneself with someone of whom we have a favorable impression.

One day in early adolescence, while Arthur was buying a hat, he looked into the three-panel mirror and saw his profile for the first time. It was a new perspective and a shock to him. He saw his protruding nose, receding chin, and large Adam's apple. He recalled this image frequently thereafter and brooded over it. Throughout his high school years, he habitually held his hand at the side of his face so others could not see his profile. He thought that, if they saw how he looked in profile, they would reject him. (The counselor regarded Arthur as a boy of average or superior appearance. To be sure, there are others who have more attractive profiles, but the counselor could see no reason for Arthur's concern. He encouraged Arthur to express his feelings freely about his physiognomy.)

Arthur would never have been able to talk about his facial features had it not been for an acquaintance he had made recently. This friend was tall, superior to Arthur in athletics, meticulously neat, had some very attractive clothes, and was well-liked by the other fellows. He had social poise and ease and seemed to accept himself and to behave with confidence. Arthur was attracted to him in friendship principally because he felt that this boy had a profile very similar to his, "yet in spite of it he was quite well-liked by others." This insight came to Arthur: Maybe a profile like mine is not a source of rejection and social failure; maybe it is only one aspect of one's personality. His perspective arose mainly through knowing this other student. It also allowed him to ventilate the whole matter with the counselor.

One is obtaining self-understanding and perspective when one can *accept* himself as not too undesirable or as one of the group, and yet see the need for personal improvement and for implementing this need with normal efforts. This is the antithesis of regarding oneself as hopelessly inadequate and of feeling that drastic and immediate changes are needed. The latter attitude amounts to rejection of and hostility toward oneself.

Inferiority Feelings as a Defense. Sometimes a youth will discover that those aspects of his behavior that irritate others and yet seem hard to control may be the results of his own feeling of insecurity and inadequacy. Such behavior is illustrated by tendencies to brag, to be conspicuously in the limelight, to be irritable, loud, domineering, and aggressive. He may realize that these symptoms of inferiority alienate him from his fellows. With this realization comes an understanding of the cause of this behavior that seems so impulsive. He may go so far as to discover that he can eradicate this behavior most effectively by attempting to gain inner security.

In raising questions about the basis for one's inferiority, it might be well to pose the following: To what extent is the unpleasantness and withdrawal that accompany the inferiority complex an example of self-punishment?

Those individuals who feel inferior sometimes find their acquaintances think more of them than they realize. The following experiment is suggested. Type off five or six copies of the *rating scale* which appears in the accompanying volume, *Teaching Personal Adjustment: An Instructor's Manual*, and present them to your friends, asking them to fill them out anonymously and mail them to you. Your associates will be glad to do this frankly if they know that others are filling out the same blanks about you at the same time, and that you will be unable to identify the authors of specific remarks, but rather see the response of your friends as a group. One might ask himself if his feeling of inadequacy is satisfying in any way. Does it protect him from the unpleasantness of making contacts? To what extent is a given inferiority complex an attempt to shield the ego, to prevent more disturbing anxiety?

Accomplishment in an "Important" Endeavor Will Assist in Removing Feelings of Inferiority. If you feel inferior in respect to physical activities, would it be well to pursue systematically some athletic game, take lessons in it, get someone who is superior to teach you, or learn by yourself through trial and error, as suggested in Chapter 5?

If you believe your deficiency is in your natural appearance, improve it as much as you can by habits of neatness, grooming, selection of attractive colors, and the like. Remember that *good looks are largely a matter of grooming*, dressing, and good social skills, as shown in Chapter 10. Too often those of mediocre looks assume mediocre habits of care. You might ask yourself what is the relative importance of innate physical traits. Are those you like best the handsomest by nature? You might start a project of meticulous grooming, of washing, dyeing, pressing, and polishing, as suggested in Chapter 10. You may notice immediately the reactions of your friends to this and your own feeling of well-being.

There are few deficiencies that the average human being cannot overcome with systematic, daily effort if he does not expect the impossible of himself. If he at no time frankly faces his deficiency and does not convert his worry into a program of work, naturally he will be depressed. This activity is a conscious form of compensation (see pages 75 to 76).

It may be that accomplishment in *some other related field* in which success is more probable will have greater value. It is important that the person who feels inferior find some avenue into which to direct his energy as soon as he has discovered the area of his assets. Children of withdrawn personalities developed initiative when allowed to play freely alone at camp, later in small groups, and finally in large ones (470). Sometimes responsibilities in group organizations give the individual a chance to excel. We can always harness our energies and receive recognition if we attack community problems or if we join organizations that have goals of service to other individuals. The best way to forget oneself is to *help others* to meet their difficulties.

There are persons who have felt inferior and have *associated themselves with groups or movements* and have with time obtained strength from this affiliation. As a result they have made a major contribution to their organization. Others have started new groups or movements and have gained confidence through their successes. Belonging to the group has allowed them to identify themselves with the strength and magnitude of the group. It consists in losing oneself in an activity outside oneself and thereby finding potentiality and growth. After having success in non-self-centered activity one might be provoked to ask himself: Why didn't I find earlier these interests, adventures, and needs that are bigger than my own petty problems? Sometimes an individual like Herbert finds a role he can play and in playing it discovers himself, his strengths and weaknesses, and adds to his social skills.

Herbert T., as a freshman in college, was extremely self-conscious—so much so that he blushed scarlet whenever he was embarrassed. He never ventured to answer questions, even though he knew the answers, was terrified whenever called upon in class, and would state that he did not know the answer rather than attempt it. He had always been a shy child, and his family's manner of living had accentuated his shyness. They were retiring as a group and protected him and his sister. Herbert always received above-average grades and was an excellent, conscientious worker. He had participated to a moderate degree in sports and had the appearance and mannerisms of a regular fellow.

At the end of his freshman year, he secured a job in the largest theater in the college town. For this job he had to be well groomed and wear a uniform. The job was an entirely new experience to Herbert because his life in a small town of a thousand inhabitants had afforded him no experience with large groups of people, especially strangers. His job required him to assume the ascendant role, since he had to speak to patrons to learn their wishes regarding seating and then seat them. At first he felt very awkward, but the night-after-night repetition of social contact, of ascendancy, produced some results. At first this behavior remained tied up with the job and did not transfer to other situations, but his attitude toward himself and his confidence gradually improved throughout college, largely because of this role he had learned to play.

Upon completing his university course, he was inducted into a professional branch of the Army, became an officer, and again slipped into a uniform with all its accompanying flourishes. After three years in this role, he was quite different in outer behavior from the freshman he had been. He seemed to be much more ascendant and confident, capable of assuming responsibility and taking the initiative in a situation.

Sometimes experience over a period of time in the sort of environment discussed in Chapter 5 will lead to a more *realistic perception of one's self—a better self-acceptance* as shown by Leonard N.

Leonard N. was a sophomore when he first consulted the counselor. He had marked feelings of inadequacy and some depression and guilt. He was the youngest of four boys who had been greatly overprotected by a doting mother. Although above average in practically all respects, Leonard was less well-built, less popular, and less athletically inclined than two older brothers, both of whom were exceptional in leadership, social poise, and athletics. Leonard had spent more time than any of the other boys with their mother and was undoubtedly her favorite. She shielded him from much of the give-and-take of childhood, and he had never developed the toughness of some of the other boys. At puberty he had been with a group of boys who had engaged in sex play, and he felt extremely guilty about this. Although he had a very superior aptitude, his grades were mediocre. His outstanding symptoms were his feeling of inferiority, his inability to get down to work and produce results, and the unevenness of his behavior. At times he could put on a front of sociality and dominance, but this balloon was easily punctured, and then he felt he was insincere and a fraud and tended to feel depressed and unworthy for a period of time. He finally graduated with a major in English and worked in publicity for a while. As soon as he left home and shifted for himself, compared himself and had contacts with the average population rather than with the highly selected group of boys in his fraternity, his perspective changed somewhat. Accomplishments on the job also boosted his morale. Frequently in college he said that the one obsession he had was that *he would be a bum* and never fit in with the demands of society. He felt that he would never stay with a job and accomplish what his brothers had. At that time he did not see clearly that he was trying to live the sort of life his brothers had lived, despite the fact that his aptitudes, interests, and whole personality pattern were different. Even the people he enjoyed were not those whom his brothers found interesting. He had failed to meet his brothers' standards but he had not failed in being the kind of person he could best be. Over a ten-year period after college, he came more and more to accept himself as he really was. He compared himself less frequently with his brothers. He gave up the notion of being eminently successful in an extroverted career, encouraged his interests in the arts and literature, and developed deeper friendships with people of similar interests. He became an officer in the early days of service and was promoted rapidly. At the end of hostilities he had accomplished enough, had gained enough perspective about people. On visiting the same counselor he had consulted many times in college, he stated without realizing it, "When I get this uniform off *I am going to be a bum.* I know that I am not one of the best contemporary writers, but writing is what I want to do, and I have an opportunity to work as a free-lance writer. I know it means being a bum, but I am going to enjoy it." Here is an individual who did not change in basic traits, but his *whole perspective and frame of reference had changed* throughout the years. No doubt his guilt had lessened and his attitude toward himself had improved.

As pointed out on page 393 in connection with the prevention of depressions, absorption with events outside of ourselves is of some help along with the other suggestions given above. For example:

One city dweller describes a hobby that makes going to and coming from work a pleasant adventure. He selects certain houses and persons and tries to imagine the life that goes on beyond the façade. He has become quite a student of human nature and architecture through this interesting hobby.

Often we under-rate our wider possibilities. We fail to call upon the capacities that are available to us. We function on a level far below our possibilities, or we try in a field for which we do not have great aptitude and overlook one in which development is possible. Now and then an ordinary person sees his potentialities, pulls himself together, realizes that it is usually single persons, working with and through groups, who solve human problems and often accomplish what previously was thought to be impossible. Sometimes individuals with conviction demonstrate the great potentialities of persons to develop, to improve astonishingly their initial performance, and with time become expert in a given field. History is replete with persons who were regarded as ordinary human beings but who *used their ordinary capacities in an extraordinary manner.* Certainly most of us, if we realize daily our abilities as average human beings, could move toward a solution of our personal problems and make a contribution to society. (For more specific suggestions see Chapters 5, 10, and 11.)

Reducing Self-Consciousness

Description of Self-Conscious Reaction

"I have a pronounced tendency to become self-conscious when I walk into a gathering of people, particularly if I think they are watching me. In extreme instances, I experience cold chills up and down my spine. If I have to talk to a group my knees tremble. The tremor in my hands does not allow me to read from a paper. My voice seems strange to me. It is impersonal, high-pitched, and strained. I am conscious of my facial movements.

"Since I have taken courses in psychology I can identify some of the physiological responses that occur. I realize that thermal sensations in the head, spinal region, or elsewhere are due to changes in blood circulation. I know that the sensations in the abdominal region are the cessation of the peristaltic movements. The increased heartbeat and breathing rate are easy to identify. I know that my increased energy is due to the adrenalin that is secreted in the blood stream. I know that I have more energy than I can control at the moment. This is why I tremble and feel awkward. I realize that the blood volume becomes greater in the periphery or limbs of my body. I realize that at some times I am conscious of these changes and at other times of other changes. This difference is due no doubt to the intensity of the changes and the direction of my attention.

"I am aware that all these sensations and reactions are *natural events in fear*. I know that if I could react in an adaptive manner I could harness some of the energy and be less disturbed. There was a time when I was embarrassed by these reactions, ashamed to let others know that I lost control of myself, but now I have an entirely different attitude. I try to behave in a manner which will help me to adjust to the situation and ignore or smile inwardly at these drastic changes in my physiological processes. This emotion no longer confuses me as it once did. I know that many people in the audience have gone through the same experience and that they will respect me if I gain control of myself, and if I don't they will be sympathetic."

Who Is Self-Conscious? Self-consciousness is often associated with feelings of inferiority. It, too, is a symptom of anxiety and conflicts in a social situation. Much that has been said previously about causes, control and personality patterns of those experiencing feelings of inferiority hold for self-consciousness. Certain facts and suggestions that may be helpful at times of self-consciousness are presented here with possible advantage to the reader.

Certain persons are more acutely and more frequently self-conscious than others. The shy, introverted individual seems to be more self-conscious than the active, social extrovert. The person who has high standards and is trying to guide his behavior in terms of these standards is also more self-conscious than others. Anyone who is learning a new skill or reacting to a new situation is likely to be self-conscious. Certainly all of us are self-conscious some of the time. Many persons believe, while they are experiencing self-consciousness, that they alone are bothered by this attitude. At some ages, particularly during adolescence, self-consciousness occurs more frequently. It has been emphasized that many of our great leaders of the past were self-conscious (645). Most individuals tend to lose their self-consciousness with middle age, or as they habituate themselves to the typical events of their lives.

Those who do not recover from extreme self-consciousness by the time they have reached middle age should seek professional advice. Similarly, those who must retire from normal social life because of the painfulness which attends meeting others would be aided by psychiatric or psychological sessions.

Suggestions for Overcoming Self-Consciousness. Below is a list of suggestions that have been made for the alleviation of self-consciousness (645). They were given to students in a class in applied psychology who rated them from 1 to 10 (10 is the highest value) on the basis of their own past experience. Accompanying each suggestion on the list is the average rating for the class.

1. Face the situation. Attend to it, not to yourself. Self-consciousness is usually a withdrawal attitude. Average, 8.3.

2. Believe in your message, your activity, your personality. Average, 7.5.

3. Achievement tends to eliminate self-consciousness because the individual realizes his success and feels he is looked up to by others. Average, 7.4.

4. Realize your auditor is probably thinking of himself and not of you. Average, 7.2.

5. Lack of adjustment is due to inertness and lack of activity. Adopt a spontaneous attitude. Go through motions. Take an aggressive attitude. Average, 6.9.

6. Self-consciousness may and does occur in everyone under some circumstances. Average, 6.8.

7. Self-consciousness goes hand in hand with the inferiority complex. Find the cause of the feeling of inferiority; remove it or see its significance. See that it comes from the past (it usually does). Average, 6.1.

8. Use special devices to produce successful experiences with others. These vary with individuals. They are acts that make individuals feel at ease. Average, 6.1.

9. Realize that self-consciousness is not suddenly eliminated. Average, 5.9.

10. Note flaws in others—cases in which others are self-conscious. Average, 5.9.

11. Realize that self-consciousness is not a disease or an ailment intrinsic to personality, but only an attitude, an introverted one, an attitude of looking inward instead of outward, an attitude of looking at oneself. Average, 5.79.

Physique and Self-Consciousness. Most men and women differ in some degree from the physical ideal that is held up to them as approximating perfection at any given time or place. Not all men, for example, fit the ideal masculine physique or have typical masculine interests and attitudes (351).

Tall men are sometimes described as prone to self-consciousness (703). One study shows, however, that they differ in their reactions to height (642). These differences no doubt are due to many factors in their background and experience, such as kidding, nagging, and inability to use standard equipment with comfort in trains, buses, automobiles, and hotels. Others regard their height as an asset and as productive of respect from women. The suggestions given to tall men do not differ from many of the others mentioned in this section, namely, not to emphasize the differences between themselves and others, but to be frank about their deviation from the norm and use it as an asset whenever possible. Many learn to dress, dance, and walk in a manner to enhance their posture. They get people to laugh with them rather than at them. They tease back if necessary, and take lessons in any skill in which they feel awkward (642).

Stage Fright an Extreme Example of Self-Consciousness. Many of the characteristics of the student who is subject to self-consciousness are accentuated in stage fright. All the fear reactions occur. It is a more complex experience because the individual *must* respond. Usually the spotlight is centered on him. He realizes this and knows that his responses fall short of what they might be, and he is chagrined.

The speaker who is in the grip of stage fright feels awkward. He has difficulty facing his audience calmly. He trembles, blanches, blushes, or becomes tense. He is somewhat less effective than he could be since his attention is divided between what he is saying, his audience's reaction, and the ignominy of failing to meet his goal. He is unable to meet the gathering in an amiable, calm, and creative manner.

WHAT THE SPEAKER DOES NOT REALIZE. The typical audience may be described as receptive. Their presence demonstrates their interest in the speaker's message. They enjoy a smooth-running performance. If the speaker fails, they suffer along with him. They are sympathetic. They therefore prefer to see him succeed. Furthermore, the typical audience is a homogeneous group. If the speaker finds the motives of this group and satisfies them, he can then proceed to deliver his message with the feeling that they are with him.

SUGGESTIONS FOR OVERCOMING STAGE FRIGHT. The suggestions that we shall give here do not differ in the main from those given earlier. We shall merely apply them to the self-consciousness that occurs when one assumes the role of performer.

1. Talk it out freely with a teacher of speech. Insist that he let you "get it off your chest" first. Find the cause of the emotional disturbance. Is the audience a sea of upturned, hostile faces or are you overly conscious of some aspect of your personality? Do you fear that you cannot finish your performance without a flaw?

2. Your next task is to associate calm responses with the performer-before-an-audience situation. This will require time and numerous experiences. Begin talking spontaneously at every opportunity such as small and more comfortable and unimportant groups. *Do not expect to do well at first.* Stay with them until you gain confidence, then move to those which seem more difficult. Speech-training courses help (267). Remedy the situation by adequate preparation and reducing all factors that may concern you during the speech, as poor grooming, pronunciation, uncertainty about facts, etc.

3. Use all the devices you find effective. Relaxation is an excellent aid to most people. (See page 449.)

One reason for your disturbance is the excess energy fear has produced in your system. You therefore tremble and are confused. It has been suggested that some of this excess energy be harnessed in some way both before and when you rise to perform. Take papers out of your pocket and place them on the lectern. Take a drink of water. Some have suggested recalling reasons why you are considered competent to speak while you await your turn.

4. Practice the techniques of successful orators to remove self-consciousness in public speaking. A few suggestions follow: Know your audience. Speak directly to them and be guided by their responses. Use vivid illustrations, anecdotes, diagrams, jokes, and other means of keeping their attention. These are important, particularly in the beginning. Have your message well organized. Do not try to teach them too much at one time. Elaborate on a *few* basic points. Most of your speech should con-

sist of illustrations. Build up to a climax. End abruptly. Do not talk too long.

As you discover that these and other similar activities win your audience, confidence in yourself will grow.

Stuttering. About 1 per cent of the population stutters. Stuttering varies from a marked, conspicuous retardation in speech to a mental disturbance of which the auditor is unaware. In the latter, the individual merely has a mental block as he is about to speak. It occurs for just a few seconds, and then he is able to go on with the conversation.

The speech mechanism of the stutterer is practically always normal. Studies of stutterers have shown them to differ from nonstutterers in having more stuttering ancestors, belonging more frequently to twinning families, and, according to some investigators, exhibiting more left-handedness and more differences in some physiological rhythms (632, 807). Factors such as pampering and disturbed attitude toward parents have been mentioned also (668, 429). The major factor at the basis of the problem of stuttering is usually an emotional one involving the whole personality (389).

SUGGESTIONS FOR THE STUTTERER. The stutterer will want to raise some questions similar to those raised in our discussion of inferiority. Does stuttering gain anything for you now or did it in the past? Does it restrict your activities, defend you from unpleasantness or anxiety? (389) Is it a form of self-punishment?

Rollie McKenna

It is not our purpose to discuss comprehensively the causes of stuttering, as specialists do not themselves agree. We shall give some of the methods for alleviating the stutterer's distress because there is some agreement on them.

1. See a specialist who is known for his ability in this field. Many universities have speech, psychological, or psychiatric clinics that aim to help the student to improve his oral language. The negative attitude that the student often holds has been acquired over a long period of time, and a new attitude cannot be established in a day or two. Usually the stutterer feels insecure, and stuttering is regarded as his most conspicuous trait. He would be more secure if he had outstanding accomplishments and interests so that he could think: "I am an individual with many characteristics, some of which are very desirable. Among my characteristics is the habit of stuttering."

2. Relaxation is very helpful to the stutterer. (See below.) Some relaxation can be achieved indirectly by acquiring attitudes that involve a sense of humor.

3. Any disturbing factor in his life should be understood. Stuttering is often regarded as a symptom of underlying anxiety and conflicts. Some stutterers are reacting to a strict father as they stutter before all persons in authority, or to a feeling of inferiority that is due to their family background. Others are responding to symbols of other events in their early life.

Relaxation an Aid to Adjustment. Most mental problems, such as fear, worry, self-consciousness, depression, and inferiority feelings cause tension. Those who are troubled by these problems become emotional and rigid. Very often this tension becomes a habit, and the individual becomes habitually high-strung. It is well, first, to *remove the cause of the problem before attempting to reduce the tension.* Once the conditions giving rise to the problem cease to operate, the habitual tension can be removed more easily. The following methods are suggested for relieving tension (373).

1. The individual must *learn* the habit of relaxing. This habit must be a substitute for the contrary habit of tensing. Once the habit has been acquired, it will not be difficult for one to think, "Relax!" and thereby arouse the relaxed behavior, just as when one plunges into the water one immediately arouses the habit of swimming.

2. Tense persons cannot relax at will, so they begin by forcing relaxation. In order to achieve this one must first *contract* the arm as completely as possible, then relax it completely. This must be done several times until the arm becomes entirely limp. The same should be done with the other arm, then with each leg successively. Finally, one should

relax the throat and eye muscles. These can be tensed and then relaxed. The eye muscles are tensed by placing the fingers on the nose and fixating on them, then allowing the eyes to relax.

3. After all the skeletal muscles have been relaxed successively, try to relax them in patterns. The two arms can be contracted together and relaxed. Then the arms and legs, then the rest of the body. This exercise will take time. The individual should go through it several times a day. Then he should practice relaxing the entire body at different times throughout the day. You may care to plan a program of relaxation exercises throughout the day and keep a record.

When we are carrying on daily activities we frequently tense more of the body than is necessary. Such tension does not make our activities more effective. Rather, excessive tension detracts from nearly every skilled act. The best dancers are those who use only the necessary muscles. All of us have had the experience of dancing with "muscle-bound" people. They are tense and make dancing a workout rather than a delightful social relaxation. This also holds for swimming, tennis, basketball, and any other athletic games.

Most persons do not realize how tense they are. They are not aware of the value of relaxation for them. To convince yourself of this, go through the relaxing exercises for the next five minutes, then attempt to relax while you read. You will notice that a certain amount of tension is necessary for you to remain alert; beyond that point tension can be excessive. Relaxation is particularly recommended to those who are self-conscious or worried, or who have other nervous habits.

Self-Confidence. The trait of self-confidence is in contrast to anxiety, inferiority, self-consciousness, and emotional instability. The more self-confident individual ventures into new territory with ease and pleasure. He views himself and others more positively. He is less rigid and can be said to have greater ego-strength (218, 44). Just as the anxiety condition is built up over a period of years as the result of many fearful experiences, so self-confidence is built up as the result of a feeling of inner security and success in areas that the individual *considers important* to him as a total person, accomplishments that affect his self-concept (779). These areas may be in personal efficiency, academic success, social adjustment, leadership in social groups, or the respect and affection of the opposite sex. Methods of achieving success in these fields have been discussed in the chapters on these topics.

The confident individual tends to face his fears and build habits of success in their stead. He is in the process of developing a *strong ego,*

. . . self-confidence . . . as the result of a feeling of inner security and success in areas that the individual considers important to him as a total person . . .

he is integrating his experiences, and is acquiring an acceptable attitude toward himself. He usually knows how he stands on important issues (has a personal philosophy of life) and is maturely motivated. The importance of these attitudes has been discussed in Chapter 7. The confident individual has learned to expect progress if he plans and works hard. His experiences have taught him that he need not worry over his role in future events. With an attitude of this type he is quite often successful, and this success increases his previous confidence.

He who lacks self-confidence may profit from the insight aroused by issues presented here. He should discover the origin of his greatest fears and the sources of insecurity, a wounded ego, and inferiority. He may strive for accomplishments first in those fields in which he has aptitudes or interests. As he develops there he may extend his efforts elsewhere.

Supplementary Readings

H. L. Ansbacher and R. R. Ansbacher, *The Individual Psychology of Alfred Adler*, Basic Books, 1956.

G. Murphy, *Personality*, Harper, 1947.

P. M. Symonds, *The Ego and the Self*, Appleton-Century-Crofts, 1951.

In addition see the references cited by number in the chapter and appearing in the bibliography of an accompanying volume entitled *Teaching Personal Adjustment: An Instructor's Manual.*

Rollie McKenna

A s a college student you desire friends, clothes, popularity, vocational success, a good school record, the mastery of certain scholarly pursuits, and supremacy for your ideals and the groups of your affiliation. You are *motivated*. But you have not attained success in all these realms. You are, to some extent, *frustrated*. Furthermore, some of your wishes and attitudes *conflict*. But you have not quit; you are constantly seeking new ways to satisfy these motives, to *readjust*. We have presented discussions of the general principles of conflict and adjustment as well as discussions and some suggestions for meeting problems in areas in which you are thwarted. It is appropriate, in the final summation, to ask to what extent you have been building traits which make it more easy for you to meet new frustrations and conflicts. To what extent have you found ways to reduce anxiety, to satisfy your needs over the long span, and build traits that enable you to live with the inevitable conflicts and anxiety that may not easily be reduced? After a brief summary of the generalizations about adjustment, we shall turn to a discussion of the nature of the adjustive and mature student, the wholesome society, and questions of mental hygiene.

452

CHAPTER 16

THE ADJUSTIVE
PERSONALITY

The Meaning of Adjustment

Generalizations about Adjustment. In Chapters 1 and 3 we saw
the adjustment process in essence as gaining perspective or broader
understanding and using it in the building of habits and attitudes or
the changing of environment to meet the thwarted or unsatisfied motives. That discussion pivoted on a simple act of adjustment as the
basic process for the complex adjustment found in the many-sided
daily life of the typical college student. Here we go beyond single
acts of adjustment to a consideration of the adjustment of a given
person. The term *adjustiveness* is more appropriate for our discussion here because we are constantly implying that the persons who
seem "well adjusted" have traits that enable them to meet the conditions of their lives satisfactorily and to learn the behavior required by
them. What generalizations can we venture concerning the adjustment of the *entire person* in a given culture? (502, 61, 777, 422)

HUMAN ADJUSTMENT IS TO SYMBOLS THAT READILY CONFLICT. First,
most of our adjustments are to *symbols:* to causes, honors, wishes,
ideals, social relationships. These symbols are laden with *emotion.*

453

We rarely inspect *all* that a symbol means. How many of us could take an examination on the meaning of American Democracy, Spanish Fascism, Russian Communism, or Presbyterian Christianity? Nevertheless, all of us *feel* definitely about them. We sometimes support two causes that are *incompatible*, as, for example, the Klansman who is convinced that he is a patriotic American, or the barely ethical businessman who believes he is a true Christian. Many of us have grown up without realizing that we hate some aspects of causes we espouse because we have never fully understood them. As we shall see shortly we are born not into a well-ordered society but into one filled with conflicts that we introject and must solve.

ADJUSTMENT IS CONTINUAL. Human beings never remain entirely adjusted. Biological and social needs are too persistent and ever-changing. With new inventions and technological progress our society changes. Furthermore, we are limited in time and abilities and cannot satisfy all the needs that arise. Adjustment is a *continuous* process. The dead man is the only completely adjusted individual. Moreover, complete adjustment might be undesirable. The individual who constantly remains in fair adjustment to his environment has been referred to as "bovine." *Plasticity of behavior* amid continuity seems to be a more desirable condition.

Frequently, *transient maladjustment* is necessary in order to motivate the individual to acquire new traits so that he may develop. We showed in our discussion of inferiority feelings that handicaps often "make a man" by causing him to compensate desirably.

The homesick freshman is maladjusted. A permanent return home would be the easiest way to adjustment. Certainly, to stay in school and fight his battle will continue the maladjustment for a time. By his senior year, however, this maladjustment will have earned a healthy growth for him. Life is a continual struggle. With traits appropriate to the demands of the individual, and with a sufficient capacity to learn and solve the problems that new conditions bring the struggle may be regarded as a satisfying and interesting game. Otherwise, it results in many psychic scars.

Definition of Individual Adjustment. The question now arises, "Who are the individuals high in adjustiveness and who are the individuals who show limited adjustiveness? When does one make a sustained good adjustment?"

You are high in adjustiveness if you can *meet broadly your long term needs with the resources available in your environment.* Your needs are specifically determined by the cultural *milieu* (customs, ideals, and attitudes) in which you live. You may recognize and assume as part of your environment all or only a *fragment* of this culture.

For example, as a college fraternity man you may think, along with your brothers, that chapter prestige, dances, dates, popularity, clothes, and campus offices are important. You may, on the other hand, get along well with the fellows but not consider their attitudes important, and therefore not attempt to adjust to them. You may find one or two of the more mature, better-read members who think as you do in terms of the importance of liberal attitudes in these times, and from then on you may associate mainly with these men.

Whether you remain adjusted to your environment depends on how much you and it change. In evaluating your adjustment you must consider all your motives (urges, wishes, and tendencies) and all the habits and attitudes that you use to satisfy your organic, social, and personal demands. You must consider your entire personality. Furthermore, you must speculate about your *future* demands and your pliability in the development of new habits and attitudes. In addition, you must know whether your behavior is compatible with that of your fellows, whether your adjustment is *socially oriented*. A humanitarian factory owner cannot live happily in luxury when he sees the low wages he pays leading to dire human need and to crime.

Effective adjustment often consists in *changing environment rather than in conforming to it*. Many of the great personages in history as well as the more obscure leaders have adjusted to their inner environment, to the truth as they and fellow thinkers saw it, rather than to the *status quo* or to high authority (340). The question always arises, of course, of the rightness of one's own convictions when they differ from the group's. Is one a leader adjusting to facts or an eccentric, a paranoid, adjusting to one's own defenses and escapes? In science the laboratory and the experimental method can be used to validate facts. Time and experience are testers of truth. The test of reason and belief has been discussed more fully in Chapter 7. Adjustment through changing an environment, by developing rather than by conforming, is a difficult but from many standpoints a higher level of adjustment.

From this viewpoint an individual may be *adjusted at one time* of life and not at another; he may be adjusted to *one aspect of life* and not to another. Many poorly adjusted adolescents may have been regarded as well-adjusted children. Some poor students are good athletes. In the cases of George N. and Henry T. in Chapter 1 we found respectively a student who was poorly adjusted in childhood and better adjusted in college and a student who is rather well adjusted to intellectual pursuits yet poorly adjusted in terms of competitive sports and extracurricular activities. In recent warfare there were frequent cases of combat fatigue in which the individual who had passed all the various screenings for emotional stability broke under continual battle pressure and, later, with proper treatment apparently recovered quite completely (155). There were, however, cases of neurotics who had long and successful combat experience without any emotional break (574). Moreover, studies of two different groups of former problem children while in service showed that many made good adjustments (475). Certainly not all well-adjusted adolescents will remain adjusted throughout life. Every change of party administration in Washington causes many politicians to be poorly adjusted. Some persons are temporarily maladjusted, and some remain maladjusted most of their lives.

Adjustment in the western world may be thought of as presenting at least four major areas: adjustment to physiological urges, to work, to people, and to one's inner standards. We saw in one of the cases of college students, Ned J. (in Chapter 4), an example of success in adjustment to school work and responsibilities but of failure in adjustment to the boys in his fraternity. Another student, Tom G., was very popular, yet he was nearly eliminated from school because of poor grades.

The mere fact that one has built traits, habits, and attitudes that clash with social environments he has met does not mean that he cannot be placed in another environment with resultant success or that he cannot gain new habits and attitudes. Jesus of Nazareth, Saul of Tarsus (St. Paul), Woodrow Wilson at the time of his death, Galileo when he published some of his results—all were out of adjustment to their environment or times. We now regard all these men as having made major contributions to the development of our civilization.

It is well established that some persons we consider "crazy" would be accepted as normal in other cultures. Some of our epileptic, senile, psychotic, and hysterical personalities could find a cultural group some place in the world where they would be accepted and even honored (60). Many of these persons have attempted to adjust to conflicting standards and, from the standpoint of the prevailing culture, they are failures.

The odds are against the successful adjustment of the individual who has traits and habits that are incompatible with his needs and who remains in or transfers to the same general type of environment. The old traits, habits, and attitudes often persist into the new, similar situation unless there has been a change of orientation, as in the case below.

Alfred K. had a year and a half of college before he was drafted. He came to rush week as a freshman, had a glorious round of parties, assumed the attitude that college was a place to have a good time, and was not initiated the first semester because of low grades. He transferred to another school, with only transient change in attitude. He still regarded studies as a bore and contacts with others as of primary importance. His grades were barely high enough for him to remain in school. In short, this prewar period was one in which he gained very little knowledge or maturity. His whole orientation was adolescent.

He returned to school after four years in the Army, two of which had been spent overseas. He had realized in this time the importance of science, geography, history, and other disciplines in the world of affairs as well as in combat. He was more serious and, although his major goal was to establish himself vocationally, he developed considerable social consciousness, a realization of the need for providing opportunities for educational, social, and economic development of all people. He regarded most of the boys who were just out of high school and very much like he had been previously as intolerable kids. He achieved a grade average that was quite admirable.

Continuous failure is another extremely frustrating condition. It destroys personal morale. Most persistently maladjusted individuals *need guidance* in order to discover their inner trends and to build habits and attitudes when placed in a new situation—this is called counseling or psychotherapy.

The Persistently Maladjusted Individual. *Neurotic and psychotic personalities.* People often regard the persistently maladjusted individual as *intrinsically* incapable of adjustment. These persons seem difficult or peculiar to those around them (neurotic), and in extreme cases psychotic or mentally ill. It is difficult to know what percentage of our population is neurotic. Much depends upon the degree of disturbance necessary for the label "neurotic" to be applied. Various more careful estimates run from 3 per cent "more or less disabled" to around 27 per cent (436).

Neurotic individuals vary greatly, are sane, sometimes "very successful" in business or creative ventures (16), but their emotional and social adjustment to life is difficult. One writer states that psychological patients in war served as long and at least as well as, and earned about as many decorations as, the average soldier (546). Persons with neuroses have severe anxieties, feelings of guilt, unresolved and trapping conflicts, or are obsessed with ideas or impulses that dominate them. Life for them is a continual emotional struggle. After qualified professional treatment, however, the majority show improved adjustment (25, 529).

Psychotic individuals suffer from a mental disorder of one type or another. They usually are hospitalized. Unlike the neurotic individuals, they often show little insight into their condition, and their contact with the real world around them is lost or distorted. The neurotic is highly anxious, in frequent conflict, and struggles with the events in his life rather than completely withdrawing from them. The psychotic may, as in *schizophrenia*, withdraw from society and exhibit behavior difficult to understand, such as mutism, silly talk and actions, belief that they are persecuted or are exalted personages; or they may become expansive, somewhat uncontrollably excited or very deeply depressed and suicidal, as in the *manic-depressive psychosis*. With proper diagnosis and appropriate professional treatment many psychotics improve and return to a more useful life in the realistic world.

THE BASES AND COURSE OF EMOTIONAL DISTURBANCES. Schizophrenia is found more frequently in families with previous histories of the disorder (402), but there are many from such families who survive the ravages of civilized life without severe emotional disturbance. The nature and the role of *constitutional weakness* in emotional disorders have not been determined. It is not known how much of the weakness is also due to early environmental frustration. A large number of psychiatrists see that adjustments to a complex social culture are important in the background of mental disorders. Emphasis is placed upon the roles the individual has difficulty in learning to play and on the *conflicts that involve the individual's self-esteem and ego* and that make him feel unworthy (122). They can point to a study such as the one which compared 100 soldiers with psychiatric illness with 1000 successful combat soldiers. No differences were found between the two groups in heritage or background, yet the groups differed in the number of neurotic traits among the 100 men (478). Others insist that such breaks as were found at Dunkirk among only a certain percentage of soldiers, while the majority showed rapid spontaneous recovery, give evidence of constitutional predisposition to emotional disturbances (22). Most authorities today see severe emotional disturbances as an *interaction* of basic constitutions and the events in the individual's development.

It has been shown through group statistics that wars, depressions, and unemployment do not lead to increases in the rate of hospitalization due to mental disease. Suicide rates even drop in war time (483, 23). However, we must ask again if wars, depressions, and waves of unemployment which affect practically everyone, if not actually at least in imagination, can be as frustrating as failure during a period of prosperity, which reflects on the individual as a person (420). Such individual factors as *shame, feeling of unworthiness as a person, and feeling cut off from others* are most devastating in effect. In war, if group or individual morale is high, and if there is no conflict within the individual, it is astonishing what he can withstand. Furthermore, it is known that, when many who show rather far-reaching abnormal symptoms are given proper treatment, the symptoms disappear. This treatment consists in removing them from the precipitating influences, allowing them to rest, giving them professional care, and providing them with opportunities to reorganize their thinking, to gain security, and possibly to get insight into their attitudes and behavior (627). An important aspect of this treatment is not deep analysis but rather positive motivation, helping the individual to identify with his group and reestablishing his place in it (271). A follow-up of some "psychotic" personalities from warfare showed that about 50 per cent of them can be characterized as "well adjusted in community" or "making acceptable adjustment with assistance" (344). Percentages of improvement run even higher in some disorders and in some cases that received modern treatment (25).

The results of organizations of ex-patients of mental hospitals (249) and the accomplishments of Alcoholics Anonymous and individuals like Clifford Beers and A. T. Boisen demonstrate the importance of the human element in recovery. Clifford Beers wrote the book *A Mind that Found Itself* (53) and established the great international Mental Hygiene movement. A. T. Boisen wrote *The Exploration of the Inner World* (83) and has been actively studying mental disorder as a pastoral counselor since his recovery in a mental hospital. Case histories of anonymous ex-alcoholics tell of individuals who have spent years as "drunks" and who have not only been able to recover and lead a normal life but have also been able to help others and to become outstanding members of their communities (6). It is well to be realistic about mental disorders and realize that they have a biological aspect, but at no time is it necessary to take a cold, detached, and fatalistic attitude, to forget that the patient is first of all a person with self-regard and human attitudes and to underestimate the tremendous therapeutic force of inspiration and faith. The individual's attitude toward himself, toward other people, and his relationship to the universe and the Deity are highly important. As one writer said in discussing the history of Reverend Boisen mentioned above:

". . . his people were given the bleak information that recovery was not to be expected. Evidently Boisen was not informed of this bleak prognosis; for he proceeded to recover. However, at first he had trouble convincing his family that the unexpected had taken place so that he was obliged to remain at the hospital longer than would otherwise have been the case. It was during this period that his interest in his own breakdown and in the troubles of his fellow-patients was born. His efforts to learn something about his own case by talking with the physicians at the hospital proved futile: the doctors, according to Boisen, being advocates of the constitutional theory, deemed it unwise to discuss symptoms with the patients" (420).

THE RELATIVE NATURE OF NORMALITY. We cannot emphasize too strongly that what may be considered normal at one time and at one place in the world may be regarded as abnormal in another; that normality and abnormality are relative and there is no absolute line of demarcation between the normal and the abnormal. One is normal if he *meets the demands of the culture he has assimilated over a period of time* (562). He is abnormal if he continues to fail to meet these demands. If he is abnormal either his inner orientation or the environment must be changed. For all practical purposes, adjustment in our culture means a change of self or perspective rather than a radical change of environment. It involves *growth toward a more mature status*, as shown later in this chapter. Most environments are sufficiently complex to allow one to adjust to one aspect even if he is out of adjustment with another. A college student may not be adjusted to the most popular group on the campus, but he can certainly find a number of students with whom he may be congenial.

Whereas adjustment is relative, there are certain minimum standards that any given society makes absolute to some degree. A simple agrarian environment with little civilized encroachment may not stigmatize the low-grade moron who cannot adjust to a high-speed technical culture. Even a mildly psychotic or mentally diseased person may "get by" in this situation or in an overprotective home that assumes responsibility for him and solves his problems. But in modern industrial society the individual who falls short in efficiency or sociality because of mental illness or incompatible traits is conspicuous. For administrative purposes in institutions of medicine, law, and education, absolute standards seem to be preferred. A person is regarded as sick or well, innocent or guilty, passing or failing, and, because of this adminstrative imperative, the differences between the extremes of the group are emphasized rather than the similarities between the borders.

Cultural Concomitants of Mental Health

What are the characteristics of a mentally fit or adjustive individual in our culture? The answer to these questions in a specific form is not easily given, mainly because it is extremely difficult to ascertain what conditions are *productive* of mental health and what conditions are *by-products* or effects of a healthy mind. Furthermore there is not one pattern of adjustment. There are many ways to reduce anxiety and conflicts so that they become motivation for individual creative growth rather than stifling to it, or leading to nonadjustive, rigid conformity or impulsive opportunism. The individual "finds himself," seeks to gain an understanding of what broadly and realistically he may become. He develops an *accurate self-concept* or self-picture that includes his limitations and his possibilities.

Some of the important signs that indicate that an individual enjoys good mental health follow; they are the result of comparisons of "well-adjusted" and "poorly adjusted" individuals (520, 13, 710). All these generalizations must be interpreted in terms of the above discussion of the complex and relative nature of adjustment. It might be well at this point to reread the cases of well- and poorly adjusted students in Chapter 1 and on pages 122 to 129 in Chapter 5.

All the characteristics may be subsumed under one major criterion: the well-adjusted individual has so ordered his life or has been so influenced that *conflict and anxiety are reduced to the minimum*. In addition, he has developed those traits of inner strength that enable him to *endure anxiety while he learns an effective way to reduce it, redirect it and grow* as discussed on page 86 in Chapter 3. Although adjustive individuals may differ greatly in various walks of life, most of the characteristics mentioned will be found in the individual with higher adjustiveness who is resolving his conflicts and growing toward emotional maturity.

HAPPINESS. One characteristic of mental health is relative happiness. Chronic unhappiness usually indicates maladjustment. It is often an index at least of a temporarily unhealthy mind. To use an analogy, it is like a fever, which indicates inner pathology. It is a symptom. The poorly adjusted individual struggles with conflicts. He continually fails to reach unrealistic goals. Most of his activities have an unpleasant background.

Studies show that the happier people are those who are concerned with matters outside themselves rather than preoccupation with their own problems (780); that the happiest period of life for most is when they are working hard bringing up children (439); and that health, faith, cheerful attitude, money, friends, pleasant family relations, and doing things for others are assets in later life.

Happy is the man who can satisfy the basic motives of life, whose bed feels good to him after physical work or play, who looks forward to his meals, enjoys his work no matter how obscure, who appreciates the minor changes and adventures in his life—a moonlit night, strains of music, a beautiful tree in a neatly clipped lawn, burning leaves, sunrises, or even a new route home from work. Particularly happy is the man who *experiences genuine love*, respect, friendships, and adventures *unmarred by the severe strictures of fear, envy, guilt, self-pity, or self-adulation* (671), who feels secure as he aspires to the goals he can reach. Happiness is not synonymous however with the absence of suffering or problems. The happy person does not, on the other hand, punish or injure himself by inordinate feelings of guilt, depressions, or dangerous, impulsive behavior. Such an individual is living *simply, purposefully*, and *realistically* and, as we shall show, attending to the present. His happiness is a by-product of the satisfaction of these motives and is not achieved through pursuit of thrills (477).

MOTIVATION. The above-described individual is purposefully satisfying needs. A youth who is in good mental health attacks the problems he meets; they are challenges, a part of the game of life, and they make life worth while and interesting. The healthy enjoy work as well as play and alternate between them. Under optimal conditions adults retain childhood vivaciousness and interest in life, which some believe is a fundamental property of mind.

Unadjusted individuals sometimes show such strong motivation in a single direction that they will become distinguished in that one field of endeavor (817). This means much to society, but these strongly motivated achievers may be unhappy and lack zest in other aspects of their lives. Their field of accomplishment may be an escape from their maladjustment. A good generalization regarding the most desirable condition of motivation in the lives of human beings is: *The man who is motivated, striving, and zestful in a number of compatible directions within the extent of his capacities and interests reaches optimal adjustment.*

We have discussed in detail the methods of avoiding conflicts between motives in Chapter 3. Under "Personal Philosophy of Life" in Chapter 7 we have seen how the individual may integrate his motives.

SOCIALITY. In our culture the man who has a healthy mind is the man who is adjusted to some of his fellows, who enjoys some human contacts. The cases of well-balanced youths described in Chapter 1 indicate the extent to which such individuals enjoy people, and are motivated by the praise, condemnation, ills, sympathy, and counsel of their fellows (520, 73). We human beings are deeply dependent upon each other for our food, clothing, protection, and indeed for the development of the characteristics that distinguish us from animals. From birth all our habit patterns are so organized around people that inability to adjust to people is a serious handicap. The situations we have learned to value most highly are friendships, social successes, honors, recognitions, and social skills. Being a part of a group that is "our own" has much security value. A sense of rejection by the group is exceedingly disturbing, and if prolonged it may have disastrous consequences.

There are those adjustive persons who are not highly social. They are, however, adjusted to *some* congenial group composed of others like themselves. They may even be opposed to some of the typical activity of the average man. Nevertheless, they may understand the more typical man and appreciate his follies. Though critical of mankind as a whole, they may seek to better his lot. They are humanitarian-minded even though they may seem unsocial. The major aspects of social adjustment were discussed in Chapters 10 and 11.

UNITY AND BALANCE. We mentioned that the adjustive individual has come to understand his goals and limitations. With understanding and resolution of his conflicts over a period of time he develops unity and *integration* of his behavior tendencies. He acquires a more accurate and realistic picture of himself and his potentialities which we have called his *self-concept*.

The "well-adjusted" youths described have many interests, hobbies, and achievements, and their motives tend not to be grossly incompatible with each other. It has been suggested that effective mature adjustment involves both broadening and deepening of interests (841).

Although some adjusted persons may not be balanced in certain *specific* traits, other traits in their personality minimize this imbalance. A very reclusive introvert may write with insight into human nature. When known well this person may be delightful company. His total personality overshadows imperfections.

The opposite of unity and balance is found in the inhibited, puzzled, thwarted youth who "doesn't know where he stands." He would like to be an athlete, but he thinks he is too mediocre. He wants to be the campus Adonis, but he sees himself as lanky and homely. He is *himself*, but he does not want to be himself. He hates and disowns certain parts of his personality. He is a Hamlet, torn between "to be or not to be." To be sure, even the adjustive have conflicts that disturb their equilibrium, but they face their conflicts at the rate at which they can effectively deal with them (73).

We have previously considered more fully the means of achieving unity and emotional stability (Chapter 14). A philosophy of life integrates and unifies the individual and helps him to gain self-consistency. We have defined it and discussed its development in Chapter 7.

ORIENTATION IN THE PRESENT REAL WORLD. The happy, motivated, sociable, integrated individual lives primarily in the present. He is oriented in the *real* world in which he lives. Studies bear this out (520). He is *objective*, does not react to situations with his feelings or take personally little events. He can see occurrences as events in life rather than fearful or depressing experiences involving him.

A comparison of "normal" women to women hospitalized with neuroses shows that they are distinguished not in terms of a lifetime of differences in experiences, but rather in terms of their *reactions to and attitudes regarding* these experiences. The women with neuroses, for example, do not report any greater number of childhood sex aggressions but give them *more significance*. These women show no differences in physical constitution, development, or medical history. The big difference in background, as we might expect from our study of development in Chapter 4, is the extent of conflict, instability, and friction in the home, and in their relationship to their parents. These factors brought about the insecurity and instability in early life (435).

Efficiency involves a characteristic usually attributed to the adjustive person. He shows initiative and interest in the world around him. He is not "in a fog." He has reasonable perspective on the events in his life. The past and the future are important only as they are related to the present. If one aspect of his wide environment does not satisfy his needs, he turns to another rather than turning inward to brood. He is oriented toward a vocation (Chapters 8 and 9). He is improving his work habits (Chapters 2 and 6). The past supplies him with experience and wisdom. His daydreams are usually not a substitute for daily events but a supplement to them. The poorly adjusted student escapes to a dream world of improbable events. He defends himself from reality and its stings by various subjective fears and attitudes of self-inadequacy. Dreams can enrich our lives, but not when they build attitudes that are at odds with the real world.

There are those who have learned the habit of looking outward and enjoying the realities of everyday life better than daydreams. They do not need to see life events in the movies to enjoy them. They appreciate the details in the architecture, landscapes, and human behavior in their own neighborhood. Many times a college student remains oblivious to the beauties of his campus until he notices them through the clever shots of the year-book photographer. He will enjoy the details of structure, form, and human action as seen in a movie or described in a novel depicting college or small town life and miss them in the life which surrounds him. If reality seems dull try seeing the details around you as though you were looking at them for the first or last time, or as though they were a part of a movie or story plot.

ADAPTABILITY. We can best summarize the mentioned characteristics of the mentally fit by saying that he is relatively adaptable. He characteristically *faces the situation as it is,* rather than turning to his inner life as an escape or a defense. As he looks at the situation squarely and *uses a trial-and-error approach,* some solutions suggest themselves. None will be the ideal, but certain solutions will be better than others. He realizes that in real life *many compromises must be made.* He must not expect to find a perfect answer immediately but will accept the best possible solution to his dilemma (533, 726).

The adaptable individual moves toward the satisfaction of his motives instead of being thrown into anxiety by the unbreakable conflict and developing nonadjustive reactions like the neurotic animal. If we are to be adaptable, *common sense and new, appropriate solutions have to be substituted for fixed ways of behavior.* The world changes, and we must change with it. We must grow emotionally, as shown in the next section. Behavior that might have satisfied us as children cannot satisfy men. We must "put away childish things." Fixations of immature behavior and regression to kid behavior will not solve the problem permanently. Similarly, escaping into daydreams or defending oneself rather than slowly facing one's anxiety will not produce effective adjustment.

Studies have shown that certain individuals tend toward an *authoritarian pattern of personality*, which illustrates low adaptability. They tend to be highly conventional, superstitious, prejudiced, destructive, cynical, concerned over sex, and desirous of power. There is evidence that many of them have experienced parental rejection or domination in childhood, have repressed the consequential hostility, and in adulthood show this hostility toward minority groups (5). (See page 194 for a more thorough and critical discussion of this.)

Sometimes adaptability is shown by getting assistance from someone else—a friend, a counselor, or a specialist. The neurotic alternative is an attitude that this experience, problem, or event is too terrible to deal with or to face. We must therefore deny it and escape from it. The adjustive individual tends to face it, says, "It is a part of life. It *has* occurred, and I must deal with it in the best possible way, however unpleasant that may be. It has happened to others before me; it has been solved before; I must solve it now." Usually, there is *strength in facing one's problems*. Many have attested to the courage obtained when facing problems rather than running away from them.

SELF-RESPONSIBILITY IMPLICIT IN ADJUSTMENT. In a complex society one may adjust on various levels of maturity. There are persons who are secure and may remain so within a certain milieu all their lives and yet are not living at a very high level of maturity or responsibility. Several of the characteristics such as adaptability and orientation assume that the individual described by them shows some responsibility and realistic attitude in ordering his life. However, sometimes the responsibility and understanding of himself that one shows is minimal, and yet he adjusts adequately. The individuals who live in a simple society show all the characteristics mentioned above as long as they are living in that society. If they are moved into a more complex framework that requires more responsibility, more understanding of themselves and their world, they become maladjusted. It has been said that the adjustive individual *must accept responsibility for himself* (777), and surely this is true in view of the fact that even a simple society may change, requiring more knowledge, less repression of the unacceptable in oneself, and more complex choices. The highest form of adjustment, then, requires maturity, which involves responsibility.

The Emotionally Mature Personality

Characteristics of the Mature Individual. Call to mind the behavior of the children under 14 years of age whom you know. Then, in contrast, run over in your mind the actions of some of your friends of both sexes who are well-adjusted, mature adults. What differences do you find?

Not all persons who are mature anatomically and physiologically are mature psychologically. The individual must possess other characteristics to be emotionally mature. The mature individual is independent. He is *becoming emancipated from the home.* He is capable of being the father and supporter of his own household. He is making contributions in the vocational world. He can arrive at his own conclusions and make his own decisions. He is not dependent upon the admonitions or security of his elders.

One of the psychological characteristics of maturity is *heterosexuality*. The mature individual regards his own sex as a means of companionship and the opposite sex as a source of companionship and of love. The highest development of heterosexuality in our culture is the selection of one member of the opposite sex as a life mate.

Maturity involves an *appreciation of* the attitudes and behavior of *others*. The person preoccupied with himself is not emotionally mature. He is like a child. His own needs and feelings are uppermost in his mind. His own pleasure is the basis for most of his decisions. The mature person, although he recognizes authority, does not feel self-conscious and inferior to every older person or authority he encounters. He is learning to meet other persons on a more unemotional, and equal basis. He learns to accept criticism, to examine it rather than to have a temper tantrum or a depression about it. He does not have to dominate a group completely or withdraw from it. As one writer puts it, he is freeing himself of the deeply colored personal relationships of childhood—his childhood fears, rivalry, jealousies and hates (841). He is a secure part of a group although not dependent upon this group for all his ideas and actions. He has social outlets for his energy, plays games, follows hobbies. He is unlikely to be a lone wolf or an eccentric. If he differs from others he is rather tolerant of their behavior.

The emotionally mature individual is *capable of delaying his responses*. The child must have what he wants when he wants it. He is unwilling to substitute remote ends for immediate goals. He cannot inhibit behavior that will be disastrous to his later existence. He lacks endurance and fortitude. The mature person shows *controlled and directed emotionality*. He is not impulsive or highly emotional in most situations. He is, rather, composed, reflective, deliberate, and calm. He has developed a certain degree of mental toughness to life's problems which we have called *frustration-* and *anxiety-tolerance*, and does not need to run for shelter as each difficulty confronts him.

But we cannot stop here. Not all persons who are heterosexual, sociable, and independent represent a high level of maturity in our complex civilization. This independence should go further. The best example of the mature person is one who not only supports himself but *controls to some extent his environment*. Instead of being completely subjected to the forces of the outside world, he takes part in molding these forces. He recognizes his talents, and he sees his place in the world, sees future goals, and moves toward them (12). Neither does he surrender to strong, repressed forces within him. He is conscious of them and of all his limitations, accepts them, and deals with them.

Maturity brings with it a *point of view of life*. If this is adequately verbalized it deserves the title of a philosophy of life. It includes the individual's convictions on matters such as ethics, morals, politics, and the nature of the world and of man. Those persons judged most mature by recognized scholars and leaders are individuals capable of devoting themselves to an abstract ideal, such as the discovery of truth. If a man can allow an ideal to permeate his life so that egocentric motives are subordinate to it, he is indeed mature. We have devoted a section of Chapter 7 to a detailed discussion of a philosophy of life.

Many of the characteristics of the adjustive individual presume a certain degree of maturity. Assuredly the mature person is adaptable, oriented in the present world, motivated, and sociable. Whether he is happy and unified depends upon whether he is behaving at a level of maturity compatible with his abilities, experience, and personality traits. The college student who is described below illustrates this.

Frank U. is 25 years old. He has had military experience. He looks and acts more like a person of 20. He has superior intelligence and vocabulary, good work habits, and above-average grades. His attitude is submissive, despite a well-developed, average-size physique and a "regular fellow" appearance. As soon as he begins to talk, he gives the impression of being younger than he is.

Hard work and high intelligence won for him an officer's rank in the Army, even though he showed few evidences of social or executive leadership. Throughout the interviews he would say, "Yes, sir," in answering the counselor. He stated that he found it very difficult to differ with anyone of any authority.

His present behavior follows an orderly development. He comes from a family of the lower middle economic class and attended a strict religious school. His mother died before he started school, and he was subsequently shifted from relative to relative as he developed. His father was a laborer. Apparently the whole attitude of the family is one of submission to authority.

During the several years that he worked after completing high school, it never occurred to him that he could pursue college work. He was greatly surprised to learn that students of his economic class had of their own initiative come to college and earned their way, even before the war. He is strongly motivated. He has improved his vocabulary by sheer effort. He has performed every job assigned him well, within the limits of his orders.

The problems he faces at present are his tendency to worry over school work, tension, insomnia, fear of mistakes, and a general lack of confidence in himself. He is engaged to a girl who apparently has much more self-esteem. She has assumed responsibility for their relationship and their future. Although he feels that many of her decisions are right, he rebels inwardly at her making the decisions for them. After his experiences as an officer and with contemporaries in college, he realizes that he is deficient in initiative and leadership capacity. Furthermore, his whole constricted personality is frustrating to him and is producing anxiety. He wants to assume more responsibility, yet his background causes him to fear every new venture that is not supported by authority.

Here is a case of an individual who made a fair adjustment on a simpler level of behavior, then he became an officer in the Army, realized his intellectual ability, but because of his insecure and authoritarian background was not prepared to adjust at the level of maturity that he saw in his contemporaries. The conferences with a counselor helped him to obtain some insight into the origins of his behavior and to see himself and his future role more clearly.

Suggestions for the Attainment of Maturity. Immaturity consists mainly in remaining emotionally at an earlier level of development, referred to as *fixation*. It may consist of returning to an earlier level or of *regression*. The traits of responsibility, objectivity in viewing problems with courage have not been developed. The individual behaves as though he wants someone to protect him. He either has not grown up emotionally or has returned to childhood because of the difficulties encountered on a more mature level. Frequently, the parents of immature individuals have rewarded the child for remaining childlike because they feared the adult life the child would have to meet. When women with neuroses were compared with normal women, the former were found to continue a childish relationship with their parents longer and were late in reaching independence (435). Similarly, college students with emotional problems showed less contact with both sexes, fewer play experiences with contemporaries, fewer memberships in clubs, less attendance at dances, and less independence than unselected (normal) students (520).

It should be stated that most college students want to grow up. They need only to see clearly what immaturity is like, why they are immature if they are, and to realize that maturity grows from assuming more and more responsibilities at a rate that allows them to be handled, responsibilities that are compatible with the student's abilities and interests. With this in mind we are presenting suggestions which aid insight and the rearrangement of one's life. Many of the following represent traits, habits, or conditions suggested by the analysis and can be regarded as a goal for trial-and-error learning activity.

Earn own money	Recognize in yourself immature
Help parents find interests	attitudes and behavior
Attend more to others	Go away to school
Join clubs, hobby groups	Date
Try your own decisions	See others like yourself
Write your philosophy of life	Learn dancing, social games
Travel and read	Cultivate mature associates
Try to understand people different	Join teams
from yourself	Plan for future

Unbalanced Maturity. Every student is acquainted with fellow students who seem mature in some respects and immature in others. Here is a good example:

Merl B. does not like to dance or date, has few friends, is greatly interested in music, literature and philosophy, and is a good student. He has developed his own philosophy of life and is motivated by commendable abstract principles. The typical college student does not like him. To his contemporaries he seems affected and supercilious. He has never passed through the stage during which he would have acquired their attitudes. He was never interested in the activities of the typical 10-year-old boy, such as athletics, sports, camping, nature lore, and collections. At no time in his life did he have the typical adolescent interests: girls, parties, dates, clothes, grooming, dancing, and luxuries. He has many of the interests of a 30-year-old man, but he is not at ease with members of his own age group. He is idealistic and socially minded in terms of major issues. He has not attained experience or skills sufficient to feel at ease with the older group either. Sex control is one of his problems. He is not a very happy person, although he would be the first to deny this.

Is Merl emotionally mature? In some respects he is mature. For years he has had the interests of an older individual. He was reading philosophy in high school. However, his growth has been asymmetrical. Merl may never feel completely adjusted as an adult and to his fellows. On the other hand, he may develop social skills with older persons who have similar interests, join their group, and eventually over a period of years be adjusted superficially to a certain type of society. The likelihood of this happening depends upon the extent to which the conditions of readjustment discussed in Chapter 5 are met.

Levels of Maturity and Adjustment. People of strong faith and simplicity are sometimes the envy of those who struggle with the problems of mankind. Many of them cannot, in view of their development, adjust effectively on any other basis. However, if all of us lived on this level of behavior, dictators and medicine men would thrive and scientific progress, and mature philosophy and theology would fall into oblivion.

The mature individual has responsibility for his choices and makes his decisions rather than uncritically accepting those of others. If the ideas of established authority seem inadequate, he turns to experiments and reason for a more valid solution.

The individual, then, who is best adjusted has reached the highest level of maturity within his capacity. Those who accept authority unquestioningly and make few decisions experience security but sacrifice the freedom to think and to choose for themselves. The degree of responsibility an individual or group will assume, the security they desire, and the amount of freedom they expect to enjoy are basic to many of the more acute economic, political, and social problems of the day (593).

The Older Years. The later years in life, near and after retirement from one's major responsibilities, bring their own adjustmental problems. Recently, there have been numerous publications on the problems of later maturity and some suggestions as to causes and remedies (39, 431, 802, 837). The causes revolve around the roles assigned to the older person in our culture, reactions of the individual to his own physical and mental changes, particularly those that intensify the problem of age rather than reduce it.

Great differences exist between individuals in their adjustment to old age. Those who make the best adjustment in the later years keep appropriately busy at constructive work that is satisfying to them and allows them to retain and enhance their self-esteem. Some have arranged to shorten hours of work and reduce heavy responsibility to adjust to their physical condition. In general, older employees who make the necessary adjustment are regarded as quite good by their employers. The individual who sees at middle age the changes that are occurring in the roles he will have to play in the future and finds new outlets more suitable to these decades of life is preparing for better adjustment in later years. Mothers whose children are grown, who find new outlets for their energy in social service or part-time employment that will occupy their time satisfyingly, are good examples of this adjustive effort.

A Wholesome Society

The Individual Is Influenced by His Culture. The child is born into a social order; during the first hour of his life its mark is implanted on him. If he is born into an urban American social order, before he leaves the delivery room he has been cleaned and oiled. His social inheritance includes race, language, customs, religion, and attitudes that include patterned prejudices and hostility. Before the first year is over, he is being molded by this society's pressures as well as by his family's idiosyncrasies. If the *culture* into which he is born is conflictory and unhealthy, he finds himself a part of these conflicts (see Chapter 11). Furthermore, as you have discovered in preceding discussions, it is difficult for an individual to break with the social structures that surround him. They become a part of the warp and woof of his individual make-up. Part of his adjustment is to work with his fellows to make a more sane society.

We cannot plan for individual adjustment without examining the social order. It is futile to try to adjust the individual to social conditions which are themselves unhealthy. By a wholesome society we mean one that tends to produce a minimum of debilitating conflicts and anxieties and tends, on the other hand, to promote the maximum realistic adjustment and mature growth in its citizens.

Changing Conditions in Society. If a society needs modification here and there, this modification must take place along with individual change. Otherwise mental hygiene becomes verbiage. Moreover, a part of the individual's adjustment involves dealing with society and assisting others in similar plight to effect adjustment. Most of us cling to present mores and customs because they consist of well-established individual reaction patterns and they represent personal security. The longer they have been a part of our way of behaving, the stronger they are. Special privilege groups defend most vehemently the *status quo* that sustains them. They fight for it, even though it may mean conflict, unhappiness, or slow death to many other people. We and they support the present way of life when it runs counter to our strongest cultural ideals and produces thereby a deeply serious conflict (398). All the modes of adjustment mentioned in Chapter 3 are ammunition. We rationalize fixed thinking. We use scapegoats. There is displaced emotion. Proponents and

Susan Greenburg

programs of change are labeled impractical, Utopian, or communistic. Prejudice, ignorance, and violence, the foes of humanity, are recruited as defenses. The inexorable changes of time and the products of a free education gradually bring the conflict into the open or resolve it by bringing about social change.

Characteristics of an Adjustive Society. A relatively ideal society, from a mental-hygiene standpoint, is one that will provide for the *development of mature, well-integrated or unified individuals* who can meet the demands of their motivation without unhealthy conflict. The previously mentioned characteristics of the well-adjusted individual (pages 461 to 466) then become the marks of a healthy society. A healthy society is one that permits its members *happiness.* It enhances *good relations* between men and harnesses hate so that man does not use it blindly against himself and his fellow men. It produces *sociality, motivation* within the limits of the personality, *adaptability, unity,* and *balance* of traits. Furthermore, it encourages *interest* in the basic *realities* of the present world but looks to a world of tomorrow (777). As we have stated previously, no thoughtful person advocates the abolition of all conflict. Those conflicts that can be resolved without being destructive to the individual are stimulating to him. The goal of those who wish a healthy society is the control of conflict, so that it may be effectively *assimilated* by the individual. The reduction of devastating conflict is an important goal, irrespective of whether personal disorganization is due to constitutional or environmental factors. In either case, conflict is an important factor.

From a negative standpoint, the mental hygienist is interested in promoting a society that will sharply reduce social ills. These are suicide, mental disease, crime, violence, wars, poverty, and the breakdown of basic institutions without adequate replacement.

Some Basic Conflicts Intrinsic to Our Society. What are some of the conflicts into which a child is born in the Western world? To what extent are the mental conflicts we as individuals experience a result of clashes between incompatible standards in our society? To what extent are they due to circumstances, brought about by society, that prevent us from reaching our ideals? Some of these conflicts were evident in the discussion of values in Chapter 7. One outstanding psychiatric writer has called attention to three conflicts intrinsic to our Western civilized society.

1. It has been suggested that our advertisement-created desires for new commodities—cars, refrigerators, clothes, gadgets—conflict with our present abilities to buy them (353). Advertising and American movies are to an extent responsible for the dissatisfaction individuals feel with their appearance since both of these media, unlike some modern art, tends not to depict people and the world as they really are but select exceptional models who are the extreme of beauty, symmetry, color blending, etc. These ideal models are incompatible with the many variations in physique, complexion, facial features, and dress found in realistic living and which are so interesting to the true artist.

2. There is the conflict between competitive success and brotherly love. Similarly, individualism frequently conflicts with the welfare of the group as a whole, but we are taught to respect both. Competitiveness is taught to the child even before he enters school. The child is taught to stand up for his rights and on the same day is told to share his toys with the neighbor child. In American social structure, even in the schools, much more emphasis seems to be placed upon competition than upon cooperation, yet many believe that the survival of human groups strongly depends upon cooperation.

3. There is the conflict between continual mouthings about the freedom of the individual and the daily experiences of limitations of that freedom. Anyone who has lived in the more backward sections of the American South knows how little real freedom the Negro enjoys. He is "kept in his place" by all kinds of threats including lynching. The North cannot be pleased about its position. It is a rare suburb in which a professional Negro is permitted to buy property. The freedom for all to rise to any heights by sheer hard work and honesty has been questioned by many psychological authors (420). The delusion that *any* American can move from rags to riches with proper living is well inculcated by many parents despite the fact that it is rare for the people of some neighborhoods or communities to attain such success. Registrations in state universities before the passage of the GI Bill showed relatively few individuals from the slums or lower middle economic and educational groups (520). As one author suggests, ambition and hard work are not sufficient to guarantee economic security, not to mention outstanding success (420). Despite this fact, children are taught this delusion only to have it conflict later with reality.

As we live in Western society we assume other conflicts which are to be added to this list. Judaeo-Christian ideals frequently conflict with Western materialism. This probably is one of the deepest conflicts American children inherit. Every Sunday they are taught and recite lessons in nonaggression, brotherhood, self-effacement, importance of inner development, and purposiveness in the universe, yet some time before the day ends they have also been taught to fight for their rights, beat the other fellow to it, "the Lord helps him who helps himself," put up a good front, and other lessons of competitive aggression. Some aspects of the teachings of Jesus seem to conflict and need to be rationalized by theologians. Jesus' emphasis on the simple life, the unimportance of property, antagonism toward ritual that kills spirit, the supremacy of brotherhood whenever it conflicts with any other allegiances, certainly seem incompatible with some modern practices of various sects. There are the existing elaborate cathedrals, the Jim-Crow practices among various sects, those congregations that promote class-consciousness among their members, and the gross materialism exhibited in the pomp and ceremony of many modern churches. There are many clergymen and religious groups, however, who are clearly conscious of these conflicts and are attempting to resolve them in favor of Judaeo-Christian ideals. Of all institutions, the church is outstanding for the examples shown by some of its leaders in their attempts to solve some of the problems of mental discord.

We have referred previously to our conflicting attitudes toward sex in the United States. Sex is blatantly and publicly exploited in advertising, moving pictures, novels, and songs, whereas individual overt sexual behavior violating the codes leads to social derogation (206).

On the positive side one critical writer after reviewing much that has been written about contemporary America sees among our many culture conflicts a *motivation and capacity for growth, a plastic strength* that has and can further shape us into a great civilization (450).

Social Conditions Inimical to Wholesome Development. Mental disease has been found to be of greater incidence in certain areas of cities—the same areas that produce crime. Usually these are the disorganized areas near the center of the city (226). Obviously, in a society in which so much prestige is placed upon clothes, cars, good jobs, and other evidences of material success, not all of the approximately 70 per cent of the population who earn less than what is considered a necessary minimum for decent living can derive comfort from the common nature of their plight (420). Severe conflicts will ensue among some of them. Low earnings usually mean poor housing, minimal education, poor health standards, and low morale. Anthropologists who have studied various primitive cultures have reported that they find few neurotic signs in those cultures that have fewer *repressive taboos* associated with strong drives (489). Many of the psychological casualties in World War II have been attributed in part to the training of English-speaking people in repression of aggression and the disapproval of expression of fear. Serious guilt resulted when men so reared had to participate in warfare (143). A psychiatrist who compared cultures in mountain communities of varying degrees of isolation and complexity found neurotic symptoms increased with *complexity* of social organization (706). The extreme gratification of the ego in our society, which allows arrogant individualism, would be considered egomania in other societies, we are told (60). It must be remembered, in discussing these generalizations, that cultures cannot be transplanted from one society to another. Any suggestions about our own society are merely hypotheses, which must be tested before being accepted as established conclusions.

Emphasis on nationalism extolling the virtues of our way of life to the discredit of differing cultures conflicts violently with the serious need for internationalism. This emphasis is particularly inappropriate in a world that has been unified technologically by rapid communication and transportation (504, 732, 806). There are many conflicts among the motives of man, but often these conflicts are promoted by insular cultures. As individuals we strive for affection and for satisfaction of our basic biological urges like hunger and warmth. Therefore the conflict between the love of goods and the love of man is one that frequently appears.

As previously indicated, there is a natural conflict between society's emphasis on the *status quo* and the need for change dictated by new inventions and new skills. Sometimes this conflict is between youth and older generations. The fast American tempo of living and our escapes into sensational experience caused by our competitive culture and our urban frustrations conflict with the need for meditation, calm, and serenity advocated by health authorities and religionists (401).

In addition to these conflicts intrinsic to our society are those that are inevitable when our differing subcultures are at odds. There are the convictions of the small businessman, the farmer, organized labor, intellectuals, big business, the clergy, the old folks, and the young set—all disagreeing on some points. These *culture conflicts* are illustrated by the incompatibility of the ideas that woman's place is at the sink and the fact that some of the greatest careers have been those of women; the exaltation of efficiency and the opposing admonition to be less machine-like and more human; parents may emphasize thrift and friends may urge on one the small satisfactions of daily spending.

The question may be raised whether there is enough emphasis in our national and international culture on vehicles for the resolution of conflict and the integration of these various subcultures. The modern church, the U.N., the free press, forum groups, and cultural interchange between different groups are all movements in that direction (739).

High Morale in a Wholesome Society. One crucial index of a wholesome society is high morale, which reflects security. The attitudes that accompany morale are the antitheses of conflict, discouragement, inertia, apathy, or surrender. Morale signifies zest, faith in the fundamental purposes of the group, belief in loyalty to the leaders. With high morale are found confidence in the group and oneself, perseverance, and a good spirit toward work and hardship. The attitude of the British after Dunkirk and during the darkest hours when they underwent hardships, frustration, and losses and showed faith in a cause that was their way of life is a present-day example of high morale (89).

Morale is always implemented by the knowledge that those around us have a similar attitude, that we and our fellows feel the same about things. The group can marshal its zest when there are *common strivings*. A leader who *knows* the way and can gain respect is essential. Faith in man and his eventual outcome has been listed as another valuable item (627, 89). Additional boosters of morale mentioned by Army manuals consist of the satisfaction of physical needs, of a sense that we are contributing to the common cause, are moving toward victory, and are "in the know," even though the news may not be good. Recreation also has been found to assist in maintaining morale (89). In industry, being a part of the firm or a team (507), knowing that he has status, that he is as important as the profit, makes a measurable difference in the worker's production. Nothing lowers individual morale more than holding a job that carries a stigma, that does not tap one's abilities and interests, or that is supervised by someone who is not respected. Group morale falls when security with regard to job status and permanence is jeopardized (544, 659). Morale as well as personal problems and social stability of the individual reflects itself in such behavior as absenteeism and punctuality (507, 188).

In a democratic atmosphere the individual develops, with fewer restrictions, into a more creative person. Morale in a community or a nation is in no way different from that in an army or industry. In a free, ideal democracy achieving morale may at first seem more difficult than in a state in which there is a single party, a controlled press, low literacy, a ruling group, and a submissive population. A free state will encourage the development of more creative and individual attitudes and less stereotyped behavior. But there are common purposes amid the different personalities, and these must be emphasized without jeopardizing too greatly individual development. In favor of the development of morale in a democracy is the opportunity for the individual to feel that he can participate in the group destiny, knowledge about the state of the nation, and the stronger assurance of civil liberties (91). This morale is endangered when theoretical freedoms of speech and worship and freedom from want and fear are not realized in actuality and when representatives in Congress represent pressure groups more than the welfare of the majority of the people. A study of differential civilian morale during war time indicated lower morale among students who prefer to be born in a "socially prominent family" or to "make a lot of money," students whose attitudes are superficial, selfish, materialistic, and lacking in inner conviction or spiritual depth (657).

Suggestions for a Healthier Society. The entire preceding discussion leads naturally to certain suggestions. To build a better society it is important (1) that *physical health* be improved and maintained. Very closely akin to this is the satisfaction of basic human wants—the need for food, shelter, clothing, status, and security. In short, it is an economic need. Therefore a wholesome society in our times requires (2) *economic and social conditions* that are conducive to personality integration rather than the mechanized man (426). This means employment that will allow the individual to experience the dignity that is intrinsic to man. Conditions should be such that he may obtain a job that is compatible with his abilities and interests and that will give him status. If man is to have any society at all, to say nothing of a wholesome society, (3) the forces at work at present must be moving toward the *prevention and redirection of man's destructive tendencies*—war and violence. In 1945 the American psychologists issued a statement endorsed by 99 per cent of the profession who responded to a communication about it (732). In it appeared the assertion that war can be avoided by educating for peace in the coming generation. Furthermore, "the frustrations and conflicting interests which lie at the root of aggressive wars can be reduced and redirected by social engineering." "Men," continues this statement, "can realize their ambitions within the framework of human cooperation and can direct their aggressions against those natural obstacles that thwart them in the attainment of their goals."

In addition, "the white man must be freed of his concept of the 'white man's burden.' The English-speaking peoples are only a tenth of the world's population; those of white skin only a third . . . The time has come for a more equal participation of all branches of the human family in a plan for collective security." The statement continues: "Disrespect for the common man is characteristic of fascism and of all forms of tyranny. The man in the street does not claim to understand the complexities of economics and politics but he is clear as to the general directions in which he wishes to progress. His will can be studied (by adaptations of the public-opinion poll). His expressed aspirations should even now be a major guide to policy."

In Chapter 5 we pointed out that, through (4) *recreation, special interest and hobby groups*, one can discover himself and socialize his inner impulses. Provision for recreation and play becomes more important every year with the increase of leisure time created by machinery. Several writers have claimed that recreational facilities reduce juvenile delinquency (150). It is true that the "well" and "poorly adjusted" differ at least in this factor, the "well-adjusted" having more social outlets of a recreational nature (520).

(5) Any form of *education* worthy of its true meaning is as individualized as possible within the framework of our present system. True education is an opportunity by which one may grow and become more creative. This means less parroting of knowledge, fewer drills, and more use of experiences to energize and socialize one's life. With this viewpoint we no longer emphasize comparisons of entirely different students through grades and other competitive means. There is a continual emphasis on the total individual rather than on segments of his personality, with a full realization that some students will excel in some subject matter or skills and be inferior in others. In college, then, knowledge will not be presented for the sake of knowledge alone but in a form that will have value for the student's growth as a personality and as a citizen in an integrated world.

(6) To these must be added the various psychiatric, psychological, educational, and social services suggested throughout the book, which will enable individuals to gain *insight into their conflicts, reduce and harness their anxieties for growth, and find their identity as persons*.

To summarize, a societal structure that permits the optimal development of a socialized personality through the satisfaction of his basic motives and the prevention of irreconcilable conflicts is desirable. This culture is one that does not jeopardize his self-esteem or integrity but promotes the conditions that allow him to *realize his intrinsic dignity*.

Mental Hygiene Precepts

Mental hygienists have attempted to formulate simple generalizations, place them in pamphlets and psychological textbooks so that individuals may reflect on them, pass them on to others, and attempt to use them in their own lives. It is obvious that mental health cannot be improved by health drills, but rather by *an atmosphere, a way of life, personal morale, self-understanding, and creative adjustment*. Following is a list of precepts taken from several previously published sources which will be helpful if they arouse and strengthen previously discovered insights and plans of action (291, 695). They have a factual basis (520) and summarize the general and specific suggestions made throughout this book, and they constitute an appropriate ending.

1. Keep yourself *physically fit* through hygienic habits of rest, exercise, diet, and cleanliness.

2. *Face your troubles*, worries, and fears; do what you can about them, then turn your attention to more satisfying things.

3. Have several absorbing *hobbies*, interests, social games, or sports in which you like to participate.

4. *Find desirable ways to express your disturbing impulses* and emotions rather than to suppress them.

5. Strive to become a *balanced personality;* try to discover what causes you to go off on a tangent.

6. Try to develop a *sense of humor;* be willing to admit your own mistakes and laugh at yourself.

7. Have several major *goals* in the line of your abilities and enjoy working toward them.

8. Acquire real *friends* and companions who will share your fortunes and troubles.

9. Avoid strain; try to develop serenity; *relax* all muscles that are not necessary for the task at hand.

10. Build the habit of *enjoying the present* by drinking in the beauties of the world around you.

11. Be *courageous* in crises; don't run from them.

12. Grow daily by creating things yourself rather than being merely a spectator, dreamer, and nonproducing consumer. There is fun in *striving*.

13. Don't be *overconscious* of your uniqueness. Realize that most of us are ordinary people.

14. Realize that *time heals* many wounds; try to be patient and hopeful.

15. *Seek* love, adventure, safety, and success—*but* be sure it is the kind that you can fully enjoy.

16. Develop your *philosophy;* know where you stand and try to adjust to the conditions you must meet.

17. There are several ways of looking at yourself, others, and events in your life; try to find the *perspective* that will help you most to develop toward maturity.

Supplementary Readings

R. M. MacIver, *The Pursuit of Happiness, a Philosophy for Modern Living,* Simon and Schuster, 1955.

A. H. Maslow, *Motivation and Personality,* Harper, 1954.

C. E. Moustakas, *The Self Explorations in Personal Growth,* Harper, 1956.

O. H. Mowrer, "What Is Normal Behavior?" in L. A. Pennington and I. A. Berg (Eds.), *An Introduction to Clinical Psychology* (2nd ed.), Ronald, 1954.

C. Tibbitts, *Living Through the Older Years,* University of Michigan Press, 1951.

In addition see the references cited by number in the chapter and appearing in the bibliography of an accompanying volume entitled *Teaching Personal Adjustment: An Instructor's Manual.*

INDEX